W9-CTW-824

THE IMPACT OF THE CHURCH UPON ITS CULTURE

ESSAYS IN DIVINITY

JERALD C. BRAUER, GENERAL EDITOR

Vol. I: The History of Religions
Vol. II: The Impact of the Church upon Its Culture

The Impact of the Church Upon Its Culture

Reappraisals of the History of Christianity

BY QUIRINUS BREEN, GEORGE A. DRAKE
CORNELIUS J. DYCK, B. A. GERRISH, G. WAYNE GLICK
ROBERT M. GRANT, RICHARD LUMAN
JOHN T. MCNEILL, JAMES D. NELSON, JAROSLAV PELIKAN
RAY C. PETRY, MASSEY H. SHEPHERD, JR.
MATTHEW SPINKA, ROBERT L. WILKEN

Edited by JERALD C. BRAUER

THE UNIVERSITY OF CHICAGO PRESS
CHICAGO AND LONDON

To JOHN T. MCNEILL

Exemplary scholar, exacting teacher,
prolific author, and a true leader
among his fellow historians of Christianity

THE UNIVERSITY OF CHICAGO PRESS
CHICAGO AND LONDON
The University of Toronto Press, Toronto 5, Canada

Library of Congress Catalog Card Number: 67–30155

Printed in the United States of America

General Editor's Preface

The present volume is the second in a series of eight books being published under the general title "Essays in Divinity." This does not appear, at first glance, as a particularly auspicious moment for such a formidable enterprise. At the very moment the so-called radical theologians announce that "God is dead," an eight-volume series investigating various dimensions of the study of religion or of theology is published. Is this not an ill-timed venture?

In point of fact, however, in America the discipline of theology was never in a healthier state. To be sure, there are no giants such as Tillich or Niebuhr on the scene, but there are many new and exciting factors in the picture. The very presence of the "God is dead" movement is evidence of a new vitality and ferment among the younger theologians. In no sense does such a movement herald the end of systematic theology or the impossibility of using God-language. It is but one of many significant attempts being made now at basic reconstruction and reinterpretation of Christian theology.

One primary fact marks this new age – the pre-eminence of dialogue in all aspects of divinity. Basic conversation between Roman Catholicism, Protestantism, and Judaism is just beginning, and its full effect on theological construction lies ahead. At the time systematic theology entered the preliminary phase of dialogue, Paul Tillich's last lecture pointed to the future of this discipline in relation to the world's religions. Dialogue is not to be understood as the "in" movement in religion today; it is to be viewed as providing a new base that will profoundly affect not only the systematic study of doctrines and beliefs but every dimension of religious studies.

Another mark of the vitality of religious studies today is its dialogic relationship to other disciplines. Studies in divinity have never been carried on in complete isolation from other areas of human knowledge, but in some periods the relationship has been more fully explored than in others. The contemporary scene is marked by the increasing tempo of creative interchange and mutual stimulation between divinity and other disciplines. Several new theological disciplines have emerged recently to demonstrate this fact. The interplay between theology and literature, between theology and the psychological sciences, and between theology and the social sciences promises to reshape the traditional study of religion, as our major theological faculties are beginning rapidly to realize.

The emergence and increasing role of the History of Religions is a case in point. Until recently it has been a stepchild in the theological curriculum. Today it is developing a methodology that probably will prove influential in all areas of theological study. History of Religions also appears to be the way that most state universities will introduce the serious and disciplined study of religion into strictly secular curriculums.

These are but a few of the factors that demonstrate the present vitality of the study of religion today. It makes both possible and necessary a series of books such as this. The particular occasion for the publication of "Essays in Divinity" is supplied by the one hundredth anniversary of the Divinity School of The University of Chicago and by the University's seventy-fifth anniversary.

The editor of this series proposed that this event be celebrated by the Divinity School faculty and alumni by holding seven conferences, each of which was focused on the works of one of the seven academic fields of the School. Out of these conferences have come eight volumes which will, it is hoped, mark the progress in the various disciplines of theological study and point to the ongoing tradition of scholarship in the University's Divinity School.

Though something may have been lost in thus limiting the roster of contributors to these books, this very limitation may have the effect of marking the distinctive genius of one theological center long noted for its production of scholar-teachers in American theology. Also, it will enable an observer to determine the extent to which several generations have been shaped by, and have shaped, a particular institution. It will be possible to note the variations of approach and concern that mark respective generations of that institution. Furthermore, it will help to assess the particular genius, if any, that a given institution possesses. It will demonstrate to what extent its graduates and professors are in the midst of contemporary theological scholarship. It is to be hoped that the series will provide both a bench mark for today's scholarly discussions and research in religion and a record from which future generations can assess the contributions of an institution at the turn of its first century.

None of these volumes pretends to be definitive in its area; it is hoped, however, that each will make a useful contribution to its area of specialization and that the entire series will suggestively illuminate the basic tendencies of religious scholarship at the present moment. The intent has been to devote each volume to a particular issue or area of inquiry that is of special significance for scholarly religious research today, and thus to keep each volume from being simply a disconnected series of essays. It is hoped that these books will be found to have, each in its own terms, a genuine unity and that the reader will note a cumulative effect, as he moves from essay to essay in each volume.

This particular volume is respectfully dedicated to one of the contributors, Professor John T. McNeill. It is not inappropriate in a series celebrating his alma mater's anniversaries to have one volume honoring this distinguished church historian. In a sense, he forms a bridge between the first and second collection of essays by Chicago historians of Christianity. Thoroughly trained and at home in the socio-historical environmental method, his work demonstrated an equal concern for the impact of Christianity on its culture. During his eighteen years as professor in Chicago's Divinity School, he educated a host of church historians, and he continued this work during his final years at New York's Union Theological Seminary. All historians of Christianity, whatever their field, are deeply indebted to the scholarly contributions of John T. McNeill. Most of the authors in this volume were students or colleagues of his; the remainder are his scholastic grandchildren. It is fully appropriate that this volume be dedicated to him.

JERALD C. BRAUER, *General Editor*

CONTENTS

Introduction

JERALD C. BRAUER

Environmental Factors in Christian History, an interesting and provocative collection of essays edited by three faculty members of the University of Chicago's Divinity School, John T. McNeill, Matthew Spinka, and the late Harold R. Willoughby, appeared in 1939. This *festschrift* in honor of the retiring dean, Professor Shirley Jackson Case, represented a landmark in the study of church history in the American scene. It was written by former colleagues and students who, together with Dean Case, developed and employed the socio-historical method which came to identify the "Chicago school" made famous by the Divinity School.

This particular method dominated American studies in church history for several generations. It emphasized the fact that Christianity was a historical religion that came into being at a certain time, in a particular context, and with its own special background. There was nothing mysterious or unusual about the origins and history of Christianity. It was to be studied as any other historical entity with methods identical to those of other so-called scientific disciplines.

Special attention was given to the total social context through which Christian institutions, thought, and life developed, because this was thought to provide the key for interpretation. If one understood the total social matrix and its dynamics, then one could understand reasons for the emergence and history of Christianity and its true nature. Perhaps Dean Case's *Jesus: A New Biography* (1927) was the most consistent and thorough exposition of the method produced by any of the members of the Chicago School. Through the reconstruction of the total environment of Jesus, Case attempted to create a new biography of Jesus.

Much is commendable in the method. It was the first serious attempt in America to make church history a responsible scientific discipline at home in the university. It made possible a serious discussion of radically different interpretations on grounds other than simple personal commitment. Above all, it forced the correlation of church historical methods and research with other disciplines such as sociology, psychology, economic, political, and social history, and philosophy. It helped to make church history a self-conscious discipline with a method and content of its own.

All historical methods exhibit certain shortcomings that become evident only after prolonged usage. They emerge as a corrective to a reigning point of view and, after a time, give way to a new development which embodies a necessary corrective. The socio-historical method emphasized the continuity of Christianity with its epoch and environment; this against the assumption that Christian religion was something totally extraordinary that miraculously appeared contrary to all historical processes. In making this point concerning the historicity of Christianity, the method tended to overlook two things.

Christianity is not only an integral part of its environment, shaped and formed by it; it is also a religion that transcends its environment and helps to shape and form it. Christianity is something more than the sum total of the socio-historical forces of a given moment in time and history. It professes to be more, so it is the historian's responsibility to assess that claim. The question is the nature and uniqueness of religious experience and its consequences in the historical process. In no sense can the historian, as such, demonstrate that Christianity is beyond the historical process. The historian must, however, carefully evaluate the nature and content of religious experience and institutions to determine their role in a given epoch.

The socio-historical method neglected to do this. It was so intent on demonstrating the extent to which Christianity was the consequence of its environment that it overlooked the equally important task of discerning the uniqueness and special genius of Christianity itself. Thus it was not concerned to explore the dynamics of Christian religious experience and its consequences over against its environment. A second result of the method was a failure to appreciate the extent to which Christianity was not only shaped by its environment but also helped to form its culture. The relationship between Christianity and culture is dynamic and fluid. They profoundly influence each other. To be sure, the influence is not always equal, but it is the historian's task to assess the pervasiveness and direction of that influence. By assuming the pre-eminence of the environment, the socio-historical method tended to overlook the genuine dialectical relation between religion and its environment.

Environmental Factors in Christian History appeared after the method had passed its peak of influence. In theology, neo-orthodoxy and the impact of process theology attempted to isolate the genius of Christian theology. The concern was with the uniqueness and particularity of Christian revelation. A similar movement was underway in historical studies of Christianity. In the 1940's and 1950's numerous articles appeared in journals demonstrating the shift in interest. Three men, all professors in the University of Chicago Divinity School's field of the History of Christianity, spearheaded the new movement. Professors Sidney E. Mead, James Hastings Nichols, and Wilhelm Pauck wrote articles on methodology expressing a concern to redefine the nature of the Christian church in order to provide a base from which to write church history. The new generation of historians were trained in the socio-historical method but were dissatisfied with its one-sided emphasis. They sought to elevate the uniqueness of Christianity and to locate the special responsibilities of the church historians.

Almost thirty years later, a second collection of essays is written by the faculty and former students of the Divinity School's department of church history. This volume also appears at the end of an epoch before a new direction is clearly discernable. It is a summary of a point of view that has prevailed through the past several decades. This view builds solidly on the socio-historical method with its disciplined approach to research. At the same time an effort is made to analyze the interplay between religion and culture or the total environment. Such an approach lacks the clarity and cutting edge of the early days of the socio-historical method. What it lacks in excitement it makes up with solidity. This is the generation of surveys and source collections.

It is fitting that this collection of essays be concerned with the impact of Christian institutions, life, and thought on culture. Christianity has shaped its culture in diverse ways, as these essays illustrate. This does not repudiate the earlier volume; it builds on it and fills out the total picture. It demonstrates the extent to which all the writers have been formed by the earlier school of Chicago church historians. At the same time it indicates how these men have continued, yet transformed, a given tradition of scholarship.

The papers represent four major areas of church historical studies—ancient, medieval, reformation, and modern. No essays on religion in America are included, because a special volume on that will be part of the total series. The essays in this volume are arranged basically in chronological order. The authors were most cooperative with the editor in limiting their studies to a specific length. This is never easy to do, and for certain authors this worked a particular hardship because of the nature of their subject. It is hoped that the various essays will together illuminate the process of interaction between Christianity and culture. Thus the impact of Christianity on its culture will be clearly evident.

1

The Prefix Auto- *in Early Christian Theology*

ROBERT M. GRANT

The study of words and their meanings has constituted a significant part of modern investigations into biblical and patristic thought, and in recent times James Barr's *The Semantics of Biblical Language* has contributed some powerfully negative thinking on the subject.[1] His warnings against premature or excessive generalizations need to be taken into account, but it remains true that for the understanding of early Christian theology the study of words is crucial. Patristic debates over philosophy and theology can be viewed as essentially logomachies. This is what one would expect. Perhaps the Christian faith transcends the words and reaches more adequate expression in cult or social action, but if one asks what it means one can hardly escape the use of words and even of definitions and propositions. In this essay I propose to investigate the history of a group of terms created by the use of the prefix *auto-*, specifically as referred to divine beings in Gnosticism and to the Father and the Son in the theologies of Origen and his successors. They do not stand alone. Two other groups are equally significant, if not more so: terms beginning with the alpha-privative and thus expressing the *via negativa* in theology, and terms beginning with *hyper-* and denoting absolute divine transcendence. *Auto-*, however, has an interest of its own, for we can see the class being employed by Gnostics and several philosophers then by Origen as something of a shorthand expression of theological views based on biblical exegesis.

[1] James Barr, *The Semantics of Biblical Language* (London: Oxford University Press, 1961).

From Philosophy to Gnosticism

Nouns and adjectives with the prefix *auto-* were current coin in Greek philosophy from the time of Aristotle onward. He did not originate the terminology but derived it from members of the Platonic Academy who were accustomed to add the prefix *auto-* to various words and thus indicate a reference to the Ideas standing behind the phenomena in question (*Metaph.* 1040b34). The terms we encounter in the Metaphysics thus include *autoagathon*, the good-in-itself or ideal good, *autoanthropos* (man), *autogrammē* (the line itself), and *autoippos*, the ideal horse.[2] His commentator Alexander of Aphrodisias (second century A.D.) even coined the term *autoelephas*, the ideal elephant.[3]

Aristotle's major works were lost for several centuries after his death, and when they were rediscovered in the first century B.C. they only gradually became influential in Hellenistic philosophy.[4] It is not clear whether or not the *auto-* terms were continuously employed among Platonists during the interval; it it probably significant that they rarely occur in the writings of Philo of Alexandria. *Autoagathon* recurs in the writings of the eclectic Platonist Numenius of Apamea, in the first half of the second century. He states that the highest god is the only one *autoagathon*, "good in himself", the second god, the demiurge, is good only because he shares in the supreme goodness.[5] Numenius' statement reflects both the new (or reviving) tendency to use words of this class and the tendency to apply them to the highest divinity. These tendencies will be reflected in the thought of Origen.

Among the Gnostics, however, the terms are employed not of the ultimate ground of being (for which words like *proarchē* and *propatōr* are often used) but of intermediate principles,

[2] *Metaph.* 996a28, 991a29 (etc.), 1036b14, 1040b33, 1084a14.

[3] *Comm. in Metaph.*, p. 761, 30 Hayduck.

[4] J. Bidez, *Un singulier naufrage littéraire dans l'antiquité* (Brussels: Office de publicité, 1943).

[5] E.-A. Leemans, *Studie over den wijsgeer Numenius van Apamea* (Brussels: Palais de académies, 1937), pp. 140–41, 143. *Autoagathon* recurs in Plotinus, *Enn.* 1. 8, 13.

often called Aeons. Thus such principles are styled *autophyes*, "self-produced," or *autopatōr* and *automētōr*, father or mother "by nature." [6] A glance at the Greek word-index to the *Apocryphon of John* [7] will show the extent to which such terms proliferated. We may add that the Valentinian Ptolemaeus could refer to divine light as *autoon*, "self-existent." [8]

Because of its use by the Gnostics, Irenaeus and other anti-Gnostic writers viewed such language with suspicion, and in his writings we find only one word of this class, *autoprosopōs*—if indeed the latest editors have correctly retranslated the Armenian version at this point.[9] In any event, the context of the word is rhetoric, not philosophy or theology. His follower Hippolytus was well aware that Gnostics used such words, since he found them in the Gnostic documents he used, and he too generally avoided them. The only exception seems to occur in a fragment on Proverbs in which he referred to Christ as *autozōē*, "life as such,"[10] presumably because he had in mind such a significant Johannine passage as John 5:26: "As the Father has life in himself, so also he gave the Son to have life in himself," or even John 1:4: "In him was life."

Origen

The theology of Origen combines motifs taken from Middle Platonic philosophy and from Valentinian Gnosticism with his

[6] Irenaeus *Adv. haer.* 1. 1, 3; Epiphanius, *Pan.* 31. 5–6; J. Kroll, *Die Lehren des Hermes Trismegistos*, 2d ed. (Münster: Aschendorffsche Verlagsbuchhandlung, 1928), p. 3.

[7] W. Till, *Die gnostischen Schriften des koptischen Papyrus Berolinensis 8502* (Berlin: Akademie-Verlag, 1955); M. Krause and P. Labib, *Die drei Versionen des Apokryphon des Johannes im Koptischen Museum zu Alt-Kairo* (Wiesbaden: O. Harrassowitz, 1962).

[8] Epiphanius *Pan.* 33. 7. 7.

[9] A. Rousseau *et al., Irenée de Lyon: Contre les hérésies Livre IV* (Paris: Les éditions du Cerf, 1965), pp. 198–99, 392–93 (*Adv. Haer.* 4. 1. 1). The word occus in a fragment (14 Harvey, II, 485. 6) ascribed to Irenaeus ("Adam in his own person received the commandment from God"), but the fragment probably belongs to the Marcionite Apelles (A. von Harnack, *Marcion*, 2d ed. [Leipzig; J. C. Hinrichs, 1924], p. 414*, n. 1). Clement of Alexandria uses verb and adverb in the same sense: *Paed.* 1. 91. 2; *Str.* 3. 71. 3.

[10] H. Achelis, ed., *Hippolytstudien* (Leipzig: J. C. Hinrichs, 1897), p. 162, l. 25.

own ideas based primarily on long and arduous study of the Bible.[11] This general statement can be confirmed in detail from his use of the *auto-* class of words, which he often employs, as A. Orbe has noted, to signify "the primal substantial form."[12]

In his great early treatise *De principiis* (1, 2, 13), Origen explicitly denies that the Son is *autoagathon.* This term, as in the philosophy of Numenius, can be used only of the Father, and Origen thus agrees with the Valentinian Ptolemaeus, who said that the Father was "good in accordance with his own nature."[13] The Savior is not *autoagathon* but—with a reference to Wisd. 7:26—the Image of God's goodness. Similarly in another early treatise, the *Commentary on John,* Origen explains that the Father as *ho theos* (with the definite article, as in John 1:1) is *autotheos,* and the "source of deity," while the Son as "source of word" (or rationality) is the *autologos.*[14] Similarly, only the Father can be called *autozōē,* for only he, ultimately, has life in himself (cf. John 5:26).[15] According to a fragment on Proverbs, however, the whole Trinity can be called *autozōia* because God as such, *ho theos,* is life.[16]

Origen is very careful to avoid using such "ultimate" terms in regard to the Son, whom he never calls *autotheos, autoagathos,* or *autozōē.* Instead, he uses no fewer than fifteen *auto-* words in speaking of the Son, and all of them are derived from the Bible.

We begin with two obvious Old Testament examples. In Ps. 17:2–3 (Septuagint) the Lord is called "my strength" and "my firmness"; Origen makes the comment that "the Lord is the *autoischys* and the *autostereōma* of the saints."[17] Similarly, on Ps. 61:2, "from him is my salvation," he says that "the *auto-*

[11] Cf. R. Gögler, *Zur Theologie des biblischen Wortes bei Origenes* (Dusseldorf: Patmos-Verlag, 1963), pp. 251–52.

[12] A. Orbe, *Hacia la primera teologia de la procesion del Verbo* (Rome: Apud Aedes Universitatis Gregorianae, 1958), pp. 419–20, 442–43.

[13] Epiphanius *Pan.* 33. 7. 5.

[14] *Ioh. comm.* 2. 3; on the definite article see Philo, *De somniis* 1. 229–30.

[15] *Matt. comm.* 12. 9.

[16] Migne *Patrologia Graeca* 17. 196B.

[17] *Ibid.,* 12. 1224C.

sōtēria is from God."[18] In both instances he obviously has Christ in mind.

The Old Testament, however, was not his starting point. His method is clearly set forth in his *Commentary on Ephesians*, where he argues that as Christ is the Power of God and the Wisdom of God (1 Cor. 1:24), so he may be called the Will of God in Eph. 1:1, just as he is Logos, Truth, Resurrection, and Way.[19] Similar arguments are set forth in regard to calling Christ "Glory" and "Peace."[20] The *auto-* terms are not used, any more than in similar passages in his homilies,[21] but he employs the same method of extension used for some of them, and it is plain that he found key passages in 1 Cor. 1:24 and 1:30. In the former passage he read that Christ was "the Power of God and the Wisdom of God"; in the latter, that Christ Jesus "became Wisdom for us from God, Righteousness (*diakaiosynē*) and Sanctification (*hagiasmos*) and Redemption (*apolytrōsis*)." The Son is therefore *autodynamis*, "power as such," [22] *autosophia*, "wisdom as such,"[23] *autodikaiosynē*, "righteousness as such,"[24] *autoagiasmos*, "sanctification as such,"[25] and *autoapolytrōsis*, "redemption as such."[26] Obviously the more important Corinthians passage was the second one; the first two nouns in it provide sixteen to twenty of our examples.

Other examples are clearly Johannine in origin. *Autologos*[27] certainly comes from the Johannine prologue, while *auto-*

[18] *Ibid.*, 1484C.

[19] J. A. F. Gregg, ed., *Journal of Theological Studies*, 3 (1901–2): 235.

[20] *Ibid.*, 398, 406.

[21] E.g., *Num. hom.* 20. 2; *Josh. hom.* 17. 3.

[22] *Ioh. comm.* 1. 33.

[23] *Ioh. comm.* 32. 28; *Rom. comm.*, p. 146, 16 Scherer; *Matt. comm.* 14. 7; *C. Cels.* 3. 41; 5. 39; 6. 47; 7. 17; cf. *Princ.* 2. 6. 2.

[24] *Jer. hom.* 15. 6; 17. 4; *Ioh. comm.* 1. 9; 2. 6; 6. 6; *Matt. comm.* 14. 7; *C. Cels.* 5. 39; 6. 47.

[25] *Jer. hom.* 17. 4; *Ioh. comm.* 1. 9.

[26] *Ioh. comm.* 1. 9.

[27] From the second century, *C. Cels.* 2. 31; for Origen, *Luc. hom.*, frag. 22; *Ioh. comm.* 2. 3; *In Pss.*, pp. 91 and 143 Cadiou; *Exh. mart.* 10; *Matt. comm.* 12. 39; 16. 16; *C. Cels.* 3. 41; 5. 39; 6. 47–48; 7. 17; cf. *Princ.* 2. 6. 2.

alētheia[28] is based on John 14:6: "I am the Way and the Truth and the Life." Two further terms are also based on Johannine language. The key verses are John 5:26–27. "As the Father has life in himself, so also he has given the Son to have life in himself, and he has given him to make judgment (*krisis*) for he is the Son of Man (*huios tou anthrōpou*)." We have seen the first part of this sentence probably employed in relation to the Father; Origen evidently used the second part as a source for his teaching that the Son is *autokrisis* (*Ioh. comm.* 2, 6) and *autouios tou anthrōpou* (32, 28), although the latter term is explicitly related to John 13:31: "Now the Son of Man has been glorified, and God has been glorified in him."

In several instances we see Origen making use of the method of extension we have already mentioned. As Christ is one or another of the substantives regarded as generally accepted, so he is also *autobasileia* (*Matt. comm.* 14. 7) or even *autonomos* (*Rom. comm.*, p. 146 Scherer[29]). Both terms are rather surprising. The first, "kingdom as such," recalls Marcion's statement that "in the gospel the kingdom of God is Christ himself,"[30] although what Origen is saying is that Christ is the kingdom itself. He is explaining the parable of Matt. 18:23–35, which begins with the words, "The kingdom of heaven is like a king." The kingdom, he adds, is described as belonging to the "poor in spirit" (Matt. 5:3) because Christ as *autobasileia* rules over them. The second, *autonomos*, is to some extent explained by the need to interpret the apparent universality of the "law" in Rom. 3:19–20, on which Origen is commenting. If it is universal it can only refer to the *autonomos*, Christ. Again, in a passage now lost from the *Homilies on Jeremiah* but known to us from Jerome's close use of it, Origen evidently interpreted the "throne" and the "sanctuary" of Jer. 17:12 as symbols of Christ. The Greek text then continues as he explains

[28] *Jer. hom.* 17. 4; *Ioh. comm.* 6. 6; *Exh. mart.* 10. 47; *Rom. comm.*, p. 146, 16 Scherer, *Matt. comm.* 14. 7; *C. Cels.* 3. 47; 6. 47.

[29] J. Scherer, *Le commentaire d'Origene sur Rom. III. 5–V. 7* (Cairo: Imp. de l'institut français d'archéologie orientale, 1957). He compares (p. 115) Rufinus' "translation," which is not very close.

[30] Tertullian *Adv. Marc.* 4. 33. 8. Kroymann (*ad loc.*) deleted the words *Christus ipse* without adequate warrant.

that "endurance" (*hypomonē*) of Israel" must also be referred to the Savior, who, just as he is *autodikaiosynē*, *autoalētheia*, and *autoagiasmos* — the last suggested by *hagiasma*, "sanctuary" — is also *autoypomenē*.[31] As in our first two examples, Origen is providing Old Testament exegesis, to be sure of a Christological kind, but not philosophical theology.

What we have seen in our examination of Origen's use of these terms is that while in regard to the Father he derives them primarily from Greek philosophy — perhaps especially Numenius — and sets them in a philosophical framework, in regard to the Son they become part of the same framework but are explicitly based on exegesis of the Bible. Theologically, the key terms are *autologos*, from John, and *autosophia*, from 1 Corinthians, Proverbs, and the Wisdom of Solomon.[32] The Son, mediating the purpose of the Father, is inferior to him alone; he can thus be called "the essential (*ousiōdes*) *autodikaiosynē*" or "the essential autoaletheia."[33] He can be called the *autourgos* of the universe, but he obeys the command of his Father.[34] The *auto-* properties of the Son are derived from those of the Father.[35]

From Origen Onward

Origen himself, probably writing after his departure from Alexandria in 231, had to defend himself against charges that he was excessively concerned with Greek philosophy,[36] and it would appear that after his departure his terminology became somewhat suspect. Unfortunately, we know the teachers of Alexandria after his time only from fragments of their writings. It is probably significant, however, that his selection of *auto-* terms is reflected in none of these fragments, even though the theological ideas expressed are much the same as his. The only exception is provided in the *Refutation and Defence*,

[31] *Jer. hom.* 17. 4.
[32] See my article in *Texte und Untersuchungen*, 92 (1966): 462–72.
[33] *Ioh. comm.* 2. 6; 6. 6.
[34] *C. Cels.* 6. 60.
[35] See the table in Orbe, *Hacia la primera teologia*, p. 443.
[36] See P. Nautin, *Lettres et écrivains chrétiens des IIe et IIIe siècles* (Paris: Les éditions du Cerf, 1961), pp. 126–29.

which Dionysius of Alexandria addressed to Dionysius of Rome. "For if God is *autoagenēton* [as such, or by nature, uncreated], and his nature, so to speak is *agenēsia* [to be uncreated], matter would not be uncreated, for matter and God are not the same."[37] This is not one of Origen's terms, but the theological conception is his; and another fragment makes Dionysius' debt to Origen clear. "The Christ always existed, since he is Logos and Wisdom and Power . . . but the Son has his being not from himself but from the Father."[38] In a statement like this he could not use *autologos, autosophia,* and *autodynamis* without making his position more ambiguous than it was.

The terminology was too valuable to abandon, however, and we find it used without any qualms by both Athanasius and Eusebius of Caesarea. What has happened to it is, as Orbe states, that it has lost *su primer tecnicismo.*[39] Building on an Origenist base now become traditional at Alexandria, Athanasius in his *Contra gentes* (c. 318) spoke of the Son as *autosophia, autologos, autodynamis idia tou patros,* and then added four more terms which he regarded as showing that the Son is the "imprint" (Heb. 1:3) and "reflection" (Heb. 1:3; Wisd. 7:26) and "image" (Wisd. 7:26). These terms are Origen's *autoalētheia* and *autodikaiosynē,* and, in addition, *autophōs* (light as such) and *autoaretē* (virtue as such).[40] The first of the new terms, we may suspect, is exegetical in origin. God is Light (1 John 1:5), and the life of the Logos was the light of men (John 1:4); indeed, we may venture to suppose that somewhere Origen referred to the Son as *autophōs,* in view of the fact that both Athanasius and Eusebius[41] so refer to him. On the same basis, Athanasius further speaks of the Logos as *autoagiasmos* (from Origen) and *autozōē*—a term which, as

[37] Eusebius *Praep. evang.* 7. 19. 3, in C. L. Feltoe, *The Letters and other Remains of Dionysius of Alexandria* (Cambridge: At the University Press, 1904), p. 183, ll. 8–11.

[38] Feltoe, *Letters*, p. 186, ll. 6–9.

[39] Orbe, *Haca la primera teologia*, p. 419, n. 1.

[40] Migne *Patrologia Graeca* 25. 93B–C.

[41] *Dem. evang.* 4. 13. 9; *De eccl. theol.* 1. 8; 2. 14.

we have seen, Origen reserved for the Father; his distinction had since been abandoned among his followers.[42]

After the outbreak of Arianism, Athanasius seems to have realized that these terms could be used in support of the unity of the Son with the Father, and thus in his fourth *Oration against the Arians* he spoke of God—Father and Son together—as *autologos* and *autosophia.*[43]

As for Eusebius, his pre-Arian writings clearly reflect an Origenist base even though, like Athanasius, he was transferring terms to the Son which Origen had reserved to the Father. In the *Demonstratio Evangelica,* written before 318, we are not surprised to find Origen's old terms *autologos* and *autosophia* with reference to the Son.[44] It is more surprising to find the "firstborn Wisdom" explicitly called *autoagathos* and, analogously, *autokalos,*[45] not to mention *autozōē* and *autophōs.*[46] The Origenist distinctions are being neglected; in addition, two new terms, both applied to the Logos-Son, are almost certainly derived from Plotinus, whose treatises Eusebius had been reading. These are *autonous* and *autoousia.*[47] These terms, all but *autoousia* repeated in Eusebius' much later work *De ecclesiastica theologia,* show the extent to which his Christology and that of Athanasius were in agreement before the Arian controversy, although the later omission of *autoousia* is presumably due to the course of the controversy itself. In his late *Address to Constantine* he calls only the Father *autoagathon tēn ousian.*[48]

Eusebius' successor at Caesarea, Acacius, insisted against Marcellus of Ancyra that as the Father's image the Son is *autoousia, autoboulē,* and essential *dynamis* and *doxa;*[49] this is the general "orthodox" view of the fourth century. Epipha-

[42] *Dem. evang.* 4. 13. 9; 8. 1. 60.

[43] Migne *Patrologia Graeca* 26. 469B.

[44] *Dem. evang.* 4. 2. 1.

[45] *Dem. evang.* 4. 2. 1.

[46] *Dem. evang.* 4. 13. 9; 8. 1. 60.

[47] *Ibid.,* 4. 2. 1; *autonous* in Plotinus. *Enn.* 3. 2. 17; 5. 9. 13; *autoousia, Enn.* 6. 8. 12.

[48] *Laus Constantini* 12. 2.

[49] Epiphanius *Pan.* 72. 6. 5.

nius, the quintessence of orthodoxy, militantly argued against Aëtius that the Son must be *autoagathos* from the *Autoagathos* and that he is *aorgētos* (free from wrath) not because he is not wrathful but because of his essential *autoaorgēton.*[50] God himself is absolutely perfect and can be called *autoaisthēsis* and *autothelēma.*[51] Just, so, the God-Logos is perfect and is *autoteleios, autotheos autodynamis, autonous,* and *autophōs.*[52] Such terms are frequently used by Basil and the two Gregories and are applied indifferently to Father, Son, and Spirit. Naturally they recur in the writings ascribed to Dionysius the Areopagite.

It is fairly obvious that the demands of philosophical theology have triumphed over the careful exegetical distinctions made by Origen. The philosophy in question is Neoplatonic. Among the terms used by Plotinus in the *Enneads* we may mention *autoagathon* and *autokalon* (1. 8. 13), *autodikaiosynē* (1. 2. 6), *autoen* (the one itself, 5. 3. 12), *autoousia* (6. 8. 12), *autonous* (5. 9. 13), and even *autopsychē* (5. 9. 13). All these terms refer to the primal realities or patterns (cf. 1. 2. 6). Later Neoplatonists added to the store of terms.

What happened was that the exegetical base of Origen's terminology was neglected or rejected, while the increasing tendency to apply to the Son terms which in earlier Christian theology had been reserved for the Father was expressed in language borrowed from Neoplatonism. The novelty lay not in the borrowing—as we have seen, Origen's own language is philosophical in derivation—but in the use to which it was put.

Conclusion

Words with the prefix *auto-*, first used technically by Platonists known to Aristotle, took a new lease on life in the second century A.D. Practically unknown to Philo and Clement of Alexandria, such words were employed by the eclectic Platonist Numenius and among the Gnostics, with whom his thought

[50] *Ibid.*, 76. 36. 10–11.
[51] *Ibid.*, 76. 37. 9.
[52] *Ibid.*, 77. 35. 2.

has some affinities. Among Christians (perhaps Gnostic?) the term *autologos* was used before the time of Celsus (c. 178 A.D.). The chief proponent of this terminology was Origen among Christians, Plotinus among Neoplatonists. For Origen the terms had a function both theological and exegetical; while he employed them in the service of a system he also kept close to biblical language and ideas, especially in matters of Christology. After his time, however, the implications of trinitarian thought, developing in a philosophical environment, seemed to make it necessary to use the term in relation to all three persons of the Trinity, and philosophical theology triumphed over exegesis.

Thus Eusebius says that the Old Testament prophets call God – who is incorporeal and immaterial and *autonous* (or rather beyond *nous* and beyond all rational expression "by nature") – figuratively spirit and fire and light, and so on.[53] Though *autonous* is Neoplatonic, Eusebius' statement is still relatively close to the Bible, at least as understood in early Christian theology.[54] Similarly, around the same time the *Dialogue of Adamantius* refers to the Christ who suffered as *autoalētheia*.[55]

The distinctions based on exegesis were already breaking down, however, and they were obliterated in the systematic theology of the late fourth century. To give only a few examples, in his early treatise *De virginitate* Gregory of Nyssa refers to "the apostle" as calling God *autosophia* and sanctification (*hagiasmos*), truth, joy, peace, etc. The scriptural passage he has in mind is 1 Cor. 1:30: from God Christ became wisdom for us. In Gregory's mind the traditional Origenist exegesis of the passage has come to be what Paul said. Elsewhere in the same treatise he uses Paul's words more exactly and refers them to fruits of the believer's heart.[56] In his later *Catechetical Oration* he speaks of the Logos as *autozōē, auto-*

[53] *Praep. evang.* 7. 15. 15.

[54] Cf. Irenaeus *Adv. hear.* 1. 12. 1, etc.

[55] *Dial.* 5. 6.

[56] Cf. *De virg.* 17. 2, with the note of M. Aubineau, *Grégoire de Nysse: Traité de la virginité* (Paris: Les éditions du Cerf, 1966), p. 458, n. 1.

dynamis, and *autosophia*.[57] In the theological orations of Gregory of Nazianzus we find the most obvious movement toward philosophical theology. He argues that in spite of references to the Father as the "only true God" in John 17:3 and as "alone good" in Mark 10:18, the common deity of Father and Son must be implied; otherwise the *autoalētheia* (i.e., of the Son) would be excluded. And when he speaks of the Spirit as revelatory, illuminative, and vivifying, he says, "or rather, *autophōs* and life."[58] Gregory's statement is based not on exegesis but on philosophical theology.

What characterizes this whole movement in the use of the *auto-* terms is not exclusively borrowing by Christians from Greek philosophical terminology but a complex interweaving of influences. The terms first arose in philosophy and then were used among Gnostics. In the thought of Origen – like Plotinus a disciple of Ammonius Saccas – they developed a life of their own in the service of both exegesis and theology. At the same time they were flourishing in Neoplantonic circles. With the continuing and renewed influence of Neoplatonism on Christianity they tended to lose the exegetical import Origen had given them and came to be vehicles of a more strictly philosophical theology.

[57] J. H. Srawley, *The Catechetical Oration of Gregory of Nyssa* (Cambridge: C. J. Clay, 1903), p. 9, l. 15; 50, 22; 65, 18.

[58] A. J. Mason, *The Five Theological Orations of Gregory of Nazianzus* (Cambridge: At the University Press, 1899), p. 128, l. 13; 184, 6.

2

Before and after Constantine

MASSEY H. SHEPHERD, JR.

The periodizing of history is a necessary speculation if one is to be fair to the continuities and discontinuities of the historical process. It is the only way to give meaning and revelance to the instruction which the study of history offers, and to elevate it to the level of a science over and beyond the mere cataloguing of chronicles and annals. True, even chronological systems of dating carry an implicit interpretation that depends upon the event or person used as a starting point, the periods chosen for organizing the data, and the selection of entries to be recorded for posterity.

The perspective of history that stems from Christian faith is essentially eschatological, if not apocalyptic. It comprehends all history as a nexus of unique and unrepeatable particularities, which are no less related inextricably by reference to a final end. The unity of history and its continuity are apprehended by faith in a providence transcending history itself; its purpose is the revelation of salvation. But the glory to be revealed does not wait for the gathering together of all things at the end of time. It is manifested in particularities of the present time, above all in the perfect "fullness of time" in the historical event and person of Jesus Christ.[1]

Thus the simplest of all periodizations of history derives from Christian faith; namely, the division into two parts, B.C. and A.D. — before and after Christ. Though the principle is implicit in the New Testament, it is explicitly stated for the

[1] Gal. 4:4. See the important essay of Georges Florovsky, "The Predicament of the Christian Historian," in *Religion and Culture, Essays in*

first time in the introductory chapters of Eusebius' *Church History*, where salvation-history is summarized with reference to the twofold dispensation (*oikonomia*) of Christ the Logos,[2] before and after his Incarnation. But the dating of events "in the year of our Lord," i.e., from his Incarnation, first appears in the Paschal computations of Dionysius Exiguus (525),[3] a reckoning adopted by Bede and through him popularized in the western world.[4] Bede also anticipated the dating of events "before" the Incarnation,[5] but this custom did not become common until the later years of the seventeenth century.[6]

Early Christian chronology was dominated by apocalyptic. On the one hand, there was the symbolic numerology of the seven millennial ages of the world, based upon the seven-day creation story of Genesis.[7] This in turn gave way to an apologetic interest designed to prove the antiquity of Christianity, the priority of the Biblical revelation over the inspired insights of Greek philosophy. For this purpose the four-empire theory of the Book of Daniel was exploited — the last of them being,

---

Honor of Paul Tillich, ed. Walter Leibrecht (London: SCM Press Ltd., 1958), pp. 140–66.

[2] Eusebius *Church History* 1. 7–8; 4. 1–15.

[3] B. Altaner, *Patrologie*, 5th ed. (Freiburg: Herder, 1958), pp. 443–44; J. Rambaud-Buhot, "Denys le Petit," *Dictionnaire de droit canonique*, 4:1131–52 ("C'est lui le père de l'ère chrétienne," p. 1138).

[4] R. L. Poole, *Studies in Chronology and History*, collected and edited by A. L. Poole (Oxford: Clarendon Press, 1934), pp. 1–37; Wilhelm Levison, *England and the Continent in the Eighth Century* (Oxford: Clarendon Press, 1946), pp. 265–79; C. W. Jones, *Saints' Lives and Chronicles in Early England* (Ithaca: Cornell University Press, 1947), pp. 31–50.

[5] Bede *Ecclesiastical History* 1. 2 — for his dating of Julius Caesar's invasion of Britain.

[6] J. H. J. van der Pot, *De Periodisering der Geschiedenis, Een Overzicht der Theorieën*, Ph.D. diss., Amsterdam (Te's-Gravenhage: W. P. van Stockum and Zoon, 1951), pp. 51–52; Oscar Cullmann, *Christ and Time* (Philadelphia: Westminster Press, 1950), pp. 17–18, n. 2, points to Bossuet.

[7] Jean Daniélou, "La typologie millenariste de le semain dans le Christianisme primitif," *Vigiliae Christianae* 2 (1948), 1–16, and *The Bible and the Liturgy* (Notre Dame, Ind.: University of Notre Dame Press, 1956), pp. 255–86. Cf. Van der Pot, *De Periodisering der Geschiedenis*, pp. 39–43. The Biblical basis is Ps. 90:4; 2 Peter 3:8; Rev. 20:2–7.

of course, the universal Empire of the Romans.[8] Through the influence of Jerome and Orosius this periodization remained dominant in medieval historiography. Its last great expression is the *De Monarchia* of Dante.[9]

If secular historians took over the Christian division of eras before and after Christ, church historians in turn have adopted from their secular colleagues the periodization of the Christian era into ancient, medieval, and modern epochs. The distinction also appears first in the late seventeenth century, in the three-volume work of Christopher Kellner (d. 1707), a professor of history at the University of Halle.[10] The classification ignores, of course, the history of Eastern Christendom; and it leaves open to continual debate the exact chronological dividing lines that separate the three epochs. Between the ancient and medieval periods the line has been drawn at various stages from Diocletian to Charlemagne, and between the medieval and modern periods from Petrarch to the founding of the Royal Society in London.

Today a new challenge to our accustomed patterns imposes itself upon the historical process. In a prophetic course of

[8] Dan. 2:31ff.; Irenaeus *Against Heresies* 5. 26. 1; Hippolytus *On Christ and Antichrist* 19 ff., *Commentary on Daniel* 2. 11–13, and 4. 2–6; Jerome *Commentary on Daniel* 2:31 ff., and 7:1 ff. (*P.L.* 25. 526 ff., 552 ff.), Augustine *City of God* 20. 23. In Christian interpretation the four kingdoms are generally identified as the Babylonian (or Assyrian), Persian, Macedonian, and Roman. But Orosius *History Against the Pagans* 2. 1, lists them as Babylonian, Macedonian, Carthaginian, and Roman. Cf. Van der Pot, *De Periodisering der Geschiedenis*, pp. 77–79, for later medieval writers. For classical parallels, see reference in G. B. Ladner, *The Idea of Reform: Its Impact on Christian Thought and Action in the Age of the Fathers* (Cambridge: Harvard University Press, 1959), pp. 14–15.

[9] 2. 8. Though Dante cites Orosius, he follows the scheme of Jerome. The four-empire theory was followed as late as the sixteenth century in the work of Johann Sleidan (1556). See Van der Pot, *De Periodisering der Geschiedenis*, p. 81; J. W. Johnson, "Chronological Writing: Its Concepts and Development," *History and Theory*, 2 (1962): 124–45.

[10] Kellner (also known as Cellarius) published three volumes of universal history: *Historia antiqua* (1685), *Historia medii aevi* (1688), and *Historia novi* (1696). See Van der Pot, *De periodisering der Geschiedenis*, pp. 121–22, 270; and the Preface by Henri Berr in Ferdinand Lot, *The End of the Ancient World and the Beginning of the Middle Ages* (New York: Alfred A. Knopf, 1931). pp. xx–xxv.

lectures prepared during the immediate aftermath of the Second World War, Romano Guardini posited without qualification his thesis of *The End of the Modern World.* His editor summarizes thus:

> Not only does Guardini reject the old gospel of progress, but he insists that there is no chance of grafting the old personal world to the new world of technologized anonymity. . . . The old aristocratic ideal of the universal man must perforce collapse in a world wherein all effort is co-operative if not absolutely collectivist. The old bourgeois ideal of a full warm life lived within the bosom of the private family cannot co-exist with a new age whose social structure is better symbolized by the factory and the barracks than by the cottage and the castle. . . .
>
> The Christian of tomorrow will be a man of the masses; he will be conditioned psychologically like his atheist coworkers. His grip on the supernatural will not be buttressed by that natural sense of the divine, that awareness of the numinous in all things, that man has until now felt as he looked out on a world other than himself. Seeking God, the Christian of the future will scan the horizon in vain; nowhere in the new age will he find Him, but only in that love which conquers the world.[11]

The disciples of Professor Arnold Toynbee have also been eager to describe our contemporary situation as "post-Christian," at least with respect to western, secular civilization.[12] Christian believers may well disdain to accept such Olympian judgments upon history. Christian faith is bound to reject as premature any designation of an era as "post-Christian." And

[11] Romano Guardini, *The End of the Modern World: A Search for Orientation*, edited with an Introduction by F. D. Wilhelmsen (New York: Sheed & Ward, 1956), pp. 11–12.

[12] Toynbee posited his view that western society could no longer call itself Christian in *A Study of History* (Oxford, 1934 ff.), 1:34; 6:344. Typical of his later expression is the following: "the tide of Christianity has been ebbing and . . . our post-Christian Western secular civilization that has emerged is a civilization of the same order as the pre-Christian Graeco-Roman civilization." — *Civilization on Trial* (New York: Meridian Books, 1958), p. 202.

in fact, neither Guardini nor Toynbee is so pessimistic about Christianity that he does not recognize, from its own history, its remarkable powers of adaptation and response to unprecedented situations.

It would be far more accurate, from a historical point of view, to describe the contemporary crisis of Christianity as the emergence of the "post-Constantinian" age. For the structures of relationship between religion and society that have dominated the Church's outlook and action, whether in the East or the West, whether Catholic or Protestant, have been rooted in the acceptance of and development from the Constantinian settlement. The broad signs of their dissolution today are evident.

They are seen not only in the decline of political control of the world by those western powers which have traditionally been "Christendom" and the direct heirs of Graeco-Roman culture and law. Within so-called western civilization itself the several explicit or implicit establishments of Christianity are rapidly being reduced to mere ceremonial vestiges. The Church no longer has an accepted patronage in the direction of public morality or a predominant role in public education, and it has in fact given up responsibility for the promotion of the arts and sciences. Two specific illustrations may be selected as indications of the new order of things in this emerging post-Constantinian era. One is the collapse of clericalism, the privileged status and influence of the ordained ministry. The other is the desperate need of the "older" churches for guidance in renewal and *aggiornamento* from the "younger" churches of its own missionary planting—churches of tiny minorities in cultures not rooted in Graeco-Roman civilization, whose only resource is the Holy Spirit and whose only privilege is witness.

It is not surprising, therefore, that in recent years there has been a remarkable revival of interest, among both secular and church historians, in the study of Constantine: both his religious convictions and policies and their impact upon the course of history.[13] One does not need to exaggerate the "great-man theory" of history in order to affirm the crucial impact of Constantine's career upon the course of human events. As a statesman and military commander he would have deserved his posthumous title of "The Great" quite apart from his religious policy. He was a revolutionary in the tradition of Alexander the Great and Julius Caesar – a fact recognized, though for petty reasons, by his nephew Julian, who described him as "an innovator and disturber of ancient laws and custom."[14]

Much scholarly ink has been expended upon an analysis of the process and character of Constantine's conversion to Christianity, though in fact a great part of the debate has centered in assessments of the authenticity and credibility of Eusebius' *Life* of the emperor. Out of recent discussion, certain judgments appear to receive a wide consensus. There is no question that Constantine was intensely ambitious, and that his will to power was undergirded by an inner sense of destiny. His personal gifts of leadership and command were evident at an early age (and there is no good reason to suppose that he was not aware of them), and these were confirmed in the loyalty of his troops, who followed him in daring risks that resulted in extraordinary successes in the battlefield. That Constantine rather consistently won his laurels against odds may be explained by his peculiar genius in military strategy, not to say also by effective rapport with his army. But he may be forgiven if he also attributed his success to divine favor.

[13] The older literature on Constantine may be found in the masterful Introduction to Eusebius' *Life*, by E. C. Richardson in A Select Library of Nicene and Post-Nicene Fathers, 2d ser., 1:411–69. A good listing of recent publications is Johannes Quasten, *Patrology* (Westminster, Md.: Newman Press, 1960), 3:322–24. This can be supplemented by the entries in the annual *Bibliographica Patristica*, ed. W. Schneemelcher (Berlin: Walter de Gruyter & Co.), for the years since 1956. See also André Piganiol, "L'état actuel de la question constantinienne, 1930/49," *Historia*, 1 (1950): 82–96; Joseph Vogt, "Bemerkungen zum Gang der Constantinforschung," in *Mullus, Festschrift Theodor Klauser*, Jahrbuch für Antike und Christentum, suppl. vol. 1 (Münster Westfalen: Aschendorff, 1964), pp. 374–79.

[14] In Ammianus Marcellinus *History* 21. 8. Cf. Joseph Vogt, "Kaiser Julian über seinem Oheim Constantin den Grossen," *Historia*, 4 (1955): 339–52.

Though Roman imperial power rested fundamentally upon military force, its effective governance demanded a high degree of political sagacity in gaining support of the ruling aristocracy, if not of the populace generally. And this required a tangible evidence of social and economic stability and religious peace. Diocletian's energetic reforms had assured the former; his persecution had wrecked the latter.[15] Constantine's decision, therefore, to place his fortune under the aegis of the God of the Christians was impelled not only by his own inner religious attractions but by the necessities of his struggle for power in gaining the *imperium*.[16] He was not alone in realizing this demand. The deathbed edict of toleration issued by Galerius admitted the problem of public order created by the persecution. All the rivals for the succession had to determine their course on the religious issue. Maximin Daia favored continued persecution, but Maxentius and Licinius, though unattracted to Christianity, sided with Constantine for toleration. It is therefore important to remember that the conflict between Constantine and Maxentius in 312 was not fought out on religious grounds,[17] and the later struggle with Licinius in 324 was by no means a "holy war."[18]

[15] The increasing severity of the persecution revolted many pagans; cf. Eusebius *Martyrs of Palestine* 9. 3. See the excellent study of the persecution by G. E. M. de Ste. Croix, "Aspects of the 'Great' Persecution," *Harvard Theological Review*, 47 (1954): 75–113.

[16] No doubt many factors lie in the background of Constantine's direction towards Christianity: influences of his family and especially the tolerant attitude of his father (Eusebius *Life of Constantine* 1. 13–17), and his personal disgust at persecution (*ibid.*, 2. 24 ff., 48 ff.; 4. 12). On the influence of Christian advisors, especially Bishop Ossius, see V. C. de Clercq, *Ossius of Cordova: A Contribution to the History of the Constantinian Period* (Washington, D.C.: Catholic University of America Press, 1954), pp. 158–61.

[17] That Maxentius tolerated Christianity has been shown by Hans von Schoenebeck, "Beiträge zur Religionspolitik des Maxentius und Constantin," *Klio*, suppl. 43, n.s., bk. 30 (1939).

[18] For Licinius' persecution, see Eusebius *Life of Constantine* 1. 49–56, and 2. 1–5; the critiques of P. Orgels, "A propos des erreurs historiques de la *Vita Constantini*," *Annuaire de l'Institut de philologie et d'histoire orientale et sslaves*, 12 (1952): 575–611; and C. Calderone, *Costantino e il cattolicesimo* (Florence: Felice le Monnier, 1962), 1: 205–30.

Constantine, however, went further than his rivals. He openly and deliberately embraced allegiance to the Christian God. Whatever the circumstances and nature of Constantine's "conversion" experience prior to the Battle of Milvian Bridge, few critics today accept the harsh verdict of Jacob Burckhardt that it was neither genuine nor sincere but a cynically calculated policy of "a genius driven without surcease by ambition and lust for power . . . , a man essentially unreligious" and a "murderous egoist who possessed the great merit of having conceived of Christianity as a world power and of having acted accordingly."[19] Burckhardt can arrive at this conclusion not only by an elimination of the admittedly biased interpretations of Eusebius but by a discounting of the pagan historians, such as Zosimus, who "fell into the same error of assuming that his conversion was genuine and not merely for outward show."[20]

One may concede that Constantine did not adopt Christianity without some element of calculation. No political figure could risk such an extraordinary change, at a time of crisis, without some premeditated consideration of its effects upon his fortunes. One is reminded of Augustine's account of the concern of the eminent rhetorician Victorinus, who had been honored by a statue in the Forum of Trajan, lest his conversion "offend his friends who were proud demon-worshippers and their enmity fall upon him."[21] Calculation is not in any case an inevitable sign of insincerity. It is simply a matter of proper timing for revealing one's decisions. Constantine took a risk that was both unnecessary and dangerous, for it is unlikely that the Christian minority in the western provinces was in any position to assist him materially in the final issue with Maxentius. In actuality, his religious conversion was revealed only to his army, and that too in a cryptic sign that indicated a

[19] Jacob Burckhardt, *The Age of Constantine the Great* (Garden City, N.Y.: Doubleday Anchor Books, 1956), pp. 281–82. The work was first published in 1852.

[20] *Ibid.*, p. 290.

[21] *Confessions* 8. 2; for the location of the statue, see Jerome *Chronicle*, for the year 3270 (A.D. 354).

divine portent. The psychological impact was without doubt useful.

Success confirmed faith — a not unusual experience. It is to Constantine's credit that he acted henceforth in conformity to his religious intuition. The genuineness of his conversion is sufficiently attested. From this time forth he not only refused the title of divinity accorded a Roman Emperor; he also disdained all personal participation in pagan sacrifice.[22] He gave Christianity official status and patronage equal to the traditional pagan cults and endowed it, from the imperial treasury, beginning with the gift of the Lateran palace to the Roman bishop and the remuneration of the straitened church in North Africa.[23] Though he was careful not to offend the predominantly pagan Senate of Rome, by the guarded and ambiguous inscriptions accompanying his official monuments, he set up a colossal statue of himself in the impressive new Basilica of Maxentius in the Roman Forum, holding in his hand the salutary sign of the Cross.[24] Within a few months after his victory at the Milvian Bridge, he sealed his alliance with Licinius by an agreement on religious policy (the so-called "Edict of Milan") and the marriage of his sister Constantia to his colleague.[25] He involved himself at once in the internal affairs of the Church, intrusting important missions to certain bishops for the unity and well-being of the churches, and instructed his chancery to draw up letters that identified himself with

[22] The best discussion of Constantine and paganism at this early period of his reign is Andrew Alföldi, *The Convention of Constantine and Pagan Rome* (Oxford: Clarendon Press, 1948), pp. 53 ff.

[23] The gift of the Lateran is attested by Optatus *On the Schism of the Donatists* 1. 23, which recounts the episcopal synod under Pope Miltiades that examined the Donatist claims; documents of Constantine's benefactions are recorded in Eusebius *Church History* 10. 5–6.

[24] Eusebius *Life of Constantine* 1. 40; *Church History* 9. 9. 10–11; Carlo Cecchelli, *Il trionfo della croce* (Rome: Edizioni Paoline, 1954). Fragments of the statue are preserved in the Capitoline Museum in Rome.

[25] For the "Edict": Lactantius *On the Death of the Persecutors* 48. 2 ff.; Eusebius *Church History* 10. 5; for the marriage of Licinius and Constantia: Lactantius *Death of the Persecutors* 43. 1; *Excerpts of Valesius* 5. 13.

the promotion of Christianity.[26] Above all, he arranged for the education of his sons under the tutelage of Lactantius, a distinguished Christian rhetorician.[27]

All these actions, within the first few years of Constantine's rule over the West, point to a decisive stance of the Emperor in commitment to Christianity and a design to favor it. They cannot be brushed aside with a theory that Constantine remained, at least until after the defeat of Licinius, as a dissembling if not confused syncretist. Though his personal aversion to the paganism of old Rome was immediate and consistent, he did not become reckless and iconoclastic with its tradition. The ambivalence and ambiguity of his coinage and public monuments were conciliatory to the pagan sentiment of the majority of his subjects, and particularly to the Roman aristocracy, whose services he continued to use generously in the civil government.[28] His legislation in this early period, insofar as it displays Christian influence, was not disruptive, but followed an *ad hoc* pragmatism—or, to use Alföldi's phrase, like that of "a good rider, now tightening, now slackening rein." [29] The supports given to family stability, the ameliorations in the treatment of the defenseless, the promulgation of Sunday as a holiday, even the harsher limitations upon the privileges of the Jews—none of these would have been particularly offensive to pagan sentiment. In the area of criminal law and procedure, C. N. Cochrane noted a new tendency "to improve moral and social conditions, with its inevitable concomitant, a growing confusion between the notions of sin and crime." [30] Perhaps the most revolutionary act in establishing the Church was the legal recognition of episcopal courts in matters of civil litigation.[31]

[26] See above, note 23.

[27] Jerome *Lives of Illustrious Men* 80.

[28] Alföldi, *Conversion of Constantine*, pp. 62 f.

[29] *Ibid.*, p. 78.

[30] C. N. Cochrane, *Christianity and Classical Culture* (Oxford: Clarendon Press, 1940), p. 203. Cochrane's whole discussion of Constantine's legislation is illuminating.

[31] *Codex Theod.* 1. 27. 1 (318); confirmed *Const. Sirmond.* 1 (333). See A. Steinwenter, "Audientia episcopalis," *Reallexikon für Antike und*

It is difficult for lesser men to comprehend genius, though the temptation to do so is irresistible. Much of the fascination of Constantine lies in the enigma of his person, more especially in the inmost citadel of his religious consciousness as it is concordant with his drive for realization of his perception of destiny. He left no diary or *sacra privata.* We depend upon the testimony of partisans. Among them only two were contemporaries and personal acquaintances; namely, Lactantius and Eusebius, both of them rhetoricians and scholars, old men who had lived through the persecution and the triumph of their faith. Both of them were honored by Constantine – Lactantius as tutor of his son Crispus, Eusebius as the court orator on special occasions. We have no evidence that either of them enjoyed prolonged or intimate personal association with the Emperor, or were treated as special advisors, such as the politically astute Bishops Ossius of Cordova and, later, Eusebius of Nicomedia. The latter (Eusebius of Nicomedia) appears to have been related to the imperial family and to have enjoyed the confidence of Constantia, the Emperor's favored sister and wife of Licinius.[32] His fortunes, contrary to all deserving in the opinion of church historians, were no doubt related to Constantine's deep emotional attachment to his family.[33]

Christentum, 1:915–17; Jean Gaudemet, *L'église dans l'empire romain* (Paris: Sirey, 1958), pp. 230–36.

[32] Ammianus Marcellinus *History* 22. 9; Philostorgius *Church History* 1. 9.

[33] For the career of Eusebius of Nicomedia, with full reference to sources, see M. Spanneut, "Eusèbe de Nicomédie," *Dictionnaire d'histoire et de géographie ecclésiastique,* 15:1466–71. The judgment of him by Louis Duchesne is classic: "The memory of this intriguing prelate, in whom one can find no single sympathetic feature, remains weighted with a heavy responsibility." – *Early History of the Christian Church* (London: John Murray, 1912), 2:169. Constantine's family devotion was stained by the execution of his son Crispus and his wife Fausta in A.D. 326 – a tragedy not mentioned by Eusebius, but recorded first by pagan historians. Ammianus Marcellinus notes simply the fact of Crispus' fate (14. 11. 20); Julian implied "murder" of kindred (*Symposium: The Caesars* 336B); fifth-century writers such as Zosimus wove a tale of incest (*New History* 2. 29). Modern biographers admit that it is impossible to be certain of the true facts. E.g., Cochrane, *Christianity,* p. 207, suspects treason; André Piganiol, *L'empereur Constantin* (Paris: Rieder, 1932), p. 170, believes that Constantine was caught in the web

Lactantius makes no claim to any direct communication from Constantine about his conversion, nor does he postulate any prophecies of its enduring effects. Strongly biased as he is, he nonetheless records facts in a treatise addressed to "a person of knowledge."[34] Eusebius first met Constantine at the Council of Nicaea – some ten years after Lactantius' contacts, at a time when Constantine's Christian commitment was indisputable. For all his enthusiasms and biases, Eusebius does not need to be downgraded as a historian. Like all historians, he made mistakes in the dating and interpretation of documents, but time and again he has been shown to be reliable in his transcriptions of sources.[35] He tells us quite frankly in the *Life* of the Emperor that his work is an encomium and that he is selective in what is worthy of praise.[36] He is honest enough to suggest that the Emperor's relation of his conversion experience was colored by time's reflection upon it; he does not ask his readers to accept it verbatim.[37]

---

of his own laws on sexual morality; A. H. M. Jones, *Constantine and the Conversion of Europe* (New York: Macmillan Co., 1949), pp. 243–46, considers the offense to have been moral but disassociates the crimes of Crispus and Fausta, respectively. Zosimus' supposition that Constantine's guilt-feelings for his action led to his adoption of Christianity, because of its claim to forgive sin – a resolution in which he implicates Ossius – is properly rejected by most historians today. See De Clercq, *Ossius of Cordova*, pp. 285–87. Burckhardt, *Age of Constantine*, p. 328, sees the affair, characteristically, as consistent with Constantine's "inconstant nature." Dorothy L. Sayers has dramatized the tragedy in the final scenes of her play *The Emperor Constantine: A Chronicle* (New York: Harper & Bros., 1951).

[34] Lactantius *On the Death of the Persecutors* 52. For a just estimate of Lactantius as a historian, see the edition of J. Moreau in Sources Chrétiennes, no. 39 (Paris: Les éditions du Cerf, 1954), pp. 22 ff.

[35] The attack of Henri Grégoire on the authenticity and reliability of the *Vita* has not been sustained (see the Bibliography in n. 13 above). A confirmation of the genuineness of the documents was published by A. H. M. Jones and T. C. Skeat, "Notes on the Genuineness of the Constantinian Documents in Eusebius's Life of Constantine," *Journal of Ecclesiastical History*, 5 (1954): 196–200.

[36] 1. 11.

[37] 1. 28. The vision related to Eusebius is not necessarily the same as that recounted by Lactantius. See the discussion of Pio Franchi de'Cavalieri, *Constantiniana*, Studi e Testi 171 (Vatican City, 1953), pp. pp. 5–50.

Apart from official documents of the chancery, Eusebius gives us very few quotations from the mouth of Constantine himself — an indication of Eusebius' care for evidence. Apart from the account of the conversion, the most notable example of verbal reminiscence is the cryptic remark of Constantine at a dinner party for bishops: "You are bishops of what is within the Church; I am a bishop, ordained by God, of what is outside."[38] Perhaps the most revealing utterance (and revealing also for its reticence) is the transcript of Constantine's address to the bishops at Nicaea, for it was at this moment that he was at the height of both his political power and his influence on the Church. It is not likely that Eusebius would have distorted this record (even if he had no written notes of it), for the impression of the occasion must have been powerful upon his conscience.[39]

In this address Constantine made two points which were crucial in all his thinking: (1) By the will and power of the "supreme God," "the universal King," "our Saviour," he has been the instrument of overthrow of tyrants and the restoration of freedom to the Church. (2) He is now primarily concerned with "peace and concord" among the bishops, since "in my judgment," said he, "intestine strife within the Church of God is far more evil and dangerous than any kind of war or conflict." It is clear that he makes no neat theological distinction between "the supreme God" and "our common Lord and Saviour." This is a matter for the bishops as theologians to decide. It is also clear that he expects their "favor" to him, their "fellow-servant," in removing the causes of disunion. We believe that any fair estimate of Constantine must admit that he worked consistently with these principles and that he held

[38] 4. 24. See Calderone, *Costantino*, pp. xi-xlv. Much of the obscurity of his saying lies in the uncertainty of the gender of the article τῶν, whether it is masculine or neuter. Calderone's careful analysis is in favor of the neuter.

[39] 3. 12. Eusebius' emotion on the occasion would be the more intense, in view of the fact that he came to the Council under a suspended sentence of excommunication passed at the Synod of Antioch in early 325. See De Clercq, *Ossius of Cordova*, pp. 206–17, 234–35; D. S. Wallace-Hadrill, *Eusebius of Caesarea* (Westminster, Md.: Canterbury Press, 1961), pp. 24–27.

them sincerely. This was the religious face that he set to the world. To probe more deeply into his inner piety becomes merely speculative. Whether the sentiments are lofty or commonplace depends upon one's point of view. They cannot, it seems to us, be described as superstitious.

If Constantine said little about Christian love, he said much about Christian peace. In his recent study *Pagan and Christian in an Age of Anxiety*, Professor E. R. Dodds—no special pleader for Christianity—has made a perceptive observation. After quoting Rostovtzeff's comment that in the world of Constantine "hatred and envy reigned everywhere: the peasants hated the landowners and the officials, the city proletariat hated the city bourgeoisie, the army was hated by everybody," he says: "Christianity was the one force which could effectively bring the jarring elements together: hence its attractiveness to Constantine."[40]

Historians are not allowed to indulge in an "if," though all succumb to the temptation. *If* Constantine had not been converted, what would have been the fate of Christianity in the ancient world? It would be easy to marshal arguments to support its ultimate triumph, apart from purely theological principles, without the intervention of Constantine. Immediately one can point to the failure of concerted effort at its suppression—as Galerius admitted in his deathbed Edict of Toleration. "Very great numbers," he said, "held to their determination."[41] Other considerations come readily to mind: the resilient organizational structure of the Church, the reasonable persuasion of its apologetic, the ability to adapt to dominant religious sentiments of piety, the discipline of its morality, the acceptance of men of whatever station in life and ability to give them hope, and a sense of meaning to their vocation. The list could be extended endlessly.

The eminent Harnack saw the root of its triumph in its

[40] E. R. Dodds, *Paganism and Christianity in an Age of Anxiety* (Cambridge: At the University Press, 1965), pp. 136–37, n. 4.

[41] Lactantius *Death of the Persecutors*, 34.

"spirit of *universalism,* by dint of which it laid hold of *the entire life of man* in all its functions," referring to Jesus the Logos "everything that could possibly be deemed of human value, . . . powers of attraction, by means of which it was enabled at once to absorb and to subordinate the whole of Hellenism."[42] Professor Dodds, already cited, puts it with disarming simplicity: "Love of one's neighbor is not an exclusively Christian virtue, but in our period the Christians appear to have practised it much more effectively than any other group. . . . Christians were in a more than formal sense 'members one of another': . . . that was a major cause, perhaps the strongest single cause, of the spread of Christianity."[43] He leans heavily upon the grudging testimony of Julian, who was at least a contemporary witness. In a letter to Arsacius, "Highpriest of Galatia," Julian wrote: "Why do we not observe that it is their philanthropy towards strangers, their care for the graves of the dead, and their pretended holiness of life that have done most to increase atheism [i.e., Christianity]? . . . The impious Galileans support not only their own poor but ours as well."[44]

Julian's compliment has enduring value. But it does not touch upon the peculiar impact of Constantine himself upon the fortunes of the Church. He was too close to the Constantinian "revolution" to understand it in historic perspective. Yet his attempts to revitalize paganism illustrate some of the very effects of the new order that we may legitimately attribute to Constantine's genius.

The day dreams of what would have happened, *if* . . . are shattered by the actual particularities of what Constantine did, whether premeditated or not, and how the Church, in large measure unprepared for him, responded. In one matter, Constantine had no choice. If he was to be a Christian, he must give up the title of divinity, and with it, implicitly, the deification of the State as an absolute end in itself. The renun-

[42] Adolf Harnack, *The Expansion of Christianity in the First Three Centuries* (New York: G. P. Putnam's Sons, 1904–5), 2:145.

[43] Dodds, *Paganism and Christianity*, pp. 136–38.

[44] *Letters* 429D, 430D.

ciation was in fact revolutionary, though it was hidden, not merely because Constantine continued the "sacral" ceremonial trappings surrounding the imperial office. It was hidden because the Emperor now assumed an aura of divine right by claim to be the chosen instrument of God. The Emperor was not God, but God's vice-gerent, and his government was an image of God's sovereignty – or, as Professor Baynes has put it, "a terrestrial copy of the rule of God in Heaven."[45] The transformation of the Hellenistic theory of kingship was subtle. The Emperor was not himself God-manifest, but as it were a "sacrament" of God-manifest, namely the Logos. Constantine was ordained by God not only as a bishop for "what is outside" the Church; he becomes within the Church – if one may judge by his final arrangements for burial in the Church of the Holy Apostles at Constantinople – a *primus inter pares* among the apostles themselves.[46]

It may be noted in passing that Julian made no effort to restore the imperial cult, and he disdained divine honors. His lack of interest in ceremonial surrounding his person in fact brought him ridicule from Christian and pagan alike. His ideals of kingship were more Hellenic than Hellenistic, more philosophical than theological.[47]

Churchmen like Eusebius responded enthusiastically to the theocratic ideology of Constantine.[48] They found a basis for it in the Old Testament monarchy. Theophany replaced eschatology, as is evident from the impressive *martyria* built

[45] Norman H. Baynes, "Eusebius and the Christian Empire," *Mélanges Bidez, Annuaire de l'Institut de philologie et d'histoire orientales*, 2 (1934): 13–18.

[46] Eusebius *Life of Constantine* 4. 60, 71. Constantine's burial near the altar, in the center of a circle of twelve cenotaphs for the relics of the apostles was unprecedented, and possibly the occasion of scandal. Bishop Macedonius removed the body, and it was placed in a separate mausoleum built by Constantius II adjacent to the church. See the acute discussion of the problems concerning the history of this edifice by Richard Krautheimer, "Zu Konstantins Apostelkirche in Konstantinopel," *Mullus, Festschrift Theodor Klauser*, pp. 224–29.

[47] Julian's ideals are set forth in his *Letter to Themistius*, esp. 259AB–267B; for the ridicule, see his *Misopogon* 343CD.

[48] Notably in his *Oration* delivered on the tricennalia.

by the Emperor and his family.[49] The older eschatology had been weakening, in any case. Even Tertullian had made his peace with the Pauline injunction about the "powers that be being instituted by God." "Caesar is more ours than yours," he had said, "since he was appointed by our God."[50] (This was written under Septimius Severus!)

There was protest, however. We may discount the sincerity of the Donatists, since they were the first to appeal to Constantine to adjudicate an intrachurch quarrel; but the principle which they raised was not successfully quieted.[51] Then there is Athanasius, with all his personal animosities and political power play. But he was fighting, even before Constantine's death, for a theological principle.[52] And that principle was one which Constantine himself had imposed at Nicaea—the *homoousios*, the unity of the Godhead.[53]

Again, it would be possible to argue that the Church would have worked out its monotheistic-trinitarian faith without interference from the State. But the fact remains that Constantine precipitated the solution; for it is unlikely that without his intervention the *homoousios* would have been adopted by the fathers at Nicaea. It does not matter if Ossius or some other bishop inspired him with its promotion. Constantine was a strict monotheist; the substantial unity of the Father and the Son would have appealed to him. Arianism was essentially polytheistic, more so perhaps than the intimations of contemporary pagan philosophy. The faith of Nicaea was a great simplification of theology and gave the ancient world a real choice of one God or many—something which Judaism had failed to accomplish because of its cultic particularities.

[49] André Grabar, *Martyrium, Recherches sur le culte des reliques et l'art chrétien antique*, 2 vols. (Paris: Collège de France, 1946), 1:204 ff.

[50] Rom. 13:1; Tertullian *Apology* 33.

[51] W. H. C. Frend, *The Donatist Church: A Movement of Protest in Roman North Africa* (Oxford: Clarendon Press, 1942), pp. 159–60.

[52] This is suggested by Athanasius' resolute refusal to obey the Emperor in restoring Arius to communion; cf. Socrates *Church History* 1. 27.

[53] That the intervention of Constantine in support of the *homoousios* was decisive is reluctantly admitted by Eusebius, in his well-known letter to his Church in Caesarea; see Socrates *Church History* 1. 8; Athanasius *On the Decrees of Nicaea* 33.

Julian's failure, theologically, was the same. Because of Nicaea, serious thinkers can no longer argue whether God is one or many, though they may argue whether there is one God or none. The collapse of paganism in the fourth century is really not so mysterious. The common man found in the Church's theological argument an interest, however crude, that is unimaginable with respect to the involved traditions of a Porphyry or a Julian. As Gregory of Nyssa remarked:

> Ask a man for change and he will give you a piece of philosophy about the Begotten and the Unbegotten. If you inquire the price of a loaf of bread, he replies, "The Father is greater and the Son inferior." If you ask whether a bath is ready, the answer you get is that the Son is made out of nothing! [54]

A third and immediate impact of Constantine's conversion to Christianity concerns the novel relationships between civil and ecclesiastical government. The change is difficult to describe precisely, for there was no break with the tradition of established religion. From one point of view it is possible to interpret the so-called "Edict of Milan" as simply an enlargement of this establishment to include Christianity and a widening of tolerance and state support to an even more pluralistic religious situation.

In actuality it did not, and could not, work out this way. An absolute sovereign was sincerely committed to a religious persuasion inherently universalistic and exclusive in its claims and not prepared to accept a status of equality among competitors. It is indicative of the "magnanimity" of Constantine that he managed to be as forbearing towards paganism as he did.[55] In a sense, he was forced by the Church itself to involve the State in its affairs — these not so much matters of broad

[54] Gregory of Nyssa *Oration on the Deity of the Son and Holy Spirit* (*P. G.* 46. 557).

[55] On the policy of Constantine towards paganism, see Luigi Salvatorelli, "La politica religiosa e la religiosità di Costantino," *Ricerche religiose*, 4 (1928): 289–328; Piganiol, *L'empereur Constantin*, pp. 185 ff.; Alföldi, *Conversion of Constantine*, pp. 105 ff.; Jones, *Constantine and the Conversion of Europe*, pp. 209 ff.; Hermann Doerries, *Con-*

civil concern but of internal schisms, first with the Donatists and then with the Arians and Meletians. No previous *Pontifex Maximus* had been faced with such problems of religious unity.

The reason was that Christianity, unlike paganism, was essentially more than a cult. It was a unitive system of theology and ethics, and in addition it had a powerfully cohesive organizational structure. It is a tribute to Julian's intelligence that he understood this difference and planned a similar program for paganism as the only possible way for paganism to recapture its predominance.[56] Julian's reign was too short, in any event, for his program to have much success, but it is questionable whether it could have succeeded. One has only to compare the religious ideology that separated Symmachus and Ambrose.[57]

It is true that episcopal synods were kept distinct from lay senates and consistories. The bishops did not become (at least for some centuries) an official part of the civil bureaucracy, though they soon came to share many of its privileges. But just as the civil and military jurisdictions were fused at the top in the person of the Emperor, so also were the civil and ecclesiastical jurisdictions. The protection of religion by the State became more than a defensive matter; it involved positive promotion of theological orthodoxy, moral ideals, and the enforcement of canon law.[58] The Church could not be satisfied with the old principle that the due honor of the divinity was needful for the security and welfare of the State. Due honor meant right honor. Constantine accepted the thesis. His sons and successors carried it through by appropriate legislation.[59]

---

stantine and Religious Liberty (New Haven: Yale University Press, 1960), pp. 23 ff.

[56] See especially his various letters to pagan priests; cf. Cochrane, *Christianity*, pp. 285–86.

[57] F. H. Dudden, *The Life and Times of St. Ambrose*, 2 vols. (Oxford: Clarendon Press, 1935), 1:256–69.

[58] Gaudemet, *L'église dans l'empire romain*, pp. 14 ff., 213 ff., 456 ff.

[59] Cochrane, *Christianty*, pp. 255 ff.; S. L. Greenslade, *Church and State from Constantine to Theodosius* (London: SCM Press Ltd, 1954); K. F. Morrison, *Rome and the City of God: An Essay on the Constitutional Relationships of Empire and Church in the Fourth Century*,

The acceptance of Christianity into the establishment thus carried with it a well-developed, structured institution – the *imperium in imperio* that earlier persecuting emperors had feared. Constantine extended its scope from a provincial and even interprovincial form to an ecumenical and empire-wide policy. There is a progression from the pre-Constantinian councils of the Antiochene patriarchate that met in the 260's to deal with Paul of Samosata, or the North African councils of the 250's under Cyprian's leadership, to the pan-western Council of Arles in 314 and then the ecumenical council of Nicaea in 325. Thus the hierarchical structure of the Church, which was originally liturgical and pastoral in character, was undergirded with a political and juridical significance, and "clericalism" was brought to birth along with the inevitable interest of the State in the selection of the episcopate.

The Church had nonetheless a weapon of its own against an absolute Caesaropapism, as Cochrane has so acutely noted:

> The fourth-century opponents of Caesaropapism . . . argued that the emperor was a member of the *ecclesia* and not its head; subject, like every one else, to the Christian law and, in consequence, to the discipline of the Church divinely appointed to be its custodian. The introduction of such ideas imparts a peculiar flavour to the Christian empire, and serves to distinguish it from the forms of Oriental monarchy with which it is sometimes confused. Their effectiveness was to be tested during the century, first in the successful resistance offered by Athanasius to political pressure at the hands of Constantius and, subsequently, in the submission of Theodosius to the stern demands of Ambrose of Milan. These heroic combats illustrate the result of committing what, from a strictly political point of view, may be accounted "dangerous authority" to the "priestly guardian of the emperor's conscience," as they also foreshadow the famous conflicts

---

Transactions of the American Philosophical Society, n.s., vol. 54, pt. 1 (Philadelphia, 1964); A. H. M. Jones, *The Later Roman Empire 284–602*, 2 vols. (Norman, Okla.: University of Oklahoma Press, 1964), 1:77 ff.; 2:938 ff.

> between popes and princes in medieval times. They are, in fact, landmarks in the growth of ecclesiastical imperialism.[60]

The Constantinian settlement has undergone many transformations and permutations in medieval and modern times. But the signs of the end of the Constantinian era of Church history are evident. The secular State gives only lip service, if that, to any supernatural allegiance, or it falls into the totalitarian stance of an atheistic deification of itself. It indeed continues to seek justice and peace, but it is indifferent to theology, to devotion, and to a morality defined in categories of sin. The Church itself accepts religious pluralism, and increasingly encourages dialogue and plays down conversion. It tolerates theologians who talk about the death of God and religionless religion, who demythologize its creed and find Biblical exegesis for "the secular city." True, it still hopes for some divine miracle that will revitalize its universal attraction, but it stumbles in efforts to find a "theology of mission." More often than not it takes its cue from nonecclesiastical movements for civil rights and the war on poverty. Few people give heed to the high-minded resolutions of ecclesiastical synods, even the majority of those who push them through by large or by close margins.

Historians will continue to argue about the precise dating of the transition from one era to another. One could argue for the French Revolution; the "Guns of August" 1914; the publication of *Das Kapital* or *The Origin of Species*; or perhaps the bomb on Hiroshima. Church historians will doubtless select more religious foci – the death of Pio Nono; the Declarations on Religious Liberty and the Non-Christian Religions of Vatican II; the birth of the Ecumenical Movement in 1910 at the Edinburgh Missionary Conference; the publication of Barth's commentary on Romans; or perhaps even the election of the first Roman Catholic president of the United States. The possibilities are endless.

[60] Cochrane, *Christianity*, pp. 187–88 (the words in quotes are from Gibbon).

The study of history is always conducive to hope. For the Christian student of history, today is peculiarly hopeful. For eschatology is reasserting itself in Christian thought and action. As Guardini said:

> The stronger the demonic powers the more crucial will be that "victory over the world" realized in freedom and through faith . . . involving a courage of the heart born from the immediacy of the love of God as it was made known in Christ. Perhaps man will come to experience this love anew, to taste the sovereignty of its origin, to know its independence of the world, to sense the mystery of its final *why*? [61]

[61] Romano Guardini, *End of the Modern World,* pp. 131–32.

3

Insignissima Religio, Certe Licita? Christianity and Judaism in the Fourth and Fifth Centuries

ROBERT L. WILKEN

> Much of the world's history is written by history's winners, and their accounts are usually cheerful reading. Winners minimize the mistakes inevitable in human enterprises and allot credit instead of sharing blame. But winners' accounts seldom offer thoughtful descriptions of the losers – one reason for reconsidering history from the point of view of losers' narratives.[1]

Since the days of Gottfried Arnold at least some historians have tried to tell the history of the Church from the point of view of the losers – whether this be through the eyes of the heretics, the lives of "pious men," or the exponents of ancient humanism. But I doubt whether any Christian church historian has ever tried seriously to write the story of the ancient Church through the eyes of the Jews. Indeed, were it not for the efforts of a few mavericks and the publication of a work here and a work there, most church historians would be hard pressed to say anything at all about Judaism and the Church after the first or second century.[2] It is not until much later that

[1] Naomi Bliven, *The New Yorker*, August 27, 1966, p. 122.

[2] See for example Leopold Lucas, *Zur Geschichte der Juden im vierten Jahrhundert*, Beitraege zur Geschichte der Juden, pt. 1 (Berlin: Mayer & Mueller, 1910); James Parkes, *The Conflict of the Church and the Synagogue* (New York: World Publishing Co., 1961; first published, 1934); Frank Gavin, "Aphrates and the Jews," *Journal of the Society of Oriental Research*, 7:95–166. Other works could be mentioned, but the

the Jews return to the scene and when they do they have been moved to the fringe of society, cast into a ghetto, viewed as a puzzling curiosity darkly reminiscent of a forgotten past.

Actually it is a colossal understatement to say that little attention has been paid to Judaism and its relation to Christianity in antiquity. Observe, for example, how slight the influence of Marcel Simon's work *Versus Israel*[3] – subtitled *Study of the Relations between Christians and Jews in the Roman Empire* – has been. First published in 1948, the book showed that during the period from 135 to 425, Judaism, far from coming to an end, was a real, active, and often effective rival and competitor of Christianity. In the essay accompanying a new edition of the work, Simon discusses his critics but observes that no one seriously questioned the central thesis. Certainly what Simon said in a work paralleling the period of greatest development of the ancient Church is supremely important for the church historian; but it is noteworthy that most reviews of his work came from other sources – ancient historians, historians of religion and of Judaism, philologists, etc.

If asked to assess the influence of Christianity on its environment, a plausible case can be made that Christianity so totally changed its environment that even modern historians fail to consider the role of the rivals in writing the history of the Church. That is, one very obvious influence of the victory of Christianity in the fourth century was on the writing of the history of Christianity itself, and this persists even to this enlightened day. But this is really too big a question to handle within the scope of this essay, though I should like to have it on record as part of the larger question to which this essay is directed. As the recent volume by Charles Glock and Rodney Stark reminds us, there *is* a relation between Christian beliefs

real evidence does not lie in the monographic studies, but in the general works. A quick look at the index of church histories of the period reveals immediately what a small part the Jews play in our interpretation of this period.

[3] Marcel Simon, *Verus Israel: Étude sur les Relations entre Chrétiens et Juifs dans l'Empire Romain, 135–425* (Paris: Editions e. De Boccard, 1964).

and anti-semitism even today.[4] In what follows I would like to explore some aspects of Christian-Jewish relations in the fourth and fifth centuries. Since it was at this time that Christian attitudes toward the Jews were hardening into fixed beliefs, we can observe in surprising detail some of the ways that the growing influence of Christianity shaped the environment.

I

Judaism occupied a unique place in the Roman world. Ever a subject of interest and fascination, men approached the Jews with a mixture of curiosity, admiration, and wonder. Of the many other religions that the empire absorbed, Judaism alone seems always to have remained "foreign," aloof, never quite ready to identify wholly with the society of the empire. Somehow Judaism remained impervious to the acids which ate away at every import to Rome, not because it was afraid or unwilling to accommodate, but because it refused to give up its own identity. Judaism appealed strongly to the religious instincts of the Hellenistic age, offering a belief in the supernatural coupled with a serious attempt to provide a comprehensive and rational interpretation of all of life. We possess only a tiny portion of what must have been a rich and impressive literature by the Jewish writers who accepted the challenge to provide such a total view of life. The boldness, even the audacity, of Philo to grapple with the primary issues of his day reflects this capability of Judaism to appeal to the best in Hellenistic culture.[5]

[4] Charles Glock and Rodney Stark, *Christian Belief and Anti-Semitism* (New York: Harper & Row, 1966).

[5] For Judaism in the Roman Empire see especially the work of J. Juster, *Les Juifs dans l'Empire Romain* (Paris: Librairie Paul Geuthner, 1914), 1:129–79. The work of Juster is fundamental, but the following studies are also of great value: Salo Wittmayer Baron, *A Social and Religious History of the Jews* (New York: Columbia University Press, 1937), vols. 1 and 2, esp. vol. 1, chap. 6, and vol. 2, chaps. 11–12; I. Heinemann, "Antisemitismus," in Pauly-Wissowa, suppl. 5, pp. 3–43; J. Leipoldt, "Antisemitismus," in *Reallexikon für Antike und Christentum*, 1:469–76: N. W. Goldstein, "Cultivated Pagans and Ancient Antisemitism," *Journal of Religion*, 19 (1939), 346–64; Emil Schuerer, *A History of the Jewish People in the Time of Jesus Christ*, 5 vols. (New York: Charles Scribner's Sons, n.d.).

Judaism also provided firm direction in moral matters, and in this way it adapted readily to the prevailing mood in the philosophical schools. Philosophy at this time was not primarily concerned with intellectual questions but devoted itself to the task of shaping men's lives along moral and spiritual lines. Judaism also offered an extensive literature of great antiquity – history, poetry *et. al.* – and bore witness to a venerable tradition of teachers and prophets who, so the argument ran, preceded the Greek sagas and actually were their teachers. As a general rule, writes Philo, men have an aversion for foreign institutions, but

> this is not so with ours. They attract and win the attention of all, of barbarians, of Greeks, of dwellers on the mainland and islands, of nations of the east and the west, of Europe and Asia, of the whole inhabited world from end to end. For who has not shown his high respect for that sacred seventh day. . . . Again, who does not every year show awe and reverence for the fast. . . . That the sanctity of our legislation has been a source of wonder not only to the Jews but also to all other nations is clear both from the facts already mentioned and those which I proceed to state.[6]

A Jew could take great pride in his religion and his people, and the very success of Judaism in the empire is impressive evidence of the truth of Philo's claims. No other people could boast that its teachings were taught throughout the inhabited world even though they were the product of a foreign nation. Of Judaism's attraction Bousset wrote:

> Judaism offered men a faith and revealed truth . . . a certainty without the eternal contradictions and the perennial doubts of schools. It was religion and at the same time it was a tightly knit community, much more stable than the fluctuating conventicles of the philosophical schools and at least as significant and powerful as the

[6] Philo *Vita Moises* 2. 20–25; F. H. Colson, trans., *Philo* (Cambridge: Harvard University Press, 1959), 6:459–61.

other oriental mystery religions which were so highly revered.[7]

Judaism made great gains in the Mediterranean world during the late Republic and early Empire. It must have grown enormously, as the passage from Philo implies. Every indication we have from ancient sources confirms the statements of writers such as Philo and Josephus. Even the satirist Juvenal, who frequently held up the Jew to ridicule, once remarked that some Romans abstain from pork, observe the Sabbath, and that their sons are circumcised and study the Torah of the Jews.[8] And Josephus says that "the masses have long since shown a keen desire to adopt our religious observances, and there is not one city, Greek or barbarian, nor a single nation, to which our custom of abstaining from work on the seventh day has not spread, and where the fasts and the lighting of lamps and many of our prohibitions in the matter of food are not observed."[9]

If the sources of the period give us a rosy picture of the extent and influence of Judaism, we must not be misled into thinking that this is the full story. During this same period we find clear evidence of a growing spirit of prejudice toward the Jews, inspired in part by the same things which had made it fascinating. Galen was mildly critical of Jews — and Christians — for the supposed religious certainty they offered. "If I had in mind people who taught their pupils in the same way as the followers of Moses and Christ teach theirs — for they order them to accept everything on faith — I should not have given you a definition."[10] No doubt not everyone was persuaded by the extravagant claims of Jews and Christians, and when compared to the tenets of other "schools" apparently they could not offer a reasonable basis for their beliefs.

But the growing prejudice against Judaism cannot be traced

[7] Wilhelm Bousset, *Die Religion des Judentums im spaethellenistischen Zeitalter* (1902), p. 174.

[8] Juvenal *Satires* 14. 96.

[9] Josephus *Against Apion* 282; H. Thackeray, trans., *Josephus* (Cambridge: Harvard University Press, 1926), 1:405–7.

[10] R. Walzer, ed. and trans., *Galen on Jews and Christians* (London: Oxford University Press, 1949), p. 48.

to the attitude represented by Galen. To many the problem lay elsewhere, namely in Judaism's "sovereign self-sufficiency," which made it appear to men as alien and foreign, unable and unwilling to assimilate new people and accommodate to new cultures. Persuaded that Israel played a unique role in history, Jews tended — in the eyes of Romans — to consider their religion and customs superior to others and to seek means to preserve, protect, and conserve their own Jewish traditions.[11] As early as the third century B.C. we learn of legends which traced Jews to dubious origins, such as the account of the Egyptian Manetho, who claimed that Jews were originally lepers who had been expelled from Egypt. Even Tacitus repeats a portion of this tale.[12]

Jewish neighbors were offended by the social practices associated with Jewish religion. Prohibitions about food such as pork, the observance of the sabbath, circumcision — all these engendered suspicion, distrust, and misunderstanding. To the outsider it appeared that Jews were exclusivistic and separatistic. When such attitudes took the form of actual separatism, as in the case of prohibitions concerning marriage between Jew and Greek, the consequences were serious. The Roman gradually grew disenchanted with Judaism, and this eventually turned into animosity, bitterness, and even hatred. Poets, satirists, historians, and orators — all mention Jews and consistently poke fun at them. Seneca, no fiery radical, a man devoted to the life of contemplation, conversation, and correspondence, charged the Jews with sloth because they rested every seventh day. Says Seneca: this practice causes men "to lose through idleness about the seventh part of . . . life, and also many things which demand immediate attention."[13]

In the famous chapter in his *Histories* Tacitus summarizes

[11] See the articles on Anti-Semitism in footnote 5 as well as Simon, *Versus Israel*, chaps. 4, 8. For attitudes of ancient writers to Judaism, see Théodore Reinach, ed., *Textes d'Auteurs Grecs et Romains Relatifs au Judaisme*, Publications de la Société des Études Juives (Paris: Ernest Lerous, 1895).

[12] For Manetho, see Reinach, *Textes d'Auteurs*, pp. 20–34, and Tacitus *Histories* 5. 1013.

[13] Cited by Augustine *De Civitate Dei* 6. 10; text also in Reinach, *Textes d'Auteurs*, p. 262.

many of the prevailing attitudes toward the Jews.[14] Tacitus' own prejudices are reflected in his uncritical adoption of popular views as well as in the way he supports prejudice by accenting just those aspects of Judaism found most offensive by Romans. Men speculate about the origin of Jews, says Tacitus, but we do not know whether they come from Crete, Ethiopia or Assyria. Though we have no certainty, most would agree the Jews once dwelled in Egypt and were expelled from the land. Here Tacitus accepts the slanderous legend passed on by Manetho. Moses, continues Tacitus, led the Jews out of Egypt to Canaan, where they settled, and he established for them a "novel religion quite different from the rest of mankind." What, then, distinguished their religion? "Among the Jews all things are profane that we hold sacred; on the other hand they regard as permissible what seems to us immoral." Thus they prohibit the eating of pork, they celebrate a meal in remembrance of their departure from Egypt, they set aside one day a week for rest and idleness. While Tacitus allows Jews the right to practise their religion as they wish according to ancient privilege, he nevertheless believes their practices are sinister and revolting. Jews are wicked and inclined to lust, they look on other men as enemies, they separate themselves by circumcision, their proselytes despise Roman Gods, and eventually shed all feeling of patriotism to Rome. In short they are a most criminal people (*sceleratissima gens*).

In light of this brief survey it seems that Simon and others are correct in claiming that Graeco-Roman anti-Semitism rests more on social than religious factors.[15] Implicitly, the superiority of Jewish mores suggested a judgment on Roman mores, institutions, traditions, and religion. And even though it was Jewish religion which promoted Jewish social behavior, we get the distinct impression that the feelings of the Romans against Jews really had little to do with religion. As early as Cicero Jewish separatism was taken to be destructive of social and political life.

[14] Tacitus *Histories* 5. 1–13.

[15] Simon, *Versus Israel*, pp. 239–45; see also Reinach, *Textes d'Auteurs*, pp. x–xx; and Heinemann, "Antisemitismus."

> Each city has its peculiar religion; we have ours. Even while Jerusalem was standing and the Jews were at peace with us, the practice of their sacred rites was at variance with the splendor of our empire, the dignity of our name, the customs of our ancestors. But now it is even more so, when that nation by its armed resistance has shown what it thinks of our rule; how dear it was to the immortal gods is shown by the fact that it has been conquered, reduced to a subject province, made a slave.[16]

In summary then, the opinions of ancient writers on Jews vary greatly, but most writers tend to emphasize the social side of Judaism. Dio Cassius accuses them of superstition,[17] Diogenes Laertius says they were sorcerers descended from Magi,[18] and Juvenal says that "Jews will sell you any dreams you please for the tinest coin."[19] Horace and Martial make fun of the sabbath; Plutarch ridicules the Jews for falling captive to Pompey because he attacked on the sabbath.[20] Sextus Empiricus mockingly derides Jews for making of the abstinence from pork a matter of life and death. Some men, he writes "would rather die than eat the flesh of pork."[21] Others attacked Jewish history, their national traditions, and their insignificant role in world affairs.

II

The attacks of Romans and Greeks on the Jews sound like the complaints of annoyed aristocrats, irritated by a troublesome nuisance, serious no doubt, but detached and aloof. The Jews were outsiders and intruders, not really here to stay. Only when the nuisance really showed potential for major

[16] Cicero *Pro Flacco* 28. 69; Louis E. Lord, trans., *Cicero The Speeches* (Cambridge: Harvard University Press, 1937), 1:441.

[17] Dio Cassius *Roman History* 37. 16–17.

[18] Diogenes Laertius *Lives of the Philosophers*, Pref. 9.

[19] Juvenal *Satire* 6. 542 ff.

[20] Horace *Satire* 1. 5, 100; Martial *Epigrams* 166. 7; Plutarch *De superstitione* 8. See also *Regum et imperatorum apophthegmata Antiochus* where Plutarch makes fun of Jews for asking for seven days to celebrate the Feast of Tabernacles when Antiochus Epiphanes was attacking; Reinach, *Textes d'Auteurs*, p. 136.

[21] Sextus Empiricus *Hypotyposes* 3. 24, 223.

unrest did reprisals follow. Reprisal against the Jews, of course, did follow in the Empire. At the time of Philo in the early part of the first century, Jews in Alexandria suffered violent persecution in the wake of a visit by the Jewish king Agrippa I. The prefect of Alexandria sided with the anti-Semites and the Jews were shut up in one quarter. When they traveled to other sections of the city they were slaughtered. Their houses were plundered and their goods stolen.[22] In Rome during the reign of Tiberius a large number of Jews were expelled by Tiberius' counselor Sejanus. But Tiberius later revoked the order and allowed the Jews to return.[23]

But these are exceptions. In the early Empire the Romans generally dealt fairly and justly with Jews, granting them rights and privileges and preserving earlier privileges. Baron writes:

> Rarely in the history of the Diaspora have Jews enjoyed such a high degree of both equality of rights and self-government, under the protection of public law, as in the early Roman Empire. Responsible exponents of Roman rule repeatedly stressed the principle that the Jews were to be treated in all legal, administrative, fiscal and, to a certain extent, political questions on an equal footing with other citizens.[24]

The earliest official dealings between Jews and Romans took place before Palestine became a province of the Empire. From the second century B.C. we know of several treaties in which Romans and Jews pledged to aid each other in times of war.[25]

[22] Victor A. Tcherikover and Alexander Fuks, *Corpus Papyrorum Judaicarum* (Cambridge: Harvard University Press, 1957), 1:65 ff. H. I. Bell, *Jews and Christians in Egypt* (London: Oxford University Press, 1924). Heinemann in Pauly-Wissowa, suppl. 6, p. 10, writes of persecution in Alexandria: "Gegen die juedische Religion als solche hat man nichts einzuwenden; der Stosz geht gegen die Rechtsund Machtstellung der Juden."

[23] See Eusebius *Historia Ecclesiastica* 2. 5. 7; Bell, *Jews and Christians in Egypt*, pp. 25, 29.

[24] Baron, *History of the Jews*, 1:240. See Baron's long footnote on page 403 concerning the legal status of Jews in the Empire.

[25] See 1 Macc. 8:23–28; Juster, *Les Juifs*, 1:130–32.

After the Jews became part of the Empire such good relations continued, as testified by the immense number of laws reproduced in Josephus.[26] For example, he cites an edict addressed by the Laodicaeans to the proconsul of Asia in which it is affirmed that "Jews may be allowed to observe their sabbaths, and other sacred rites, according to the laws of their fathers."[27] Josephus writes as an apologist for Judaism and is clearly interested in presenting Jewish privileges in a favorable light. But this does not detract from the cumulative effect of the number of laws he cites. What we miss in Josephus, however, are materials which would tell us about legislation concerning Jews in private life.

After the time of Josephus there are only a few references to legislation concerning Jews and few—if any—actual legal documents. Between the first and fourth century legal sources are almost wholly silent. In a number of places we learn of repressive legislation, especially in the time of Hadrian. Thus in the *Historia Augusta* it is reported that during Hadrian's reign Jews were "forbidden to practise circumcision (*quod vetabuntur mutilare genitalia*)," and that Jews were prohibited from setting foot in the country around Jerusalem.[28] The *Historia Augusta* also reports that during the time of Septimius Severus Jews were forbidden to proselytize. "He forbade conversion to Judaism under heavy penalties and enacted a similar law in regard to the Christians."[29] But these are the sum of references during the centuries from Josephus to Constantine. More important than prohibitions of circumcision or proselytizing were efforts begun in Egypt which led to the humiliating tax on Jews, the *fiscus Judaicus*. This tax, imposed on all Jews in the Empire, had profound effects on the development of ancient Jewry. The amount of the tax was not too great—two denarii—but socially it tended to segregate Jews further from the rest of the population.[30]

[26] Juster, *Les Juifs*, 1:132–58.
[27] Josephus *Antiquities* 14. 10, 8; Juster, *Les Juifs*, 1:152–54.
[28] Aelius Spartianus *Hadrian* 14. 2.
[29] Spartianus *Septimius Severus* 17. 1.
[30] Tcherikover and Fuks, *Corpus Papyrorum Judaicarum*, 1:80–82.

Surveying these bits and pieces it appears that legislation against Judaism comes as a result of specific problems with Jews, such as the uprising under Hadrian. As a general rule, imperial authorities are reluctant to impose restrictions, and when they do, they seem to follow directly on danger—or alleged danger—to the stability of the Empire.[31]

III

In the first section we sketched the developing animosity toward Jews among writers in the Empire. And though the picture was growing darker, the hostility of Roman writers was not matched by legal or social measures designed to restrict the rights of Jews or segregate them from the life of the society. When we turn from a Seneca or a Tacitus to a Tertullian or a John Chrysostom we sense immediately just how radically the scene has changed.[32] Now we are dealing, as it were, with an internecine feud, a conflict devoid of reason and logic, a bitter war, the spoils to be nothing less than life itself. Both Jew and Christian claim to bear an ultimate truth, each supports this claim by appeal to the same book, and each realizes that the fate of the one is somehow dependent on the other. Either Christianity or Judaism!

The passion that fired Christian-Jewish antagonism resulted in part from their common origin, and this was heightened by the practice of outsiders to group Christianity and Judaism together, as in the passage cited above from Galen. Pagan critics of the Church chided Christians for unfaithfulness to Jewish traditions. Christians did not obey the law, did not practice circumcision, nor did they observe the sabbath. As

[31] Simon, *Versus Israel*, pp. 131 ff.

[32] For the writings of Christians against the Jews, see A. Lukyn Williams, *Adversus Judaeos: A Bird's Eye View of Christian Apologiae until the Renaissance* (Cambridge: At the University Press, 1935); Robert Wilde, *The Treatment of the Jews in the Greek Christian Writers of the First Three Centuries*, The Catholic University of America Patristic Studies, no. 81 (Washington, D.C.: Catholic University of America Press, 1949); A. B. Hulen, "The 'Dialogues with the Jews,' as Sources for the Early Jewish Argument Against Christianity," *Journal of Biblical Literature*, 51 (1932): 58–70; Juster, *Les Juifs*, 1:43–76.

a consequence Christians not only had to defend their beliefs to outsiders, but also to justify them to Jews and Greeks who knew Jewish arguments. Inevitably Christians found it necessary to subvert the claims of Jews while upholding their own convictions. And it is this which gives to Christian attitudes toward Jews such a radically different character than pagan attitudes.[33]

Christianity brought a wholly new element to relations between the society of the Roman empire and the Jews, and this was a theological interpretation of Judaism. Christians sought to account for the rejection of Jesus by the Jews, and this laid the foundations for the eventual estrangement of Judaism from the life of the empire. Christians, however, seldom objected to Jewish practices on social grounds, and during the first centuries Christianity had no effect on official attitudes toward Jews. But what Christianity brought was a view of Judaism which saw misfortunes of Jews as resulting from the divine will and wrath. Christianity made it possible to look upon the Jews as committing the ultimate crime—turning their backs on God by their blindness, stupidity, and sin.

Roman writers attacked Jews because of circumcision, observance of the sabbath, and other Jewish practices. Christians too made the same charges, but the reasons offered were quite different. As early as Ignatius we read of opposition to the Jewish Sabbath, but now it is not because of laziness that the Sabbath is rejected but because of the resurrection of Jesus and the Christian celebration of the Lord's day. If one has come to "newness of hope," writes Ignatius, one no longer lives "in antiquated customs" such as "keeping the Sabbath," but lives "in accordance with the Lord's day." For "if at this date we still conform to Judaism then we own that we have not received grace." Christians should "put away the deteriorated leaven, a leaven stale and sour, and turn to the new leaven, that is Jesus Christ." Ignatius concludes. "It is absurd to have Jesus Christ on the lips, and at the same time live like a

[33] For a summary of the arguments, see Simon, *Versus Israel*, pp. 189–213.

Jew."[34] Now these comments are purely theological and tell us nothing about how Ignatius viewed Jews socially or personally. But they do give hints as to how Christianity is going to view Judaism and the difference between Christian and pagan attitudes.

In Ignatius we find a relatively pure statement of the theological judgment of Judaism, but Christian authors sometimes merge a social and a theological point of view. Thus at a much later date Cyril of Alexandria wrote about the Sabbath.

> Jews keep the Sabbath according to the law, holding back their bodies from any labor and pursuing sloth in their bodily activities. But this kind of Sabbath was rejected by God and he who enters into the rest which Christ brings keeps the Sabbath spiritually, truly rests from his own deeds. . . . Note that the shadow of the law is reversed and the ancient things of the law are made ineffective.[35]

Cyril repeats the familiar charge of Jewish laziness, but gives the whole passage a theological setting. What really disturbs him is not alleged Jewish laziness, but their persistence in celebrating the Sabbath according to the law and not according to Christ.

Christian criticism of Jewish institutions does not arise out of a vacuum. Apparently Christians were responding to Jewish claims that the Church, by deserting ancient practices, proved itself unfaithful to the legacy of ancient Israel. Justin, echoing the criticism of the Jew Trypho, wrote: "Is there any other fault you find with us, my friends, save this, that we do not live in accordance with the Law, and do not circumcise the flesh as did your forefathers, and do not keep the sabbath as you do?" Trypho replied that Christians "despise this covenant" and "neglect the commands," practising none of the

[34] Ignatius *Magnesians* 8–9; translation from Robert M. Grant, *The Apostolic Fathers* (Camden, N.J.: Thomas Nelson & Sons, 1966), 4:63.

[35] Cyril of Alexandria *Commentary on Isaiah* 5. 3 (PG 70 1248a–b); see also Paschal *Homily* 6 (PG 77, 521d).

things men do who fear God.[36] Almost precisely the same sentiments are expressed in Augustine's *Tractatus adversus Judaeos* several hundred years later.

> For they (Jews) say to us: "What is the reading of the Law and the Prophets doing among you who do not want to follow the precepts contained in them?" They base their complaint on the fact that we do not circumcise the foreskin of the male . . . and do not observe the Sabbath . . . nor do we celebrate the Pasch as they do. . . .[37]

From Rabbinic sources it appears that these were precisely the criticisms made of the Minim. To cite only one example from Rabbi Eliezer of Modi: "He who defiles the sacred food, despises the festivals, abolishes the covenant of our father Abraham, gives an interpretation of the Torah not according to the halachah and publicly shames his neighbor . . . has no portion in the future world."[38]

These few passages serve to illustrate the shift that has taken place in attitudes toward Jews. Because Christians and Jews claimed to be faithful to the same history and shared a common sacred book, inevitably questions between Jews and Christians became exegetical questions about the interpretation of the Old Testament. In his famous chapter on interpreting the Bible in *De Principiis* Origen puts his finger on the problem when he writes: Those of the circumcision "refused to believe in our Savior because they think that they are keeping closely to the language of the prophets that relate to him, and they see that he did not literally 'proclaim release to captives' or build what they consider to be a real 'city of God' . . . or 'eat butter and honey,' and choose the good before he knew or preferred the evil." Assuming that the Messiah had in fact come, Christians had to answer the ques-

[36] Justin Martyr *Dialogue with Trypho* 10. 1–3.

[37] Augustine *Tractatus adversus Judaeos* 3; trans. Sister Marie Liguori in *Saint Augustine: Treatises on Marriage and Other Subjects*, ed. Roy J. Deferrari (New York: Fathers of the Church, 1955), p. 393.

[38] Sanhedrin 99a; *The Babylonian Talmud* (London: Soncino Press, 1935 ff.).

tion: why are the messianic prophecies not fulfilled? Why for example does the wolf not lie down with the lamb? Jews answered: the Messiah had not come.[39] In defense the Christians had to construct an interpretation of the Bible and of history which supported the Christian claim and undercut the obviously telling evidence Jews could present. The extent to which Christian-Jewish relations in antiquity were exegetical debates about the meaning of the Old Testament serves to emphasize that the new factor Christianity brings is none other than the religious factor. Whereas in earlier attacks on Jews it was the social consequences of Jewish religion which troubled the Romans, for the Christians it was Jewish religion itself that was the object of attack.

Christianity not only had to defend its religious practice against Jews but it also received criticism from Greeks on "Jewish questions." In the writings of Christian apologists to Greeks there is frequently a discussion of such questions because pagan critics of the Church recognized that Christianity's relation to Judaism was one of its more vulnerable points. This can be seen in numerous passages of Origen's *Contra Celsum* and at a later date in Julian's *Against the Galilaeans*. Julian said that he wanted to explore the question "what can be the reasons why they (Christians) do not adhere to the Jewish beliefs but have abandoned them also and followed a way of their own." And elsewhere: "Now since the Galilaeans say that, though they are different from the Jews, they are still, precisely speaking Israelites in accordance with their prophets, and that they obey Moses above all and the prophets who in Judaea succeeded him, let us see in what respect they chiefly agree with those prophets." Julian then shows that Christians do not agree with Moses and the prophets, and concludes: "How then does this agree with the teachings of Moses?"[40] In response to just this kind of objection to Chris-

[39] Origen *De Principiis* 4. 2; G. W. Butterworth, trans., *Origen. On First Principles* (New York: Harper Torchbooks, 1966), p. 267.

[40] Origen *Contra Celsum* 7. 18; Julian *Against the Galilaeans* 43a, 253a, 262c; Wilmer Wright, trans., *The Works of the Emperor Julian* (London: William Heinemann, 1923), 1:393.

tianity, apologists sought to justify Christianity historically and to explain how it could shun circumcision, avoid the eating of pork and the keeping of the Sabbath, and yet remain faithful to the traditions of Israel.

We know from numerous sources that Christians continued to have contact with Jews and consciously responded to Jewish objections. The most impressive body of evidence for Jewish-Christian contact in the period after Constantine comes from catechetical literature. In his *Oratio Catechetica Magna* Gregory of Nyssa wrote: "We must adapt religious instruction to the diversities of teaching; we cannot use the same arguments in each case." For example, says Gregory, "a man of the Jewish faith has certain presuppositions; a man reared in Hellenism, others. . . ." And elsewhere: "It does no good to heal the polytheism of the Greek in the same way as the Jew's disbelief about the only begotten God." Cyril of Jerusalem, too, observed that when dealing with Jews we "silence them from the prophets," and "Greeks from the myths promulgated by them (Greeks)." Those of the circumcision, continues Cyril, lead "you astray by means of the Holy Scriptures, which they pervert if you go to them." [41]

One form the exegetical debate took can be seen in Augustine's work on the Jews mentioned above. Here Augustine expounds a number of Psalms with the superscription "for those things that shall be changed." Apparently the Septuagint translator and the Vulgate mistook the word "lilies" for "shall be changed" because of the similarity of the Hebrew root. Augustine immediately concludes that the psalms should be read Christologically. Commenting on Psalm 45 (Vulgate 44) he writes: "Christ is named, in fact, from the word 'annointing' (vs. 7) which in Greek is *chrisma.* He himself is God annointed by God, who changed this corporeal into a spiritual annointing, along with the rest of the sacraments." Next Augustine turns to Psalm 68 which "sings of the passion of our Lord Jesus Christ," . . . for the psalm speaks of Christ in the work

[41] Gregory of Nyssa *Oratio Catechetica Magna,* Pref.; Cyril of Jerusalem *Catechetical Lectures* 13. 37; 4. 2; 12. 27–29.

"and my offences are not hidden from you." [42] If these psalms so clearly refer to Christ, why do the Jews not recognize this? With other writers Augustine decides that the Jews must be blind, if not stupid, and this blindness results from their rejection of the Christ. Misreading of the Old Testament eventually becomes the equivalent of unbelief and rejection of God.

Christians also had to give a satisfactory account of Jewish history and Christianity's relation to this history. The destruction of the temple, the crushing of the rebellion under Hadrian, and eventually the victory of the Church provided the raw material for a Christian interpretation of Jewish history. In the opening of his *Ecclesiastical History* Eusebius states as one of his purposes the recording of "disasters . . . that fell upon the whole Jewish nation immediately after their plot against our Savior." Throughout the *History* he takes every occasion that arises to remind his readers of God's vengeance on the Jews, as demonstrated in their history. Speaking of the destruction of Jerusalem he advises the reader to turn to Josephus if he wishes to see how great the disaster was that befell the Jews. Eusebius only wishes to let his readers know that "God's vengeance was not slow to descend upon them for their wickedness against the Christ of God." [43] Augustine, too, writing after the Church's triumph, interprets passages such as "a mountain would be prepared . . . to which all peoples were going to come" as fulfilled in the history of the Church. When he read "sacrifice is offered from the rising of the sun to the going down . . ." this too confirmed Christian claims. "Open your eyes," writes Augustine, "at any time, and see from the rising of the sun even to its setting . . . the sacrifice of the Christians is being offered." [44]

[42] Augustine *Tractatus adversus Judaeos* 4–5.

[43] Eusebius *Historia Ecclesiastica* 3. 5; see also 2. 5–6. He tells only so much of Jews under Gaius "as shall inform my readers clearly as to the misfortunes which befell the Jews then and shortly afterwards, because of their crimes against Christ." Chrysostom writes: "It was not by their own power that the Ceasars did what they did to you; it was done by the wrath of God, and his absolute rejection of you."—*Homilies against the Jews* 6. 3.

[44] Augustine *Tractatus adversus Judaeos* 7.

Augustine and other Church Fathers could point to the New Testament and such passages as Gal. 6:16 where the Church is called the "true Israel," as well as statements in the Apoc. 2:9: "I will make those of Satan's synagogue, who claim to be Jews but are lying frauds, come and fall down at your feet . . ." What they frequently forgot were Paul's statements about the wild olive. In Rom. 11:17–18 Paul wrote: "But if some of the branches have been lopped off, and you, a wild olive, have been grafted in among them, and have come to share the same root and sap as the olive, do not make yourself superior to the branches. If you do so, remember that it is not you who sustain the root; the root sustains you." Augustine was quite ready to grant that Paul had given this warning to Christians, but this did not alter the fact that the Jews were "broken off on account of their unbelief," and the "wild olive was grafted on and shared in the richness of the true olive tree after the natural branches had been cut off." [45] For the Church Fathers of the fourth and fifth centuries Judaism had forfeited its rights to the ancient inheritance because they had turned their back on the One sent from God.

It is perhaps unfair to compare Paul and Augustine. Augustine wrote almost four hundred years after Paul. Paul lived with a hope, tempered by disappointments. Augustine lived with the reality of four hundred years of Christian history. What hope there was was rapidly disappearing as the disappointment gradually grew into bitterness. The four hundred years separating Paul and Augustine changed forever the relation between Judaism and Christianity. During the intervening centuries Christians had forged new answers that were different from Paul's. Paul's comments about the wild and cultivated olive sound quaint in the fifth century, and their very quaintness is a sign of their irrelevance. At first Paul's approach was modified, but gradually it was transformed into a new exegetical system and a theology of history. By the time we reach the fifth century the die is cast and few significant changes will occur.

[45] *Ibid.*, 1.

IV

At the beginning of this essay we asked the question to which this volume is addressed: how and to what extent did Christianity shape its environment in the fourth and fifth centuries? If there is any period in Church history where the influence of Christianity dramatically changes its environment it must be the time of the later Empire. What was begun then took centuries to reach maturity, but it is here that men planted the roots of the Christian civilization of the West and the Byzantine Empire of the East. The most dramatic change was, of course, the proclamation of Theodosius I in 380 that all men in the empire should confess by "the sole deity of the Father and of the Son and of the Holy Spirit." Since the time of Constantine a steady stream of laws rapidly transformed the life of the Empire. In the year 313, provision was made for subsidies to the Church and clerical exemption from public duties; in 320, clerical exemption from taxation; in 321, recognition of Sunday; in 330, clerical exemption from senatorial service; in 365, exclusion of bakers from the clericate; in 368, amnesty for prisoners at Eastertide; in 380, suspension of criminal cases during Lent. Taken together the mass of new laws during the period give clear testimony of the influence of Christianity on its environment.[46]

Christian influence on legislation came as a direct consequence of Christian beliefs. What Christians confessed in their creeds and read in their Scriptures formed the basis for the enactment of laws to govern all men, not only the Christian community. This was also the case in the Church's atti-

[46] *Codex Theodosianus* 16. 1–2; for the influence of Christianity on Roman law, see especially the recent volumes of P. R. Coleman-Norton, *Roman State and Christian Church,* 3 vols. (London: S.P.C.K., 1966), bibliography on this question in 1:lxvii. See also Jean Gaudemet, *L'Eglise dans l'Empire Romain* (Paris: Sirey, n.d.), pp. 487 ff.; Gaudemet, *La Formation du Droit Séculier et du Droit de l'Église aux IVe and Ve Siecles* (Paris: Sirey, 1957); James Everett Seaver, *Persecution of the Jews in the Roman Empire,* University of Kansas Humanistic Studies, no. 30 (Lawrence, Kans.: University of Kansas Publications, 1952). The specific legislation cited here can be found in *Codex Theodosianus* 16. 2, 10; 2, 7; 14. 3, 11; 9. 38, 4; 35, 4; and Eusebius *H. E.* 10. 6–7.

tude toward Jews. The picture of Judaism created by the Church was not an idle construct hastily patched together after-hours while Christian apologists rested from their debates with Greeks. And what Christian theologians thought about Jews took concrete shape in the lives of Christian people, particularly through catechetical instruction and the liturgy. For example, Juster has shown conclusively how thoroughly Christian attitudes toward Jews permeated the ancient liturgies.[47] What Christians thought about Jews also caught the attention of the emperors. In a striking passage recorded by the Church historian Socrates, Constantine shows just how completely he is dominated by the new Christian attitudes. Speaking of the Jewish celebration of the Pasch, Constantine said that Jews are

> a people who having imbrued their hands in a most heinous outrage, have thus polluted their souls, and are deservedly blind. Having then cast aside their usage, we are free to see to it that the celebration of this observance should occur in future in the more correct order which we have kept from the first day of the Passion until the present time. Therefore have nothing in common with that most hostile people the Jews. We have received from the Savior another way; for there is set before us a legitimate and accurate course in our holy religion: unanimously pursuing this, let us, most honored brethren, withdraw ourselves from that detestable association. For it is truly absurd for them to boast that we are incapable of rightly observing these things without their instruction. For on what subject will they be competent to form a correct judgment, who after that murder of their Lord, having been bereft of their senses, are led not by any rational motive, but by an ungovernable impulse, wherever their innate fury may drive them? Thus it is that even in this particular they do not perceive the truth, so that they, constantly erring in the utmost degree, instead

[47] Juster, *Les Juifs*, 1:304–37.

of making a suitable correction, celebrate the Feast of Passover a second time in the same year.[48]

There is nothing to match this in any writer or imperial official prior to the advent of Christianity. Not only does the statement reflect the depth of the estrangement between Christianity and Judaism, but it also bodes evil for the way Judaism will be handled as Christians gain power and influence in the Empire. What elements of justice were present in the earlier Roman treatment of Jews—and there were many—are now replaced by holy vindication. The status of Jews in the Empire will be radically transformed.

It is one of the merits of Simon's study that he exposes at length the character of Christian anti-Semitism as it crystallized in the later Empire. Christian attitudes to Jews went far beyond those of the ancient Greeks and Romans and were nourished by the highly developed theology. Whereas we may rightly speak of a moderate anti-Semitism prior to Christianity, it was more like a "spontaneous reaction, elementary and instinctive, a social defense rather than a preoccupation reflecting a religious defense. Religion is only a factor in that it isolates, singularizes and opposes them (Jews) to the surrounding world." This earlier and milder form of Jewish prejudice provided the ground for Christian anti-Semitism but it does not account for the nature of Christian anti-Semitism. Writes Simon: "The anti-Semitic disposition of the pagan world represents, in any case, part of the cause, the substratum on which is developed with some characteristics in part inherited, but more largely original, Christian anti-Semitism."[49] There is a madness in speaking of the "originality" of Christianity's anti-Semitism. But Simon chose his word carefully. What grew on the soil of the Gospel at the hands of the Church's bishops was *new*. Just how new can be seen in the legislation of the fourth and fifth centuries.

[48] Socrates *Historia Ecclesiastica* 1. 9, 5; translation in *Nicene and Post Nicene Fathers*, ed. Philip Schaff and Henry Wace (New York: Christian Literature Co., 1890), 2d ser., vol. 2, p. 15.

[49] Simon, *Verus Israel*, pp. 243, 245.

From Constantine to Theodosius II (d. 450) an enormous body of legislation appeared dealing with the Jews. Indeed, on the basis of materials collected in the *Theodosian Code*, and to a lesser degree in the *Code of Justinian*, there are almost fifty laws dealing directly with Jewish matters.[50] The breadth of the legislation is striking, especially after one has observed the sparsity from the time of Josephus to Constantine. No doubt the great number of laws is due to the care of the compilers of the *Theodosian Code*, who preserved materials which under other conditions would have been lost. But even so, this cannot really account for the presence of such extensive legislation.

The laws reflect a strange ambivalence, conditioned no doubt by the state's evident concern to respect its traditional principles of justice and to preserve to Jews their ancient privileges. At the same time such privileges increasingly conflicted with the Christian interpretation of Judaism, and as the Empire became more thoroughly Christian it grew increasingly restless with traditional Jewish privileges. Already in 315, Constantine went on record favoring Christians over Jews. "We will that it should be made known to Jews and their elders and patriarchs that if after this law anyone shall have dared to assail with rocks or with another kind of madness . . . anyone who has fled their *deadly sect* and turned his attention to God's cult, he must be delivered immediately to the flames." The law also prescribed punishment for those who turned to Judaism. And this mandate was issued only nine days short of Constantine's vision of the Cross.[51]

In the years following this first declaration numerous specific questions concerning Jews were dealt with by the emperors. Here are some examples. In 352 Constantius II issued the following mandate: "We have ordered by the established

[50] See especially *Codex Theodosianus* 16. 8. For a listing of laws on Jews from Constantine to Justinian see Juster, *Les Juifs*, 1:163, 168–72; see also Gaudemet, *L'Église*, pp. 623 ff.; Giannino Ferrari Dalle Spade, *Scritti Giuridici* (Milan: A. Guiffre, 1956), pp. 267–304; and Seaver, *Persecution of the Jews*.

[51] *Codex Theodosianus* 16. 8. 1; citations of *CT* from Clyde Pharr, *The Theodosian Code* (Princeton: Princeton University Press, 1952).

venerable law that if anyone, having become a Jew from a Christian, should join their sacrilegious assemblies . . . his property shall be claimed for the ownership of the fisc."[52] In 404 Jews were excluded from serving in the imperial service. This was reaffirmed in 418.[53] Eventually Jews were prohibited from constructing new synagogues, though they were assured that old ones would not be taken from them.[54] Jews were forbidden to contract marriages with Christian women, and if they did, such unions were considered adulterous.[55] They were prohibited from acquiring new slaves who were Christians.[56]

While these laws were being passed, a steady string of laws appeared which guaranteed Jewish privileges. One cannot help being impressed here by the attempt of the emperors to guarantee rights long cherished by the Romans and to maintain a sense of justice. But we sense a growing uneasiness about granting such privileges because of unhappy incidents between Jews and Christians. Apparently Jews and Christians frequently attacked each other and ridiculed each other's religion. The laws reaffirming Jewish rights reflect this social unrest. We learn of Jews burning an effigy of the cross and know of incidents such as the destruction of the synagogue at Callicinum by Christians.[57] In a mandate to the Count of the Orient: "Your sublime Magnitude will, therefore, after receiving this order, restrain with proper severity the excesses of those persons who, in the name of the Christian religion, presume to commit certain unlawful acts and attempts to destroy and to despoil the synagogues."[58] Elswhere the ancient right is affirmed that Judaism "is forbidden by no law." And a comment follows: "We are gravely disturbed that their assemblies have been forbidden in certain places." In 412 it was decreed, following custom, that no summons be served on the Sabbath. Synagogues were not to be burned indiscrimi-

[52] *Ibid.*, 16. 8. 7.
[53] *Ibid.*, 8. 16; 8. 24.
[54] *Ibid.*, 8. 27.
[55] *Ibid.*, 3. 7. 2.
[56] *Ibid.*, 16. 9. 1–5.
[57] See Seaver, *Persecution of the Jews*, pp. 41 ff.
[58] *Codex Theodosianus* 16. 8. 18.

nately, and if they were, recompense was to be made. One law – reflecting the social situation – says that a man should not be declared guilty simply because he is a Jew.[59]

Church law is even more revealing than civil laws. In the *Apostolic Constitutions* we read: "Endeavor therefore never to leave the Church of God; but if anyone overlooks it, and goes either into a polluted temple of the heathens, or into a synagogue of the Jews or heretics, what apology will such a one make to God in the day of judgment, who has forsaken the oracles of the living God." And in the *Apostolic Canons*: "If anyone, either of the clergy or the laity, enters into a synagogue of the Jews or heretics to pray, let him be deprived and suspended." There are regulations against clergy who "fast with Jews, or keep festivals with them." More importantly the Canons of the Synod of Elvira, actually a pre-Constantinian synod, prohibit intermarriage between Jews and Christian girls, unless the Jew is willing to be converted. There are canons against accepting Jewish hospitality. Other canons prohibit adultery with Jewish women, probably referring to concubinage. These and other canons were to have great social significance and contributed to the pressures which moved Judaism off to the edge of society and eventually prohibited it from having any significant role in the society.[60] The results of the changed attitude in the Empire toward the Jews are only beginning to become apparent in the fifth century, but the outlines of the picture are plain.

If Tertullian at the end of the second century could say that Christianity hid under the umbrella of that "most illustrious religion which was certainly legitimate" (*insignissima religio certe licita*),[61] by the time Christianity had won the Empire this was no longer such an open question. Take several illustrations. The most dramatic is of course Ambrose's violent reaction to Theodosius' order that Christians rebuild the burned synagogue in Callicinum. Even reading Ambrose's letters to-

[59] *Ibid.*, 8. 9. 12. 20–21.

[60] Synod of Elvira *Canon* 16. 78. 50. 49; *Canons of Laodicea* 16. 29. 37; *Apostolic Canons* 62. 65. 70–71; *Apostolic Constitutions* 5. 20.

[61] Tertullian *Apologeticum* 1. 21. 1.

day, one is struck by the boldness and audacity of his statements. He refuses to budge an inch. "It is a serious thing to hazard your faith for the sake of the Jews." Why should you countenance the building of a "place of unbelief, a home of impiety, a refuge of insanity, damned by God Himself?" It is only one building which was burnt, says Ambrose, and because it is a synagogue, why should the emperor take vengeance on the Christians? To whom is the victory? The Jews? Or the Church? The Jews will number this day among their great festivals and remember it for years to come. The emperor must decide for Christianity or for Judaism.[62]

Or take the case of the Jews in Alexandria who, under the instigation of the Christian bishop Cyril, were expelled from the city because of an uprising (414 A.D.). The precise course of events is not known to us, but even the Christian historian Socrates gives us enough information to know that it was not the Jews alone who were culpable here.[63] As the bishops looked upon Israel's misfortunes as resulting from divine wrath, so the historians gave space in their histories to Jewish misfortunes resulting from God's wrath. When the attempt to rebuild Jerusalem under Julian failed Sozomen immediately concluded that God had brought the earthquake on them. And when they began to build they failed to realize that "this unexpected earthquake was a manifest indication that God was opposed to the re-erection of their temple."[64]

V

The contrast between Christian and pagan attitudes in the later Empire can be seen in the relatively unknown Latin poet Rutilius Manatianus, who lived in the fifth century, well after the time Christianity had begun to influence the official attitude of the government toward Jews. Rutilius was an aristocratic and well-educated Roman born in Toulouse, a man of literary knowledge and taste, and an adherent of ancient paganism. On a trip from Rome to Toulouse in the autumn of

[62] Ambrose *Epistula* 40. 26. 14.
[63] Socrates *H. E.* 7. 13.
[64] Sozomen *H. E.* 5. 22; Socrates *H. E.* 3. 20.

416 he kept a diary of his travels and eventually wrote a lovely poem called *De Reditu Suo*, an account of his adventures, the sea and countryside, and the people he met. One of those he met was a Jew and Rutilius, in relating this experience, reveals the attitude toward Jews represented in earlier Roman and Greek writers. He had sailed to Falese (modern Porto di Faliese) and had disembarked there.

> Landing, we seek lodging, and stroll within a wood; we like the ponds which charm with their shallow enclosed basin. The spacious waters of the imprisoned flood permit the playful fish to sport inside these preserves. But we were made to pay dear, for the repose of this delightful halting-place by a lessee who was harsher than Antiphates as host. For a crabbed Jew (*querulus Iudaeus*) was in charge of the spot—a creature that quarrels with sound human food. He charges in our bill for damaging his bushes and hitting the seaweed, and bawls about his enormous loss in water we had sipped. We pay the abuse due to the filthy race that infamously practises circumcision: a root of silliness they are: chill Sabbaths are after their own heart, yet their heart is chillier than their creed. Each seventh day is condemned to ignoble sloth, as 'twere an effeminate picture of a god fatigued . . . The infection of this plague, though excised, still creeps aboard the more; and 'tis their own conquerors that a conquered race keeps down.[65]

This passage presents a sharp contrast to the Christian writers we have considered and even to some of the phrases which occur in the legal documents. For example, Judaism is here called a *gens obscaena*, a reference to Jews as a people whose customs offend Romans; whereas in the *Theodosian Code* we meet terms such as *nefaria secta*, highlighting not so much the race of Jews as their religion. Here too we find the traditional complaints: circumcision, sabbath, abstention from cer-

[65] Lines 375–98, cited from J. Wight Duff and Arnold M. Duff, *Minor Latin Poets*, Loeb Classical Library (Cambridge: Harvard University Press, 1934), pp. 797–99.

tain foods, and just as earlier writers, Rutilius is offended by the social side of Jewish religion. They are, he says, slothful, stingy and separate themselves from others by the distasteful practice of circumcision.

When Rutilius is placed alongside Augustine or Cyril of Alexandria — contemporaries — the differences are plain. Rutilius represents a conservative Roman approach which recalls the complaints of earlier days, almost oblivious to the rise of Christianity and its new attitude toward Judaism. His comments are more innocent and less passionate than those of Christians — the reflections of a man who is irritated by a Jew he has met but thinks that this is perhaps the way most Jews are, and is quite unconcerned about Judaism except as it crosses his path now and then. After his brief outburst he returns to the story of his poem and never finds reason to refer to the Jews again.

Rutilius has not been touched by the rise of Christianity, neither in his personal beliefs nor in his social attitudes. But his mores were a thing of the past, and even men like Rutilius would eventually be influenced by the growing influence of the Church. But he provides an interesting sidelight — a lonely figure, somewhat off the center of the stage, as the main drama takes place elsewhere.

"Most of the world's history is written by history's winners. . . . Winners minimize the mistakes inevitable in human enterprises and allot credit instead of sharing blame." This is surely the case for the history of the Jews in the later Empire. The tale told here is not new, but it has been overlooked and obscured by Church historians. If Church history keeps alive the memory of the Church's past, it has suffered amnesia here. What happened in the fourth and fifth centuries had enormous consequences, for as Seaver said, "many of these laws passed naturally into the tradition of western Europe by way of the Church." And as later history demonstrated, the attitudes developed during this time changed the relation of Judaism to Western society. "The later sad history of the Jews in western Europe is largely a consequence of the misfortunes which befell them in the fourth century."[66]

We are driven then to conclude: The influence of Christianity on its culture has not always been wholesome; indeed, at times it has been detrimental and destructive. The influence of Christianity on Judaism in the fourth and fifth centuries is just such an instance. But the historian cannot be content with this conclusion, not because it is untrue, but because it is insufficient. Why did Christianity respond to Judaism in the fashion it did? If nothing else, Christian anti-Semitism in the fourth and fifth centuries not only tells us something about Christians; it also says something about Judaism. Christians are not anti-Semitic in a vacuum. Perhaps we have been dazzled by the brilliance of the great men of the time — Athanasius, Basil, Augustine, Cyril — and therefore forgotten the light which shone from Zion. Perhaps we have not yet broken free of the icy grasp of Harnack and persist in viewing the early Church solely in relation to Hellenistic culture. Whatever the reasons for previous neglect of Judaism in this period, we can no longer forget its presence and overlook its influence. The virulence of Christian anti-Semitism is a sign of the vitality of Judaism in the later Empire. And for the Church historian this is worth noting.

[66] Seaver, *Persecution of the Jews*, pp. 81–83.

4

The Russian Church and the Rise of Moscow

MATTHEW SPINKA

From the very beginning of its introduction into Russia, the Church has played a most important role, not only in the religious, but also in the political and cultural life of the country. The conversion of Prince Vladimir to Christianity (987), and the subsequent Christianization of the country, was of tremendous transforming significance. Vernadsky summarizes its effect as follows: "It was not a purely religious event: Christianity, for Russia, meant at that time a higher civilization. In the eyes of the Russians themselves the conversion made them part of the civilized world."[1] Although our preeminent interest is in a later period, when the influence of the Church was potently exerted upon the rise of Moscow, it is by way of introduction that we cast a brief glance at the beginnings of this process.

The adoption of Christianity on the part of Kievan Russia is entangled in obscurities and legendary accounts of contradictory sources which are extremely difficult to unravel.[2] The popular legend of the *Povest' vremennykh let* (translated under the title of *The Russian Primary Chronicle*),[3] which has been long but erroneously ascribed to monk Nestor of the

[1] George Vernadsky, *Kievan Russia* (New Haven: Yale University Press, 1948), p. 69.

[2] Matthew Spinka, "Conversion of Russia," *Journal of Religion*, vol. 6 (1926); Francis Dvornik, *The Slavs: Their Early History and Civilization* (Boston: American Academy of Arts and Sciences, 1956), pp. 204–9.

[3] *Povest' vremennykh let* (Moscow and Leningrad, 1950) 1:59–61; S. H. Cross and O. P. Sherbowitz-Wetzor, trans., *The Russian Primary Chronicle* (Cambridge, Mass.: Medieval Academy of America, 1953), pp. 96–98, 110–11.

Pechersky monastery in Kiev, is today discredited as folklore.[4] It asserts that Prince Vladimir (978–1015) sent emissaries to the Moslem, Jewish, Roman Catholic, and Orthodox centers and that, upon their return and report, he chose Byzantine Orthodoxy as the state religion. Actually, Vladimir, a pagan, had hired Varangian troops to seize the rule from the hands of his half-brother Yaropolk because the latter favored the Christian Varangian party in that city. Christianity had existed in Kiev ever since the rule of Igor (912–942). Princess Olga, the grandmother of Vladimir, was a Christian, as was his own mother Malusha. Vladimir did conquer Kiev (978) and united it with Novgorod. He at first exerted himself in strengthening Slavic paganism; he ordered the people to worship the Slavic pagan deities and revived human sacrifices. In the course of time, however, being a truly religious man, he increasingly recognized the pre-eminence of Christianity and was drawn toward its acceptance. What induced him toward this radical change? Was it an external force or an inner compulsion? Metropolitan Hilarion in his *Word about Law and Grace*, written c. 1051, knows nothing about the popular story told in the *Primary Chronicle*, and emphasizes exclusively that Vladimir's conversion was brought about by his own initiative. He writes: "And having heard all this, Vladimir desired with his heart and longed in his spirit to become a Christian, he and his mother."[5] According to Hilarion, the three impulses leading to Vladimir's conversion were (1) his innate reason; (2) his desire to introduce Byzantine culture into his realm; and (3) "God's visitation." The same interpretation is strongly upheld by the recently deceased Church historian A. V. Kartashev in his massive two-volume work, which is among the most recent treatments of the subject.[6] Another of the early sources, Monk Jacob's *Eulogy of the Russian Prince Vladimir*, ascribes his

[4] A. V. Kartashev, *Ocherki po istorii russkoi tserkvi*, 2 vols. (Paris: YMCA-Press, n.d.), 1:107; but Vernadsky credits the legend with having some historical foundations, *Kievan Russia*, p. 62. Also, *idem*, *The Origins of Russia* (Oxford: Clarendon Press, 1959), pp. 294—95.

[5] Quoted in Vernadsky, *Origins of Russia*, p. 295.

[6] Kartashev, *Ocherki*, 1:108–9.

conversion almost entirely to the influence of Princess Olga and thus also makes the conversion due to an inner compulsion. Kartashev adds to Olga's influence the urgings of Vladimir's Christian mother and his Christian wives, particularly of the Czech Adlogia. It may, therefore, be concluded that it was by a voluntary act on Vladimir's part, by his free choice, that he accepted Christianity.

Further controversy is waged over the date of Vladimir's conversion. Many of the chroniclers agree on the year 987, although 988 and 989 are given as well. Monk Jacob informs us that "after the holy baptism, the blessed Prince Volodomer lived twenty-eight years."[7] Since he died in 1015, the year indicated is 987. According to him, Vladimir was baptized by the Varangian Christian priests either at Kiev or—as Kartashev supposes—at his own residence of Vasilev. Furthermore, Bardas Phocas, the Byzantine general, proclaimed himself emperor on September 14, 987. Thereupon, the legitimate emperors, the brothers Basil II and Constantine, appealed to Vladimir for aid. They promised him, as an inducement, the hand of their sister Anna in marriage "if he would become a Christian." Vladimir's armies were at the time helping the Bulgars against the Byzantines. The imperial brothers, therefore, had to make the offer sufficiently alluring—a marriage with a real Porphyrogenite, "a princes born to the imperial purple"—to convert an enemy into a friend. According to other sources, it was Vladimir who made the demand on Basil II that Anna be given him in marriage, for which reason he promised to be baptized. He also demanded that the Byzantines organize a Russian Church and grant it a large degree of autonomy; and last, that the Russian claims to eastern Crimea be recognized. The imperial embassy reached Kiev early in 988 and accepted the conditions. Vladimir, on his part, agreed to the plea for aid, for it afforded him the possibility of a brilliant alliance with the most civilized empire of the time, from which cultural influences could transform Russia into a

[7] Jacob's "Eulogy of the Russian Prince Vladimir," quoted in E. E. Golubinsky, *Istoriya russkoi tserkvi* (Moscow, 1900–1901), 1:245.

veritable part of civilized Europe.[8] He was then baptized in Kiev. Thereupon he sent a force of 6,000 in aid of the imperial brothers and defeated Bardas Phocas at Abdydos in the same year.

After the victory, which firmly seated the emperors on their throne, Basil refused to make good his promise to give Anna in marriage to the much-married Vladimir, although he had already been baptized. He thereupon invaded Crimea, which had been promised him as part of the agreement entered into the year before, and took the principal city of Kherson. It was only then that Basil hastened to send Anna to become Vladimir's wife. Vladimir thereupon gave Kherson back to her as her dowry. Moreover, for her sake he dismissed five of his wives and 800 concubines (so the sources say!). According to Greek sources, he was then baptized, receiving the name of Vasily, i.e., Basil, after the Byzantine emperor. Christianity had long been established in Crimea: the oldest Byzantine eparchy existed at Tmutorokan, ruled by an Archbishop Anastasius. There were five other bishoprics besides.

The *Primary Chronicle*[9] has still another version of the events. Having first invaded Crimea and conquered Kherson, Vladimir sent a message to the Byzantine emperors demanding the hand of Anna. They reluctantly agreed on condition that he receive baptism. Vladimir accepted the condition. The emperors further requested that he be baptized before Anna arrived. Vladimir, however, urged that she bring the priests along with her. This was done. But then, having been afflicted with an eye disease, he was baptized by the bishop of Kherson, who is suddenly introduced into the narrative. Thereupon he married Anna.

It is this kind of interpretation of the events connected with the baptism of Vladimir which has been accepted, in various combinations, by a large number of Russian historians. Vernadsky[10] may be cited as typical of these scholars, even though

[8] Vernadsky, *Origins of Russia*, p. 297.

[9] Cross and Sherbowitz, *Russian Primary Chronicle*, pp. 112–13.

[10] Vernadsky, *Origins of Russia*, pp. 298 ff; cf. also *idem.*, "The Status of the Russian Church during the First Half-Century Following

they differ from each other in various details. He inclines strongly to the view that Vladimir was baptized in Kherson in 989, apparently by the Greek ecclesiastical authorities in Tmutorokan. Vladimir also secured there the clergy for the introduction of Christianity into Kiev and the rest of the Russian land. He obtained from this source not only the priests but also church vestments, sacramental vessels, icons, and liturgical books. Thus, during the earliest years, the ecclesiastical authority over the nascent Russian Church was exercised not by the patriarch of Constantinople or some dignitary sent by him, but by the archbishop of Tmutorokan, who acted as a provisional supervisor of the Church. Whether he did this by mere extension of his Crimean archdiocese or by patriarchal permission is not clear. Nor do the sources reveal how the Greek priests (or were they *Rus*, since Tmutorokan had been under their control since the ninth century?), using Greek language at the services and in the missionary work, could so quickly succeed in converting the people. Nevertheless, the presence of Bulgarian priests using Slavic liturgical books is admitted in passing but not explained.[11] One may also ask—although in vain—what was the relation of the native Varangian Christianity to the new ecclesiastical establishment. Despite all these difficulties, this appears to be the preferred interpretation of the introduction of Christianity into Vladimir's dominions.

After spending about a year in Crimea, Vladimir and Anna returned to Kiev, accompanied by Archbishop Anastasius. Thereupon, Vladimir ordered the destruction of Slavic gods.[12] Perun was dragged at the tail of horses to Dnieper and thrown into it along with the other gods. Pagan temples were destroyed and Christian churches built in their places. People were ordered baptized en masse in the river. The prince ordered a stone church to be built—the Dormition of the Mother of God—which he "entrusted to Anastasius of Kher-

Vladimir's Conversion," *American Slavic and East European Review*, 1 (1941): 297 ff.

[11] Dvornik, *Slavs*, p. 210.

[12] Cross and Sherbowitz, *Russian Primary Chronicle*, pp. 116–17.

son."[13] Christian missionaries then ranged the rest of the Kievan principality and entered other realms as well.

Kartashev, however, strongly repudiates this kind of interpretation of the introduction of Christianity into Russia. He insists that the sources upon which it rests were written from the Greek point of view when the patriarch of Constantinople wielded sway over the country during the reign of Vladimir's successor Yaroslav. Instead of receiving Greek clergy from Tmutorokan, with whom he returned to Kiev to administer baptism to all its inhabitants, Kartashev, following an earlier writer M. D. Priselkov, offers the theory that Vladimir first submitted to the ecclesiastical jurisdiction of the Bulgarian patriarch at Ochrida. Bulgaria had been a Christian country ever since the conversion of Tsar Boris (865).[14] As such, it possessed an autocephalous ecclesiastical rule. This theory, if true, would explain what has hitherto been an insoluble puzzle; namely, how could the Greek priests, not knowing the Russian language, evangelize the pagan Slavic population immediately upon entering the Kievan territory. The Bulgars had the Church Slavonic version of the Bible, the creedal and liturgical books, as well as a flourishing general literature. "Newly converted Russia," Fedotov writes, "received from the Bulgarian Slavs an enormous treasure of translated Greek sermons, lives of saints, and Patericons (i.e., collections of legends . . .)."[15] Originally, the translations of the basic books had been made by the Greek missionaries Cyril and Methodius, who had been called to Greater Moravia in 863 by Prince Rostislav. After Methodius died in 885, his disciples were driven out of the country by his German successor Wiching and found refuge in Bulgaria. In such a fashion that country, particularly under Tsar Symeon (893–927), became the radiating center of Slavic culture,[16] which reached a high degree of development. Thus the theory that the Russian

[13] *Ibid.*, p. 119.

[14] Cf. Matthew Spinka, *A History of Christianity in the Balkans* (Chicago: American Society of Church History, 1933), pp. 29 ff.

[15] G. P. Fedotov, ed., *A Treasury of Russian Spirituality* (New York: Sheed & Ward, 1948), p. x.

[16] Spinka, *Christianity in the Balkans*, pp. 50–56.

Vladimir received Bulgarian priests who spoke a language closely related to the Russian and brought with them a complete set of ecclesiastical texts necessary for religious services and ministration as well as the propagation of the faith, if tenable, would make sense, even though it lacks documentary evidence.

Nevertheless, where there is so much strife among the authorities, it would be foolhardy "to rush in where angels fear to tread." Fortunately, it is not necessary to our purpose to decide such a complicated problem in a brief study such as this. It amply suffices to accept the bare fact that Vladimir was converted to Christianity and introduced it into his vast territory in an astonishingly short time. A chronicler credits him, although with the customary hagiographical exaggeration, with having "baptized all the Russian land from one end to the other."[17] It must not be assumed that he succeeded immediately in eliminating all traces of paganism from among the people. For many centuries there has existed what is known as "*dvoeverie*" — a mixture of Christianity with paganism. Nevertheless, the tremendous cultural influence which the Church thus exerted throughout Vladimir's realm, and later throughout other principalities, formed the basis of Russian culture in all its ramifications until the Revolution of 1917. Even the Cyrillic letters of its alphabet are to this day a heritage of it in all countries affected by these influences. The Byzantine contribution to Russia, both through Bulgaria and later directly, has been summarized as follows: "Byzantium brought to Russia five gifts: Her religion, her law, her view of the world, her art and writing."[18] Without the civilization created and inculcated by the Church, Russian culture in general would be wholly unthinkable.

The peaceful development of Russian political life and culture was rudely and catastrophically interrupted by the

[17] Quoted in Kartashev, *Ocherki*, 1:122.

[18] Quoted in Sidney Harcave, ed., *Readings in Russian History*, 2 vols. (New York: Thomas Y. Crowell Co., 1962), 1:100.

Mongolian invasion. Mongols, organized by Temuchin (1167–1227)[19] into an irresistibly destructive military force, carried all before them like a tidal wave. Temuchin dreamed of establishing a Mongolian empire which would ultimately embrace the world. He was proclaimed Chingis-khan (the Great Sovereign or Emperor) in 1206 at the all-Mongolian assembly (Great Kurultay) which met on the banks of the Onon River. This same assembly decided upon a military conquest of all their neighbors. Chingis-khan's first campaign, from his seat at Karakorum, was directed against northern China. In this expedition he was successful, and by 1212 he was the acknowledged master of the vast territory extending to the provinces south of the Yellow River. Three years later he set up his new capital at Khanbalyk (the present-day Peking). This conquest, immensely important in itself, was likewise significant for the fact that it enabled the khan to incorporate Chinese officials into his trained administrative corps, whose services proved invaluable. This was particularly true of Eliu-chu-tsai, a scholar and a statesman, who henceforth ranked high in the Mongol service. Chingis-khan continued his conquests by adding to his territories, after 1219, Tibet, part of India, Turkestan, Khiva, Bokhara, and Khorezm. Having created the greatest empire ever known, he died in 1227, after having divided his conquests among his three sons and the son of his fourth, who had predeceased him. The result took the form of four khanates, among which Karakorum ranked the highest. Its ruler, Chingis-khan's favorite son Ugedei, reigned as the grand-khan, who exercised supreme authority over the other three.

The first invasion of Russia occurred in 1222–23, under the leadership of two of the khan's generals Jebe and Subuday. They were returning from an expedition into Persia and were seeking to return through the lands of the Cumans. Their khan, Kotian, who had organized a defensive action with the aid of ten Russian princes, among them the prince of Kiev, Mstislav III of Galicia, opposed their passage. The battle oc-

[19] George Vernadsky and Michael Karpovich, *A History of Russia* (New Haven: Yale University Press, 1953), 3:20–21.

curred on the River Kalka where, after an initial victory in a preliminary skirmish, the Cuman-Russian forces suffered a crushing, overwhelming defeat. Nine of the ten Russian princes, among them Mstislav, and a large number of common soldiers, lost their lives. Since the Mongols then had no intention of attacking Russia, they proceeded on their homeward way beyond the Urals.

In 1235 the Mongol grand assembly adopted a plan of invasion which this time included all of Russia. The leader of the expedition was Batu, the grandson of Chingis-khan. First of all, the Mongols attacked the Volga Bulgars, who stood in the way of invasion of northern and western Russia. During the winter of 1237–38, they conquered the principalities of Riazan and Vladimir, the latter the seat of Grand Prince Yuri II Vsevolodovich. They defeated him at the battle on the Sit' River on March 4. Thereupon the Mongol horde, having burned Moscow, Kolomna, Suzdal, Rostov, Yaroslavl, and Tver, proceeded through Northern Russia to Novgorod, but receded from it because of the impassable roads made soft by the melting snow. They applied everywhere "the scorched earth" policy; wherever their armies passed, they left in their wake heaps of dead bodies, smoldering ruins, and utter devastation of the lands. They conquered not only by overwhelming numbers but by superb strategy as well. After some five or six months, Batu retired with his army southward to the mouths of the Don and Volga rivers. The Cumans, who held these steppes, were cut down and scattered in all directions, mostly to Hungary.

During 1239 Batu renewed his invasion, but this time against the southern Russian principalities. He burned Pereyaslavl and Chernigov. His army finally reached Kiev, but retired, not feeling strong enough to take it then. During the winter of 1240, however, Batu, with his entire army, assaulted and conquered Kiev on December 6. He plundered and burned it, putting all inhabitants who did not save themselves by flight to the sword. The two magnificent churches, the St. Sophia Cathedral and the Church of the Tithes, were leveled to the ground. The same fate overtook that cradle of

Russian monasticism, the Monastery of the Caves (*Pechers-kaya Lavra*). Kiev, the mother of Russian cities, the seat of the metropolitanate, was so utterly devastated that only some two hundred houses remained standing. Friar John of Plano Carpini, who traveled with papal letters to the great khan in 1245–47, describes the desolation that was Kiev as follows:

> When we were traveling through this country, we found an innumerable multitude of dead men's skulls and bones lying upon the earth. It was once a very large and populous city, but it is now in a manner brought to nothing; for there do scarce remain two hundred houses, and the inhabitants of these are kept in extreme bondage.[20]

Thereupon, Batu's armies proceeded westward through Poland, Silesia, Moravia, and Hungary and then turned southward to the Balkans. Batu returned home in great haste in 1242 upon hearing that Grand Khan Ugedei had died. This perhaps saved Europe from sharing the fate of Russia. He chose the region near the mouth of the Volga River for his permanent settlement and built himself there a magnificent capital called Sarai. Since then his contingent called itself the Golden Horde.

Having become masters of Russia, the Mongols or Tatars, as they may be called, because they were now mixed with many other Asiatic racial groups, particularly the Turkomen, treated the country and its people as valuable property, to be exploited for profit rather than wantonly and senselessly ruined. Not that periodically outbursts of rage, either of a particular group or of the whole khanate, did not devastate this or that region of Russia. Solovev asserts that Russia was invaded by punitive and other Tatar incursions forty-eight times between 1236 and 1462. But on the whole, peace prevailed. The Mongols allowed the native princes to rule over their territories, although each had to secure in person at Sarai an official investiture from the Khan. This humiliating ceremony was aptly known as "beating

[20] Manuel Komroff, ed., *Contemporaries of Marco Polo* (New York: Boni & Liveright, 1928), p. 22. Cf. also Harold T. Cheshire, "The Great Tartar Invasion of Europe," *Slavonic Review*, 5 (1926–27): 89–105.

the ground with one's forehead." The metropolitans were likewise required to secure the khan's approval to their exercise of office, although they had been appointed to it by the patriarch of Constantinople. Otherwise the Russians were left undisturbed to practice their religion as they pleased. No wars were allowed to be waged among the grand princely or appanage principalities. The inhabitants were carefully enrolled in a census for taxation purposes. New currency was coined known as *dengi* — the Russian word for money to this day. At every change on the Golden Horde's throne the princes and the metropolitan were required to secure the new khan's *yarlik*.

Since Kiev lay in ruins, its inhabitants sought refuge by migration to safer regions. The flight took, for the greater part, two directions: to the southwest into Galicia-Volynia and to the northeast into the region between the upper Volga and the Oka rivers — the provinces of Vladimir-Suzdal, Kostroma, Yaroslavl, Moscow, and Tver. It was Vladimir-Suzdal which emerged as the northeastern grand principality; its counterpart was the grand principality of Galich. Since the northeastern regions had been settled by Finns, the influx of the Kievan Russians resulted in a racial mixture which produced the "Great Russian" type, clearly differentiated from the "Little Russians" of the south.

This mass immigration greatly strengthened the newly rising settlement of the hitherto insignificant hamlet of Moscow, built on the gentle rise of land on the River Moskva, not far from where it merges with Oka. The first mention of the settlement occurs in a chronicle entry of 1147. A few years later it was surrounded by a palisade. Its rulers were younger sons of the more important neighboring princely houses. One of these, Prince Vladimir, perished in the destruction of the city by the Mongols in 1237. It was, however, only when Prince Daniel, the youngest son of Alexander Nevsky, was its ruler that the principality came into prominence.[21] He expanded it by seiz-

[21] Nicholas V. Riasanovsky, *A History of Russia* (New York: Oxford University Press, 1963), pp. 106 ff. Cf. also Arthur Voyce, *Moscow and the Roots of Russian Culture* (Norman, Okla.: University of Oklahoma Press, 1964), pp. 3 ff.

ing the mouth of the Moskva River from the Riazan prince, thus extending his control of it over its lower course and making it an important commercial waterway. Daniel's son and successor Yuri III (1303–1325) enlarged the territory further by annexing the lands of his neighbor, prince of Mozhaisk, thus securing control of the whole length of the Moskva River. In 1317 or 1318 Yuri married the khan's sister and along with her received the grand princely rank, held hitherto by Prince Michael of Tver. Yuri's advancement led to a war with Tver, during which his wife was taken captive and died in prison. The Tver prince, tried at the khan's court, was sentenced to death. But in 1322 his eldest son Dmitry again regained the title of grand prince.

Since Kiev was utterly ruined in 1240, the metropolitans could no longer reside there, although they continued to bear the title of that city. They traveled all over the newly settled territories, using the two grand principalities Galich and Vladimir alternately as their temporary residences. The rulers of these principalities tried to attract them to their respective sees permanently, because of the prestige of the metropolitanate—the only unifying center in all Russia. Thus the metropolitanate possessed a great political significance as a centralizing force. The princes also sought to secure the appointment of their own native candidates, in order to possess a surer and firmer hold upon them than they could exercise over a Greek.

In the very year of the Mongol invasion of Russia (1237) there arrived in Kiev a new metropolitan, a Greek by the name of Joseph. After Kiev was conquered three years later, he apparently returned to Constantinople, for no further mention is made of him. After a short interval (in 1242), Grand Prince Daniel Romanovich of Galicia-Volynia chose as the candidate for the vacant post one of his subjects, the archimandrite Cyril,[22] and when he arranged his relation to the Mongols, sent him to Nicaea to secure the patriarchal consecration. Patriarch Manuel II resided at Nicaea, because Constantinople had

[22] For the metropolitanate of Cyril, cf. Kartashev, *Ocherki*, 1:290–95.

been occupied by the Latins since 1204 in the course of the Fourth Crusade; they even established there their own patriarchate.[23] Manuel approved and consecrated Cyril, who thereupon returned to Russia in 1249.

The patriarch probably did not choose a Greek for the post, but consented to a Russian, because a Greek would not wish to go into a country under Mongol domination. Cyril himself did not settle in the midst of ruins that had been Kiev but took up his residence at Vladimir on the Kliazma River. This was a significant new development. The fact that Cyril, a native Galician, would choose Vladimir rather than Galich as his residence was even more remarkable. Furthermore, although he traveled a great deal over his vast archdiocese, there is no mention of his ever visiting Galicia-Volynia. On the contrary, he gave a clear indication of his intention of residing at Vladimir permanently by keeping its episcopal see vacant until 1274 and performing the episcopal duties there himself.

Why did Cyril avoid Galicia-Volynia in such a marked, even provocative, manner, since he was, after all, metropolitan of all Russia? The reason must be sought in Daniel's pro-papal policy. In 1245 Daniel found it necessary to submit to the suzerainty of the khan in order to be able to defend his territories against the attacks of the Hungarians and the Poles. He deeply resented this subjection. It happened that in the same year Pope Innocent IV had sent Friar John Plano de Carpini with a letter to Grand Khan Guyuk. Innocent had ordered Carpini to stop at the court of Daniel to offer the latter inducements to accept papal jurisdiction. The Galician prince, however, did not happen to be at home at the time. Upon his return, he entered into negotiations with the pope. He entertained the hope that Innocent might help him throw off the Mongolian yoke and perhaps grant him the royal crown. Therefore, he immediately sent a reply to the pope, asking his help. Innocent answered in 1246 that, "consenting to his sup-

[23] Matthew Spinka, "The Effect of the Crusades upon Eastern Christianity," in J. T. McNeill, Matthew Spinka, and Harold R. Willoughby, eds., *Environmental Factors in Christian History* (Chicago: University of Chicago Press, 1939), pp. 267–72.

plication," he accepted Daniel and his land under his and St. Peter's protection. Thereupon, he sent him his legate, the bishop of Prussia, with the royal wreath. For some reason, Daniel refused to accept the royal insignia from him. Such was the situation when Metropolitan Cyril returned from Nicaea; no wonder he refused to enter Daniel's territories! In 1253 Innocent made another attempt to gain Daniel for the Roman Church, and at that time he succeeded. Daniel was crowned king of Galicia; but since the pope failed to send him troops along with the crown, he again returned to Orthodoxy. In view of these circumstances, Cyril's preference for the northeastern principality is understandable, particularly when one remembers that Alexander Yaroslavich of Novgorod in 1240 heroically defended Orthodoxy by defeating the invading Roman Catholic Swedes on the River Neva. He has been known as "Nevsky" ever since. When, two years later, the Teutonic Knights took Pskov and came within twenty miles of Novgorod, Alexander drove them onto the frozen surface of Lake Peipus and inflicted such a defeat upon them that thereafter they left the Russians severely alone. In 1245 he repeated the feat in dealing with the invading Lithuanians. This zeal for Orthodoxy could not but impress the metropolitan.

Another interesting circumstance of Cyril's long term of office was the fact that Khan Mangu-Temir of Sarai gave him (in 1267) a *yarlik* which specified that (1) Russians were assured a free confession of their faith without any interference or ridicule; (2) their priests were free from all payments, gifts, and civil duties; and (3) the title to ecclesiastical lands and properties was recognized and confirmed as inviolable and that all servants and serfs belonging to ecclesiastical establishments were free from corvée duty. Penalty for publicly insulting or dishonoring the faith was death with torture.[24]

Cyril's administration of the Church was noteworthy for several important accomplishments, particularly the Sobor he called in 1274 at which his "Rule" was adopted. It sought to correct a number of abuses in the lives of bishops, clergy, and lay people. His long reign, lasting some forty years, came to an

[24] Golubinsky, *Istoriya russkoi tserkvi*, 2:33.

end with his death on December 6, 1281. Although he died at Vladimir, he was buried in the Cathedral of St. Sophia in Kiev.

Cyril was succeeded by a Greek, Metropolitan Maxim (1287–1305).[25] He at first settled at Kiev. Nikon's *Chronicle* informs us that it was his custom to travel all over his vast metropolitanate. He thus visited Vladimir, Novgorod, Pskov, and even Galich. But in 1299 the Mongols again frightfully plundered Kiev, thus sending its inhabitants northward. Maxim now decided to leave Kiev permanently. He left, with his entire suite and the cathedral staff, for Vladimir in 1300. Kiev eparchy was left to be administered by a substitute. Moreover, in Vladimir Maxim transferred the local eparchial bishop to the vacant see of Rostov and he himself assumed his functions.

The permanent removal of the metropolitan to Vladimir had an unpremeditated result: the Galician-Volynian eparchies now demanded that they be set up as a separate metropolitanate. Grand Prince Yuri I of Galich petitioned both the ecumenical patriarch and the emperor for a Galician metropolitanate, entirely independent of the Kievan-Vladimirian. His demands were actually granted by Patriarch Athanasius and Emperor Andronicus II Paleologus sometime in 1302 or 1303. According to a later report, the first Galician metropolitan was a certain Niphont, of whom nothing is otherwise known. Maxim died in 1305, and Niphont seems to have ended his life about the same time. Maxim was buried in the Cathedral of the Assumption in Vladimir.

Yuri Lvovich thereupon promptly dispatched as his candidate for the vacated see of Galich the hegumenos of the Ratsky monastery, Peter. The grand prince of Vladimir, Michael Yaroslavich, likewise sent a request to Constantinople, asking that the hegumenos Gerontius of Kiev be consecrated as Maxim's successor. Of course, since there now existed two metropolitanates, both these candidates could have been appointed to their respective posts. Patriarch Athanasius, however, who had created the second metropolitanate of Galicia-Volynia, now changed his mind; he abolished his re-

[25] Kartashev, *Ocherki*, pp. 295–98.

cent creation and reunited it with the Kievan metropolitanate. Furthermore, he appointed Peter to this unified metropolitanate, embracing both Galicia-Volynia and Vladimir-Suzdal as well as the rest of Russia.

The appointment of Peter (1308–1326)[26] had most important consequences. Both grand princes resented the patriarch's act. Yuri Lvovich was displeased because he had thereby lost ecclesiastical autonomy and because Peter had chosen to reside at Vladimir. Since he died the same year, however, his resentment had no practical significance. Michael of Vladimir, on his part, resented the appointment because Peter had not been his candidate to begin with. Nevertheless, Peter was obliged to reside at Vladimir, for after Kiev it was the recognized see of the metropolitan. He was treated with decided hostility by Michael Yaroslavich who, although he resided in Tver, was the grand prince of Vladimir (for this dignity was passed around by the khan in accordance with seniority and the amount of money offered for the rank). In his hatred, Michael went so far as to seek Peter's deposition. He instigated Bishop Andrew of Tver to accuse Peter to the patriarch of simony. The latter immediately sent a secretary to investigate the charge. The trial was held in Pereyaslavl before a packed assembly, in which only two bishops participated. The majority consisted of hegumenoi, priests, princes, and boyars. The proceedings were stormy, occasionally bursting into an armed conflict. Despite its hostility, the Sobor found the charges against Peter trumped up and cleared him of all guilt. This angered the grand prince, so he was thereafter opposed to Peter more than ever and brought to the Patriarch another charge against him. The new patriarch Niphont (1312–1315), probably bribed by Michael, cited Peter to Constantinople and to all appearances was ready to depose him. Fortunately for Peter, Niphont himself was deposed, even before the trial could be begun, for having loved money more than justice.

Under these circumstances, Peter sought relief from the constant harassment at the friendly court of Moscow, then

[26] *Ibid.*, 1:298–304.

ruled by Ivan I, surnamed Kalita, i.e., the Moneybag (1325–41). He was an ambitious, far-seeing, parsimonious person, but above all a shrewd politician. He not only obsequiously submitted to Khan Uzbek of the Golden Horde (1313–1341); he secured for himself the appointment as tax collector of the extremely heavy tribute money in place of the Tartar functionaries performing the service hitherto. This operation netted him considerable profit. Thus enriched, he extended his dominions by prudent purchases and attracted new settlers to his territories by aiding them to make a start. This more than doubled his tiny patrimony. At the Sobor of Pereyaslavl his predecessor had taken Metropolitan Peter's part. Ivan also showed himself friendly to Peter, manifesting thereby his animosity toward Michael of Tver, whose grand princely dignity he coveted. Peter, therefore, in his need of a peaceful shelter, gratefully accepted Moscow's hospitality, although for the time being he could not transfer his metropolitan see there, since Moscow was then a mere appanage principality.

Nevertheless, astute Ivan secured from Peter a promise that, if he should build in Moscow a stone church (the first of its kind there), Peter would consent to be buried there. All these schemes to secure the transfer of the metropolitanate to his city found a happy solution when Ivan himself became grand prince in 1328, although Peter did not live to see the day. Before his death, tradition says, he "prophetically consecrated the poor little town of Moscow as the future ecclesiastical and political capital of the land of Russia."[27] He died in December, 1326, and was buried in the unpretentious Uspensky church built within the walls of the Kremlin (the present day *Uspensky Sobor*). It was not yet finished at the time of his death. Thus Peter deliberately aided Ivan's ambitions, although his ability to do so was considerably limited.

That Peter was seriously helping to make Moscow the dominant political power in central Russia is seen in his schemes, before he died, to secure as his successor someone who would

[27] Vasily Klyuchevsky, "St. Sergius: The Importance of His Life and Work," in *Readings in Russian History*, ed. S. S. Harcave (New York: Crowell, 1962), 1:157.

remain in Moscow rather than return to Vladimir. He and Ivan agreed on Archimandrite Theodore, a Muscovite. Immediately upon Peter's death, Ivan sent Theodore to Constantinople with the request that he be consecrated metropolitan. However, the grand prince of Tver, Alexander Michaelovich (1326–28), protested against this usurpation of his right to nominate the candidate for the metropolitan's post. Diplomatically, to ingratiate himself with the patriarch, he suggested that a Greek be appointed to that office. It was Theognost, a Greek, who was consecrated metropolitan of Kiev and repaired to Russia in 1328.

Theognost (1328–1357),[28] upon reaching his destination, took up his residence in Vladimir. But that same year an event occurred that radically changed the political complexion of affairs. Khan Uzbek had sent, the year before, an emissary Shevkil, with his retinue, to Tver. This man had acted haughtily and had provoked the inhabitants to such a fury that they killed him with all his retinue. Grand Prince Alexander had to seek refuge from the khan's wrath in Pskov. Uzbek thereupon deprived him of his grand princely rank and bestowed it on Ivan Kalita, with the proviso that he seize and deliver Alexander to him at Sarai. From that time the grand princely honors, with a few short intermissions, were held by Moscow. Furthermore, Ivan simply annexed Vladimir to his territories, thus expanding his realm several-fold. The newly arrived metropolitan was induced to excommunicate Alexander, who was then seized by Ivan and brought to Sarai. The khan ordered him to be beheaded. Thus Ivan rid himself of a strong rival and realized his dream of becoming the grand prince. This was the first step of the Muscovite principality's rise to hegemony among the central Russian principalities and to its ultimate aggrandizement in the empire.

Nothing now stood in the way of a legal transfer of the metropolitanate from Vladimir to Moscow. Theognost promptly made the change and effectively aided Ivan in the transformation of the insignificant city into one more worthy of the grand princely rank. The Uspensky church, in which Metro-

[28] Kartashev, *Ocherki*, 1:304–7.

politan Peter had been buried, was now completed. Several other churches were built thereafter. In his own court monastery Ivan built the small Church of the Savior in the Wood.[29] Three years later he erected a similar church of Archangel Michael (now the *Arkhangelsky Sobor*). Even with five such small, newly built stone churches, Moscow was far behind the other large Russian cities, such as Vladimir; yet it had made a beginning of the transformation which followed. Metropolitan Peter even in his death served to magnify his chosen city; miracles were reported to have occurred at his grave, and in 1339 he was canonized as a saint by the patriarch of Constantinople.

The rise of Moscow was naturally resented by greater cities, which regarded themselves as more suitable for the honors and privileges. Indications of such jealousy are noticeable in the Novgorod Chronicle, which records that Metropolitan Theognost during his visit to that city was given but poor hospitality by the bishop and the monastery.[30] They resented his spending their money for the building of the Moscow churches. They even complained of him to the patriarch.

Although a Greek himself, Theognost was so devoted to the interests and welfare of Moscow that he took thought how to secure a like-minded man as his successor. The rise of that city to its political eminence was so rapid and so much resented by other principalities that the next metropolitan, by supporting an opponent of Moscow, could undo the work of Peter and Theognost. What was needed was to obtain the election of a native Muscovite. Such a person was found in the court-favored monk Alexis, the most learned man of the time. Theognost died on March 11, 1353, of the Black Death plague, which had spread from Western Europe into the East.

Alexis (1353–1378),[31] a forty-year-old monk of the Monastery of the Epiphany, was entirely worthy of the high office

[29] Samuel H. Cross, *Medieval Russian Churches* (Cambridge, Mass.: Medieval Academy of America, 1949), pp. 63–64, remarks that this church "was dismantled within the last few years and now destroyed." He gives a picture of it in Figure 64.

[30] Kartashev, *Ocherki*, p. 306.

[31] *Ibid.*, pp. 307–13.

which was entrusted to him. The ecumenical patriarch at first did not wish to grant him the Kievan metropolitanate, desiring to appoint a Greek instead. Moreover, he feared the growth of Russian nationalism, which might lead to a demand for ecclesiastical autocephaly. Nevertheless, Alexis appeared so eminently suitable a candidate that the patriarch hesitated to reject him outright. He subjected him to all kinds of examinations, tests, and further instruction; altogether, he kept him in Constantinople for a year. When he finally consecrated him, he hedged the appointment about with all kinds of unusual requirements, the most resious of which was that Alexis must personally come to Constantinople every two years and make a report on his administration.

Before Alexis left Constantinople, he fully explained and justified the transfer of the metropolitanate from Kiev to Vladimir and asked that the patriarchal synod officially approve the change. The patriarch acknowledged the reasons for the removal as valid, and the synod thereupon issued a decree stating that, although Kiev was still the official see of the metropolitanate, its actual transfer to Vladimir as its second residence was both necessary and legal. Henceforth, Alexis bore the title of the metropolitan of Vladimir, even though he actually resided in Moscow.

Alexis' appointment provoked a continued and aggressive protest. The Lithuanian grand duke, Olgerd (1341–1380), whose large territories included many of the former Russian western provinces and extended southward into Kiev, renewed the struggle for an independent metropolitanate of Kiev. In the last year of Theognost's life there appeared in Constantinople a certain ecclesiastical adventurer, Theodorit by name, seeking appointment to the Kievan see on the pretense that Theognost had already died. The patriarch, whose suspicions had been aroused, sent an emissary to Moscow to inquire about the truth of the claim. Thereupon Theodorit, knowing that the statement was false, ran away to Trnovo in Bulgaria, where he secured the desired consecration from the Bulgarian patriarch. He next arrived in Kiev, proclaiming himself its legitimate holder. Olgerd now utilized this opportunity for carrying out his ambition not only to restore the Kievan metropolitanate but to make its occupant the ecclesiastical head of *all* Russia; he would thus subordinate to it, or altogether annihilate, the Vladimir-Moscow see. For that reason he supported Theodorit. In the meantime, Theognost had died and Alexis had been dispatched to Constantinople to secure appointment as his successor. Seeing that Alexis was assured of victory, Olgerd now abandoned Theodorit, without, however, giving up his plan. He thereafter supported the candidacy of his relative on his wife's side, Roman, and appealed to the patriarch for his appointment as the metropolitan of Kiev. Furthermore, Olgerd planned to detach Tver from the Vladimir-Moscow jurisdiction and attach it to the projected Roman's ecclesiastical province, thus making him essentially a Lithuanian metropolitan. Patriarch Philotheos, however, decided to make Alexis the metropolitan of Kiev and *all* Russia.

In 1355, when there was a change on the patriarchal and imperial thrones, Olgerd and Roman tried once more to carry out their plans for a separate metropolitanate. Nevertheless, their efforts again proved in vain. Even thereafter Olgerd continued to repudiate Alexis' jurisdiction over his Russian provinces. When in 1358 the metropolitan visited Olgerd's territories, the latter had him arrested and kept him in prison until 1360. After Roman died, Olgerd again renewed his request to the patriarch that the metropolitan live in his territories: this time he formulated his argument in the sense that, since Kiev was the original see of the metropolitan, Alexis should transfer his residence from Moscow to Kiev. But even this scheme failed.

Even more serious was the undertaking of the Polish king Cazimir the Great (1333–1370) who, when he had conquered Galicia and part of Volynia, sought to establish a separate metropolitanate for those territories. In 1370 Cazimir sent his candidate Anthony to Constantinople with the petition that he be consecrated for Galich. He not only pleaded that Galicia-Volynia had always had a metropolitan of its own and that "now the land perishes for the lack of rule," but even threatened that if Anthony be not appointed, he would have to seek relief from the Roman Catholic authorities. Anthony was consecrated metropolitan by Patriarch Philotheos in 1371.

Thereupon, however, Olgerd of Lithuania renewed his request for a separate metropolitanate for his territories. Philotheos sent his official Cyprian to Russia, to investigate this matter. Cyprian managed the affair so cleverly that he himself secured the appointment as metropolitan of Kiev and all Russia (1375), even though the legitimate metropolitan Alexis was still alive. This was contrary to all canonical rules. Cyprian thereupon sought the deposition of Alexis. The final result, however, was that, although Alexis remained the metropolitan of Vladimir-Moscow, there existed two other metropolitanates – those of Galich and Kiev.

In turning now to Alexis' administration of his office, we note that he gave the Moscow princes even more effective and valuable service than his predecessors had given. He exercised not only the supreme ecclesiastical authority in all Russia – unless forcibly prevented from doing so – but took part directly in the work of the government. The grand princes, on their part, trusted him implicitly. Simeon Ivanovich, Ivan Kalita's successor, advised his two brothers prior to his death (1353) to obey Alexis in all things.[32] His successor, the weak Ivan II Ivanovich (1353–58), entrusted him with wide powers. Alexis was his intimate advisor and eminent statesman, respected by both the boyars and the common people. He was esteemed highly even at the khan's court, because he had cured the khan's wife Taydula of an eye infection. The Moscow principality now steadily extended its territory and power over other princes. Because of its prosperity, immigrants willingly flocked into the Moscow principality, and many boyars from elsewhere entered the service of the grand prince. Moreover, peace reigned throughout his lands.

After Ivan's death, Alexis served as the regent of the realm during the minority of Dmitry Ivanovich (1359–89). Kartashev declares that this was "the only event (of the sort) in all our history,"[33] either forgetting or not regarding the cases

[32] *Ibid.*, p. 310.
[33] *Ibid.*

as comparable, that Patriarch Philaret participated in the early part of the reign of his son Michael Romanov (1613–45).[34] According to Greek sources, Ivan had not only left his eleven-year-old son in Alexis' care but had entrusted Alexis with "the rule and defense of his principality, not trusting anyone else because of his many enemies."[35] Alexis was thus the real ruler of Moscow lands during Dmitry's minority and, after the latter assumed the rule, his most intimate counselor and guide. That enemies there were is evident from the fact that in 1360 Dmitry Konstantinovich of Suzdal secured from the khan the title of grand prince; but within two years the boyars and the metropolitan succeeded in winning its restoration to Dmitry Ivanovich. Alexis also built a number of churches in Moscow. He built two monasteries for men and a convent for women. In one of these monasteries, the Chudov, he was buried in 1378.

Besides the aid rendered the Moscow princes by Alexis, the famous national saint Sergius, the most outstanding spiritual leader of the Russian people, contributed much to the upbuilding of Moscow power and to the spiritual renewal of all Russia. In fact, in the fifteenth century he became the patron saint of Moscow and, by his saintly reputation, helped to unify all Russia under the overlordship of Moscow.

Sergius,[36] whose original name was Bartholomew, was born in Rostov (*c.* 1314–23), the son of a wealthy noble Cyril, who was later reduced to poverty. The family moved to Radonezh, after which place Sergius is usually known. He received a good education; having been brought up in piety, he desired to become a hermit but waited to carry out his plan until after his parents' death. Thereupon he induced his brother Stephen to accompany him in seeking out a suitable place where they could establish themselves. They found the place in a thickly wooded region about forty miles northeast from Moscow (the present day Zagorsk), and built themselves a rough log cell

[34] Riasanovsky, *History of Russia*, p. 194.

[35] Kartashev, *Ocherki*, p. 310.

[36] The sketch of Sergius' life is based on the hagiographical *Life* written by Epiphanius, a monk of the Trinity monastery, during the saint's lifetime. It was published in a greatly shortened version by Fedotov, *A Treasury*, pp. 54–84.

and a chapel, which they dedicated to the Holy Trinity (now the *Troitsko-Sergievskaya Lavra*). Stephen then left Bartholomew, who remained there alone. But not for long: gradually, like-minded men gathered about him. It was then that he received the tonsure of a monk from an abbot and assumed the name of Sergius. With the increase of the community, it became necessary to choose an abbot to rule the brethren. Sergius was earnestly besought to assume the office, but in his characteristic humility he steadfastly refused. The need, however, was great and at last Sergius went to the bishop of Pereyaslavl to request one of his clerics to be ordained an abbot for the monastery. The bishop insisted that Sergius himself assume the office and the latter, after a struggle, yielded.

After the monastery had existed for about fifteen years, the vicinity began to be populated by peasantry, who felled the forest and built their huts in the clearing. The fame of the saintly abbot of Trinity rapidly spread about, and he was visited by a great many, both low and high, seeking cures, comfort, and advice. Sergius now spread his influence for moral education of the Russian people. Even the patriarch of Constantinople wrote him a letter. The monastery received many gifts and expanded both in size, charity, and influence. Among those who sought Sergius' services were Metropolitan Alexis and Grand Prince Dmitry. The latter asked Sergius at one time to intercede with the fierce Prince Oleg Ivanovich of Riazan and dissuade him from attacking Moscow. Sergius succeeded in persuading Oleg to abandon the project. Indeed, when the metropolitan lay on his deathbed (1378), he implored Sergius to become his successor; but the latter steadfastly refused. The Epiphanius *Life* recounts Alexis' pleading with Sergius:

> Dost thou know why I sent for thee? I desire, while I yet live, to find a man able to feed Christ's flock. I have doubted of them all, thee alone have I chosen as worthy. I know with all certainty that, from the puissant prince to the lowliest of his people, thou art the one they want.[37]

[37] *Ibid.*, p. 79.

Nevertheless, Sergius, in his profound humility, refused to be moved. Instead, he saw his task as that of being the spiritual leader of Orthodoxy. He now extended his mission throughout the land, and his pervasive influence wrought moral transformation.

This was done, besides other means, by the spread of new monasteries. From time to time the monks of the Trinity monastery "swarmed" out to establish new homes on the order of Trinity. Such monasteries counted almost the fourth part of the new establishments. Hitherto there existed relatively few monasteries: from 1240 to 1340 only thirty were founded,[38] and those mostly in cities and their environs. The next century witnessed the founding of nearly one hundred and fifty, located chiefly in deep forests northeast of the Volga River. These communities became centers of busy and expanding peasant settlements, thus populating regions hitherto entirely uninhabited. The monks taught the settlers new methods of farming and of raising stock, as well as practical piety. "So the combined efforts of monk and peasant, imbued with the spirit which St. Sergius had breathed into Russian society, created a new Russia beyond the Volga."[39]

Despite his youth, Grand Prince Dmitry boldly extended his power over the neighboring princes. In 1367 he even dared to erect stone walls around the Kremlin, thus defying the strictest Tatar order that no Russian city be surrounded by any stronger walls than wooden palisades. Thereupon the khan transferred the grand princely title from Dmitry to Prince Michael Alexandrovich of Tver, Moscow's sworn rival. But Michael did not keep it long. Although he secured the cooperation of his son-in-law Olgerd of Lithuania and the combined forces attacked Dmitry, the attack failed. The stone walls of the Kremlin stopped them. Soon peace was restored. But Dmitry's victory had infuriated the new khan Mamai, who had seized hegemony at Sarai. He promptly sent an advance guard against Moscow. The contingent burned Nizhni Novgorod, but when it collided with Dimitry's army, it was defeated (1378). This

[38] Kliuchevsky, "St. Sergius," p. 161.
[39] *Ibid.*, p. 162.

was the *first* time that the Russians succeeded in inflicting a defeat upon the Tatars. Enraged, Mamai now gathered an army estimated at 200,000 and secured another army of the same size from the Lithuanian Grand Duke Yagailo. Dmitry was confronted with a decision upon which depended not only his own life but the fate of the grand principality and perhaps of all Russia. Fortunately, the other Russian princes, with the exception of Novgorod, Pskov, Nizhni Novgorod, Tver, and Riazan, supported him, having in the moment of supreme danger laid aside their petty feuds and rivalries. The Tatars, on the other hand, were divided among themselves. Yet Dmitry was loath to assume responsibility for deciding such a momentous issue. Since Alexis was dead by this time, he turned to Sergius. Again the Church, in this critical time, came to the aid of the state. Sergius gave Dmitry his blessing and—as Epiphanius' *Life* recounts—said to him:

> It behoveth you, Lord, to have a care for the lives of the flock committed to you by God. Go forth against the heathen; and upheld by the strong arm of God, conquer; and return to your country sound of health, and glorify God with loud praise.[40]

The decisive battle between the two armies was fought on the River Don at Kulikovo field, on September 8, 1380. Dmitry decided to attack the host of Mamai before the Lithuanian army joined the fight. Moreover, he chose terrain where Tatar cavalry could operate only with difficulty. At first the Russians, numbering less than Mamai's host (some 150,000), suffered defeat, and many soldiers panicked. That moment a courier from Sergius arrived on the scene with the encouraging message: "Be in no doubt, Lord, go forward with faith and confront the enemy's ferocity; and fear not, for God will be on your side." Thus encouraged, Dmitry renewed the battle with new determination. A small detachment of reserves, held back until the Tatars exposed their rear, assaulted them and drove them to flight in confusion. Despite enormous losses, which included the flower of the Muscovite realm, victory was won

[40] Fedotov, *A Treasury*, p. 77.

by the Russians. Dmitry, since then known as "Donskoy," was not able to throw the Tatar yoke altogether, but merely to ease it. In 1382 the new khan Tokhtamysh made another incursion into Russia, took Moscow and other important cities, and burned them. Dmitry had to resume the payment of tribute and to give his two sons into the khan's keeping as hostages. Russia for another hundred years was not strong enough to free herself.

And yet, the battle of Kulikovo proved that the Tatars were not invincible and that the path of freedom lay in unification of Russia under a single supreme ruler, the grand prince of Moscow. This, then, was to be the firm policy of the rulers of Moscow. In this policy, over the last hundred and thirty years, ever since the metropolitanate of Cyril, the Russian metropolitans faithfully and efficiently cooperated with the state authorities in supporting the grand princes in their efforts at consolidating the state. Whether this preference for Moscow on the part of the metropolitans, who after all were ecclesiastical heads of *all* Russia, was wise or just, does not come into consideration here. We are interested primarily in the fact that Moscow gained its pre-eminence with the efficient aid of the Church. Its very loyal services should be acknowledged as contributing mightily to the rise of Moscow to its ultimate greatness.

5

The Reforming Critiques of Robert Grosseteste, Roger Bacon, and Ramon Lull and Their Related Impact upon Medieval Society: Historical Studies in the Critical Temper and the Practice of Tradition

RAY C. PETRY

Re-creating tradition, critically, means practicing the greatest of all crafts, namely that of judicious receptivity and discriminating deliverance. Robert Grosseteste, Roger Bacon, and Ramon Lull made reforming history as critical exploiters of the Christian heritage.[1] Theirs constituted a genuine, though strictly medieval, attempt at reform. That is, they contemplated no reshaping of the entire social order in keeping with humanly engineered dynamics. They did envision a slowly burgeoning development at the divine behest within the stable

[1] Texts and representative literature are exemplified in S. Harrison Thomson, *The Writings of Robert Grosseteste, Bishop of Lincoln 1235–1253* (Cambridge: At the University Press, 1940); D. A. Callus, ed., *Robert Grosseteste: Scholar and Bishop* (Oxford: Clarendon Press, 1955); Rogeri Baconis, *Moralis Philosophia*, ed. F. Delorme and E. Massa (Turici: in Aedibus Thesauri Mundi, 1953); R. Carton *et al.*, *Roger Bacon*, 3 vols., Etudes de philosophie médiévale, vols. 2, 3, 5 (Paris: J. Vrin, 1924); *Obres de Ramon Lull*, 1st ed., Commissió Editora Lulliana, vols. 1–21 (Palma de Mallorca, 1905–53); Ramon Lull, *Obres Essencials*, ed. M. Batllori *et al.* (Barcelona: Editorial Selecta, 1957–60), vols. 1–2; and *Raimundi Lulli: Opera Latina*, ed. F. Stegmüller (Palma de Mallorca, 1959–63), vols. 1–4). Cf. the fundamental work of Tomás Carreras y Artau and Joaquín Carreras y Artau, *Historia de la filosofía Española: Filosofía Cristiana de los siglos XIII al XV* (Madrid: Real academia de ciencias exactas, físicas y naturales, 1939), vols. 1–2, esp., 1:233 ff., 272 ff., through vol. 2.

framework of human transformation. They viewed *reformatio* as the distinctive province and expression of the critical mind. It operated under God within the historic environment. Divinely sustained renewal constituted the chief levelling and elevating force. Through it, tradition could become dynamically rigorous in its commitment to received deposit and transmissive vitality. Collectively, these three innovators recapitulated the roles of university thinkers, linguists, translators, and preachers. They comprised mendicants, inquisitors, administrators, missionaries, and mystics. Theirs was a productive mélange of gospel acumen and professional sophistication, of historical astuteness and contemporary expendability. They were goads to public opinion and persimmon-like aperitifs for social taste. They did not hesitate to deliver themselves on morals and aesthetics, philology and dogmatics, theology, and canonics. Their sweeping preoccupations were based on a premise we do not collectively espouse. The deepest and most pervasive action was held traceable to the most inward, and sometimes the least perceptible, *contemplatio. Theoria* and *praxis*, with overtones strange to our ears, were always conjoined in them.

Robert Grosseteste (c. 1175–1253) was an Oxford preceptor of Franciscans and a scholar, teacher, and translator of distinction. He was a dedicated bishop quite able and willing to send a peregrinating pope into apoplectic fits. This he did while cheerfully subscribing to the pontiff's unlimited commission as a "servant of the servants of God." Roger Bacon (c. 1214–92/94) was a thoroughly medieval son in the spirit of Master Robert of Lincoln. None could call him a modern man except, perhaps, in his laboratory and temperamental explosiveness. He was a Franciscan scholar and self-established authority on practically all fields of experimental, metaphysical, and theological knowledge. Apparently, he alternated between inspiring a few Christians to new feats of active rapture and stigmatizing virtually all others as ignorant of their basic inheritance.[2] Ramon Lull (c. 1232–1315/16) was, and remains,

[2] *Compendium studii philosophiae*, cap. 1 (J. A. Brewer, ed.) RS 15:398–404.

an enigma of scholarship and devotion. That is, he provided a clear martyrdom. He also witnessed through turgid scholastic theses and summas. Yet he was the author, too, of moving, mystic treatises.[3]

These men have been the subject of excellent researches. There has been all too little imaginative regard for their central stance as relentless critics of the Christian pilgrimage, which they supported with passionate loyalty. Viewing them historically requires a keen sense of their doctrinal and social orientation.

All these men were eschatological, according to classic Christian usage. They actually believed the coming judgment and final Kingdom to be imminent. The Church's business was to explicate, in its earthly disposition of clerical rules and lay obedience, the heavenly mandate for human salvation. The majestic concern of the celestial hierarchy was to empower terrestrial hierarchs for true deification and human service. The beloved *patria* beckoned to a wayfaring society en route to heaven for the exercise of social critique and inwardly reforming action. The heavenly city elicited and empowered the earthly commonwealth.

Grosseteste's eschatology was the practicing critique of a living, though blunted, tradition. His strictures on a decadent Church and a static society stemmed from his commitment to divine creation and redemption. These acts were a cosmic deliverance, a holding forth of salvation and a summoning to judgment. Human acceptance of them through the Church constituted the most realistic prosecution of tradition possible. Grosseteste was eschatological in that he was biblical. He was evangelical in his acceptance of Old and New Testament covenanting between God and man. Therefore, he shouldered his share of the heavenly commission for responsible curacy and soteriological proclamation. He served these ends through the Church. This was the sum and substance of his elevating

[3] Consult my *Late Medieval Mysticism*, Library of Christian Classics, vol. 13 (Philadelphia: Westminster Press, 1957), pp. 142 ff.

the hierarchical role of popes, bishops, priests, and of his own *cura pastoralis.* Here was the nub of his insistence upon visitation prerogatives. It was the validation of his using mendicant shock troops in the heavenly war of reform, waged in his diocese.[4]

His most blistering criticism of a bloated papacy and curia was his *Memorandum* of 1250. It was preceded and supported by a whole series of administrative, sermonic, and biblically documented propositions.[5] Actually, its genius lay in its systematic discernment of historic institutions and social motivation. This was a reforming appeal to free the Church to the condition in which Christ had delivered it. It was currently being hemmed in for clerical aggrandizement in the name of Petrine servantship. In a sheaf of correspondence on hierarchical privilege and obligation, Grosseteste accepted his part of the task. A vital deposit required liberal transmission. This must come through vicarious service by way of the Church's divine gratuities. All of his episcopal statutes were grounded in diocesan responsibility. Reformation, correction, and inquisition in the sense of disciplinary visitation were operative principles.[6]

In Bacon, nothing was clearer than the function of eschatological *theoria* in everyday *praxis.* This was the music of heaven delineated by Augustine and reinvoked by Master Robert. It was the dance of living theology, the ascetic and aesthetic cult of salvation, the proclamation of kerygmatic preaching by way of gesture and genuflection. Poetic rapture and rhetorical summation spoke through it, as well as measured hermeneutics and homiletical exposition.[7] But the throb-

[4] See Ep. 14–16, 20, 41, and esp. 34, 58 (RS 25:59–63, 71, 133–34, and 121, 179, 181). Cf. his own description of his visitations in texts edited by F. M. Powicke and C. R. Cheney, *Councils and Synods* . . . (Oxford: Clarendon Press, 1964), 2:261–65.

[5] Consult Thomson, *Grosseteste*, pp. 141 ff.; E. Brown, *Fasciculus rerum expetendarum et fugiendarum* (London, 1690, 2:250–57. Cf. W. A. Pantin, in Callus, *Grosseteste*, pp. 209–15, for a good analysis of the *Memorial* and related documents.

[6] Powicke and Cheney, *Councils and Synods*, 2:265.

[7] *Opus tertium*, cap. 75 (RS 15:303–10); cf. cap. 14 (RS 15:52). *Compend. studii phil.*, cap. 5 (RS 15:425–28). Cf. E. de Bruyne, *Etudes*

bing heart of man's destined salvation was experienced supremely in sacrament and eucharistic grace.

Bacon's major works were replete with references to the soteriological ends of moral philosophy. Beatitude and the felicity of eternal life were recurrent themes. The *beata vita* awaited the test of Antichrist and the Last Judgment.[8] Effective critique and reforming vitality alone could withstand Antichrist's assault. Otherwise, reformation would have to be by Turk or Saracen. But reform would come as surely as God reigned.[9] *Resurrectio, vita futura,* and all the other classic terms of Christian eschatology dotted Bacon's *opera.*[10] The practical, operative thrust of moral philosophy conduced man to his ultimate considerations of God, neighbor, and himself.[11] God, angels, and demons called for decision on the future life, punishment, and glory. The life of the body was not overlooked in the emphasis on the soul's existence. The best part of moral philosophy did not exhaust itself in strictly ethical considerations. It dealt, also, with the heavenly objectives of Christian community and the revealed evidences of Christian triumph. The chief concern of all human endeavor in social context was the long trajectory of man inclined toward the Fatherland.[12]

Human hierarchy had, therefore, to follow divine gradations. Pope and priest required nice articulation with the purposes of salvation. Preaching might be effected by logical analysis or by mystical testimony, or both. It remained, however, the prerogative of the Church's confessional faith, never the premium of theological debate.[13] In the Eucharist, especially, the Incarnation was perpetually activated. Here, Christ's own living deliverance of himself, vicariously, to the

d'esthétique médiévale (Bruges, 1946), 2:234–38; R. Carton, *La synthèse doctrinale de Roger Bacon* (Paris, 1924), pp. 89–91.

[8] *Moralis philosophia,* pt. 1 (Delorme, ed.), 15–17; pt. 4, no. 6, pp. 147–50.

[9] *Compend. studii phil.,* cap. 1 (RS 15:403–4).

[10] See the index to the Delorme edition of the *Moralis philosophia.*

[11] *Moralis philosophia,* pt. 1, Preface (Delorme, ed.), pp. 3 ff.

[12] *Opus tert.,* cap. 14 (RS 15:48–52).

[13] *Compend. studii phil.,* cap. 5 (RS 15:427).

whole world became the capstone of tradition. Throughout history, all who would might eat his body and drink his blood. These acts constituted the most vital liberation of personal faith and social hope. Liturgical chant was instituted to echo celestian praise. It dared not countenance random tempos and denaturing falsettos. The language and the operation of the cultus called for meticulous purity. In them revolved the hub of eternity redeeming the waning times of earth.

Lull was no less cogent than Bacon in his scholarly treatises. He was even more eloquent in his mystical tracts. He predicated his entire delineation of hierarchy, cult, preaching, university curriculum, and contemplative regimen on eschatological grounds.[14] In introductory works and massive, contemplative cryptograms the divine economy was enunciated. Endless damnation and perdurable bliss sharpened human choice and footnoted divine Providence. Christ as the lodestar of human redemption became the focus of history. As the balance wheel of active contemplation, he synchronized the energies of social dedication. Ramon's works were endless variations on Christ's incarnation, historical pilgrimage, and harrowing death. They enshrined his glorious resurrection and ascension to heavenly glories. Terrible judgment and redeeming love were inseparably narrated. Lull wrote handbooks for cavaliers, preachers, and prospective converts. In them he traversed all the sequences of the world's ages. He also depicted Antichrist's coming, the roles of angels, men, and demons, and the magnetic impulses of hell and paradise. The bent of all this doctrinal preoccupation was outlined in his trite systematics. His coruscating raptures suffused his more strictly contemplative opera.

In all this, the eschatological fulcrum supported the full leverage of divinely incarnated love in Christ. Herein, the union of Lover and Beloved was celebrated. What fused them was a poetic paradigm of poverty and self-immolating charity.

[14] Typical passages are to be found in the *Doctrina pueril* (*Obres doctr.* 1, caps. 2–12, 55, 59, 96–100, etc.), and the *Liber clericorum* (*Obres doctr.* 1, caps. 11–14). Cf. the *Libre de contemplació* (OE, 2:205 ff.), 2, no. 11, caps. 50–58.

The spirit of the Poverello hovered close. Contemplative ecstasy prompted social action. Doctrinally precipitated meditations were invariably the launching points for his endless critiques of missionary failure. They also precipitated an inexhaustible array of ingenious plans for evangelizing heathen and schismatics.

The dedications of the Fool for Love in the romantic epic *Blanquerna* recorded an agape critique. Here the sordid vacillation of earthly hierarchs gave way at last before heavenly yearnings for the lost. Everywhere, Lull's stubborn belief in God's love engendered through Virgin Mother and Virgin Son burst out into febrile, evangelizing schemes. Through these resourceful assays he sought to infuse gospel deliverance into papal and curial lag. In the *Blanquerna*, the final triumph of the poor Fool's idiocy was consummated. The pope and his court here projected in epic romance what Lull in his lifetime of travail could never bring about.[15] This was the marshalling of the Church's spiritual and military resources for world mission. Mongols, Tartars, Bulgarians, Nestorians, Russians, Chinese, and many more, rushed to eternal fire. Unless, that is, they could find procurators to help rescue them from their erratic course to eternal life.[16] The soteriological energy of Christ's very incarnation, together with his judgmental glory, constituted the dynamo of Lull's missionary activity. Its electrifying current surcharged his mystical dedications and his rapturous time tables of infidel conversion.

The whole gamut of grief and glory is unfolded with fiery passion and massive abbreviations in the *Great Book of Contemplation*. It is treated more briefly in dozens of other works. In all these, it was the heavenly Lord of Glory who gave himself in eschatological surrender for lost humanity. Lull's plan of action for world mission was at once a trenchant criticism of the status quo and a reforming appeal to a stagnant Church. Christianity desperately needed to capitalize Christ's own

[15] See the *Blanquerna*, cap. 80, viz., Petry, *Late Medieval Mysticism*, pp. 149–56 (OE, pp. 229–32).

[16] *Doctrina pueril*, cap. 72 (cf. R. S. de Franch, *Raymond Lulle* [1954], pp. 94–95).

tradition of gracious mercy. The Church's very life depended on its vicarious ministry to the entire world.

Lull never ceased to belabor the curia, the princes, and university authorities with his plan for language schools and spiritual commandos. He would have made them all a vast bureau for the propagation of the faith. Their main reason for existence would have been the training of youth, and indeed the buttressing of every stronghold of life, for a martyr witness. They would have re-enacted Christ's living death. Every range of hierarchy, both spiritual and secular, was to be enlisted. Pontiffs and prelates, kings and barons, learned friars and lay merchants—all were to weave together at the loom of salvation.[17] The so-called *Hymn of Ramon* was actually an eschatologically oriented paean of redeeming love. In it the College of Miramar was especially set aside for evangelistic action, contemplatively inspired.[18]

For our three reformers the cult was, indeed, central to any gospel critique. Pure worship through Christian sacrament was the heart of genuine tradition. It was also the guarantor of reform. In Grosseteste's diocesan program of moral and spiritual resurgence, the life of the cult was eschatologically predicated. That is, it was liturgically practiced and doctrinally preached. Most needed was the creative indoctrination of the people in keeping God's commandments and employing his redeeming sacraments. The most detailed examination of parish vagaries and the most precise injunctions for their reform in statues and constitutions were directed to cultic procedures. These provisions called for the practiced ministry of a clergy devoted to God's Word. Sacramental observance and evangelical preaching had, too often, been neglected as a pair. They must become renascent as a unity. Exaggerated emphasis on either, out of context, could only damage both.

For Grosseteste, the *cura animarum* was primary. The food

[17] *Tractatus de modo convertendi infidelis.* See generous portions available in French translation of De Franch, *Lulle*, pp. 131–43.

[18] Also in De Franch, *Lulle*, "Cant de Ramon," pp. 143–45.

and drink of Christians was, literally, the eucharistic bread and wine. They must be evangelistically offered as the provender of heaven. Regular visitation of all parishes by diocesan, decanal, and parochial clergy was in anticipation of the bishop's determining and supplying pastoral needs. This is why he enlisted friar preachers in the work of confession and indoctrination; why, also, he held refresher courses in pastoral curacy for rural deans and parish priests. The pattern was one of inquiry, correction, and reformation, flatly demanded.[19] Grosseteste brushed aside all carping criticisms designed to scuttle his acts as arbitrary novelties. With historical sagacity he quickly sized up the stakes of old and new in men and movements. He reactivated canons so old they were almost fresh and innovated out of ancient wisdom that was forever contemporary. He doubtless thought of this as freeing the Church's historic sluices for unjammed transportation of wayfaring souls. Is it too bold to surmise that much of what Bacon was to condemn as sources of error and the bottleneck of tradition, he observed in the frontal assault Master Robert made upon them?

What Grosseteste planned to obliterate was precisely the accumulated errors that consolidated themselves in the bastions of purported authority. These abuses were locked in popular mortmain and crystallizing custom. And these, as Bacon noted in all his writings, were almost impervious to the liberating critique of valid innovation.[20] The bishop of Lincoln was as undaunted in his battles against them as Bacon was to prove. We need only advert to Lull in passing. For he was continuously squirting out into the open river, past the well-tended marshes of curial impassé.

We are convinced from contemporary protests and Grosse-

[19] See the "Statutes of Lincoln," in Powicke and Cheney, *Councils and Synods*, 2:263 ff., 268 ff., esp. nos. 2, 3, 17, 22, 27–28, 36, etc. "Ego post meam in episcopum creationem consideravi me episcopum esse et pastorem animarum . . ." (p. 265).

[20] *Opus Majus*, pt. 1, cap. 1; *Opus tert.*, cap. 1 (RS 15:398 ff.); *ibid.*, cap. 9 (RS 15:25 f.). Note the similarity with Grosseteste's problem: "Una est quod es, quae dico et quae dicenda, sunt contra exemplata et consueta, et vulgata."

teste's own log book that he resurrected the hoary canons of England and such statutes as those of London for the indictment of pastoral defection.[21] He planned the liberation of the people from ecclesiastical exaction. Principally, what the bishop needed was a reformed corpus of tradition that would feed flocks, bodily and spiritually, and declare good news, from pulpit and altar. Lascivious priests and cash-collecting quaestors were to go.[22] Friars of both orders were brought in to preach and instruct. The people were admonished to hear these trusted assistants rather than the mendacious indulgence sellers. *Scotales* were proscribed. Fraternization with Jews was discouraged. For Grosseteste, business as usual was liturgical renewal and homiletic revival.[23]

How could the bishop of Lincoln do otherwise, when he conceived prelates and doctors as being the very eyes of Christ's body?[24] Were they not the shepherds of God's flocks, the perilously responsible governors of eternal souls? Had they not the God-fearing administration of eucharistic graces fashioned according to the very form, virtue, and consummation of Christ's precious body and blood?[25] For such as these, the integrity of gospel proclamation and sacramental participation inhered in disciplinary administration. Privileged authority freely conceded to the pope meant authoritative answerability to God, episcopal as well as papal. Nothing less than the living repudiation of a now moribund tradition would bring parish visitation, correction, and reformation.

At this point also, Bacon made his analysis of cultic and homiletic enfeeblement. He based his reform on a renewal of cultic probity and preaching efficacy.[26] He sent his blueprint

[21] Powicke and Cheney, *Council and Synods*, 2:261–63; also p. 245, on Canons of London.

[22] Ep. 107 (RS 25:317–18); Powicke and Cheney, *Councils and Synods*, 2:479–80, Mandate to Archdeacons.

[23] *Ibid.*, 2:480. Cf. Ep. 127 (RS 25:357 ff.).

[24] *Sermo ad prelatos* [73], *Dictum* 41, as edited by E. J. Westermann, "A Comparison of Some of the Sermons and the *Dicta* of Robert Grosseteste," in *Mediaevalia et Humanistica*, 3 (April, 1945): 54.

[25] Ep. 110 (RS 25:328 ff.).

[26] His interesting criticisms of oversimplified and currently erroneous doctrines of transubstantiation related to Aristotelian physics and theo-

for a refurbished liturgy and revitalized church music to the pope. It was wrought, together with a newly established pattern of homiletics and philosophical theology, into a graded brochure of metaphysical and experimental planning. The entire syllabus of comprehensive disciplines, religious and moral, mathematical and scientific, political and juridical, was posted on to the chief hierarch. After all, he was historically commissioned for traditive freedom and reformation.[27]

Philosophy was, indeed, useful to God, as were the source texts of the Christian gospel. All were in the keeping of the historic *ecclesia*, together with its laws. But because of growing ignorance, philosophy and the first-hand knowledge of sacred texts had almost withered away. Actually the Sacred Scriptures, the holy doctors, and canon law alike stood committed against current errors. The truly liberating deliverances of the historic Church had always condemned unsupported authority and the lay definition of consensus. Tabooed, also, were the pressure tactics of the unlettered crowd and the concealment of selfish ignorance under the guise of apparent wisdom. But only the Holy Father could advantageously mount a spiritual reactivation of both speculative and experimental science. His backing was uniquely necessary to cultic purification and homiletic urgency. Moral philosophy stood ready as the likeliest vehicle of scientific reform and the most practical rehabilitator of fiducial Christianity. Linked closest to theology, which was the noblest of all sciences, the operative agency and the end product of all philosophy focused its attention on vices and virtues. It discriminated the ways of misery and felicity in the life to come.[28]

At the very outset of his *Moralis philosophia* Bacon celebrated the eschatological destiny of man revealed by God in

---

ries of time and place are found in *Opus tert.*, cap. 41 (RS 15:145–48). Easter chronology is treated in cap. 56 (RS 15:218 ff.); his critique of music in relation to liturgy and Scripture, caps. 59 ff. (RS 15:228 ff.); calendar reform, caps. 58–71 (RS 15:274–303); chanting and psalmody, caps. 72–74 (RS 15:295–303); and preaching, caps. 75 f. (RS 15:303 ff.). Cf. the *Compend. studii phil.*, cap. 5 (RS 15:425 ff.).

[27] RS 15:3 ff.

[28] *Moralis philosophia*, pt. 1, Preface (Delorme, ed.), pp. 3 f.

Scripture and cult. Revelation must guide the search impossible to man's own unaided knowledge. So, too, the role of a mediatorial hierarchy and spiritual vicarage on earth was incontestable. Thus holy writings and canon law were made authoritatively operative through the inspired Church. They eventuated in proper ecclesiastical government and cultic illumination. God promised future felicity to those living in accordance with divine government.[29] A horrible future awaited evil livers.

In the realm of civil order there was a natural concern with public laws. Yet their very existence was cued to the primacy of divine worship.[30] A preponderant part of moral philosophy emphasized Christian evidences. And Christian evidences pointed unerringly to the altar itself, from which they stemmed.[31]

Here was the supreme end of God-fearing mysteries and the center of rapturous devotion. The certifications of the Eternal, the resurrection, and the future life emanated not from immoral Muslims and "generation-minded" Jews but from the law of Christ and of his cultus. From this divinely validated law and gospel sprang the uniquely perfect maxims of virginity, voluntary poverty, and the obligation of one man to the will of another. It was in contemplative rapture that reality was to be sought, if the sum of all knowledge was to be apprehended. To be ignorant of what pertained most to salvation was to be comprehensively unaware. And ignorance, here, of the very lifeline of the historic community was all too widespread.

Yet, what was universally revealed in the sacraments as the basis of all Christian proofs was Christ the Lord himself. He was indeed true God and true man. He was the heavenly bread which, unlike the decaying manna of old, gave life eternal.

Bacon recounts, unflinchingly, the miracles from sacred text

[29] *Ibid.*, pp. 8–9.

[30] *Opus tert.*, cap. 4 (RS 15:50).

[31] *Opus tert.*, cap. 1 (RS 15:400); *Moralis philosophia*, pt. 5, no. 3 (Delorme, ed.), pp. 222 ff.

and venerable "histories" that witnessed the eucharistic vitality for communicating believers.[32] One such story involved a heretical bishop and some ultimately truth-witnessing demons. Confronted with the body of Christ carried to a sick man, they capitulated to the dictum: "at the name of Jesus every knee shall bow in heaven, on earth and in hell." The heretical hierarch, seeing their obeisance, became a true Christian and subsequently preached the faith of Christ to the confusion of heretical depravity.

Again, in the order of Franciscans, a brother who had hitherto been unable to communicate learned, by the sage counsel of a more experienced friar, that his own baptism might have been incomplete and his eucharistic participation thus nullified. On inquiry, the troubled Minorite discovered that through priestly carelessness at a double baptism, his own had indeed been left unaccomplished. Once having been baptized properly, he joyously entered into full communion.

Thereupon, Bacon launches into a panoramic unfolding of the whole drama of Creation, Fall, and Redemption. These events have all been cosmically encompassed and graciously hedged about with eucharistic munificence. Quite fittingly, therefore, every man standing under grace ought to receive his salvation from what the Church ordains. Original sin cannot be cancelled without a proffered victim. Satisfaction for mortal sins that daily multiply is available only from the vicarious Host. Having taken human form and suffered the passion of death for man's redemption, Christ gives afresh of his body and blood in eucharistic sacrifice. Man's salvation and his very deification is wrought through the Eucharist.

In every part of the Sacred Host resides the entire Christ. His total benediction is gloriously extended to man. Actually, through such participation he not only receives an increment of faithfulness but is also literally joined to God in Christ. Here temporal life is sustained for the eternal. In such sharing with God and Christ we are deified and Christified. In participation with the Lord we become Christs. The Scripture says

[32] *Moralis philosophia*, pt. 5, no. 3 (Delorme, ed.), pp. 225–27.

"you are gods" (Ps. 81:6 Vulg.) and "do not touch my Christ" (Ps. 104:15 Vulg.).[33] Not only participation with Christ is asserted but conversion as well. This transformation is not wrought physically but spiritually, to be sure, yet no less really. In this sense of our becoming not simply Christians but Christs we are indeed united unto him, and John 17:22 is fulfilled. We are become one with God and Christ, as Christ and the Father are one. With burning desire we ought therefore to seek such union through consecrated devotion and contemplative rapture. We have, therewith, a joyous confidence in our eating and drinking to eternal life. Grievous ignorance of what Christ has delivered to humanity is to be thus overcome. True humanity and divinity are both received through the divine power.[34]

Bacon is convinced that in the Christ thus daily offered the entire Christian tradition is solidified and energized. Meditation on past truths, such as incarnation and passion, joined with future expectations, amounts to present receptivity. One knows in joyous faith that Christ transcended the body of death to universal life in the Eucharist. So, too, every faithful Christian may be joined intimately with him now in the enduring life of the Trinity.[35] There follows a long and triumphant recapitulation of how the process of deifying glorification overcomes all impediments. Here is the exhilarating junction of contemplation and action. Now, the grades of contemplation and the stages of knowing may be fully appropriated. No doubt remains that, for Bacon, the apex of true action is experienced in liturgical contemplation.[36] This is why, in the *Opus*

[33] *Ibid.*, p. 233: "Deinde ex participacione Dei et Christi deificamur et christificamur et fimus dii. . . . Et ideo participacione Christi fimus Christi; et propter hoc dicit Scriptura: 'Ego dixi: "Dii estis," et "Nolite tangere Christos meos." ' " (Ps. 81:6 and 104:15 Vulg.). Cf. *Opus tert.*, cap. 1 (RS 15:400).

[34] *Ibid.*, pp. 233–34. *Compend. studii phil.*, cap. 1 (RS 15:400): ". . . et comedimus Ipsum, et bibimus, et convertimur in Ipsum, ut fiamus Dii et Christi. Quia non convertitur in nos his panis coeli, sed nos in ipsum, ut simus quod non fuimus, sed magis deificemur et christificemur."

[35] *Ibid.*, pp. 234–35.

[36] *Ibid.*, pp. 235–43. Cf. *Opus majus*, pt. 6, cap. 1 (Bridges, ed.), 2:170–71. Cf. *Moralis philosophia* (Delorme, ed.), p. 239.

tertium, for example, so much space is given to the restoration of the debauched cultus. From every chanted syllable to the apex of cosmic music, the human is vitalized from divine potency.

Again, Lull's closely reasoned theological treatises traverse similar ground, though with less eloquence. His mystical works transcend Bacon, if possible, in adapting the intimate compassionship of sacramental life to the re-creative disciplines of missionary endeavor. Bacon, Grosseteste, and Lull find the same ground for preaching to the faithful and indoctrinating the heathen and schismatic. Soteriological reform springs from cultic vitality. Present in all his works, to some extent, Lull's burning evangelism fairly erupts from his mystical tracts. In works on chivalry, priesthood, and homiletics one may find the sacramental genesis for his pleas in the little work on contemplation and in the *Lover and the Beloved.*[37] Throughout, the voluntary debasement of Christ in eucharistic poverty takes the common route to the Lord's Golgotha and to the Poverello's Mt. Alverna. One may scarcely doubt that, just as Lull retraces St. Francis' steps that lead to and from Christ, so Lull reincarnates in his martyr's soul the searing love of the Poverello's stigmata.

For both Bacon and Lull, the emphasis on Christian cultus was, at once, corrective and procreative; corrective of a disrupted tradition, procreative of a divinely sustained reformation. Directly involved was an indictment of stagnant, crusading barbarism and revelational access to missionary triumph.[38] Neither man was a pacifist. Both made a place for necessary military action. Each transferred the emphasis from

[37] A Catalan text of the *Art de Contemplació* is edited by J. H. Probst, "La mystique de Ramon Lull et l'Art de Contemplació," in C. Baeumker, *Beiträge zur Geschichte der Philosophie des Mittelalters* . . . (Münster i. W.: Aschendorffsche Verlagsbuchhandlung, 1914), 13:2–3, 1–124. The large treatise on contemplation, *Libre de Contemplació en Déu*, is vols. 2–8 in the Mallorcan edition, vol. 2, pp. 97–1258 in the *Obres Essencials*. There are copious extracts in De Franch, Lulle, pp. 119 ff.

[38] See *Opus majus*, pt. 3, caps. 13–14 (Bridges, ed.), 3:120–25; cf. *Libre de Contemplació en Déu* (De Franch, *Lulle*, excerpts from cap. 346, pp. 119 ff.), and *Tractatus de modo convertendi infidelis* (*ibid.*,

warfare's attritional disillusionment to a new concept of vicariously informed missionary zeal.

Hierarchy, social ministry, and mendicant mobility were intimately conjoined in the emphases of these reformers. Grosseteste was suffused with a medieval sense of Dionysian hierarchy and *analogia*. He had translated much of the Dionysian corpus. What he deduced was a hierarchy of divine order, let down from heaven for earthly hierarchs, and a mystical dedication to contemplative ascents.[39] Through a stormy career as bishop he pressed a reformation program in the name of hierarchy. His was one of the highest views of papal prerogative held by any medieval thinker.[40] None was more uncompromising in his interpretation of the responsibility entailed thereby. Grosseteste regarded his own episcopal authority and obligation as having like character because of its devolving from similar hierarchical principles.[41] He declared his authority to be from the law itself, both Mosaic and evangelical. His indictment of the Church's debility was a call to reincarnate Christ's humility. In Franciscan fashion, he paraphrased the Poverello's emphasis upon Christ's having left heavenly glory to accept earthly priority in ministry alone.

The bishop imported friars into his diocese, not to bypass hierarchs, but to trigger them for action. He wanted to incul-

pp. 131 ff.). Bacon says (*ibid.*, cap. 13, p. 122): "Praeterea fides ingressa non est in hunc mundum per arma sed per simplicitatem praedicationis, ut manifestum est."

[39] See Thomson, *Grosseteste*, pp. 78 ff., for analysis of texts of the Bishop's translation and commentaries. Cf. D. A. Callus, "Robert Grosseteste as Scholar," in his *Grosseteste*, pp. 56–60. Note the helpful study of F. Ruello, "La *Divinorum Nominum Reseratio* selon Robert Grossetête et Albert Le Grand," *Archives d'histoire doctrinale et littéraire du moyen âge*, 26 (1959): 99–120; also Y. M.-J. Congar, ". . . Le querelle entre mendiants et séculiers . . .," *ibid.*, 28 (1961): 114 ff.

[40] See Pantin, in Callus, *Grosseteste*, pp. 183–95, and the signal role of key letters and discourses (in translated excerpts). See Ep. 36 (RS 25:126–27).

[41] Ep. 127 (RS 25:364).

cate the friar tradition of flexible, popular evangelization. The great episcopal letter, 127, was a statement of positive spiritual credo. It was a declaration of faith in the vitality of reforming critique. The measure of Grosseteste's biting indictment was the nobility of his reforming zeal. The criterion of his episcopal administration was the critical initiative of the gospel itself. Letter 127, like the *Memorandum* of 1250, was a review of all the biblical figures of pastor, physician, mother, lawgiver, patriarch, and suffering servant.[42]

The *Memorandum* was an attack on papal and curial defection from gospel tradition. It was, even more, a positive vindication of his own episcopal career. His pilgrimage remained oriented to Christ's critically affirming servantship. This was now menaced by papal and curial possessiveness. Grosseteste's translation and commentary on the Dionysiac hierarchies supplied impetus for his sermonic adaptation of biblical lessons and practical *Dicta.*[43] His entire perspective was one of a Franciscan-inspired devotion to Christ's vicarious poverty. The Master's headship implied pastoral discipline and curial reformation. Jesus' dedication to the Kingdom had led to his challenging the status quo and regnant Jewish ecclesiasticism. His disciples and one apostle, especially, finally grasped a precedence of self-surrender. They interpreted this rightly as an earnest of a soul-saving Church. The papal lordship and every episcopal and priestly participation in it was intended to be a vicegerency in self-giving. Their mandate was in Christ's suffering *ecclesia.* Christ the Lord had left heaven's glory to be born of a poor virgin. That was his *traditio* — ascent by descent, elevation by renunciation.

The early Church fought against accepting such a mad commission but nobly succumbed to it. The fourteenth-century hierarchy threatened to protect its vaunted primacy by absconding from its sacrificial ministry. Purported papas, vicars, and pastors sometimes looked and acted more like minions of

[42] Cf. RS 25:357–432.

[43] Cf. Brown, *Fasciculus,* 2:250–57. See Thomson, *Grosseteste,* pp. 160–91, 214–32, on the *Sermons and Dicta.*

the devil than commissars of the Gospel. Schism replaced unity. The mission to the heathen was shamefully in default. Gospel poverty was scorned by heavily endowed churchmen. The tradition of *potestas pastoralis* was replaced by *defectio fidei.* Pastoral defection spelled evangelical dilution where curial consecration formerly guaranteed missionary dilation.

The cause of widespread parish and diocesan corruption in England and elsewhere was in curial example.[44] The supreme hierarchy of a militant, suffering Church had clearly been instituted as the agent of the hierarchy transcendent. It now gave the chief example of pastoral prostitution. The sheep were being starved by their own shepherd. A recreant pope could no more compel obedience than a false shepherd could expect to fool a trusting sheep. He who refused to honor the papal claims of a false officiant dignified the hierarchy by his very apostolic disobedience. Alas, a Christlike presidency seemed now to be giving way to the praesidium of Antichrist. The Lord's very seat had become the center of worldly business and official exaction. The only alternative to reformation was the defamation of Christ and subjection to eternal punishment.

Bacon agreed, even as he pondered in his *Opus majus* the Mosaic pre-eminence under the old law and evangelically commissioned headship for cultic propagation under the new. So he called on the pope for reform measures, even as Grosseteste had. For Bacon, also, the purpose of papacy was pastoral vicariousness. He was a true pope who acted like one. Barring the intervention of a truly good pontiff and the genuinely deifying participation of the people in the sacraments, disaster must surely come. Lacking the rapturous, dancelike ecstasy of properly effected chant and the Scripturally abetted tradition of primitive Franciscan preaching, Antichrist, or at least Turk or Saracen, must precipitate God-willed deliverance.[45]

Lull's scholastic treatises are replete with doctrinally approved defenses of historical tradition and traditional hier-

[44] *Ibid.*, p. 252: "Causa fons et origo hujus est hac CURIA . . ."
[45] *Compend. studii phil.*, cap. 1 (RS 15:403–4).

archy. But, as usual, it is in his praise of Lover and Beloved that he is most convincing. In his adoration of Virginal humility and Minorite poverty he is undeniably affecting.[46] His is the victory song of the Church Militant. Its intrepid hosts are launched and transported by the Church Triumphant.

Perhaps Lull was never downright sneaky, but he was an adroit martyr. He described and practiced the Church's world mission in disarmingly empathetic fashion. That is, his own disingenuous commitment was designed to focus the divine miracle of heathen conversion; also to reflect uncomfortable warmth upon hibernating officialdom. Popes and kings, monks and mendicants felt their collars growing tight. Indeed, every ecclesiastical gradation sensed an unpredictable freezing and thawing in the Church's weather.

Meanwhile, Lull felt, and acted, like the true Franciscan renunciant buttressed by a sense of Dominican gospel confrontation. Thus he argued, loved, and established anew the vicarage of gospel poverty as the long dormant vitality of the historic church and hierarchy. In good pope Blanquerna, the hero of his spiritual romance, Ramon re-creates a saintly papal image with edifying curial reflections. The pontiff's apostolicity recalls an ascetically refined *caritas*.[47] Sadly enough, this was, almost wholly, literary make-believe. A treatise on how to convert the infidel makes the hierachy bear the burden of simulated Franciscan-Dominican dispossession.

Veritably, hierarchy for Lull meant all grades of ministry: lay and clerical, papal and mercantile, chivalric and academic, university-sired and language-trained. Especially, however, was such graded vicariousness the infusion into crusade and mission of the Poverello's renunciatory forte. It was the disciplined program of Dominic's learning and preaching. For Lull

[46] *Art de Contemplació* (Probst, ed.), cap. 1, pp. 67–8; cap. 5, pp. 77 ff. Cf. *Sermones de Christo* (58 [De Christo 6]), *Op. lat.* (Stegmüller, ed.), 4:228–30. On Dominic's poverty, see sermon 89 [De sanctis 21]), *Op. lat.* (Stegmüller, ed.), 4:349–52; on that of Francis, 92 (De sanctis 24), *Op. lat.* (Stegmüller, ed.), 4:360–62. See his wide-ranging critiques of "prelati boni et mali," in *Op. lat.*, 4 (Index): 530–31.

[47] Cf. cap. 80, *Blanquerna.*

and Grosseteste, alike, the friars must carry the brunt of hierarchical dedication.[48]

Bacon, of course, gave backhanded salutes to "the boys" at Paris.[49] Nonetheless, the all-disposable phalanxes of true mendicancy must outflank rigid dialectic and spiritual mendacity. Like his master Robert and his Minorite associate Ramon, friar Roger was a mendicant at heart. His tribute to the boldly improvising, often rudely haranguing Berthold of Regensburg was but a reassertion of the confessional spontaneity of the first generation Minors.[50] It was not that Bacon thought theologians could not be preachers. Rather, he wanted to see theology and popular evangelizing, alike, revitalize the content and form of their appeals.[51]

Evangelical preaching, Christian indoctrination, and world mission were closely articulated in the reform programs of Grosseteste, Bacon, and Lull. Perhaps Grosseteste served preaching best through his fusion of scholarly patristic studies and translation projects.[52] These ventures into diocesan reform had much to do with his own indoctrination of the friars. He had exhorted them originally to a more regularized, scholarly attitude toward predication. He later envisaged for them a progressively more effective union of peripatetic ministry and reform agency.

Unfortunately, most of Grosseteste's own sermons and *Dicta* are still locked in unedited manuscripts. But enough is known of them to warrant both an admission of their fundamentally

[48] Cf. Powicke and Cheney, *Councils and Synods*, 2:265, 480. Cf. De Franch, texts as cited above.

[49] *Compend. studii phil.*, cap. 5 (RS 15:425 ff.): "Hi sunt pueri duorum ordinum studentium, ut Albertus, et Thomas, et alii . . ." (p. 426).

[50] *Opus tert.*, cap. 75 (RS 15:310): "Sed licet vulgus praedicantium sic utatur, tamen aliqui modum alium habentes, infinitam faciunt utilitatem, ut est Frater Bertholdus Alemannus, qui solus plus facit de utilitate magnifica in praedicatione, quam fere omnes alii fratres ordinis utriusque." Cf. Carton, *La synthèse doctrinale*, p. 89, n. 1.

[51] *Ibid.*, cap. 75 (RS 15:303 ff.).

[52] Cf. Callus, "Robert Grosseteste as Scholar," in his *Grosseteste*, pp. 1–69, and B. Smalley, "The Biblical Scholar," *ibid.*, pp. 70–97.

unexciting nature and an assertion of their resourcefulness for evangelical appeal. They incorporated a forthright impetus to biblical hermeneutics and popular homiletics. The source consciousness and language editions involved in the bishop's historical and Testamental researches were greatly admired by Bacon as all too rare. They were immediately funnelled into the doctrinal and missionary assumptions of parish evangelization. In Grosseteste, then, we have that rare bird, a bishop who can preach and does. We have an even more staggering innovator. Here was a diocesan whose scholarly proclivities were not an avocational oddity. They were the precipitating cause of his collaborative, gospel projects in parish learning and teaching. Grosseteste was forever on the hunt for resource materials, in Eastern and Western literature, that could become grist for his mill of improvising exhortation and graded diocesan indoctrination.

Bacon's right to homiletic fame lies in his trenchant critiques of preaching in relation to cultic reformation and popular crusading; also, in his broadening of the homiletic base to reconsider the subtleties of popular communication and devotional experience. Perhaps no one actually knows just how he proposed making preaching more scholarly and the message more universally applicable, at the same time. One may rest assured that this was all tied up with his faith in sacramental life as the heritage of humble men and his confidence in the contemplative gospel, yearned for by every heart.

We need to take more seriously Carton's and De Bruyne's closely related insistence. Bacon's regard for preaching was far more than the previewing of upgraded theological systems. He takes great pains to say that preaching belongs to the Church more than it does to the School. This is precisely because evangelical homiletics dispensed in the parish bears the confessional testimony which must save the world. Summa-making youngsters at Paris were busy aping source-shy masters. This was not calculated to set them on fire with the living gospel. Admittedly, indulgence hawkers let loose on parochial ignorance were not any more likely than college professors to bring gospel and people to the throne of grace. Perhaps this is exactly why the university curriculum and professoriat were at once the despair and the last hope of the irascible Bacon. He excoriated university faculties for the gospel astigmatism they tended to foster, yet he looked to them for the realization of an unprecedented potential in human resourcefulness. Theology might well learn to tailor its disciplines to the teaching of eternal verities more ingenuously and forthrightly uttered.

Bacon's most overlooked emphasis was upon the necessity for bringing both professional ministry and scholarly preparation into a closer conjunction. Meanwhile, he would preserve the unitary distinctiveness of university research and popular serviceability. Therefore, he insisted on preaching that was closely allied to contemplative witness and musical communication.

We must not forget that Bacon's recovery of musical impetus and preaching arts, together, goes back to Augustine's *De Musica* and *De Doctrina*. It comes forward again with Grosseteste's modified Augustinian theories of the musically harmonious and mathematically disposed cosmos. Furthermore, Bacon was pretty much of a practicing mystic, whose emphasis on preaching stemmed from a kind of contemplative rhetoric. It grew out of inspired gesture and rapturous theological dance as much as from any *artes praedicandi*. Bacon venerated Greek prototypes and Augustinian models in science, music, and speech. He was even more enthralled by Grosseteste's researches in astral physics and *De Musica*. These definitely involved celestial harmonics and light mathematics. Coupling these insights with his own discoveries in experimental sciences and liturgical music made Bacon a fertile seed ground for reforming impulses.[53]

In any event, what Bacon objected to in the regnant Parisian form of source-pruned, dialectical preaching was its stuffy recession from the vibrant energies of mendicant evangelism. He was at one with Grosseteste, and, strange as it may seem, with Lull's essential spirit. True, any one reading the recent

[53] Apropos of Augustine, Grosseteste, and Bacon, see my *History of Christianity* (Englewood Cliffs, N.J.: Prentice-Hall, 1962), pp. 417–32. *Opus tert.*, cap. 75 (RS 15:303–10).

editions of Lull's Latin preaching manuals and sermons can easily get the wrong impression.[54] When Ramon constructed sermons to demonstrate his own *exempla* he was successful almost to the point of emasculating his hearers, the gospel, and himself. Yet, built upon this seemingly wooden scaffolding was a fabric of doctrinal and pastoral wisdom not to be sneered at.[55] His influence on Arab philosophers and Muslim cultists is somewhat debatable. But he was a resourceful person; especially when he joined his scholastic ingenuity to his native talents as lambent poet, epic novelist, and contemplative writer. What he yearned for, most of all, was an intellectual progression in university disciplines and curial propaganda offices that would put contemplative dedication on the road. From it might follow gospel preaching and missionary action.

The university's role is central in all this—historical and theological, mystical and aesthetic. Here the function of the academy in projecting the reforming critique of tradition is paramount.[56] Fortunately, we cannot pontificate in concluding retrospect or prospect. We cannot, and must not, forget that all these men were university oriented. All believed in the efficacy of learning and in the significant, if ancillary, role of human knowledge in answering to divinizing wisdom. What they desired was a unitive thrust of the Christian tradition proceeding from university colloquium and collation to parish testimony. They worked to integrate the impulses of research scholarship with the propagation of Christian evidences in the market place. University disciplines were the potential founts of critically edited, original texts. They were the proving grounds of historically deducible principles that governed and released a reforming tradition.

[54] His *Liber de praedicatione* is in *Op. lat.* (Stegmüller, ed.), vols. 3, 4; his sermons in vol. 4.

[55] The comprehensive index (*ibid.*, vol. 4) illustrates the wide range of his themes and applications.

[56] De Bruyne, in his three volumes, is invaluable for the nexus of university ideology in relation to the larger aspects of aesthetics and social taste, or criticism,

So Grosseteste set forth new standards of critical-minded source use. He applied these in the recovery of Eastern Patristics, Greek philosophers, and of historic reformers.[57] These were capitalized for rural curacy and urban parishes. He sparked a biblical resurgence in diocesan churchmanship. He tried to regalvanize Dominican and Franciscan renunciation for contemporary parochial service. Bacon fought the stereotyped summas that deflected the force of biblical texts. Such sterile exercises thwarted the study of philosophy and the canons in supporting evangelical reform principles.[58]

At university and language school, in council chamber and on missionary location, Lull circulated his theses for systematic indoctrination. He prepared the logistics of Christian world expansion. In his way, he was almost as completely sold on the reclamatory role of education as Erasmus was. Certainly, he was no less a true son of Francis because he followed Dominican manuals of university preparation. Nor was he false to the Dominican ideal when he became a Franciscan.[59] The Franciscans convinced him that gospel renunciation was the way of Christ. The Dominicans proved that a prime servant of renunciation was intellectual dedication. For this reason they, too, preached poverty. Lull claimed both orders as patrons of the Christian heritage.

In all these men the ascetic was procreatively aesthetic. Contemplation and action were in balance. The rapture of *theoria* was united to the *praxis* of the *vita activa*. By them, the intellectual propositions of the university don were translated to parish church and social scene. These three were not essentially revolutionists, or existentialists, or positivists, or eclectics or revisionists, or any other kind of modern men. Yet, impact

[57] See Thomson, *Grosseteste*, pp. 42 ff.

[58] *Opus tert.*, cap. 4 (RS 15:425 ff.).

[59] De Franch, *Lulle*, pp. 53 ff., 65 ff. A useful collection of texts is P. G. Golubovich, *Biblioteca Bio-Bibliografica della terra santa* (Florence, 1906), 1:361–92.

they did have, as stubborn protagonists of penetrating critique in the service of the historic tradition. And the heart of all this they found in the precarious equilibrium of the contemplative and the active lives.[60] Their activism was not essentially demolitory but internally regenerative. They were not individualistically isolationist but societally sensitive.

Unquestionably, the faith of Lull the systematician is poetry at the last. Here is the inadmissable madness of the Gospels, where to save is to lose and to give is to have. Ramon's often derided spasms of love are precisely what the world rejected in Jesus and patronized in Francis. Yet Lull's total field of affection is his total humanity. His ultimate concern in university syllabus and martyr manifesto is the temporal welfare and the eternal salvation of Christian and Jew, Muslim and pagan – in a word, the good of all men.[61]

So, also, one admiring the hard-bitten administrator Grosseteste must remember what he owed to the contemplative tradition, both monastic and mystic. The *Dionysiaca,* however denatured in translation and commentary, is, for him, a bell ringing through the Christian ages of mystical theology; a sweet exhalation of the celestial and terrestrial hierarchies girdling the spheres of earth and outer space. Its light and its

[60] Carton's *L'expérience mystique* documents this (pp. 153–68, 262–82). See page 263 on the contemplative and active, the affective and the practical. Note how, on page 270, he ties up Bacon's "mysticism" with Grosseteste's work on the Pseudo-Dionysian corpus. Cf. also Ruello's studies and texts cited in our note 39. Cf. the *Memorandum* of 1250, in Brown, *Fasciculus,* 2:254–55. As noted, the *Libre de contemplació* is edited in critical texts, both Mallorcan and from Barcelona. See our note 1. Cf. A. Llinares, *Raymond Lulle: Philosophe de l'action,* Université de Grenoble Pub. da la Fac. des Lettres et Sciences Humaines, 33 (Paris: Presses Universitaires de France, 1964), pp. 419–23, for example; also pp. 169, 181, 235, 300, 337, 367, 405–15. J. S. Barbera, *Raimundo Lulio: Genio de la filosofía y mistica Española* (Madrid: Ediciones y Publicaciones Españolas, 1963), is a useful, if somewhat overenthusiastic, collection of texts and appreciations (for instance, pp. 113, 131). His commentary on the great book of contemplation is pp. 481–500.

[61] Cf. the *Arbre de filosofía d'amor* 4. 1. 8, and n. 43, p. 81 (*Obres Essencials,* 2:46, and the Mallorcan *Obres,* vol. 18): ". . . en aquest libre qui és comú a tots hòmens, a crestians, jueus, sarraíns e pagans . . . car no eren sabudes e amades per tots homes . . ."

music are the tempos of celestial symphonies and the invigoration of man's quest through the ages for the *Beatitudo.*[62]

How, finally, does one measure impact? These three churchmen were, at least, effective catalysts for many in their own day, as they may be for some in ours, who have never even heard their names. Like ourselves, they may often have been too self-consciously judgmental and far too much given to self-righteous jeremiads. They were, from our centennially assured perspective, hardly radical at all, given our smug standards of overt, evangelical eruptiveness. It may be doubted that they were even as cumulatively critical or reforming as I have led you to believe. Perhaps not even as traditional either; unless, of course, one really means, as I do, that they practiced their criticism as integral with their tradition, while retransmitting the impulses of their historic faith in keeping with the gospel critique.

[62] See a passage from Grosseteste's *De artibus liberalibus* via Baur's *Werke*, in Petry, *History of Christianity*, pp. 426–27. Thomson, *Grosseteste*, p. 55, gives the references of Grosseteste's translation according to the *Dionysiaca.*

6

A Conciliar Suggestion

RICHARD LUMAN

Debate about the sources, meaning, and influence of the decrees of the general councils of the fifteenth century (Pisa, 1409; Constance, 1414–18; Basle-Ferrara-Florence-Rome, 1431–48) has never ceased. Gallicans have praised them, Ultramontanes have damned them. As recently as the beginning of this century, Salembier could say:

> Such in their schismatical essense are the famous articles of Constance . . . [they] are merely an act of war and ill-feeling, the outcome of a hasty vote at a time of trouble by an incompetent assembly. . . . There is every reason to believe that the human spirit in its weakest inspirations had a greater share in all these deliberations than the Spirit of God.[1]

He adds that the "thesis of the superiority of the Council over the Pope" was unknown before the Schism except among heretics and a few desperate spirits (for example, the professors of Paris in the 1380's), who put forward the idea "merely as a means of bringing the Schism to an end."[2]

The general agreement of scholars in the early years of the century was that the "thesis of the superiority of the Council over the Pope" had its origin either in the crisis of the Schism, or in the heretical tradition of *Volkssouveränität* flowing from Marsilius of Padua ("We have hardly read a worse heretic

[1] L. Salembier, *The Great Schism of the West*, trans. "M.D." (London: Kegan Paul, Trench, Trübner & Co., 1907), pp. 301–2.
[2] *Ibid.*

than this Marsilius," said His Holiness the Lord Clement P.P. VI in an address of 10 April 1343) or William of Ockham, or both.[3] Paul de Vooght, writing in 1960, clung to this belief. While, he granted, the *Defensor pacis* can no longer be considered as "l'acte de naissance" of conciliarism, nevertheless the influence of the book on the conciliarists cannot be denied – indeed one finds his arguments "chez Conrad de Gelnhausen, Henri de Langenstein, Gerson, d'Ailly, etc."[4] It is true that other suggestions for the origins of conciliarism have been made over the years: but rarely have they contemplated orthodox sources for conciliarism. The great J. N. Figgis, for example – in a survey of the movement which is still extremely useful and suggestive – focused his attention on the supposed significance of the hint given the conciliarists by the growth and development of representative assemblies in the Western monarchies.[5] John T. McNeill called attention to the importance of John of Paris, the Dominican theologian and polemicist in the days of Boniface VIII and Philip IV.[6] The common assumption of scholarship before 1950 (reinforced, I think one can say, among those loyal to the Apostolic See by the bitterness of the Gallican-Ultramontane contest) was that – however justified by the event – the conciliar program had its origins in at best dubious and at worst heretical or altogether non-ecclesiastical sources. Conciliarism was an *opus alienum*, not an *opus proprium*, of the medieval Catholic constitutional tradition.

[3] An excellent discussion of the historiography of conciliarism in modern times will be found in Brian Tierney, *Foundations of the Conciliar Theory* (Cambridge: At the University Press, 1955), pp. 7–14.

[4] Dom Paul de Vooght, "Le conciliarisme aux conciles de Constance et de Bâle," in *Le concile et les conciles*, ed. P. de Vooght, Y. Congar, and J. Gill (Namur, 1961), pp. 143–44. (The quotation is from p. 144.)

[5] John Neville Figgis, *Political Thought from Gerson to Grotius*, 2d ed. (New York: Harper & Bros., 1960), pp. 44–48. For comments, see Tierney, *Conciliar Theory*, pp. 11–12, and E. F. Jacob, *Essays in the Conciliar Epoch*, 2d ed. (Manchester: Manchester University Press, 1953), pp. 1–23.

[6] John T. McNeill, "The Emergence of Conciliarism," in *Medieval and Historiographical Essays in Honor of James Westfall Thompson*, ed. James L. Cate and E. N. Anderson (Chicago: University of Chicago Press, 1938), pp. 269–301.

But the common assumption was not the universal assumption, and even scholars who supported the received view frequently acknowledged qualifications to their general thesis, or, sometimes, saw other possibilities but failed to exploit them adequately because of the conviction that orthodox ideas could have played little part in the development of conciliarism. While Salembier dearly hoped to annihilate utterly any claim by the supporters of Gallicanism to any sound foundations in the Tradition for their ideas, other scholars tentatively explored more ecclesiastically reputable possibilities. As early as 1907 Albert Hauck suggested that the views of Innocent III on papal responsibility might have contributed to conciliar ideas, a possibility also discussed by McNeill in 1938.[7] H. X. Arquillière (followed by V. Martin) investigated the importance of certain canonistic texts, especially *Decretum Gratiani, Dist.* 40, c. 6: "(Papa) a nemine est iudicandus, nisi deprehendatur a fide devius." They had, in fact, been anticipated in the discussion aroused by the first council of the Vatican in 1870.

This last line of investigation flowered in the brilliant book *The Foundations of Conciliar Theory*, by Brian Tierney (1955), which argued that the elements of conciliar theory were not new in 1378, or even in 1324, but rather were already present in Decretist speculations on certain texts of the canon law which implied or stated papal limitations, and in Decretalist teaching on corporation law. He argued further that these elements, synthesized in John of Paris, reached mature development in the *Tractatus de schismate* of Francis Cardinal Zabarella, the legal architect of the Council of Pisa and "a man who" (as they still say in political circles) – had he not died prematurely – would surely have been *papabilis* in 1417. John Watt has summarized Tierney's "standard conciliarist": "In Zabarella, [one sees] the type – distinguished canonist, prominent conciliarist."[8]

The "Tierney thesis" has had a wide vogue and a powerful impact. It was published at just the right time. The discovery

[7] McNeill, "Emergence of Conciliarism," pp. 271–72.

[8] John Watt, "The Early Medieval Canonists and the Formation of Conciliar Theory," *Irish Theological Quarterly*, 29 (1957): 14.

of "sources of unquestionable orthodoxy"[9] for the "good elements of the conciliar theory"[10] has become an object of serious interest among the reforming theologians of the Roman communion (for example, Hans Küng) who have flourished since "the new Pentecost" of John XXIII. Indeed, the authority of the decrees of Constance (which is of course closely tied with the question of precisely what the Fathers of the Council meant by them when they adopted them, which also, in turn, depends upon the question of where the ideas came from, in what sort of ideological packaging [whether in a theological plain brown wrapper or clearly labelled and if so, how] the Fathers found them) has become a live issue once again among Roman Catholics. *In effect*, of course, they have been ignored for five hundred years. But they are "on the books"; they do provide, "properly understood," constitutional possibilities post-Vatican I Roman Catholicism has not wrestled with; they are part of (but how?) the tradition. Thus, conciliar thought is being discussed by contemporary Roman constitutional writers, and the literature concerning the great reform councils and their decrees, concerning the conciliarists and their thought, and concerning the constitutional tradition of the later Middle Ages (which of course involves the orthodoxy of the sources of conciliarism), which has especially flourished in the shadow of the assembling of the second council of the Vatican, is substantial and growing. It is being written not only by historians but also by theologians, and it is being written for today. If one *must*, in order to satisfy the demands of utilitarians, justify history's usefulness, he should find the importance of exact scholarship such as Tierney's in today's discussion adequate for his purpose.

The search for orthodox beginnings has led also to the investigation of the theological tradition as well as the canonistic tradition, and to the investigation of political and ecclesiological theory, not only from the canonistic side, but also from the

[9] *Ibid.*

[10] Hans Küng, *The Council in Action*, trans. Cecily Hastings (New York: Sheed & Ward, 1963), p. 62.

side of theology. M. J. Wilks has called attention[11] to the importance of medieval Aristotelian political thought—St. Thomas Aquinas as well as Marsilius of Padua—in developing the view that the community has both certain rights and certain powers against an irresponsible or incompetent executive, and he places the conciliar issue in the context of the whole Aristotelian revolution in Western thought. Conciliar readers of Thomas—such as John of Paris and Conrad of Gelnhausen—could acquire their views on the mutual responsibility of ruler and ruled, therefore, from the very soundest theological tradition, and receive comfort thereby. Thus, Tierney found conciliar roots in the supposedly absolutist stronghold of the canon law and its commentators. Wilks found conciliarism in "extreme" papalist Aristotelians, such as Augustinus Triumphus of Ancona, and found conciliar roots in the theological citadel of Thomas.

Curiously, Protestant historians have shown less interest than Roman Catholics, although John T. McNeill argued in 1930 that conciliarism was the "Protestant constitutional principle" and that the Reformation could be interpreted as the separation of the absolutist and conciliarist trends in late medieval Catholicism, a view which he repeated in 1962.[12] Protestantism's great ecumenical body is called the "World *Council* of Churches" and illustrates Dr. McNeill's remark that

> the founders of the Reformation and their successors have characteristically reflected leading principles of the conciliarists and have sought to employ the method of conferences, synods, and councils, local or general, as the means toward a widening communion, ultimately contemplating a union of the entire Christian Church.[13]

[11] M. J. Wilks, *The Problem of Sovereignty in the Later Middle Ages* (Cambridge: At the University Press, 1963).

[12] John T. McNeill, *Unitive Protestantism*, 1st ed., 1930; 2d ed. (Richmond, Va.: John Knox Press, 1964), pp. 89–129.

[13] John T. McNeill, "Dr. Blake's Proposal: Some Historical Observations," *McCormick Quarterly*, 15 (March, 1962): 10.

It would be interesting if it were Roman Catholicism rather than Protestantism which in this generation acknowledged the truth of Pierre Cardinal d'Ailly's remark of five hundred years ago: "Nec vera unio sine reformatione, nec vera reformatio sine unione."

In any case, whatever the interest and significance of the discussion, the difficulties of the period are remarkable, even for professional historians. The new interest may be as dangerous as it is beneficial, for it may tend to reinforce the confessional issues (of which scholars like Tierney are largely free) which have made the understanding of Christian history in the fourteenth and fifteenth centuries so hard for so long. Heiko Oberman, who has done very interesting work on Gabriel Biel—a man about whom an enormous amount has been said while little has been known—remarked in 1963, and repeated in 1966, a point which might be worth quoting here:

> There are few fields of historical inquiry where the impact of vested religious interests lingers on so persistently as in the area of late medieval thought. Due to a coincidence of interests, there is, however, a remarkable agreement in the over-all conclusion that this is an era of disintegration. From differing vantage points this period has been declared a no-man's-land and has been so thoroughly raked by Protestant and Roman Catholic shells that it has become almost impossible for the historian of the period to discover paths through this field. Although there are now signs of a more balanced approach, the predominance of this view of late medieval thought may well be regarded as a major factor in the interest shown by both Protestant and Roman Catholic scholars to establish a discontinuity between the medieval era and one's own particular tradition in the sixteenth century.[14]

[14] The original citation is to Heiko A. Oberman, *The Harvest of Medieval Theology* (Cambridge: Harvard University Press, 1963), p. 1. The present quotation is from the same author's *Forerunners of the Reformation* (New York: Holt, Rinehart & Winston, 1966), p. 34. One might wish to compare the remarks of J. B. Morrall, *Political Thought in Medieval Times* (New York: Harper & Bros., 1962), p. 119.

He adds that it therefore becomes important to prove that, while one's own discontinuity is pure, the connections of one's opponent with this baleful period are rich and significant—and indeed, this sort of thing can be done with the most charitable of intentions. The whole question is of course much complicated by the debate over the meaning of "Renaissance" and "Middle Ages," and by the great upheavals and changes of life in these centuries. A more positive understanding of conciliarism might therefore alter our views of not only the period concerned, but also of the ages before and after it. This is well illustrated by the increasing interest in the influence of the conciliarists on later political thinkers.[15] The search for orthodox sources for conciliarism is, therefore, a complicated essay not only in the ecclesiastical thought of another age, but also a study in the ways in which Christianity and culture have interacted, not only in other ages, but also in our own, and is therefore probably a good work.

The purpose of this article is to suggest another line (or perhaps two separate lines) of investigation which might shed further light on the problem of the sources of conciliarism. In order to understand these suggestions, it will be necessary to once again take note of the historiography of the problem.

When earlier scholars read the conciliarists, they noted (they could not *help* noting) the frequent and detailed references to the canons. Yet few of them took this formidable legal documentation seriously. Since they were convinced that the genuine sources of conciliar thought were quite other than the canons (again with exceptions)—for most of them assumed that the law was firmly absolutist and papalist, and that therefore conciliarism *had* to be subversive of the law so understood—they could only consider the legal references as windowdressing, an elaborate orthodox facade for a fundamentally unorthodox view, or at the very least a highly ingenious but probably disingenuous twisting of the law to purposes quite other than its previously accepted intent. This

[15] One might mention, as an example, the excellent book by Francis Oakley, *The Political Thought of Pierre d'Ailly* (New Haven: Yale University Press, 1964).

view became the *doctrina recepta,* in spite of evidence to the contrary and the opinion of important scholars that there might be more to it than that. The problem with this *doctrina recepta* was that the men who proposed the *via regalis concilii* were not obvious heretics themselves, but rather respected theologians (Gerson, for instance), canon lawyers (Zabarella, for example), cardinals, bishops, professors of piety and learning, and responsible churchmen, who cited neither Marsilius nor the other heretics proposed as the sources of their thought. They *did* cite the law and the Scriptures, the example of the early Church, eminent theologians and canonists. Thus, the people they were supposed to have read were less often quoted, at least explicitly; and those they were subverting were quoted right and left. Research of course did show that unacknowledged dependence, particularly upon Ockham, could be demonstrated in some of them: medieval authors are notorious for leaving vague their footnotes to recent writers and contemporaries. Yet there were still the positive quotations, the legal argument.

Brian Tierney suggested that the proposal of the *via regalis concilii* so early in the Schism and its widespread adoption by sound churchmen who in other situations were known to be responsible in practice and orthodox in faith, argued that they were, in this situation as in others, relying on the tradition of the Church as they knew it, on the law they had learned in school, and which they had administered all their lives.[16] Suddenly, all those canonistic references made sense — and Tierney's careful study of preceding canonistic commentary demonstrated precisely *how* they made sense.

Tierney's argument was, of course, most effective when treating known canonists: people like Gelnhausen and Zabarella. The conciliarists, however, borrowed so much from one another and from the general atmosphere of canonical studies that almost all of them reveal no little acquaintance with theories of canonist origin.

The conciliarists also studded their treatises with two other

[16] Tierney, *Conciliar Theory,* pp. 245, 10.

sorts of arguments: arguments from Scripture and arguments from the practice of the early Church. Scripture and history, they say, show that Mother Church, when faced by insoluble crises, always resorts to prayer, penance, and general councils.[17] These references have, as were those to the canons, been received with a certain skepticism by modern historians. John T. McNeill, for example, acknowledges that the citation of the example of the early Church is frequent, but he concludes:

> Some influence, too, must be assigned to the church's memory of the councils of the ecumenical period; though it is possible that the appeal of the conciliarists to the early councils should in most instances be regarded rather as debating strategy than as evidence of an original impulse from that source.[18]

Once again, there is not perfect agreement. M. Seidlmayer, for example, believes that "die Rückbesinnung auf die alte Kirche" – to the Fathers and the "vier ersten allgemeinen Konzilien" – is "ein weiteres grundlegendes Element des Konzilsgedankens."[19] In any case, the references are there. What are we to make of them?

The Middle Ages (assuming that there is such a unity) were saturated by the Vulgate. Its phrases, its words, its imagery, its characteristic style, came naturally to the minds of most medieval writers. It is therefore not surprising – prima facie – that the conciliarists quote Scripture, any more than it is surprising to find canon lawyers quoting the *Decretum*. But, for that matter, it is a well-known fact that the demons also quote Scripture, although not to their salvation. Nevertheless, as with the canonists, it would seem *more* unusual to find people quoting Scripture and *not* deriving ideas therefrom, than the

[17] Henry of Langenstein, *Epistola concilii pacis*, in H. von der Hardt, *Magnum oecumenicum Constantiense concilium* (Frankfurt and Leipzig, 1697), vol. 2, cols. 2–60. This letter will be cited hereafter by the name of the author, the chapter, and the column number in Von der Hardt. The present reference is to Henry 4. 6.

[18] McNeill, "Emergence of Conciliarism," p. 269.

[19] M. Seidelmayer, *Die Anfänge des grossen abendländischen Schismas* (Munster, 1940), pp. 178, 191–92.

contrary. If *lex orandi est lex credendi*, why not *lex legendi, lex credendi*, when in both cases constant practice and reflection are presupposed? Therefore, let us look at a specimen conciliarist, Henry of Langenstein, to discover if there is a pattern of passages or interpretation of passages which would lead one to believe that he is dealing with something more than "debating strategy." The same procedure can be followed in regard to the example of the early councils of the Church – indeed, in some measure the two arguments are difficult to separate. Henry's argument might be summarized as follows: the Schism is caused by sin. We must repent of the sin and follow the best method, one decreed by God himself, for healing the Schism, and for seeing that it does not occur again. How has the Church, under divine guidance, solved such problems in the past? She has resorted to general councils. We can see this among the Apostles, who surely intended their action to be normative. We can see it in the great days of the Constantinian Church when there were certainly easier ways to do things. We see it among the Visigoths, who rejoiced when a council was called for the reformation of the Church. And what was so good for the Church of the past must be good for us. The two elements of Apostolic practice and early example thus intertwine themselves.

It is proposed, therefore, to outline the usage of Scripture and the early councils in Henry of Langenstein's *Epistola concilii pacis* of 1381. This treatise is not chosen at random. Although the first conciliar treatise, properly so called, was that of Conrad of Gelnhausen (". . . l'Epistola Concordiae, oeuvre solide et vigoreuse qu' on regarde avec raison comme le premier exposé dogmatique et complet de la théorie conciliare, fut composée, à Paris, au mois de mai 1380, par un autre docteur allemand, Conrad de Gelnhausen . . ."),[20] it was Henry's little book which first combined the demand for

[20] Noël Valois, *La France et la Grand Schisme d'Occident* (Paris: Alphonse Picard et Fils, 1896–1902), 1:324–25. He is citing A. Kneer, "Die Entstehung der konziliaren Theorie," *Römisches Quartalschrift*, Supplement I, 1893, who says (p. 126): "Als den wahren Vertreter und als den Begründer der sogenannten konziliaren Theorie müssen wir fortan Konrad von Gelnhausen betrachten."

reunion and a general council with that for regularly-called reform councils to prevent future scandals. Conrad's work was not originally intended for public circulation. Henry's was. Henry's work was widely read and quoted (for example, by Pierre Cardinal d'Ailly in his famous work *Tractatus super reformatione ecclesie* at the Council of Constance).[21] Gerson also used his pamphlet at the same council.[22] Jacob suggests that the decree *Sacrosancta* is remotely based on Henry's book.[23]

Henry and Conrad were not the first to call for a council: indeed, it had first been suggested in those confused months in 1378 before the election of Clement VII. All the early calls for a council, however, had foundered because the issue between the *contendentes* was regarded as an issue of fact (*quaestio facti*). The law declared that *synodus maior est papa* only in matters of faith. Conrad and Henry justified the calling of a council by raising the issue from a matter of convenience for the settling of an issue of fact to a necessity for the settlement of an issue of faith: schism is an attack on one of the fundamental doctrines of the faith, namely, that the Church is "one, holy, catholic, and apostolic." A papal schism undercut the center of unity which God had given his faithful. Thus, said Conrad: "Casus hodiernus est maximus casus fidei eo quod tangit caput fidei in terris."[24]

Finally, however, although one must credit Conrad with the appeal to ἐπιείκεια,[25] one must recognize that Henry surpasses

[21] This is demonstrated very well, in James Kerr Cameron's unpublished Hartford Seminary Foundation dissertation, "Conciliarism in Theory and Practices, 1378–1418," 1953, vol. 2, app. The second volume is made up of translations of several important conciliar treatises, including that of Henry, part of which were published in Matthew Spinka, ed., *Advocates of Reform* (Philadelphia: Westminster Press, 1853).

[22] *Ibid.*, 1:37.

[23] Jacob, *Conciliar Epoch*, p. 10, n. 3.

[24] Conrad of Gelnhausen, *Epistola concordie*, ed. F. Bliemetzrieder. *Literarische Polemik zu Beginn des grossen abendländischen Schismas* (Vienna: Publikation des österreich historischen Instituts in Rom, 1909), p. 119.

[25] Paul Sigmund, *Nicholas of Cusa and Medieval Political Thought* (Cambridge: Harvard University Press, 1963), pp. 100–101.

him in two ways: (1) Henry incorporates most of Conrad's treatise in his own (especially the canonistic arguments—but then, Conrad was a canonist and Henry a theologian, so why should he not?) and (2) combined with it material of his own which he used to build up the final conciliar constitutional program. Therefore, it is to Henry rather than to Conrad that we turn.

Ludwig von Pastor described Henry as "the most eminent German theologian of the day."[26] He was, at the outbreak of the Schism, the vice-chancellor of the University of Paris. In 1368, Henry wrote a *Quaestio de cometa*, disproving the use of these heavenly bodies for the foretelling of the future. This treatise was so successful that he later—at the request of the University—wrote three more. He also attacked astrologers and prophets who, in the time of the Schism, sought to reveal the future by means of the stars. He adopted the University's skeptical attitude toward the Joachimite excesses. In all this he comes off rather better intellectually than his reborn and enlightened humanist successors Pico della Mirandola and Melanchthon. He wrote three other astronomical treatises, some fifty works of ascetical theology, letters, sermons, defenses of the Immaculate Conception, and eighteen works on the Schism.[27] His views changed over the years. Disillusionment with the protracted and vicious Schism convinced him at the last that the *via concilii*, although still the best way, would never work.[28] He seems to have come to the same conclusion as Gerhard Groote, the founder of the Brethren of the Common Life, who hoped "quod ambo pontifices cum omnibus cardinalibus cantarent in coelo empyreo gloria in excelsis, et alius verus Elyachim poneret pacem et unitatem in terris."[29] One wonders who did not feel this way before it was all over. Henry was called by Albert of Austria to help organize the

[26] Ludwig von Pastor, *The History of the Popes* (London: J. Hodges, 1891), 1:154.

[27] Michael Ott, "Henry of Langenstein," *Catholic Encyclopedia* (New York: Robert Appleton Co., 1910), 7:236–37.

[28] Henry of Langenstein, *Epistola de cathedra Petri*, edited by Kneer, "Konziliaren theorie."

[29] Pastor, *History of the Popes*, 1:147, n*.

theological faculty at the University of Vienna. He remained there until his death, teaching, in addition to canon law and theology, the Holy Scriptures: he therefore knew the Bible as a scholar. Like Luther, his lectures on Genesis were not characterized by haste: "Ibi Genesin explicare coepit. Atque suam lectionem per multos annos continuavit. Erat autem adeo copiosus, & ad omnes occurentes quaestiones promptus, ut vix multis annis ad quartum caput libri per veniens, totidem volumina complerit."[30] He died in 1397.

These, then are Henry's qualities: he was a professional scholar of the Scriptures, an eminent theologian, and one of the significant formulators of the conciliar view. Unfortunately, his *Epistola* — like the works of some of his even more famous successors — has not been edited since the seventeenth century. The last publication was Du Pin's reprint (1706) of Von der Hardt's edition of 1697. Chapters 1, 2, 12, 13, and 15 are "ganz und gar"[31] from Conrad's *Epistola concordiae*. The Epistola is divided into twenty chapters. The first is short, establishing the profundity and seriousness of the causes of the Schism, which he regards as cold-heartedness, avarice, nepotism, gaudy and expensive display, a worldly, debauched, and litigious clergy who, instead of preaching the Word of God are spending their churches' money on lawsuits. It is particularly simony which he regards as the root of the destruction of parishes, the corruption of monasteries, the perversion of bishoprics: *radix omnium malorum avaritia* indeed! He foresees even more disastrous results as heresy spreads and the Faithful rebel at the stupidity of their leaders. Even the two popes encourage this by excommunicating and heaping filth upon one another. How unlike the Council of Ephesus, which called upon Nestorius to return to the fold in charity, even though condemning his heresy! Thus men no longer fear the sword of Peter, and "Tandem victor sedebit in solio majestatis princeps tenebrarum, artifex iniquitatis . . ."[32]

[30] Henry Pantaleon, *Prosopgraphia virorum illustrium Germaniae,* quoted in Von der Hardt, *Constantiense concilium,* 2:10.

[31] Kneer, "Konziliaren theorie," p. 84.

[32] Henry 2.5.

It is apparent, Henry believes, that a great crisis which involves the whole life of the Church has come about through demonstrable corruption and decay. The solution is to turn this tribulation into an appropriate reformation of the Church.[33] God, says the Prophet Amos, chastens those he loves.[34] We should therefore humiliate ourselves under the hand of God, do penance for our sins, undertake works of sacrifice, offer prayers, and summon a general council for reunion and the purging of the Church: reformation by *poenitentia, precibus, et concilio generali*, as Von der Hardt's headings put it. *Why a general council*? Again Von der Hardt's summary presents Henry's argument: "Exemplũ Patrum in convocandis Conciliis Provincialibus ac Generalibus." Says Henry: "Ecce via pacis, via trita praecedentium Patrum, via salutis."[35] Such a council would assemble — as was true in earlier days — to settle causes, and correct laws. What fathers does he mean? First he mentions Charles the king of the Franks, who assembled a council of forty-one bishops, in which the king said that he should do nothing without the judgment of his bishops, "qui throni Dei sunt dicti, in quibus Deus sedet, & per quos sua decernit judicia. . . ."[36] Hence, in the time of the Schism, kings and princes should have recourse to an ecumenical council for judgment of the cause. Henry brings forth a curious series of acts from Visigothic councils of the sixth and seventh centuries as further evidence. These passages do not come from the *Decretum*. They come instead from the Pseudo-Isidorean Decretals. He apparently used a text of the Decretals

[33] Henry 3. 4.

[34] Henry 3. 5.

[35] Henry 4. 6–7. The whole passage following this remark is important. "Ad quam summo studio assumendam Deo placentem viam, & indilatae *executioni mandandam*, valde movere debet Reges & Principes Christianos modernorum doctrix, veterum *memoria historiarum*: Insinuans, Regum devotione, patrocinio & hortatu, olim in retroactis Ecclesiae necessitatibus *Episcoporum synodos provinciales & generalis* sic providente Domino plerumque *convocatas* fuisse, atque se, suarumque litium causas & leges corrigendas & emendandas sacro *conciliorum* suorum *judicio* devote submisisse. Ut conscriptis conciliorum gestis clarum patulo intuitu."

[36] Henry 4. 7.

which differs from that we know today, for some of the passages he quotes are not found in modern editions.[37] They are omitted from modern translations of Henry, presumably because they are not very comprehensible or exciting for the modern reader. Yet Henry regards them very highly,[38] for they appear in chapters 5, 6, 8, 9, 10, and 19. He must have gone to considerable trouble to assemble them, for they constitute the only legal passages which he does not take from Conrad, and they come from a source Conrad did not use.

What does Henry seek to prove by these long quotations? These councils demonstrate, he says: (1) that councils, by the wise decisions of the Fathers, should be frequent;[39] (2) that councils are the proper forum for the enforcement of the good old laws, the reform of those who have fallen away from them, the settlement of disputes and the reconciliation of disputants, and the strengthening of the clergy for teaching, preaching, good living, and combating evil;[40] (3) that councils are the proper forum for the making of wholesome new laws and the clarification of obscurities in law or faith;[41] (4) that councils are the best means to secure the healing of schism and the extirpation of heresy;[42] (5) that the secular authorities act most properly when they both assist in the convocation of a necessary council and humbly obey its decrees.[43] Disputing prelates should be equally amenable to the virtues of a council.[44]

[37] For example, the long quotation from the Ninth Council of Toledo, which ends c. 9. I owe the information on these councils to the notes in Cameron's translation, referred to above (n. 21).

[38] Henry's taste in councils was excellent: *The Catholic Encyclopedia*, 14:758, says: "Famous in the history of Toledo are its councils, held in greatest veneration by the sovereign pontiffs, and the source of the purest religious and moral doctrine." It is interesting that Marsilius of Padua also drew upon this series of decretals, although not for the same purposes as Henry.

[39] Henry 8. 14–17, Toledo 11; Henry 9. 16–17, Braga 2.

[40] Henry 5. 8, Braga 1; 9. 16–17, Braga 2; 5. 8–9, Toledo 4; 8. 14–17, Toledo 9.

[41] Henry 5. 9, Toledo 8.

[42] Henry 6. 10–11, Toledo 12; 9. 16–17, Braga 2; 7. 10–12, Toledo 8.

[43] Henry 7. 12–13, Toledo 8; 4. 7, Savonières.

[44] Henry 8. 14, Toledo 8.

He includes two chapters (9 and 10) which are specifically designed to prove the zeal of the prelates and the popes of the primitive Church for the convocation of councils. He quotes Pope Leo I and Pope Innocent II (concerning a council celebrated in Rome in 1139 – a passage which can no longer be found).[45]

Henry explained in his last work on the Schism, the *Epistola de cathedra Petri*, that he had advocated the calling of a council in the early years of the Schism because

> non est conveniencior et securior via terminandi ipsum quam consilium generale omnium prelatorum . . . hec enim est via sepius a prelatis ecclesie practicata, est via qua usi sancti patres exortas quomodocunque credenda et agenda dubitaciones et dissensiones in ecclesia primitiva sancto spiritu invocato abstulerunt et pacem reducerunt.[46]

All this seems to indicate that Henry consciously turned to the conciliar solution in part because he accepted a norm derived from the experience of the early Church. It is hard to see his despairing remarks in the *Epistola de cathedra Petri* (1395) as "debating strategy."

Chapters 12–15 take up objections to the calling of a general council and reply to them. Much of this material is borrowed from Conrad. It contains Henry's appeal to Apostolic practice. It would not do to go through each point of Henry's argument. Chapter 12 lists eight objections to the assemblage of a council. These are taken from Conrad, who in turn adapted them from earlier canonistic opponents, such as Petrus Cardinal

[45] Henry 10. 18–19 (Leo, 18; Innocent II, 19). The organization of these two chapters was first called to my attention by Seidlmayer, *Grossen abendländischen Schismas*, p. 192, n. 73. That the ancients rejoiced in councils is proved by quotations from Toledo 9 (Henry 8, 14–17) and Toledo 8 (Henry 9. 16).

[46] Henry of Langenstein, *Epistola de cathedra Petri*, ed. Kneer, "Konziliaren theorie," pp. 138–39. Approximately half the citations in Conrad's treatise are from the law, most of the rest from Scripture. In one place he quotes both, plus Aristotle and Aquinas – Bliemetzrieder, *Literarische Polemik*, p. 129.

Amelii and Pierre Flandrin, the Cardinal of St. Eustace.[47] The most interesting of these arguments, from our point of view, is the eighth: that the early Church depended upon councils because the position of the papacy had not yet been made clear. But now the decrees of earlier councils have clarified the Faith and the pope can guide the Church through appropriate legislation.[48] Besides, times have changed since the days of the primitive Church, and new methods are needed to combat new troubles. Indeed, there have been schisms before: but history does not record that they were solved by general councils.[49]

Chapter 13 undertakes, in fourteen arguments, to defend the *via concilii.* In the first argument, Henry cites the example of the Old Testament (numbers 27, etc.) and the example of the Apostles:

> In Novo vero Testamento patet, discurrendo per quatuor concilia, per Apostolos celebrata, Act. I, Act. VII, Act. XV, et Act. XXI. Et cum Apostoli potuissent sine convocatione concilii per epistolas vel aliis modis faciliter causas & negotia terminasse, videtur, quod hoc in exemplum suis successoribus fecerint. Est enim Apostolorum actio nostra instructio sicut & Christi; juxta illud: Imitatores esto mei, sicut & ego Christi. Igitur in casibus magnis & arduis concilium congregandum est.[50]

The Apostles held, in all, four councils: for the election of the successor of Judas, for the election of the seven deacons (and here they were joined by the multitude of disciples), for deciding the question of the applicability of the law to the Gentiles, and for the meeting with Paul. Now it is perfectly apparent, says Henry, that the Apostles could read and write—after all, we have their letters—and that therefore they could have conducted their business by letter had they chosen. They

[47] The works of these men are published in Bliemetzrieder, *Literarische Polemik*, and the development of the argument may there be traced.

[48] Henry 12. 24–25.

[49] Henry 12. 25–27.

[50] Henry 13. 26.

did not so choose because *they intended to leave a norm for the Church.*

Argument two quotes Isidore of Seville's *Etymologiae* 7. 17, that before the time of Constantine it was not possible for Christians to assemble in council; therefore, they were much divided by schism and heresy. Of course, as soon as Constantine was able, he began to assemble councils to reform the Church.[51]

> Item, si tempore devotae primitivae Ecclesiae quando sancti praesidebant Papae & Praelati, ut Sylvester, & alii, fiebant concilia generalia, fortassis saepe in casibus minoris periculi vel praejudicii quam est casus praesens: Cur modo, jam multiplicatis hominibus, & malitiis, & variis erroribus, & Ecclesiasticorum exorbitationibus, concilia aggregari non deberent, pro corrigendis & abstergendis hujusmodi maculis a facie universalis Ecclesiae?[52]

The Emperor Constantine, when he wanted to give the Church material goods only, assembled councils. This matter is a matter of faith, and certainly deserves at least what temporal possessions received.[53]

Argument eight cites Augustine's demand, in *Liber de gratia et libero arbitrio,* for the convocation of councils to deal with Pelagius.

The opponents of a council tell us that the cardinals ought to be presumed honest. Indeed, says Henry, they should, had they not lied and confused everyone. In any case, presumption of honesty is not infallibility: the universal Church, which is represented by a general council, is superior to the Cardinals and the Pope, and is not able to err ("Universalis Ecclesia, cujus concilium generale est repraesentativum, est superior collegio Cardinalium, & omni alia particulari congregatione fidelium, & omni, cujuscunque digniatis, & praesidentia persona, etiam Domino Papa . . ." and "Ecclesia universalis non

[51] Henry 13. 26.
[52] Henry 13. 26.
[53] Henry 13. 27.

potest errare.").[54] Why this is so? Because Scripture teaches us that the gates of Hell shall not prevail against her (". . . et portae inferorum non praevalebunt adversus eam." Matt. 16:18).[55] Hence, there have been heretical popes, such as Anastasius II and Marcellinus—as indeed we read in the *Decretum* and in the histories of the supreme pontiffs. In addition, the servant is no better than the master: and Scripture teaches us that Peter betrayed his Master, and the other Apostles ran away from the Christ.[56] Augustine, Jerome, and St. Gregory the Great testify to the superiority of the Church universal to the pope and the college. Gregory announces his adherence to the first four councils in this way: "Sicut sancta Evangelia quatuor, sic quatuor concilia suscipere & venerari me fateor. . . ."[57] There then follow a number of quotations from the canons, the glosses, and canonists, which have been thoroughly investigated by Tierney. They include the familiar gloss *synodus maior est papa*, and list a number of popes who humbled themselves before councils, such as Sixtus, Leo III, and Innocent IV. Then he remarks, But if it is said that these acts were done of great humility, I reply: why do not present pontiffs imitate this magnificent humility?

He finally concludes that "ubi multa concilia, ibi salus."[58] A reform council should have been called a long time ago. They should meet regularly.

In chapter 14, Henry takes up the question of the election of a pope. The Scriptures tell us that Christ established the papal office. But He did *not* establish a method of election of popes. Therefore, the method of election is left to the Church. He concludes that the power of election resides in the episcopate, and in great crisis, ultimately in the whole Church. Hence supervision of the papacy lies in the episcopacy and, in times of crisis, in the whole Church. He then has a considerable discussion of the means of settling the Schism, choosing

[54] Henry 13. 28. Cf. *Sacrosancta* at Constance.
[55] Henry 13. 29.
[56] Henry 13. 29.
[57] Henry 13. 30.
[58] Henry 13. 32.

a general council, and of the possible ways of assembling such a council.

Chapter 15 takes up the doubts raised in chapter 12. Henry quotes a number of passages of Scripture in his replies. He uses Matt. 18:20 as a proof that the highest work is a general council.[59] He cites examples of the fathers who did not hesitate to acknowledge their errors, and refers particularly to the time when Paul withstood Peter to his face in Antioch. This passage (Gal. 2:11, 14) is referred to in the *Decretum*, C. 2, q. 7, and is used by Wessel Gansfort.[60] He several times refers to the position of Christ as the head of the Body of the Church, which, while it reflects corporation law, also reflects Paul. It is from this primary and indefectible headship of Christ that Henry derives both the secondary role of the papacy, and the power of the Church to cure herself of her ills. He has a long passage in which he worries about the consequences of his condemnation of avarice: perhaps the Church would have been better off without the wealth Constantine gave it? Perhaps it should have remained in primitive poverty? Perhaps the Church was richer, not poorer, without power and honors? He takes up the Scriptural passages on Apostolic economy. Yet, he concludes, different times require different solutions, and what is acceptable under persecution might not be adequate under favor. Any other analysis of God's intentions, he believes, is speculation. He is obviously worried by the criticism of the Church for its wealth made by the Spiritual Franciscans and others. He loves asceticism, but he is also bound by the orthodox view that it is not the possession but the abuse of goods which is evil.[61]

His final remarks in this chapter are directed to the charge that conditions have so changed in the Church that councils are unnecessary or inadequate. Persecutions, he says, far from being a prerogative of the early Church, have never ceased. They have simply changed from fire and sword to gossip and

[59] Henry 15. 38.

[60] Wessel is quoted in Oberman, *Harvest of Medieval Theology*, p. 411, n. 153. Marsilius also quotes the passage, *Defensor Pacis* 2. 16. 6.

[61] Henry 15. 46–47.

heresy. A council is just as secure a means against such evils today, he thinks, as it was in the days of the primitive Church. It may be true that earlier councils have provided adequately for all contingencies. But, if so, who today obeys their canons? Once again he invokes his favorite Visigothic councils: the Seventh Council of Toledo complained that in its day it was necessary to reenact the good old laws once again, simply to get people to obey them. In the time of the Schism, new corruptions have come into being, and no law can pretend to deal with all possible evils. Therefore there is always need in the Church for a council. He compares the Church to a house, which constantly requires repairs here and there: unless the house is examined every year, and repaired where it is decaying, it will fall into ruin.[62]

The next four chapters, 16–19, were republished in tracts of their own at the Council of Constance by D'Ailly and Gerson.[63] In these chapters, Henry describes the evils which have arisen and which require correction by an ecumenical council. In chapter 19 he returns to the Visigoths: he concludes with a strong plea that such wickedness can be corrected only by regular provincial and ecumenical councils. He quotes the acts of a Council of Braga, of the third Council of Carthage, of the sixth Council of Toledo, and of the fourth Council of Toledo, all of which enjoin the assembly of regular (annual or semi-annual) provincial councils for the reform of the Church. And, he concludes, by analogy, regular general councils should meet for the reform of the whole Church.[64]

There are thus intertwined two groups of historical arguments, one referring to the example of the early Church, the other to the Scriptures, a far more heterogeneous group of citations. Clearly Henry wants to establish something with which Conrad did not deal: the calling of regular reform councils, which will not cease with the extirpation of the present schism. He does not draw his arguments in this section, by and large, from the same sources Conrad drew his, and which

[62] Henry 15. 47–49.
[63] Spinka, *Advocates of Reform*, p. 134, n. 50 (See above, nn. 21, 22.)
[64] Henry 19. 56–57.

Tierney has so carefully examined, but from sources of his own, particularly some sixth- and seventh-century Visigothic councils. In addition, he remembers the ecumenical councils of the fourth and fifth centuries, and the Apostolic councils of the New Testament.

His Biblical quotations fall into several groups. Many are illustrative, or simply a striking way of saying something. But many of them go directly to the heart of the problem: the passages which are the title deeds of the papacy (for example Matt. 16:18); the images Scripture uses for the Church (e.g., Paul's metaphor of the body of Christ); and examples of resistance to papal authority (such as Gal. 2:11 ff.). This list, in fact, neither exhausts the number of Henry's quotations from Scripture, nor does it begin to include all those Scriptural passages which were of concern for the conciliarists, but which are not cited by Henry. In the latter category, for example, are 1 Cor. 14:12 and 2 Cor. 10:8, both of which assert that authority in the Church is given for edification, not for destruction.

This essay is no more than that: it is designed simply to call attention to the fact that one conciliarist, Henry of Langenstein, took seriously both the Scriptures and the practice of the early Church, in his constructive work as a conciliar theorist. Some of his examples come to him through canon law; others were no doubt interpreted in the light of recent constitutional developments dominated by canon lawyers. Yet there was an independent tradition of the Scriptural exegesis and commontary. Would not an investigation of the Scriptural commentaries on, let us say, Acts 15 and other similar passages yield some new insight? And would it not be good to know the medieval historiography of the early councils? How had historians and theologians prior to Henry understood the normative role of the early Church? The present writer is in no position to answer these questions. He can only call attention to them, in the hopes that some enterprising student will investigate the suggestion.

Hans Küng[65] has called for an examination of the theologi-

[65] Hans Küng, *Structures of the Church* (New York: Thomas Nelson & Sons, 1964), p. 290. This paper is developed from a part of a doctoral

cal resources available to the conciliarists, parallel to the study Tierney has done of the canonists. May one then add to this the suggestion that a study of Scriptural exegesis and of the historiography of the ancient church might also bear fruit?

---

dissertation submitted in the History Department of the State University of Iowa, 1965, director, Donald W. Sutherland. Needless to say, Dr. Sutherland is in no way responsible for this paper, although his advice was freely given and helpful; I alone am responsible for the paper and its conclusions.

7

Humanism and the Reformation

QUIRINUS BREEN

The reformation we have in mind is the movement associated with, of course, Luther, Melanchthon, Zwingli, and particularly with Calvin. What humanism was is another matter, and not so readily described. The very best specialists in Renaissance studies disagree. For example, Professor Eugenio Garin and Professor Paul Oskar Kristeller have for years held competing views. The most recent clash (it was an amicable one) came in 1963 at a meeting in Mirandola to commemorate the 500th anniversary of Giovanni Pico della Mirandola's birth.[1] Both agreed that Pico was a humanist in the sense of having facility in the classical languages and literatures; there was no disagreement on his ability to write an elegant Latin. Both also agreed that Pico was a philosopher, a clear proof to be his Oration on the Dignity of Man. But now came the conflict of opinion. Garin held that Pico was a philosopher qua humanist, Kristeller that Pico was a humanist but in addition a philosopher. Garin held that the difference was largely verbal. But Kristeller viewed it as basic; he has consistently held that the humanists as such were not philosophers at all. A man could be a humanist and also a philosopher, in the sense that he may be an eloquent orator *and* a philosopher; but the root of oratory is one, that of philosophy is an utterly different one.[2]

[1] Istitutio Nazionale, Florence, *L'Ojera e il Pensiero di Giovanni Pico della Mirandola della Storia dell' Umanesimo*, Convegno Internazionale (Mirandola, September 1963, 15–16), 2 vols; see 1:32–33, 134–37. See also P. O. Kristeller, "Humanism and Scholarship in the Italian Renaissance," in *Studies in Renaissance Thought and Letters* (Rome: Edizioni di Storia e letteratura, 1956), p. 561.

[2] See Herschel C. Baker, *The Dignity of Man* (Cambridge: Harvard

Kristeller's point poses a distinction between the philosopher as philosopher and humanist as humanist. It is apropos to use as illustration Pico as the author of the Oration because the view is still current that in it he voiced the humanists' conviction of man's dignity. So perceptive a scholar as Professor Lewis Spitz, writing of Luther, says, "Luther was not in 1521 a humanist in the sense that he emphasized the dignity of man in the manner of Pico, *which was, after all, the core of humanism* [italics mine]."[3] Generally the humanist felt himself most at home in the tradition of Isocrates and Cicero as orators or rhetoricians. How very different is the philosophical tradition from the sophistical or rhetorical: Plato-Aristotle vs. Isocrates! Each in its kind is necessary: so to say the philosopher to man-as-man, the rhetorician to man-in-society.[4] Each may cross the line between them; the rhetorician may speak of philosophic topics, the philosopher may use oratorical art. But a rhetorician as such does not philosophize nor a philosopher as such orate.

Moreover, each can confer a kind of dignity or nobility. But they should not be confused, for the dignity with which the philosopher endows men has to do with man-as-man, and involves him in, e.g., question of epistemology; the rhetorician bestows it on man as man-in-society. In any case, the dignity Pico had in mind was poles removed from anything a Renaissance humanist had ever thought of. Pico conceived of a dignity bestowed on Adam, which consisted in the power to control his own destiny. Pico's sources for this have been explored with rich suggestion by Dr. Frances Yates of the Warburg Institute.[5] As for the humanistic idea of man's dig-

University Press, 1943), pp. 370–74; Q. Breen, "The *Antiparadoxon* of Marcantonius Majoragius, or, How a Humanist Became a Critic of Cicero as a Philosopher," *Studies in the Renaissance*, 5 (1958): 38–48.

[3] L. Spitz, *The Religious Renaissance of the German Humanists* (Cambridge: Harvard University Press, 1963), p. 239.

[4] See Charles Trinkhaus, "A Humanist's Image of Humanism: The Inaugural Orations of Bartolomeo della Fonte [1446–1513]," *Studies in the Renaissance*, 7 (1960): 96–97.

[5] Frances Yates, *L'Opera e il Pensiero di G. Pico della Mirandola nella*

nity, much suggestion comes from the studies in civic humanism by Dr. Hans Baron.[6]

What has been said so far illustrates how fruitful is Kristeller's sharp distinction between the humanist and the philosopher. A further question is why the name of humanist was given to the scholar concerned with the classics, and not to the philosopher inquiring about ontology, epistemology, and the like. One need not doubt the good right of the classical scholar to the name of humanist, but why should it not as well fit the philosopher? In fact, the philosophical achievement of the Greeks has generally been held in higher esteem as humanistic than their philology (e.g., Homer criticism) and their rhetorical prowess.

All such prompts us to distinguish two kinds of humanism in the Renaissance era.[7] Thus we have, on the one hand, what we shall call general humanism (philosophy, etc.) and, on the other, particular humanism (classical philology and rhetoric). In the next section the discussion will pertain to general humanism and certain of its parallels with, and relations with, the reformers. The last section will deal with particular humanism (philology and rhetoric) and how it affected the reformers.

General humanism embraces all that men have done in every age (also in the Renaissance) to explore the infinite variety of man's nature and relationships, so as to know and express his exaltation or abasement. Some cultures and eras have left us more information, say, through literature and art than others; but in no culture or era was it likely for a man to have no wonder about his nature and possibilities. We may assume that the themes of man's baseness to his dignity ob-

---

Storia dell' Umanesimo in Convegno Internazionale (see n. 1 above), pp. 159–202; E. Cassirer, "G. Pico della Mirandola: A Study in the History of Renaissance Ideas," *Journal of the History of Ideas*, 3 (1942): 123–44, 313–46; particularly 123.

[6] See below, note 82.

[7] See C. Trinkhaus, *Studies in the Renaissance*, 7:90–125.

tained wherever man dwelt. They are etched with variety and sharpness in Israel's Old Testament, in Greek literature from wrathful Achilles to the philosopher-king, and (to mention no more) in literature from St. Benedict's Rule to Chaucer.[8]

There are some striking Renaissance parallels with a certain crucial concern of the Reformation, to wit, its assertion of autonomy in religion. We point to them, but to save space we do not enlarge on them. We begin by saying what we mean by the reformers' claim to autonomy.

It is characteristic of the reformers to speak with great conviction of the certainty of their faith. They sometimes found a bitter foe in *Anfechtung*, when they felt their certainty threatened. But they held their ground, for they believed they spoke through the Holy Spirit's inspiration. Zwingli[9] said he preached "by the grace and inspiration of the Holy Spirit," Luther translated the Bible "under inspiration."[10] Calvin said the only ground for believing Scripture to be divinely inspired is the "secret testimony of him who inspired it, the Holy Spirit." The Bible is self-authenticating, however, only to those to whom the Holy Spirit reveals that it is God who speaks as with a living voice through Moses and the prophets, the Gospels and the Apostles. "Such a conviction requires no reasons . . . [It is] such feeling that can be born only of

[8] The monk as seen by St. Benedict deserves a better assessment than many in the Renaissance and since have made. In the annals of general humanism, he can find an honorable place. Dom Jean Leclercq has done much to set the record straight; one should consult at least his *The Love of Learning and the Desire for God* (New York: Fordham University Press, 1961). Werner Jaeger, *Early Christianity and Greek Paideia* (Cambridge: Harvard University Press, 1961), suggests that back of the Rule lay the best thinking of Gegory of Nyssa; to wit, that to produce (as counterpart and advance over the Greek) ideal of man as man-in-Christ. Jaeger says that Erasmus "the monk" aimed at this, which Otto Herding confirms: "Nothing is comparable to the dominating role which Christ plays for the moralizing pedagogue Erasmus; it is only Christ who fully illuminates the Structure of Man." — *Studies in the Renaissance*, 13 (1966): 229.

[9] S. M. Jackson, ed., *Selected Works of Huldreich Zwingli* (Philadelphia: University of Pennsylvania Press, 1901), p. 48.

[10] Werner Schwarz, *Principles and Problems of Biblical Translation* (Cambridge: At the University Press, 1955), pp. 167–212.

heavenly revelation."[11] The reformers believed that when they heard Scripture they were inspired to hear it as God's voice with the same force the Bible writers experienced when they wrote at the dictation of the Spirit. What they "heard," therefore, became the standard for judging what the hierarchy, the councils, and all tradition said. The reformers spoke as inspired men.[12] The counterpart of this is evident in certain Renaissance general humanisms, which declared a comparable autonomy. This finds illustrations in what took place in poetry and mathematics.[13]

Poetry and mathematics are secular. This secularity alone does not characterize them as Renaissance phenomena, for the Middle Ages was far from being all other-worldly. We have to name only feudalism, the Commune, the liberal arts curriculum, and the higher faculties of law, medicine and theology.[14] Besides, the era was not alien to poetry and mathematics. The difference was rather one of emphasis and, so to say, of prestige. Poetry as a literature of the imagination, intended to delight, was not trusted with first truth; mathematics was by itself not considered a way of knowing the structure of the

[11] *Calvin Institutes of the Christian Religion* 1. 8. 5. See J. T. McNeill's notes in The Library of Christian Classics, vol. 20 (Philadelphia: Westminster Press, 1960), pp. 74, 76; also E. Dowey, *The Knowledge of God in Calvin's Theology* (New York: Columbia University Press, 1952), pp. 106–12.

[12] In a brief reference to his conversion Calvin mentioned *reverentia ecclesiae* as in effect inspiring his former loyalty to the Church. Now he yielded only to the Word of God, obedient to the Holy Spirit's prompting. Calvin thought of himself as a "*doctor*" of the church (*Inst.* "To the Readers"). Calvin's use of the term illustrates his supreme self-assurance. See F. Wendel, *Calvin: Origins and Development of His Religious Thought*, trans. Philip Mairet (New York: Harper & Row, 1963), pp. 38–39, for "reverence for the Church."

[13] There are other parallels, e.g., art.

[14] A point should be made of theology; even when thought of as "sacred theology," its professors taught on secular territory. The adjective "sacred" owed everything to its subject matter which was the Christian faith; but actually its method was philosophical, hence secular. It could never properly command conscience; it was not the faith itself, but a rational discourse about it. Theologians in effect had since the Apologists declared reason, in its kind, to be autonomous to the extent that without it theology itself would not exist.

universe; would-be reformers disapproved by the church were distrusted, if not also reckoned as heretics or schismatics. In the Renaissance, poetry declared its autonomy with Dante's *Divine Comedy* (begun c. 1307);[15] the poet himself felt free as a poet to treat the most exalted themes. As it were, poetry claimed for itself, in its kind, an autonomy equal to that of theology.[16] A like thing happened in mathematics. A pioneer was the mystic Nicholar of Cusa (1401–64), and there was, of course, Copernicus (1470–1543). Its autonomy was not substantially recognized till Descartes (1596–1650). Striking are the poets' invocations of the Muses, and of the Holy Spirit, and the mathematicians' consciousness of the divine source of

[15] It will appear that whatever Dante and Shakespeare wrote between A.D. 1300–1600 is claimed for the Renaissance. Renaissancists generally agree on these dates as the termini of the period. Every periodization is perhaps a bit arbitrary, but a given periodization is dependable when it can be shown to have a "physiognomy" of its own. (This is Kristeller's phrasing used in various works. See, e.g., *Eight Philosophers of the Italian Renaissance* [Stanford: Stanford University Press, 1964], p. 147.) A.D. 1300–1600 is such a period. If one varies the termini, e.g., 1100–1550, or any other, the problems are not simplified. A lineament of 1300–1600's physiognomy is the distinguished national literatures with world classics at each terminus.

[16] Of much importance was the influence of Aristotle's *Poetics.* A translation by Giorgio Valla was published in 1499. J. E. Spingarn says that with a translation of 1536 and a critical edition of 1548 poetic criticism really began. *Literary Criticism in the Renaissance* (New York: Harcourt, Brace & World, 1963), pp. 12–13. Note should be taken of Charles Trinkhaus's "The Unknown Quattrocento Poetics of Bartolomeo della Fonte," *Studies in the Renaissance*, 12 (1966): 40–122. He shows that with this work (c. 1490–92) "the *Studia Humanitatis* evolved to the composition of a formal *Poetics*" (p. 95), though "Fontius was without benefit of Aristotle" (p. 46). See also William Rossky, "Imagination in the English Renaissance Psychology and Poetic," *Studies in the Renaissance*, 5 (1958): 49–73; C. G. Osgood, *Boccaccio on Poetry* (Princeton: Princeton University Press, 1939), p. xxxviii, to show influence of traditional apologetic for poetry; E. R. Curtius, *European Literature in the Latin Middle Ages* (New York: Pantheon Books, 1953), pp. 238, 475, 221–29. Curtius recommends M. D. Chenu, *Introduction à l'Étude de Saint Thomas d'Aquin* (Montreal and Paris: Institut d'études Médievales, 1950), pp. 93 f. For an early Tudor poet and his strong belief in writing under inspiration, see S. E. Fish, *John Skelton's Poetry* (New Haven: Yale University Press, 1965), pp. 8–13, 33–35.

their art.[17] It is interesting to know that Calvin honored mathematics as a gift of God.[18]

The autonomy, then, of poets and mathematicians runs parallel with that of the reformers. The principle received recognition in both the sixteenth and the seventeenth centuries, though the recognition was unfriendly. Professor Chester has shown that the term New Learning (Nova doctrina) was not associated with humanistic scholarship, but with Luther's and other reformers' claim to be proper translators and interpreters of Scripture and as rethinkers of the faith.[19] It was the radical-

[17] Francis R. Johnson, "Thomas Hood's Inaugural Address as Mathematical Lecturer of the City of London (1588)," *Journal of the History of Ideas* (hereafter cited as *J.H.I.*), 3 (1942): 94–106; E. Cassirer, "G. Pico della Mirandola," *J.H.I.*, 3 (1942): 321. For Cusa, "there is no absolute up or down, no [lower] and [higher] sphere. No place in the universe differs in its nature from any other, . . . and can with equal right claim to be the center of the world." – *Ibid.*, p. 323. See Leopold Prowe, *Nicolaus Coppernicus* (Berlin: Weidmann, 1883–84), 1:526–35; also Q. Breen, "The Subordination of Philosophy to Rhetoric in Melanchthon," *Archiv für Reformationsgeschichte*, 43 (1952): 24–25.

[18] *Inst.* 2. 2. 15; "What shall we say of all the mathematical sciences? Shall we consider them the ravings of madmen? No, we cannot read the writings of the ancients on these subjects without great admiration. We marvel at them because we are *compelled* [my italics] to recognize how pre-eminent they are. But shall we count anything praiseworthy or noble without recognizing at the same time that it comes from God?" See also McNeill's comment, Library of Christian Classics, 20:274, n. 58. Whence this enthusiasm for mathematics? A clue is that when he attended the Lecteurs Royaux, Oronce Fine was teaching mathematics there. Calvin could have met him later in Marguerite of Navarre's circle, which Fine also frequented. (See below, nn. 54–55.) As to the quotation from Calvin, the entire passage will be discussed in a forthcoming publication of my essay "Calvin's Defense of Secular Studies: His Doctrine of Common Grace." This may have relevance to the question whether Calvin, like Melanchthon, rejected the heliocentrism of Copernicus. Doubt has been cast on this by Edward Rosen in "Calvin's Attitude to Copernicus, *J.H.I.*, 21 (1960): 431–41; 22 (1961): 386–88. Had Calvin known the astronomer's book, it may be asked if he could have resisted its mathematical compulsion. See also W. H. Coates, H. V. White, and J. S. Shapiro, *The Emergence of Liberal Humanism*, vol. 1: *From the Italian Renaissance to the French Revolution* (New York: McGraw-Hill, 1966), pp. 78–80.

[19] See Calvin's reply to his teaching as "new" in his "Prefatory Address to King Francis I," Calvin's *Institutes*, Library of Christian Classics,

ness of their claim that was new. For the Twentieth Century, it may suffice to call attention to Professor Herbert Weisinger's article "The Attack on the Renaissance in Theology Today."[20] Catholics, Hebrews, Greek Orthodox, and Protestants are hostile to this principle (p. 176). Representative are Berdyaev (p. 177), Gilson (p. 178), Reinhold Niebuhr (pp. 179, 181–82). Almost all agree on condemning Renaissance science, especially Descartes (pp. 181–82).[21] Many of the detractors have made valuable contributions to religion in our times, but as Renaissancists they are arguing for a doubtful case.[22]

A man's autonomy in religion strengthens autonomy in his work, whether as poet, philologist, biologist, etc. It can also enlarge the vision of his work, as well as his sense of responsibility. Thus he becomes truly "sovereign in his sphere."[23]

21:14–18. Other charges are that it is "doubtful and uncertain," "unconfirmed by miracles," "against . . . many holy fathers . . . and most ancient custom," "it is schismatic," and produces "a heap of sects." McNeill, Library of Christian Classics, 20:16, n. 8, says, "These were staple arguments against Luther and other reformers from the beginning" (see his references). Allen G. Chester, "On 'The New Learning': A Semantic Note," *Studies in the Renaissance*, 2 (1955): 139–67. The modern use of the term to refer to the revival of classical learning, says Chester, came after the publication of two influential books: Frederic Seebohm's *The Oxford Reformers* in 1862 (with an important section called "The Rise of the New Learning 1453–1492") and J. R. Green's *Short History of the English People* in 1874 (with a section "The New Learning 1509–1520"). Chester suggests that the original meaning of the term would exclude Bishop Fisher and Sir Thomas More; though he approves of the modern interpretation as "useful." *Ibid.*, p. 146.

[20] Herbert Weisinger, "The Attack on the Renaissance in Theology Today," *Studies in the Renaissance*, 2 (1955): 176–89.

[21] See J. Maritain, *The Dream of Descartes* (New York: Philosophical Library, 1944), who gives a clear, though very critical, discussion.

[22] Besides, e.g., the idea that "scientism began with the Renaissance" is hardly tenable. During our Christian era it was already begun by a medieval man (Averroes, d. 1195), the excitement of whose "scientific physics" not even the Thomistic synthesis diminished. See, E. Cassirer, "G. Pico della Mirandola," *J.H.I.*, 3 (April, 1942): 134–36.

[23] An approximate translation of Abraham Kuyner's "souvereiniteit in eigen kring." Somewhere in this essay I should make clear that the reformers' claim to autonomy in religion did not imply lack of responsiveness to the ecumene, to the testimony of history, and such. It astonishes how much they retained of traditional Christianity. A crucial issue,

So much for parallels with autonomy in the Renaissance and Reformation. We turn now to the relation of the reformers to philosophy, particularly to that of the Florentine Academy.

Professor Roy W. Battenhouse has presented a pertinent discussion of it in his article "The Doctrine of Man in Calvin and in Renaissance Platonism,"[24] which has been justly praised as "stimulating and perceptive."[25] Battenhouse cites Calvin's connection with Marguerite of Navarre and her circle as an influence, and P. Jourda (building on Abel Lefranc) describes the intense interest of Marguerite in Platonism, in Plethon and Ficino. In 1530 the interest was greatly increased, and it was in the early 1530's that Calvin was of the circle.[26] It is also known that Oronce Fine (1495–1555) was of the circle; he was a mathematician who in the last months of 1530 began teaching at the Lecteurs Royaux,[27] that is, when Calvin attended there. Well-known Calvinists appear to have been admirers of the Florentine Platonists. Battenhouse names Philip Mornay (1549–1623)[28] and Edmund Spenser (1552–99).[29] Similar harmony existed between Milton and the Cambridge Platonists. For Luther, reference is made to A. W.

however, was the right to *libre examen* and *libertas prophetandi*. Comparisons of the Reformation as progressive and the Catholic Church as stagnant are often odious and senseless. While the latter condemned Protestant autonomy, it was a rare Protestant that realized the importance of the Catholic Church's preservation of the idea of a legal structure for a universal Christianity, which is as important in its kind as having an effective international law. Not even Calvin could structure a Church polity which provided for a face-to-face confrontation of representatives of all bodies and institutions of ecumenical Christianity.

[24] Roy W. Battenhouse, "The Doctrine of Man in Calvin and in Renaissance Platonism," *J.H.I.*, 9 (1948): 447–71.

[25] C. Trinkhaus, "Renaissance Problems in Calvin's Theology," *Studies in the Renaissance*, 1 (1954): 59.

[26] P. Jourda, *Marguerite d' Angoulême, Duchesse d'Alençon, Reine de Navarre (1492–1549)* (Paris, 1930), pp. 1032–35.

[27] *Ibid.*, p. 1035.

[28] Mornay was called the "Huguenot Pope," largely because of his influence on Henry IV before the latter's turning Catholic.

[29] For discussion touching Spenser, see Baker, *Dignity of Man*, pp. 52–53.

Huizinger, *Luthers Neuplatonismus in der Psalmen Vorlesung von 1513–1516* (Naumberg, a.s., 1905).[30]

On Zwingli, there is more direct evidence. S. M. Jackson says that Zwingli's first "emancipator" was G. Pico della Mirandola (1463–94). During 1502–6 he studied in Basel; it was there he is known to have approved certain of the thirteen condemned theses of Pico's 900 Theses, and in 1510 he was "still interested in Pico." [31] There is the famous passage in Zwingli's *An Exposition of the Faith*, in the section on "Eternal Life." [32]

> . . . You may expect to see the communion and fellowship of all the saints and sages and believers and the steadfast and brave and the good who have ever lived since the world began. You will see the two Adams, the redeemed and the Redeemer, Abel, Enoch [and twenty other Biblical persons]; Hercules, too, and Theseus, Socrates, Aristides, Antigonus, Numa, Camillus, the Catos and Scipios.[33] . . . In short there has not lived a single good man . . . from the beginning of the world to the end, which you will not see there in the presence of God.[34]

[30] Battenhouse, *"Doctrine of Man,"* p. 448.

[31] S. M. Jackson, *Huldreich Zwingli: The Reformer of German Switzerland 1484–1531* (New York: G. P. Putnam's Sons, 1901), pp. 84–85. Jean Rilliet, *Zwingli: Third Man of the Reformation*, trans. Harold Knight (Philadelphia: Westminster Press, 1964), p. 37, reports that Pico della Mirandola was represented in Zwingli's library in 1516, and G. Oorthuys, *De Anthropologie van Zwingli* (Leiden: E. J. Brill, 1905), pp. 10, 35 f, discusses his Platonism.

[32] G. W. Bromiley, ed., *Zwingli and Bullinger*, Library of Christian Classics, vol. 24 (Philadelphia: Westminster Press, 1953), pp. 75–76.

[33] In January of 1531, the year of his death, Zwingli and his compatriots of Zurich staged the *Pluto* of Aristophanes in Greek. Zwingli composed the music for it, perhaps the overture and more certainly the choral pieces. See Charles Garside, Jr., "The Literary Evidence of Zwingli's Musicianship," *Archiv für Reformationsgeschichte*, 48, no. 1 (1957): 71–74. The author acknowledges the help of the only work on the subject, Arnold Hug, *Aufführung einer Griechischen Komödie in Zürich, 1 Januarie 1531* (Zürich: Höhr, 1874).

[34] The editor remarks that Zwingli's "thinking always included a persistent and fundamentally perhaps an *alien* [my italics], humanistic element." — Bromiley, *Zwingli and Bullinger*, p. 243. Anent the inclusion of pagan worthies, the editor (in n. 64, p. 349) says, "Luther at-

This may remind one of Pico's "syncretism." [35] Zwingli's writing on the Providence of God begins with a quotation from Pico's Oration on the Dignity of Man.[36]

As to Calvin and the Florentine thinkers, Professor Battenhouse has shown that for language and imagery Calvin in many places is in their debt. What of his substance? Battenhouse takes up his doctrines of depravity (pp. 451–53), of faith (453), the image of God (454–56), the relation of soul and body (457–59), the Incarnation (459–61), revelation (461–63), the history of salvation as a drama (463–65), in-the-world asceticism (465–67), and eschatology (467–69). Battenhouse describes his comparisons as "frankly exploratory and tentative," and he suggests that Calvin's turning to theology and from "reason to revelation seems to have been a rejection more often of conclusions than of basic definitions and conclusions" (469). Historians of Platonism and of theology should assess all this, for the comparisons are impressive.

Calvin's frequent use of Neoplatonic idiom alone makes one wonder how he acquired it. One can reasonably think of his connection with Marguerite of Navarre and her court.[37] The period of this connection issued in his conversion to Luther's doctrine. If there was a relation between the circle's conversations about Ficino and Pico, and the conversion, it might appear that in it there would be a parallel with St. Augustine's experience, for whom the route to conversion also went

---

tacked the idea as itself pagan . . . although he [Luther] had hazarded a similar view in his sermon on Genesis 20 [*W. A.*, 24:364 f.]."

[35] It used to be common to speak of Pico as a mere syncretist. Important qualifications were made by E. Anagnine, *G. Pico della Mirandola: syncretismo religioso-philosofico* (Bari: G. Laterza & Figli, 1937), and especially by E. Garin, *Giovanni Pico della Mirandola, vita e dottrina* (Florence: F. Le Monnier, 1937). Ernst Cassirer, "G. Pico della Mirandola: A Study in the History of Renaissance Ideas," *J.H.I.*, 3 (April, 1942): 123–44, argues persuasively for Pico's syncretism as having inner philosophical coherence. See also the important paper of Paul Oskar Kristeller, "The Sources of G. Pico della Mirandola," in *L'Opera e il Pensiero di G. Pico della Mirandola nella Storia dell' Umanesimo* in Convegno Internazionale (see above, n. 1).

[36] Battenhouse, "Doctrine of Man," p. 448.

[37] See above, notes 26–27.

through philosophy. At eighteen he knew only rhetoric, then read Cicero's Hortensius (in praise of wisdom), which was the first step. Then, when after his Manichaean period he had become a skeptic, he read "the books of the Platonists (Neoplatonists rather). Then came the conversion.[38] Calvin had labored over his *De Clementia* commentary, as a philologist, with his whole mind. His book was published in April of 1532. It did not sell,[39] but this could not have motivated his conversion. He still kept his reverence for the church,[40] but he may have felt "at loose ends." Then he fell in with Marguerite's circle. Was this his first effective exposure to philosophy? There is no record of any earlier, except that of the Scholastic at Paris (which seems not to have set him on fire). It may be assumed that young Calvin read in the Florentines, though he does not mention any. The conversations and reading in the Marguerite circle may have shaken him; they may have been an important factor in disintegrating his reverence for the church.[41]

In his Oration on the Dignity of Man (Cassirer *et al.*, *The Renaissance Philosophy of Man*), Pico addresses the scholars of his time, inviting them to debate on his 900 Theses. He is aware of a common opinion that he is too presumptuous, especially because of his youth: "I was born I admit but twenty-four years ago." Incidentally, Calvin was perhaps twenty-three when he entered the circle of Marguerite. Pico makes a moving statement of the compelling force of philosophy; who

[38] Augustine *Confessions* 7. 9, 20.

[39] Q. Breen, *John Calvin: A Study in French Humanism* (Grand Rapids, Mich.: Eerdmans, 1931), pp. 92–93.

[40] See note 12 above.

[41] All this is mostly speculative. Still one can sense an influence of Pico. Calvin wrote against judicial astrology (*Inst.* 1. 16. 3), besides a tract against it in French (see McNeill's n. 8, p. 201). Calvin did not oppose it for the same reason as Pico, however. See E. Cassirer, "G. Pico della Mirandola," *J.H.I.*, 3 (1942): 338–44. There was also the eloquent assertion of Man's prerogative to determine his own destiny, in the Oration, which may help to account for Calvin's way of dealing with man's freedom. See Cassirer, "G. Pico della Mirandola," pp. 123–44, 319–46. The most accessible translation of Pico's Oration is in E. Cassirer, P. O. Kristeller, and J. H. Randall, Jr., *The Renaissance Philosophy of Man* (Chicago: University of Chicago Press, 1956), pp. 223–54.

teaches it for money has lost it: "Philosophy herself has taught me to rely on my own conscience rather than on the opinions of others . . ." (par. 22). "Surely it is the part of a narrow mind to have confirmed itself within a single Porch or Academy" (par. 26). "What were the gain if only the philosophy of the Latins were investigated, that is, of Albert [the Great], Thomas [Aquinas], [Duns] Scotus?" (par. 28). "It is surely an ignoble part to be wise only from one notebook (as Seneca said) and, as if the discoveries of our predecessors had closed the way to our own industry and power of nature were exhausted in us, to produce from ourselves nothing which, if it doesn't actually demonstrate the truth, at least intimates it from afar — a tiller of the soil hates infertility in his field, and a husband in his wife . . ." (par. 28). No humanist philologist and rhetorician ever spake thus, unless he was also a philosopher.[42] Though no direct evidence is known of Calvin's having read Pico's Oration, it is hard to believe that he had not. In any case, it was the spirit of philosophical autonomy manifested in Pico, it can be assumed, that made possible his conversion. One may believe that Calvin had felt the attraction of Luther's position before, but always *reverentia ecclesiae* had stood in the way. This reverence had to be dissolved if conversion should occur. Philosophy would be a solvent. The philosophical aspect of the conversion also helps account for the change of profession. Though he continued to admire the classics, he no longer would devote himself to them as a professional humanist.[43] His profession would be that of theologian,[44] to reassess or rethink the Christian religion.

[42] How different was Melanchthon, who in effect said that all philosophy had been treated by the ancients and that consequently no new problems should be raised in the university disputations. See Q. Breen, "The Twofold Truth Theory in Melanchthon," *Review of Religion* (1945), pp. 120–32, for discussion of his "Leges Academiae Wittenbergensis," *Corp. Ref.* 10. 992–1024.

[43] Melanchthon remained professionally a professor of Greek.

[44] I assume that theology is philosophy as to spirit and method. The fruitfulness of this assumption has been shown by Professor H. A. Wolfson in his *Philo* and in his *The Philosophy of the Church Fathers.* See my review of the latter in *Encounter*, vol. 22, no. 4 (1961), esp. pp. 391–418 (Christian Theological Seminary, Indianapolis, Ind.).

In our view, this began in Marguerite's circle; at least there is no other clue to the provenance of the language and imagery of the Florentines in Calvin's writings. His tract against the Nicodemites[45] was aimed against a "progressive" group in France, who were friendly to reform but outwardly conformed to the Catholic Church. Bohatec has shown that among others Marguerite was one of them.[46] Perhaps some were his old associates of 1533. In any case, Calvin had gone far beyond them.

In a general assessment of Platonism in Calvin, we say that to hold he was predominantly a Platonist is as serious an error as to hold that Augustine was more a Platonist than a Christian. The language and imagery are there, such as the body is the soul's prison; but such had been used for centuries by Christians. Even St. Paul's "body of this death" must not be taken too literally. As we see it, the importance of Calvin's brush with the Florentines is that they as philosophers opened the way to a freedom necessary to conversion.[47]

This section tells of the influence on the Reformation of that particular Renaissance humanism which pertained to the revival of the classical languages and literatures. It was more

[45] See notes 25–26.

[46] J. Bohatec, *Budé und Calvin, Studien Zur Gedankenwelt des französischen Frühhumanismus* (Graz: H. Böhlaus Nachf., 1950); relevant are pp. 142–48 to Marguerite and her circle, the character of its men, the popularity in it of Ficino and Pico; see pp. 271–72 for parallels in Pico and Calvin with respect to astrology.

[47] Calvin was far from being a Neoplatonist, but like Augustine he was not untouched by it. For one thing, the Florentines, animated by the true philosophical spirit, helped shatter his awe of the church. Then both from his preference for Plato among the philosophers and from St. Augustine as his favorite among the Fathers he derived that uncertainty about the status of nature characteristic of Platonism. Hence comes that preponderance of concern with the deity of Christ over his humanity; in fact the reformers generally suffer from a touch of practical if not theoretical Monophysitism. Calvin was in line with the classical position of Christian doctrine in beginning the *Institutes* with the loci of God the Father as creator and providence. For a fuller discussion of the conversion, see J. T. McNeill, *The History and Character of Calvinism* (New York: Oxford University Press, 1967), pp. 107–18.

than that: the humanists were a professional class of scholars who saw in these a world of knowledge, of well-defined and well-exemplified moral virtue, and of refinement, which they strove to comprehend and transmit.[48] The Latin mainly pre-occupied the humanists during the first century (c. 1300–1400),[49] the Greek was almost entirely recovered by A.D. 1500.[50] A good humanist was a hard worker. He had to acquire command of Latin vocabulary and grammar for speaking and writing, with many rivals ready to blacken his name because of scholarly shortcomings. Often he had to work with bad manuscript copies, emendation of which was often long and painful.[51] By his commentaries on the classics the students learned what use to make of them.[52] There were dictionaries and grammars to make, besides model letters and orations (declamations). Knowledge of antiquity was mainly from literature, which was taken up in courses in grammar, poetry, rhetoric, history, and moral philosophy.[53] It was reckoned thus to provide a rounded education and produce a man of sound intelligence, moral sense, and refined taste. Late in the fifteenth century a professor of classical language and literature was called a "humanist."[54] Besides showing that in

[48] There was a certain awe of the classical writers, a reverence for their memory, manifested in the thrill felt when Livy's bones were recovered, and the shock at Malatesta's destruction of Virgil's statue.

[49] Petrarch (1304–74) had predecessors, e.g., Albertino Mussato in Padua and Giovanni del Virgilio in Bologna. But, though a second generation humanist, Petrarch far excelled those who had gone before. See Kristeller, *Eight Philosophers*, p. 162.

[50] Manuel Chrysloloras began it in Florence (1396).

[51] See e.g., W. H. Woodward, *Vittorino da Feltre and Other Humanist Educators* (New York: Columbia University Press, 1963), pp. 10–13, for Gasparino Barzizza (at Padua 1407–14, then at Venice), who was "the first to approach Cicero in a thoroughly scholarly spirit."

[52] There is no reason to think that the humanist neglected the knowledge content of the classics, but in his commentaries stress was given to philology – text criticism, style, varieties of saying the same thing, and so on.

[53] See Kristeller, *Eight Philosophers*, pp. 150–56; also, *idem*, *Renaissance Thought* (New York: Harper Torchbook, 1961), and *Renaissance Thought II* (New York: Harper Torchbook, 1965).

[54] Late fifteenth century student slang corresponding to *artista, legista.* Kristeller, *Eight Philosophers*, pp. 150 f., also his "Humanism and

general the profession of teacher was considered to be *the* humanist's profession,[55] it possibly indicated that his courses were associated with the all-around well-trained man, who because of having become *humanus* was better as a man (homo).[56] It suggests the Platonic ideal of obtaining virtue through knowledge. It could also describe Erasmus' view.

Were the humanists' educational aims compatible with the Christian religion? Some humanists had doubts, even though they continued to pursue them. Petrarch implied uncertainty in his dialogue with St. Augustine about his sonnets to Laura and his desire for post-mortem fame, and again in his reading from the *Confessions* upon reaching the summit of Mt. Ventoux. Rudolph Agricola (1444–85) had gone to Ferrara to perfect his Greek under Battista Guarino, but within a year he decided to switch to Hebrew so as to occupy himself with the "worthier" substance of the Old Testament.[57] On the other hand, there were humanists who were certain on this point, exemplifaction of which was Vittorino da Feltre (1378–1446). So serious was he about religion that till he was forty-five he was debating whether to become a monk, and throughout his entire distinguished career as a teacher faithfulness to, and reverence for, religion provided motivations no less than love of learning for the development of his remarkably attractive character.[58]

Scholasticism in the Italian Renaissance," in *Renaissance Thought: The Classical, Humanist, and Scholastic Strains* (New York: Harper Torchbook, 1961). Revealing is Augusto Compana, "The Origin of the Word 'Humanist,'" *Journal of the Warburg and Courtauld Institutes*, 9 (1946): 60–73; at the time of writing his article, Campana had suspected but not found the word "humanist" in writings prior to 1500. On pp. 68 and 73 he tells of Kristeller's having found the word in a manuscript letter of 1490.

[55] See Eugene Rice's Foreword to Woodward, *Vittorino da Feltre*, p. viii.

[56] Vittorino regarded a humanistic training in letters the best for those aspiring to the graduate courses "in law, Medicine, Theology, or the public service, . . . the finest preparation for a life of dignity and usefulness in their several callings." – Woodward, *Vittorino da Feltre*, p. 59; see also *ibid.*, pp. 37, 60–61.

[57] See Q. Breen, "Melanchthon's Sources for a Life of Rudolph Agricola," *Archiv für Reformationsgeschichte*, 52 (1961): 58–73.

[58] W. H. Woodward, *Vittorino de Feltre*, pp. 48–49, 58, 67, 92.

To Vittorino, of course, religion meant to be a serious Catholic. In the Reformers' experience this amounted to salvation by works. There remained, however, the humanist's ideal of virtue through knowledge, which justified his educational curriculum. This curriculum was largely taken over by the Reformers for their colleges; like Vittorino, they held this curriculum to be an adequate prerequisite for the ministerial, legal, and medical professions' training. What interests us at this point, however, is whether the Reformers in any sense recognized the humanist's belief of "virtue through knowledge." Could a man who had a college degree or its equivalent, however obtained, be better as a man for it? And being a better man, would he, if a Christian, be a better Christian? It was an old question, argued much in the ancient church.[59]

A fundamental question concerns the status of the order of nature, e.g., natural reason and what springs from it: classical literature. In general the Reformers defend such learning as useful for understanding the Bible and the Fathers.[60] But this sort of defense was as old as hermeneutics. The question raised by Professor Rice is pertinent: whether the Renaissance had produced a new, say, eighteenth-century, concept of wisdom as having a status in its own right as a secular wisdom apart from its apologetic or other use.[61]

There is reason to hold that Calvin defends the autonomy of secular learning. Particular reference is made to the *Institutes* 2. 2. 13–17. To realize the full import of these sections, one must appreciate the significance of Calvin's devotion as a

[59] Jaeger, *Early Christianity and Greek Paideia.* The expression "better Christian" is perhaps unfortunate, for there are various gifts. There are St. Francises and St. Bonaventures, Thomas à Kempises and Erasmuses.

[60] E.g., Hieronymus Zanchius, the sixteenth century Reformed theologian (1516–90), explains the importance of the distinction between literal and figurative speech for interpretation of Scripture, particularly with respect to "This is my body" for a proper understanding of the Lord's Supper. See Q. Breen, *Mario Nizolio: De Veris Principiis et Vera Ratione Philosophandi contra Pseudophilosophos* (Rome: Fratelli Bocca, 1956), p. lvi.

[61] Eugene Rice, *The Renaissance Idea of Wisdom* (Cambridge: Harvard University Press, 1958).

professional humanist to the classical literature, intensive investigation of whose fuller import has till recently not been made.[62] As of 1532, when his Seneca Commentary was publicized, Calvin gives no reason to suppose that he was concerned about a religious reason for his classical enthusiasm. His conversion involved a reassessment of everything, not only his relation to the Catholic church, but also his humanist profession. The latter meant that he had to consider whether the classical literature was in its kind as important as the preaching of the Gospel.

In effect the answer was yes, and it is given in the *Institutes* 2. 2. 15. Here he praises the secular learning of the classical (*profani*) writers: jurists, philosophers of nature,[63] dialecticians, physicians, mathematicians. Their writings are "God's excellent gifts." To "reject" or "despise" them is to "dishonor the Spirit of God." To hold in light esteem the gifts of the Spirit is to "contemn and reproach [or disgrace] the Spirit himself. We cannot read the writings of the ancients on these subjects without great admiration. We marvel at them because we are *compelled* [I italicize] to recognize how preeminent they are. . . . Let us, therefore, be ashamed of such *ingratitude*, into which not even the pagans fell, for they confessed that the gods had invented philosophy, laws, and all the useful arts." (2. 2. 15.)

Important are two words: "compelled" and "ingratitude." Calvin is "compelled" to admire the classical writers. This is on a line with his statement of not wanting to go against common sense (section 13). In addition, it appears that his response to the Spirit's terrestrial gifts is as irresistible as his response to the truth of the Scripture. In each case his response is to the same spirit. As a believer he accepts the testimony of the Holy Spirit concerning the Scripture's truth, as one of the

[62] See the pioneer work of Dr. A. M. Hugo, *Calvijn en Seneca: Een inleidende studie van Calvijns Commentar op Seneca, De Clementia, Anno 1532* (Gronigen: J. B. Wolters, 1957). In press is a much larger work on the Seneca Commentary by A. M. Hugo and F. L. Battles.

[63] Calvin here admires only the philosophers who presented "fine observation and artful description of nature." The omission of the Platonistic seems deliberate.

human race he is a theist because the Spirit has endowed him with a sense of divinity.[64] Besides, not to recognize God as the source of the good in the classics is to be ungrateful, which to Calvin is the blackest of the vices.

Calvin's discourse about this as a theologian is not always clear. Thus he distinguishes the natural gifts as a "good" from the celestial as the "true good."[65] Again, he says the natural gifts of God are gifts of God's "grace," a term that cannot well be separated from the idea of the tender love of God for sinners; yet he regards the non-elect as objects of God's continuous wrath.[66] Moreover, Calvin's doctrine of depravity is such the good things produced by the noblest among the non-elect cannot possibly spring from their natures as men.[67]

Yet the record of *Institutes* (2. 2. 13–17) stands. It is such a spirited statement—so eloquent, so pointed in its rhetorical questions—that his defense could scarcely be stronger. It is as if he were answering objections to his continuous love of classical learning, objections of men who wondered about its consistency with evangelical zeal, consistency also with his doctrine of depravity, and whether it would not have been enough for him to approve the form but not the content of the classics.

We take it that he did not come to the conclusion of 2. 2.

[64] Dowey, *Calvin's Theology*, pp. 50–56, probes Calvin's idea of *sensus divinitatis* with much good sense.

[65] Calvin's expostulation that only the "celestial" are the "true Good" cannot cancel out that a terrestrial good coming from God is, of its kind, good in quality as the celestial; it is as much a true good as the celestial. Calvin's experience with the classics is the elemental thing. His apprehension or fear of equating the terrestrial with the celestial is afterthought.

[66] Calvin's use of the word "grace" in this context is bothersome, and in view of his idea of double-predestination it is inexcusable; unless we take him to mean that although the non-elect are expendable, the divine gifts to them are not expendable. It is also possible that Calvin means to adopt Scriptural language for God's goodness to all men. Calvin the commentator of Scripture also here would take precedence over Calvin the systematic theologian. This would confirm the view of Wendel, *Calvin: Sources*, pp. 354–60. See also E. Harris Harbison, *The Christian Scholar in the Age of the Reformation* (New York: Charles Scribner's Sons, 1956), p. 156.

[67] See *Institutes* 2. 2. 3.

13–17 at once upon conversion. These sections do not appear in the first edition of the *Institutes* (1536). If he had by then so concluded, the feeling manifest in these sections would have prompted their expression in 1536. They appear first in the second edition (1539). This was seven years after the *Seneca Commentaries*. The sections would remain in every subsequent edition.

Calvin's religious defense of humanistic classical studies implied at least two things. First, for the believer it meant that he could be in conscience free in the pursuit of the higher learning. He could conceive it as his calling or profession which, in its kind, was as holy as the minister's in its kind. Second, secular learning was to be cultivated in accordance with its nature. Thus in the natural sciences, natural reason should have its way.

It is interesting to observe that, in his defense, Calvin does not adduce a celestial argument for the terrestrial or secular learning. He is compelled to recognize the good substance of the classics for what it is, and because it is good it must be from God. Of course, he used what he knew from literature to interpret Scripture, but he could be doubly confident of such use because in itself it was good.

Calvin made a significant breakthrough for the good right of the Renaissance secularistic emphasis.[68]

The humanists were the beginners of modern philology.[69] Petrarch exemplified it brilliantly in his textual criticism and

[68] As said in note 60, the breakthrough was not coherently stated, but it was fundamental because it was based on a religious experience. See Hendrikus Berkhof, *The Doctrine of the Holy Spirit* (Richmond, Va.: John Knox Press, 1964), pp. 100–104, where suggestive ideas are developed concerning the relation of the Holy Spirit to the sciences and arts and, in fact, to modern "secularism."

[69] There was a medieval philology, especially in the twelfth century. See Beryl Smalley, *The Study of the Bible in the Middle Ages* (Notre Dame, Ind.: University of Notre Dame Press, 1964), particularly chap. 4: "Andrew of St. Victor." To acknowledge the triumphs of humanist scholarship does not warrant depreciation of the medieval. In general it was not philological. Medieval scholars are generally more concerned

emendations of a manuscript text of Livy. Even more distinguished was Lorenzo Valla (1406–57), whose philological labors were approved by the Reformers.[70]

The philologist's concern with linguistics had an aesthetic aspect—his good taste was formed by attentive reading of Latin classics. In a lecture on Petrarch, Professor Chandler B. Beall[71] said that when Petrarch read Cicero he heard bells ringing in his head. The humanist was offended by the indifference of scholastics to style and to the general boorishness of much everyday Latin. Leonardo Bruni (1396–1444) admonished a young woman to be "supremely careful in our choice of authors, lest a . . . debased style . . . degrade our taste," and warned against reading authors who are "utterly destitute of sound and melodious style."[72] Perhaps even more important was the growth of a conviction that has been the best line of defense for philology, namely, that a document has, so to say, a moral right to be seen in its original form and to be understood in the light of its time. Ever increasing prominence was given to the thesis that content and form are equally important. Renaissance philology had its foes to contest this (as

with content. To appreciate the difference between the two, compare the twelfth-century glossators of the Corpus Juris Civilis with the humanist specialists in Roman Law. See Q. Breen, "The Twelfth Century Revival of Roman Law," *Oregon Law Review*, 24 (March, 1945): 224–87; and "Renaissance Humanism and the Roman Law," *ibid.*, 38 (1959): 289–302.

[70] On Petrarch and Valla, see Giuseppe Billanovich, "Petrarch and the Textual Tradition of Livy," *Journal of the Warburg and Courtauld Institutes*, 14 (1951): 137–208, and his "Le 'Emendationes in T. Livium del Valla' e il Codex Regius di Livio," *Italia Medioevale e umanistica*, 1 (1958): 245–64. The Reformers were indebted to Valla's "In Novum Testamentum Annotationes," published by Erasmus in 1505. They naturally approved his exposé of the Donation of Constantine. For a brief but useful account of Valla, see Harbison, *Christian Scholar*, pp. 43–49. Harbison also shows (p. 47, and n. 19) that recent scholars hold Valla's loyalties were definitely Christian (e.g., Mancini, Toffanin, Trinkhaus, Grimm).

[71] Professor of Italian at the University of Oregon and editor of *Comparative Literature*.

[72] "Concerning the Study of Literature: A Letter Addressed to the Illustrious Lady, Battista Malatesta," in Woodward, *Vittorino da Feltre*, pp. 124, 127.

Jerome had in Augustine for some twenty years),[73] and the battle still goes on.

In matters of taste there should be no dispute, but the goodness of "good" taste may be used without judgment. While still at Tübingen young Melanchthon hoped to join in a venture to translate Aristotle's Greek into elegant Latin, because Cicero had spoken of Aristotle's "golden stream of eloquence."[74] Taste also influenced doctrine. Thus Calvin argued against a literal eating of the "body" in the Eucharist, because it seemed in bad taste;[75] thus aesthetics played a role in determining that "this is my body" must be figurative speech.

As a philologist Calvin made significant use as a Scripture commentator of what he called "accommodation," which in effect was a recognition of what today is called form criticism. He speaks of "Moses accommodating himself to the rudeness of the common folk";[76] again, God "accommodated himself to men's capacity, which is variable and changeable."[77] To the piety of the Reformer, and to that of modern Christian scholars, it has seemed outrageous that God should be limited to only a straight literalness in revealing his mind; in fact, it would be impeaching his sovereignty. Calvin was convinced that God teaches men at whatever level they stand and in accordance with their understanding. A sixteenth-century Reformer could perhaps not imagine the lengths to which the principle of accommodation would be applied today, but it allows of them nevertheless. As a hermeneutical method, it would not be alien to R. Bultmann's "demythologization." So much for the humanists (and Reformers) as scholars.[78]

[73] See Harbison, *Christian Scholar*, pp. 18–19.

[74] Cicero says this in *Acad. Quaest.* 2. 38, 119, stating that the style of writing of the younger Aristotle was now a lost art. We know that Melanchthon's (and our) Aristotle has no golden style.

[75] *Calvin's Tracts Relating to the Reformation*, trans. Henry Beveridge (Edinburgh: T. & T. Clark, 1846–60), 2:518. See discussion in Breen, *John Calvin*, pp. 148–53.

[76] *Inst.* 1. 14. 3.

[77] *Inst.* 2. 11. 13. See also 1. 18. 13; 2. 7. 2, and McNeill's note 3; 2. 16. 2; 3. 18. 9; and "In Vera Ecclesiae Reformandae Ratio," *Corp. Ref.* 7. 44, where he says the important thing is the "spiritual truth."

[78] The humanists as philologists, whether Catholic or Protestant, were

The humanists not rarely considered themselves as mentors of society, in the meaning expressed by Isocrates, Cicero, and Quintilian.[79] Their ideal man was the orator who, as conversant in all learning, human and divine, and who, by nature and nurture having become eloquent, could lead society to desirable goals. To guide society by speech was eminently civilized, for the alternative was force or violence. Athens was the home of eloquence.[80] When her independence was lost, oratory became declamation, and so it was under the Roman Empire.[81] In medieval times, deliberative speech revived in connection with the communes; the so-called *ars arengandi* now could be adapted for a public which was undertaking something new (non-ecclesiastical and non-noble): the third estate was coming into being. When by about A.D. 1400 Italian towns had come to be ruled by despots, deliberative oratory was again lost, except in Florence. As illustration of our present thesis

the most eminent scholarly class. The effort was immense whereby they mastered classical languages and literatures, wrote lexicons, grammars, and commentaries. This brought them great prestige. When such men became Reformers their reform message might shock many but it was *heard.* See Harbison, *Christian Scholar*; for Luther's scholarship see Robert H. Fife, *The Revolt of Martin Luther* (New York: Columbia University Press, 1957). To the extent that they were humanists, Catholic and Protestant scholars spoke and wrote with respect for each other, though in religion they were enemies. Alardus of Amsterdam, who wrote violent pamphlets against Protestants, carried on amicable correspondence with Melanchton about scholarly interests. See Q. Breen, "Melanchthon's Sources for a Life of Rudolph Agricola," *Archiv für Reformationgeschichte*, vol. 52 (1961).

[79] See the Loeb Classics for the works of Isocrates, translated and edited by George Norlin, whose Introduction (vol. 1) is informative and suggestive. For Cicero, *The Orator* is important, and for Quintilian, *The Institutions of Oratory*, bk. 12.

[80] The Sophist movement arose in the Age of Pericles, who in certain respects exemplifies the orator's role at its best. Athens was as truly a democracy as any town ever has been; so to say, laboratory conditions for testing the potential of eloquence were ideal.

[81] This statement about declamation is too broad. There are three kinds of oratory: (1) forensic or court-room, which could be free even under despotic public law; (2) epideictic, pertaining to praise or blame, which could take turns in which freedom was not altogether lost; (3) deliberative, or having to do especially with politics, whose freedom was gone. All three flourished under the Roman Republic, but deliberative oratory was lost under the empire.

this exception of Florence is important. The Visconti "empire" suddenly collapsed with Giangalleazzo's death in 1402. Throughout the years of crisis and decades afterward some of the chief spokesmen for liberty were humanists. Such humanists are known as civic humanists.[82] They contributed much to the fame of Florence as the Athens of Italy. Civic humanists were the Moderns; those who did not participate in civic life but remained aloof in their ivory towers were the Classicists. The latter [the Classicists) could pursue their philological studies both under a despotism and in a free city alike. They could be good tutors at despotic courts. But they contributed almost nothing to that freedom which is necessary for great rhetoric to live.[83] For our immediate purpose, however, the Modernists interest us, particularly those like Bruni who gave Florence her great reputation.

There is a rough analogy between Florence and the towns made notable by the Reformers: Wittenberg, Zürich, and Geneva. These were the centers from which they spoke and wrote; they were, so to say, the capital cities of their more or less extensive realms or spheres of influence. Each, especially

[82] The best study of the survival of freedom in Florence under conditions of the acute crisis brought on by Giangalleazzo Visconti's imperialism is Hans Baron, *The Crisis of the Early Italian Renaissance*, 1st ed., 1955; 2d ed. rev. (Princeton: Princeton University Press, 1966). Confirming much and supplementing Baron's first book is what Baron calls a "fundamental work": Lauro Martines, *The Social World of the Florentine Humanists, 1390–1460* (Princeton: Princeton University Press, 1963), which shows from archival documents that humanists' participation in civic life went beyond A.D. 1402 for decades, also that they were at times most signally honored.

[83] Some of the greatest humanists were Classicists rather than Moderns: Petrarch, Valla, Erasmus, whose accomplishments argue sufficiently that the Classicists were not to be scorned. Averse to civic involvement, they produced no oratory espousing a political cause in the marketplace, so to say. They did make declamations, however, on many occasions such as funerals, opening of the academic year, inauguration of a new pope. Modernists likewise performed at such functions. Historians have often charged the humanists with inflicting on unwilling audiences their long-winded speeches. Professor Kristeller refutes this: "Public oratory was a favorite form of entertainment, comparable to the role played at some time or other by musical or theatrical performances or recitals of poetry." (*Eight Philosophers*, p. 154.)

Wittenberg and Geneva, achieved an immense reputation. This came about because the Reformers were "involved" men. Their involvement was "civic" in the sense that they were respectively identified with their towns,[84] with their compatriots, and with their followers.[85] But their involvement with church reform was a much bigger thing than Bruni's with the liberty of Florence. Their reform called for rethinking and reassessment of all doctrine and polity of the Catholic church, for councils in which their views would be freely aired, and meanwhile the freedom to preach and publish them uncensored. This was a freedom of which the humanists as a professional class had not dreamed, not even the brightest Modernist, let alone the Classicist. It was a freedom comparable to that of the Apologists of the second and third centuries of the church. This demand, fired by religious passion, for *libre examen*, for *libertas prophetandi*, produced great rhetoric. Allowing for excesses, it, like the writings of the Apologists, had something to say. In this sense it can be said that Renaissance rhetoric reaches its apogee in the Reformers.

The following characteristics of humanistic rhetoric had significant relevance to the Reformation:

1. The rhetorician considered speech as man's most distin-

[84] See above, note 33, to which we add George Binder's proud Prologue to the play: "Athens is dumb, silent is Greece, yet Zürich stands; here lingers Attica's Muse. All things are changed by time. Once Hellas shone when Zürich's folk were raw barbarians in the land. Yet now this folk has built an Attic theater. Therefore I present a new Greek proverb to you: Worthless are the other cities around Zürich."

[85] Luther appealed to German patriotic sentiment; we mention here his plea for public schools, in his "Letter to Mayors and Aldermen." Cr. R. Ulich, *3000 Years of Educational Wisdom* (Cambridge: Harvard University Press, 1963), pp. 218–49. Melanchthon earned his title of Preceptor of Germany. Zwingli is justly famous for his opposition to the national demoralization brought on by the Swiss mercenaries. Calvin with his own hand translated his *Institutes* into French (1541), and gave direction to the French Huguenot movement. See R. Kingdon, *Geneva and the Coming Wars of Religion in France* (Geneva: E. Droz, 1956): on p. 128, Professor Kingdon suggests "further studies of the organization of revolutions at other times and places in history – of the role of London in the Puritan revolution, . . . Moscow in the Communist revolutions." We suggest the role of rhetoric is worth looking into.

guishing mark. This contrasts with contemplation idealized by Plato and Aristotle, who said it was man's highest activity. To avoid empty loquacity, eloquence was to be wedded to wisdom, as in Cicero. The orator must be conversant with all learning, human and divine, so that he may be a good leader or mentor of human society. Striking is the parallel with the Protestant preacher, long the best-informed man in his community, for whose training most colleges were founded. His pulpit was the most prominent feature of the church, more often than not replacing the altar altogether. The word prevailed.

2. The art of rhetoric persuades; unlike philosophy it does not aim at convincing. The orator addresses the whole man: mind, feeling, and will, while philosophy addresses the cool mind only. The audience (or reading public) of the orator or rhetorician is not a specially trained group, say, in philosophy; it is a cross section of society, of normal intelligence. The orator may speak on the most important themes of human discourse; yet he must use language a man of average mentality can understand. The orator must be clear in his exposition, keep his hearer's attention by appropriate devices, and persuade to action. The Protestant minister was such a rhetorician. He translated to a cross section of society all the rethinking and reassessment of theology. It has often been pointed out that in the Protestant tradition every layman is likely to be a theologian. Protestantism has been a force in the making of democracy in that it is based on the premise that unspecialized folk can grasp great thinking.

3. According to an influential man like Agricola, rhetoric found the content for a speech by means of dialectic, and dialectic was concerned with probable propositions only. That is, all questions are open ones. The orator must argue on the side of the most probable answer. To be sure, the Protestants held to the existence of absolute truths, and often they thought they had a corner on them. But Protestant splintering proved that belief never died and that definitions and system must remain open.

4. A fact already recognized by Aristotle was that the final

judge[86] of a speech is the audience. Here again the rhetorical posture of Protestantism tended to favor popular institutions. Sometimes we tire of disputatious laymen, so as to wish that theological disputes were held in Latin. But better counsels prevailing, we rather conclude that no specialized group can decide matters of greatest moment for us. Let the people judge![87]

5. Since classical antiquity rhetoricians used common places as sources for content of a speech, they were also cues for remembering. Since Boethius (d. 524 A.D.), no writing on them appeared till Agricola's thoughts[88] on them caught the imagination. Melanchthon, under Luther's influence, used them for interpreting Scripture. In effect, he saw the whole Bible in terms of two commonplaces: law and gospel (or, sin and grace).[89] Their influence on Protestant exegesis was extensive. It is evident that the commonplaces of Luther and Melanchthon reflected intensely personal religious experiences. Others could share these and, besides, add other commonplaces which were highly meaningful to them. Protestant exegesis was motivated by vital concern.[90]

[86] Judge particularly of forensic and deliberative oratory; see Aristotle *Rhetoric* (Loeb Classical Library) 1. 3. 1–3.

[87] Genuine participation of all is an important phase of the modern Catholic concern with the "lay apostolate."

[88] Rudolph Agricola *De Inventione Dialectica* (Cologne, 1539). For a brilliant exposition of the common places, see W. Ong, *Ramus: Method, and the Decay of Dialogue* (Cambridge: Harvard University Press, 1958), chap. 2.

[89] See my "The Terms *Loci Communes* and *Loci* in Melanchthon," *Church History*, 16 (December, 1947): 197–209.

[90] For rhetoric in Calvin, see my "John Calvin and the Rhetorical Tradition," *Church History*, 26 (1957): 3–21.

8

The Religious Initiative in Reformation History

JOHN T. McNEILL

In the study of church history none of us here would be disposed to underestimate the importance of those environmental factors which have often shaped the course of events and the trend of institutional change. A movement once begun may be altered almost out of recognition in a generation or two through the responses it meets in different environments. For this reason we ought to be alert to discern real distinctions between the original character and creative force of any historical movement and its later manifestations and directions of growth. The political, social, and economic involvements of the Reformation, vastly important as they are, ought not to obscure for us the fact of its genesis in the area of religion. In some degree, I believe, the study of the Reformation and of the Counter-Reformation in our day tends to lose clarity and historical soundness through a disinclination to recognize the force of religious experience and thought as an originating element in the vast mutations of history.

The outer fringe of this pattern of historical interpretation is represented by Karl Marx and Friedrich Engels and their disciples. The Marxist theory of history holds that "the production of men's ideas, thinking, their spiritual intercourse appears as the direct efflux of their material condition."[1] *The Communist Manifesto* begins with the dogma: "The history of all hitherto existing societies is the history of class struggles,"[2] and elsewhere Marx ridicules the Young Hegelians for

[1] *K. Marx and F. Engels on Religion* (Moscow: Foreign Language Publication House, 1957), p. 73.

[2] Marx and Engels, *Communist Manifesto*, opening sentence.

"finding the birthplace of history, not in the gross material production of earth, but in the misty cloud formation of heaven."[3] It is very easy, though it is not important for us, to point to certain variations from, and even contradictions of, this doctrinal position. While for Marx it is an oft-reiterated generalization that historical movements arise from material concerns, in some references to Luther he seems to recognize an exception to this rule. Thus in 1844 he wrote in his sententious style: "Luther, we grant, overcame bondage out of devotion by replacing it by bondage out of conviction. He shattered faith in authority because he restored the authority of faith. He turned priests into laymen because he turned laymen into priests." And again, "The Peasant War, the most radical fact of German history, came to grief because of theology."[4]

Thus, in an over-all materialistic interpretation of history, religious impulses thrust themselves into recognition. For Karl Kautsky they had a fascination. Early Christianity was explained as a revolt of the poor against the rich; did not Jesus in the parable of the Rich Man and Lazarus consign the Rich Man to hell?[5] Sixteenth-century left-wing religious communism enlisted Kautsky's eager research.[6] For all Marxists, however, the historical role ascribed to religious phenomena is characteristically not creative but derivative. Religious acts and experiences are the gestures of men in the grasp of economic mechanism. So it comes about that a contemporary Marxist, P. C. Gordon Walker, in an essay of 1937 on "Capitalism and the Reformation" which has been reproduced in a

[3] Quoted by Lewis W. Spitz, ed., *The Reformation, Material or Spiritual* (Boston: D. C. Heath & Co., 1962), p. ix. Cf. *K. Marx and F. Engels on Religion*, pp. 79 f.

[4] *K. Marx and F. Engels on Religion*, p. 61, and (on Luther and Münzer) pp. 107–11.

[5] S. K. Padover, "Kautsky and the Materialistic Interpretation of History," in *Medieval and Historiographical Essays in Honor of James Westfall Thompson*, ed. James Lee Cate and Eugene N. Anderson (Chicago: University of Chicago Press, 1938), pp. 439–64, esp. pp. 458 ff.

[6] Karl Kautsky, *Communism in Central Europe in the Time of the Reformation*, trans. D. L. Milliken and E. G. Milliken (London: Unwin, 1897).

highly useful volume edited by Lewis W. Spitz, can simply ignore virtually all data of a religious color while dogmatically affirming, in a variety of language, that the Reformation was "the reaction to a force external to itself," namely, a prior "industrial revolution" which had wrecked the price structure of former times.[7] This is straightforward and easy to grasp. To be convincing it requires of the reader only that he have an unsullied ignorance of what most men of the time felt and thought and contended for.

The Freudian approach, unlike the Marxist, is concerned with the personal experience of leading figures in the Reformation, and has often been used to seek a verdict against them on the evidence that they suffered from the gravest personality defects and aberrations which discredit all that they thought and did. Since Hartmann Grisar's industrious and detailed assault with psychological weapons on Luther,[8] the Reformer has been psychoanalyzed by numerous experts with somewhat variant results. In agreement with Grisar, Preserved Smith, in an excursion into psychology, stressed, with no serious evidence, Luther's alleged, uncontrollable sexual impulses.[9] Paul J. Reiter in a two-volume work on Luther's environment and personality concludes that "he suffered from a manic-depressive psychosis," but without determining whether this was the cause or the result of his religious anguish and frustration.[10] Erik Homburger Erickson in *Young Man Luther: A Study in Psychoanalysis and History* succeeds in presenting a more

[7] P. C. Gordon Walker, "Capitalism and the Reformation," in Spitz, *Reformation*, pp. 28–46. Reprinted from *Economic History Review*, 8 (1937): 3–19. Another Marxist note is sounded by Roy Pascal, who lays emphasis on Luther's alleged class-consciousness in *The Social Basis of the German Reformation* (London: Watts, 1935).

[8] Hartmann Grisar, *Luther*, trans. E. M. Lamond, 6 vols. (London: K. Paul, Trench and Tübner, 1913–17).

[9] Preserved Smith, "Luther's Early Development in the Light of Psychology," *American Journal of Psychology*, 24 (1913): 366–89.

[10] Paul J. Reiter, *Martin Luthers Umwelt, Charakter und Psychose*, 2 vols. (Copenhagen: Levin & Munksgaard, 1941). See especially the final chapter, "Diagnosis," 2:549–83, with attention to p. 559. Cf. Horst Beintker, *Die Überwindung der Anfechtung bei Luther* (Berlin: Evangelische Verlagsanstalt, 1954), p. 72.

balanced treatment, which, however, is not entirely convincing.[11] That Luther's early problem was one of escaping his father's control, and his solution of it the substitution of surrender to God for subjection to his father, is an argument hard to establish without having the live Luther stretched for long periods on the psychoanalyst's couch. And one may ask whether, if such a view is accepted, it sheds much new light on the motivation of his work or the origin of the Reformation. It is more to our present purpose to say that Erikson does recognize in Luther a religious personality; if he has delusions and egocentricities, these lie in the religious realm. He gives prominence to Luther's own remark: "I did not learn my theology all at once. I had to search deeper for it where my temptation took me."[12]

In the name of Freudian analysis, Oskar Pfister has performed an operation on the reputation of Calvin, making him a helplessly psychopathic person driven by an irresistible compulsion to transform the Gospel of Christ into a harsh theology and to perform acts of cruel fanaticism.[13] To obtain this result Pfister has to ignore a vast body of contrary evidence. Psychology may indeed yield valuable service to history. But the Freudian analysis of any historical personage long dead may be all too readily employed as an instrument of mere defamation.

I am not suggesting that either Marx or Freud today controls the interpretation of Reformation history. Our approved historians do not represent themselves as social philosophers or psychologists. They industriously assemble historic facts, seek to evaluate them, and only cautiously generalize on them. Inevitably, in their eager search for facts, the selection and

[11] Erik Homburger Erikson, *Young Man Luther: A Study in Psychoanalysis and History* (New York: W. W. Norton & Co., 1958).

[12] Erikson, *Young Man Luther*, p. 251.

[13] Oskar Pfister, *Calvins Eingreifen in der Hexer- und Hexenprozesse von Peney . . . Ein kritischer Beitrag zur Charakteristik Calvins* (Zurich: Artemis Verlag, 1947). For comment on some of Pfister's opinions, see Richard Stauffer, *L'Humanité de Calvin* (Neuchâtel: Delachaux et Niestlé, 1964), pp. 16 f., and John T. McNeill, *History and Character of Calvinism* (New York: Oxford University Press, 1954, 1967), pp. 229 f.

evaluation of them is colored by certain preconceptions and value judgments, but of these they are in most instances largely unaware. They believe they are not making a case, but illuminating an era. The historiography of the Reformation is marked by great variety and even greater industry, and is stronger in research than in interpretation. A great many historians with the best intentions build approaches to the movement by means of a dutiful portrayal of the complicated Western society of the era before Luther—the political, economic, and cultural factors; ecclesiastical deterioration and abuses; wars, alliances, and enmities. In front of this variegated tapestry, but not convincingly connected with it, Luther steps out. We are told, with varying degrees of penetration, the story of his *Anfechtungen* and of his "breakthrough," his clash with authority in the hierarchical Church, and his alliance with authority in the German states; and, so far as Germany is concerned, we come out again into a realm of politics and economics, of leagues and wars. There follows a comparable treatment of Anabaptism, Calvinism, and the Counter-Reformation. In all this factual material the standard of accuracy may be high and the balance between alienated parties, at least by intention, just. But the total effect is to leave the reader unaware of the motivation on which the whole great stir of the sixteenth century had its inception, whence came the driving force by which reforming leaders were sustained, and whether anything happened that can be properly called "Reformation." Indeed, there has been more use of such words as "upheaval," "schism," and "revolt" than of "reform" or "renewal." The conscientious and competent historian has conducted us into every factual nook and corner and made all the facts interesting. But he has failed to convey any adequate impression of what I, at least, regard as the essential drive of the sixteenth century—the impact of truly religious experience and ideas on the genesis and development alike of the Reformation and of the Counter-Reformation. These two movements were nearer together than their proponents were aware. Taken together, in my judgment, they constituted a vast revival of religion. Christianity in Europe was, in its various units of organization, far more of a reality in 1600 than in 1500. The religious initiative was maintained in large degree throughout the century. We are here concerned almost entirely with the period before 1550.

I am using the word "religious," in preference to "theological" or "ecclesiastical," as being more comprehensive and applicable to all classes of the Christian people with or without position in the structure of the Church. It is true that the leaders were men instructed in the lore of the ecclesiastical world and steeped in the learning of the schools. But the generating source of their word and deed did not lie mainly in that realm. We have all been busy, and justifiably, with their backgrounds as well as with their approach to secular issues. But it is unrealistic to elaborate these topics while we lose from view one central fact common to them all. This fact is that all the prominent personalities by which the Reformation in Germany and elsewhere was instituted were converts whose religious experiences colored everything they said on any subject all their lives after.

I do not overlook the fact that the Protestant Reformers all knew and continued to read the Church Fathers, or that they had a good deal of familiarity with the Schoolmen of various schools. Ockham may have been in some sense Luther's springboard; a springboard merely enables a jumper to make the most of his own muscles. It was not Ockham or Biel or Staupitz who made the Luther of history. Luther's theology was wrought in his own forge, slowly and painfully, out of his private encounter with God in Holy Scripture and his public encounter with the ecclesiastical power that disowned him. In Loyola's case an intense conversion experience was no less central. The Society of Jesus would never have come to exist, never have made its contribution to the restoration of the Roman Catholic Church, had not Ignatius agonized at Manresa. There, he told Luis Gonzales, "God dealt with him as a teacher with a scholar."[14] Calvin's conversion, as we shall see, was by no means less determinative of his whole

[14] William J. Young, ed., *Saint Ignatius' Own Story, as Told to Luis Gonzales de Camara* (Chicago: Henry Regnery Co., 1956), p. 22.

later activity. Calvin's colleague and successor Beza—brilliant, handsome, and gay—on what he felt to be a divine call left his irresponsible way of life and the glitter of the French court, abandoning his incomes and possessions, to devote all his talents to the service of the Reformed Church.[15] Zwingli early learned from Thomas Wyttenbach to prize some of the evangelical doctrines, but it required a decade of study and struggle to make him the eager Reformer he became. A recent biographer Jean Rilliet even compares his inner struggles with those of Augustine; they involved "the torturing problem of the flesh." It was about 1515 that he resolved to devote himself wholly to the study of Scripture. "I began," he says, "to implore God for his light and the Scripture became much clearer to me."[16] Like Calvin, Zwingli graduated from humanism to the Reformation, and in his case also the transition involved a life commitment, a very personal matter that cannot be explained on the basis of any known background. Oecolampadius, humanist and patristic scholar, willingly read Luther from the first but was driven to self-questioning and led to enter a monastery for reflection, whence he soon emerged a zealous recruit to the Reformation.[17] Bullinger was

[15] Henry Martin Baird, *Theodore Beza, the Counsellor of the French Reformation* (New York: G. P. Putnam's Sons, 1899), chaps. 1, 2. In this work (pp. 355–67), Baird has a translation of Beza's long letter to his former teacher Melchior Wolmar, published in Geneva in 1560 as *Confessio christianae fidei et ejusdem collatio cum papisticis haeresibus*, which shows the pressure put upon him by relatives and friends to continue the pursuit of secular learning and wordly honor. For some fresh light on the conversion of Beza see the close study of his relations with Jacques Peletier by Natalie Zemon Davis, "Peletier and Beza Part Company," *Studies in the Renaissance*, 11 (1964): 188–272.

[16] Jean Rilliet, *Zwingli: Third Man of the Reformation*, trans. Harold Knight (Philadelphia: Westminster Press, 1964), pp. 34, 43–47. Cf. McNeill, *History of Calvinism*, p. 26. On Zwingli's primary emphasis on evangelical preaching rather than on ecclesiastical politics, see G. W. Bromiley, ed., *Zwingli and Bullinger*, Library of Christian Classics (Philadelphia: Westminster Press, 1953), p. 29. See also the revealing study by Fritz Blanke, "Zwinglis Urteil über sich selbst," in *Aus der Welt der Reformation, fünf Aufsätze* (Zurich, Zwingli Verlag, 1960), pp. 9–17.

[17] Ernst Staehelin, *Das theologische Lebenswerk Johannis Oecolampads* (Leipzig: M. Heinsius Nachfolger, 1939), pp. 114–57.

versed in the Scholastics when he became impressed by their dependence on the Fathers for the best they had. When he searched the Fathers he found them relying on the Scripture. So he followed them back to the fountain.[18] Without considered attention to the religious quests and inner conflicts of the men who gave leadership in the Reformation, any treatment of the movement is bound to be superficial and misleading.

If these matters are to be understood, they must be studied in the sources themselves. It is not helpful to repeat some stereotyped treatment of them constructed by another. The matter, indeed, is one of great difficulty and deserves the closest attention. Of the vast body of source documents on the Reformation, the category of autobiography is the least satisfactory. The ranks of the Reformers contained no Vespasiano or Cellini. But each of them has, if only incidentally, left some evidence of the motivation behind his life's effort. To the facts thus disclosed, contemporaries, who were in most cases their associates, added a good deal. In the light of this body of evidence, it can be said with all confidence that in every instance the motives which animated them were truly and even narrowly religious. If their opponents at the time imputed to them motives of sensual pleasure or worldly ambition, this was done for controversial effect and without factual basis. It is not here a question whether their religion was good religion or not, but whether they were moved by religious considerations.

Luther clearly ties his campaign against the theology of works with his personal experience of grace after untold conflict. Some years later he wrote to his counselor John Staupitz, deeply grateful to the latter for his consoling words which on a certain occasion "came like a voice from heaven" assuring him that true penitence begins with a longing for the righteousness of God. These words of Staupitz, however, brought not only relief but also challenge; they "pierced him like the

[18] Emil Egli, ed., *Heinrich Bullingers Diarium (Annales vitae) der Jahre 1504–1574* (Basel: Basel Buch- und Antiquariatshandlung, 1904), pp. 5 f.

sharp arrow of a mighty man." Then he eagerly studied the uses of the Greek word *metanoia* and found it meant a transmutation of the mind and feeling under divine grace. Then, he writes, came the indulgence mongers, who cried up indulgences for the forgiveness of sins without that inner penitence. He has ventured to call in question their false teaching, citing on his side the doctors of the Church; and he is charged with assailing the pope's authority. Thus it is that he, who loves obscurity and would prefer the role of a spectator, has had to come to the front.[19]

In the Preface to his Latin Works, dated March 5, 1545, we see how vividly Luther had stored in his memory the psychic event of his life, the clarification of Paul's teaching on justification. We are not here concerned with the question whether his memory is accurate for time and circumstances, but with what that new light was by which he felt his soul illumined. *Justitia Dei* had been a frightening and hated expression. "I did not love, indeed I hated, a just God who punishes sinners," he records. Searching the Scriptures for light, by God's own grace he was led to see that "justice of God" is to be understood by means of the words in the same verse, "the just shall live by faith." That Paul himself has shifted Habakkuk's meaning in this passage is neither here nor there. God's justice thus becomes for Luther not the active, punishing justice before which man the sinner has no claim, but the passive justice by which a man who could never attain righteousness for himself, becomes just and lives by God's gift of faith—*justus dono Dei vivit, nempe ex fide*.[20] "Here," says Luther, "I felt myself born anew, and entering heaven by open doors."[21]

I am not here discussing as a theologian Luther's doctrine

[19] Luther to Staupitz, May 30, 1518. Luther, *Werke*, Weimar Ausgabe, *Briefe*, 1:525 f.; Otto Scheel, *Dokumente zu Luthers Entwicklung* (Tübingen: Mohr, 1929), pp. 9 f. Translated by C. M. Jacobs in *Works of Martin Luther* (Philadelphia: Muhlenburg Press, 1931), 1:39–43.

[20] Luther, *Werke*, W. A., 54:179–87; Scheel, *Luthers Entwicklung*, pp. 186–93. The passage has been translated by Lewis W. Spitz, Sr., in *Luther's Works*, ed. Jaroslav Pelikan (Philadelphia: Fortress Press, 1960), 24:327–38.

[21] Scheel, *Luthers Entwicklung*, p. 142.

of justification, but how it was that he became a Reformer. It was out of his deep need for assurance, an assurance of his own salvation that had long eluded him. This may not be the highest of religious motives, but it is unquestionably a religious motive, and it is idle to invent any worldly motivation. Otto Scheel has conveniently presented evidence from Melanchthon's recollections at the time of Luther's death. Luther was often assailed by the old terrifying thoughts of God's wrath. Melanchthon has seen him cast himself on a bed in consternation and keep repeating for his comfort Rom. 11:32, "For God has consigned all men to disobedience, that he may have mercy upon all." What Melanchthon adds in this context shows Luther's early, very personal appropriation of the creedal phrase *Credo remissionem peccatorum* and his use of Bernard's accordant teaching in his Sermon on the Annunciation.[22] On justification Luther's theology remained constant despite the moods of dark depression that assailed him at times during his later years. These recurring experiences, which are well illustrated in Roland Bainton's essay "Luther's Struggle for Faith,"[23] testify to his continued preoccupation with religion as against all external issues. Bainton has made a good case against Boehmer's view that his later anxieties arose from problems about his reforming work rather than about his faith and salvation. We shall perhaps never quite know how it was that this religious genius, often desperately disturbed about his own acceptance with God, was also steadfast, clear-eyed, and unhesitating in his leadership of the Reformation he had set in motion. It was his faith, not his fears, that triumphed.

It has sometimes been said that though Luther was persistent in the affirmation of his theology he was inconsistent in the course of the shaping of the Lutheran Church, yielding to political forces, and that even if the German Reformation began on an essentially religious impulse it allowed itself,

[22] Melanchthon, *Opera*, Corpus Reformatorum ed., 6:158; Scheel, *Luthers Entwicklung*, pp. 198 f.

[23] Roland Bainton, *Here I Stand* (New York: Abingdon-Cokesbury Press, 1950), pp. 359–72.

with Luther's consent, to be religiously lost in German politics. This viewpoint poses questions too large for treatment here. I believe it may be fairly contended that if Luther conceded to the secular power more than later wisdom approves it was never his intention to leave to governments the control of religion or the direction of souls. He remained at heart true to the brisk remark he made in a letter to Spalatin, November 4, 1520: "If the Gospel could be either propagated or preserved by the powers of the world God would not have confided it to fishermen."[24] Ranke was "almost tempted to wish" that Luther had been content to associate himself with the "grievances" of the princes against the Papacy, a course which might have brought Germany to an inner unity. "But," he at once adds, "the answer to this is, that the strength of a mind like his would have been broken had it been fettered by any consideration not purely religious."[25] To the insurgent peasants Luther wrote: "The Gospel does not take worldly matters into account." Let them not use it to gain advantages in things temporal.[26] But this is not the whole story. He often stressed the outworking of faith in love and service amid the common life of the world, and on this basis he criticized both the peasants and their lords. His wild words against the peasants, provoked by their atrocities and their rejection of his advice, were uttered in the context of a refusal to allow his teaching on the freedom of faith to be made a political instrument. It was, you will recall, only slowly and under much persuasion that he acquiesced in the formation of the Schmalkald League.

It is easy to assume that a secular ruler is a secular-minded person and gives priority always to his worldly interests. But this is by no means uniformly the case; witness Alfred the Great, Stephen of Hungary, Louis IX of France, Oliver Crom-

[24] Luther, *Werke*, W. A., *Briefe*, 2:210; Preserved Smith, ed., *Luther's Correspondence and Other Contemporary Letters*, 2 vols. (Philadelphia: Lutheran Publication Society, 1913–18), 1:286.

[25] Leopold von Ranke, *History of the Reformation in Germany*, trans. Sarah Austin (London: Routledge, 1905), pp. 238 f.

[26] Luther, *Werke*, W. A., 18:321. See C. M. Jacobs, trans., *The Admonition to Peace: A Reply to the Twelve Articles of the Peasants, Works of Martin Luther*, 4:219–44; these words, p. 237.

well. It ought not to be forgotten that the Saxon princes who lent support to Luther were men of religious interests and scruples. Luther's *Fourteen of Consolation*, a rich devotional book, was written for Frederick the Wise during the elector's illness in 1519.[27] Luther was most ready to minister to his prince's religious needs, but remarkably indifferent about his political protection. He freely and avowedly disobeyed Frederick by returning to Wittenberg from the Wartburg in 1522, and therewith urged the elector to do nothing in his behalf; he was, he said, "under far higher protection."[28] By this Luther did not mean that God would surely shield him from danger; rather that he was in God's hands. He had actually for some time expected to meet death in the cause. With this in mind, as early as August 18, 1520, he wrote to John Lang: "Perhaps I am the forerunner of Philip [Melanchthon], whose way I am sent to prepare."[29] Among Bainton's numerous illustrations is an anonymous representation of the Crucifixion with Frederick the Wise kneeling on one side and Luther on the other.[30] Frederick may have had little understanding of theology, but his piety was not in doubt. It was at the request of John the Constant, who succeeded to the electorate in 1525, that Luther gave suggestions for the appointment of visitors to reform the parishes. By 1530 Luther rejoiced, in a letter to prince John Frederick, who was then at the Augsburg Diet,

[27] Luther, *Werke*, 6:99–106. See Theodore Tappert, trans., *Luther: Letters of Spiritual Counsel*, Library of Christian Classics (Philadelphia: Westminster Press, 1955), pp. 26 ff. See also A. T. W. Steinhaeuser, trans., *The Fourteen of Consolation*, with Introduction, *Works of Martin Luther*, 1:105–72.

[28] "Ich komme gen Wittenberg in gar viel einer höhern Schutz den des Kurfürsten." – *Werke*, W. A., *Briefe*, 2:455. Translated in Preserved Smith, *Correspondence*, 2:95; in Gottfried G. Krodel, *Luther's Works*, vol. 48, 1963, p. 391; and in Tappert, *Luther: Letters*, p. 320.

[29] "Forte ego praecursor sum Philippi." – *Briefe*, 2:167. Numerous similar remarks appear in his letters and *Tabletalk*. Less than two weeks before his death he humorously reproved his wife for her anxiety about him "as if God were not almighty and could not create ten Dr. Luthers if the old one were suffocated in the Saale. . . . I have a better protector than thou and all angels." – February 7, 1546. See Margaret A. Currie, trans., *The Letters of Martin Luther* (London: Macmillan & Co., 1908), p. 472.

[30] Bainton, *Here I Stand*, p. 248.

that in Saxony "the young people are so well instructed in Scripture and Catechism that I am deeply moved when I see that young boys and girls can pray, believe and speak more of God and Christ than they ever could in the monasteries, foundations and schools of bygone days."[31] In one letter to John, after some political advice, he exclaims: "Ah, Lord God, I am far too much of a child for these worldly affairs," and asks indulgence for his "unintelligible prating."[32]

When the future elector John Frederick was a lad of seventeen, Luther sent him a copy of his new book *The Magnificat*, an impressive inspirational treatise that he had written on his way to Worms, in which he treats with insight and devout feeling the religious experience and example of the Virgin Mary. The hortative letter that went with the book is characteristic. "How important," says Luther here, "it is that so great a prince, upon whom the welfare of so many depends, should be graciously directed of God, for how much mischief may one do left to himself!"[33] Thus Luther habitually related himself to his rulers. He thought of them as Christians in high and God-given responsibility and in need of religious counseling, never as masters in the world of religion.[34] If there was an

[31] Luther to the Elector John, December 12, 1930. *Briefe*, 5:324–28. See Tappert, *Luther: Letters*, pp. 140–44. For a similar remark in Luther's *Sermon on Keeping Children in School* (1530) see Tappert, p. 142, n. 6; from Luther, *Werke*, 30 (2): 546 f.

[32] To the Elector John, December 12, 1530: "Ach herr gott, Ich bin solchen weltsachen zu kindlich." – *Briefe*, 5:699. See Currie, *Letters of Luther*, p. 257.

[33] March 10, 1521. *Werke*, 7:544 f. See Currie, *Letters of Luther*, p. 66.

[34] Cf. V. H. H. Green, *Luther and the Reformation* (New York: Capricorn Books, 1964), pp. 155 f.: "In theory Luther was as much an exponent of the Gelasian separation of powers as any early medieval writer. He did not believe that the secular power should properly intervene in spiritual matters. . . . For while he believed that the Prince was obliged to maintain the true religion, it was not his office to declare what the true religion was." Edgar N. Carlson has observed of the crisis in Swedish Lutheranism, 1593: "The Swedish nation thus broke from the principle *cujus regio eius religio* which prevailed in Germany. The Swedish people were determining the religion of the ruler rather than the ruler determining the religion of his subjects." – *The Reinterpretation of Luther* (Philadelphia: Westminster Press, 1948), p. 23.

alliance between Luther and the Saxon princes, it was on this religious basis and was in no sense a bargain for his protection.

For Calvin the data are not so abundant as for Luther. He rarely talks about himself except in his letters to his more intimate friends. We need not here interest ourselves in the nowadays thinned-out stream of the literature of mere disparagement. Most of Calvin's detractors mount the attack in the area of his character and disposition and the severity of his discipline, leaving to inference his deplorable religious state. His religion may have been represented as fanaticism, but it is hardly possible to represent him as other than a religious man. Church discipline for him belonged clearly within religion, since its purpose was to protect the Holy Supper, the Sacrament of communion with Christ and with fellow-Christians, from profanation through the participation of persons of scandalous and evil life.

Calvin, we know, was impelled to enter upon his course of reform as a result of an experience of conversion and what he felt to be an inexorable divine call. God, he says, "by a sudden conversion subdued my heart (Latin: "*animum*"; French: "*coeur*") to teachableness."[35] This meant that he must tear himself from his attachment to, and expectations in, the unreformed Church and cast in his lot with the persecuted evangelicals. Calvin had been from boyhood an exceptionally "teachable" type. Having absorbed the learning of the universities and acquired the literary competence of the humanists, he stood at a high point in the intellectual world of his day. But now the trained and gifted scholar turned to devote his labors to the understanding of the Bible, the great textbook of God's teachable ones. He soon found himself surrounded by inquirers who wanted his Bible-centered instruction. He had to flee his country and change his name in order to have opportunity to write without distractions and dangers. He tells us

[35] *Calvini Opera*, Corpus Reformatorum ed., 31:22. On Calvin's conversion see: François Wendel, *Calvin*, trans. Philip Mairet (New York: Harper & Row, 1963), pp. 37–45; John T. McNeill, *History and Character of Calvinism*, chap. 7. I have not followed any of the numerous translations of the passage but used a literal rendering.

that his object in publishing the *Institutes* in 1536 was: to defend "my brothers whose death was precious in the sight of the Lord" and to win sympathy for them from others. Shortly afterward the commanding voice of Guillaume Farel, uttered with imprecatory insistence, enlisted him all unexpectedly for Geneva.

After his early Seneca Commentary (1532), all Calvin's works reflect his alert, continuous, and detailed attention to the Bible. His copious production of commentaries, on fifty-four of the sixty-six books of the canonical Scriptures, bears testimony to his constant application to this study. At every decisive point in his reforming career he believed himself acting in obedience to God. Had he remained where he was before resigning his benefices in 1534, presumably the motive of ambition would have carried him on to high success, either in Law, where his father hoped he would make himself rich, or in the ranks of the French clergy, to which he had been originally directed. His own apologia for his ministry can be patched together from his writings. One passage in point is found in his *Reply to Sadoleto*, 1539:

> I heard from thy (God's) mouth that there was no other light of truth which could direct our souls into the way of life, than that which was kindled by thy Word. . . . But when I turned my eyes toward men I saw very different principles prevailing. Those who were regarded as leaders of faith neither understood thy Word nor greatly cared for it. . . . Among the people themselves, the highest veneration paid to thy Word was to revere it at a distance, as something inaccessible.

He has observed that the essentials of doctrine and the purity of worship have been lost in error and superstition, but, he adds:

> That I might perceive these things, thou, O Lord didst shine upon me with the brightness of thy Spirit; that I might comprehend how impious and harmful they were, thou didst bear before me the torch of thy Word; that

> I might abominate them as they deserved, thou didst disturb my soul. . . . My conscience told me how strong the zeal was with which I burned for the unity of thy Church, provided thy truth were made the bond of concord.

When he voices the plea of the layman who has joined the evangelical party, he stresses the inadequacy of the received teaching to ease a man's conscience, the dread of God's judgment at the Resurrection, the claimed value of good works and acts of expiation, the advice to take flight to the saints from the dreadful presence of the heavenly Judge.

> For whenever I descended into myself or raised my mind to thee, extreme terror seized me which no expiations or satisfactions could cure. The more closely I examined myself, the sharper the stings with which my conscience was pricked.

Then had come the new teachers who, on the basis of the Word, "spoke nobly of the Church" while discounting the claims of the Roman pontiff.[36]

Here no doubt Calvin speaks for himself as much as for his lay brethren. He allowed the Word in Scripture to speak to his own needs. Sometimes in a sermon he will interject an application of the lesson to himself. Thus in one of his series on 1 Timothy he exclaims: "Woe is me when I mount the pulpit here and set forth the doctrine of salvation, if I do not profit from it on my own part."[37] Calvin is never personally disengaged from what he teaches; always existentially involved in it.

Perhaps in all this I am wasting persuasion on those already

[36] *Calvini Opera Selecta*, ed. Petrus Barth and Gulielmus Niesel (Munich: Kaiser, 1926), 1:480, 485. See John K. S. Reid, trans., *Calvin: Theological Treatises*, Library of Christian Classics (Philadelphia: Westminster Press, 1954), pp. 24 f., 251.

[37] *Calvini Opera*, 53:208, 17th Sermon on 1 Timothy. Cited with other such materials by Richard Stauffer in his study "Le discours à la première personne dans les sermons de Calvin," *Regards contemporains sur Calvin: Actes du Colloque Calvin, Strasbourg, 1964* (Paris: Presses Universitaires de France, 1965), p. 212.

persuaded. I am at least bringing to attention at the moment some matters that are often allowed to sink into the background and are sometimes quite overlooked. Perhaps we need to keep more definitely before us the distinction between the Reformation and the Reformation era. I am not disposed to use the term Reformation as a designation of the total upheaval of the sixteenth century or to speak of it as a revolutionary movement or as a religious eddy in the general maelstrom of affairs in that age. I believe that the Reformation and Counter-Reformation together occurred in a Europe increasingly in the grip of religious forces. The age of secularization was to follow, but not in the sixteenth century. The eminent personalities of that century were those who came to leadership in a great effort toward the revival of religion and the renovation of the Church. Their story should be told with insistence on the fact that they were religious persons. I do not mean, either, that the Reformation begins and ends with the intention of these leaders. In many respects they were responding to other men's needs and half-formed wishes; to that we shall come.

Meanwhile let us ask: how is the theme of this lecture related to the Reformation in England? Many historians are content to represent the English Reformation as the handiwork of an autocratic king and his servile instruments. For them it takes its inception from Henry VIII's attempt to resolve his marital problems and secure the royal line. Hans Hillerbrand puts this view with a flourish:

> The Reformation in England began with the marital problems of King Henry VIII, that crowned head of England who, as Charles Dickens melodramatically observed, was, "a most intolerable ruffian and a blot of blood and grease upon the history of England." [38]

[38] Hans J. Hillerbrand, *The Reformation: A Narrative History Related by Contemporary Observers and Participants* (New York: Harper & Row, 1964), p. 298. Actually the words quoted from Charles Dickens form the closing sentence in that author's *Child's History of England*, though the language is hardly adapted to tender minds! It is fair to say here that Hillerbrand's book is in general a work of scholarly quality.

By way of contrast, perhaps I may cite another Dickens, whose metier is history and not fiction. A. G. Dickens, professor of history in King's College, London, begins chapter 5 of his book *The English Reformation* with the sentence: "The English Protestant Reformation arose and grew largely in opposition to the will of Henry VIII."[39] Both these statements are in books published in 1964.

Professor Hillerbrand has better support for his judgment than Charles Dickens. Sir Maurice Powicke in 1941 declared: "The one definite thing that can be said about the English Reformation is that it was an act of state," and he finds it "one of the most mysterious things in history" that Englishmen accepted the religious changes that came with it.[40] This does seem mysterious, if we assume that the movement at its inception was a device of King Henry, who was allergic to the religious changes. Now Professor Dickens reaches only at chapter 5 the point at which he introduces us to the policies of the king. He has earlier explained various aspects of late medieval religion in England, and described the Lutheran and Christian humanist elements of the years before Henry saw the light in Anne Boleyn's eyes. At the close of chapter 3 he makes the judgment that even in Wolsey's time it was too late to forestall "either the state-revolution of Henry VIII or the subsequent conquests of Protestantism." Pointing gently to some misconceptions here, he admonishes the reader not to forget that at this time

> Protestant beliefs exercised positive claims upon certain types of mind . . . and that most of their holders cannot be dismissed as rebellious neurotics, politicans, or self-deluded profiteers. Some men were drawn to Protestantism by understanding and love; some by hatreds and heady enthusiasms; some by the belief that it was the escape-route from the broad road to damnation. But the

[39] A. G. Dickens, *The English Reformation* (New York: Schocken Books, 1964), p. 63.

[40] Maurice Powicke, *The Reformation in England*, 4th ed. (London: Oxford University Press, 1953), pp. 1, 7.

> magnetic process was real enough and it came to operate quite extensively throughout English society.[41]

The approach of H. Maynard Smith, Canon of Gloucester, in his *Henry VIII and the Reformation*[42] is noteworthy, though not by any means unique. This writer treats "The Political Reformation" in part 1 of his book, and "The Religious Reformation" in a shorter, but substantial, part 2. He thus brings into the story Frith and Tyndale and the White Horse Tavern evangelicals, all of whom Henry had taken pains to outlive, only after the hero of the "political Reformation" has been duly laid to rest. Since the researches of John Strype (d. 1737),[43] few writers before our time have taken an interest in these pioneers of the Reformation in England. But Ernest Gordon Rupp[44] and, more recently, Marcus Loane[45] and William A. Clebsch[46] have given us books in which their names and deeds are made familiar.

The short, endangered lives of these men were lived out under the constant hostility of the Defender of the Faith and his ministers and were, in many instances, ended at the stake before Henry's marital miseries produced any ecclesiastical fruits. The nascent Protestantism of the 1520's, as Professor Dickens and others have shown, owed something to the sprinkling of Lollards who had survived to that time. It also owed a good deal to the fresh reading by Cambridge scholars of the New Testament made available in Greek and Latin by

[41] A. G. Dickens, *English Reformation*, p. 58.

[42] H. Maynard Smith, *Henry VIII and the Reformation* (London: Macmillan & Co., 1948).

[43] John Strype, *Ecclesiastical Memorials relating chiefly to Religion and the Reformation of It . . . Under King Henry VIII, King Edward VI and Queen Mary the First*, 3 vols. (London: John Wyat, 1721), vol. 1, chaps. 7–8, 22–23, and Appendixes 19–22, 44.

[44] E. G. Rupp, *Studies in the Making of the English Protestant Tradition* (Cambridge: At the University Press, 1947).

[45] Marcus L. Loane, *Pioneers of the Reformation in England* (London: Church Book Room Press, 1964).

[46] William A. Clebsch, *England's Earliest Protestants, 1520–1535* (New Haven: Yale University Press, 1964). To the three works just mentioned may be added: David Broughton Knox, *The Doctrine of Faith in the Reign of Henry VIII* (London: J. Clark, 1961).

Erasmus. Prominent among these men was Thomas Bilney. The twenty-five Cambridge men who were burned for their biblical heresy in the twenties and early thirties had nearly all felt his influence. He tells how, about 1519, allured by the Latin style of Erasmus, he bought a copy of his Greek-Latin New Testament and:

> At the first reading (as I well remember) I chanced upon the sentence of St. Paul (O most sweet and comfortable sentence to my soul) in I. Timothy 1:15, "It is a true saying and worthy of all men to be embraced that Christ Jesus came into the world to save sinners, of whom I am chief and principal." This one sentence through God's instruction and inward working which I did not then perceive, did so exhilarate my heart, being before wounded with the guilt of my sin, and being almost in despair, that immediately I felt a marvellous comfort and quietness in so much that my bruised bones leaped for joy.[47]

Little Bilney, as he was affectionately called, was apparently the chief recruiter, as Robert Barnes was the presiding figure, of the group meeting for dinner and discussion in the White Horse Inn near St. John's, King's and Queen's colleges, Cambridge. In this company, to quote Marcus Loane, "the Reformation found its cradle."[48] Barnes, an Austin friar, was Bilney's convert, as was also the renowned Hugh Latimer, whose voice was not silenced till Mary's time. It is thought likely that Tyndale and Frith were present on occasions at the beginning, but at most they were fleeting visitors. The total number of those certainly or probably associated with the group during the decade 1520–30 is thought to have been fifty or sixty. From their interest in Luther the tavern came to be dubbed "Little Germany." But some of the White Horse men were never out-and-out Lutherans; they were, rather, highly individualized. The influence of Zwingli and Oecolampadius was not absent. In the case of Tyndale and of Frith the

[47] The passage is quoted more at length in Rupp, *English Protestant Tradition*, p. 23.

[48] Loane, *Reformation in England*, p. 4.

Zwinglian strain is clearly seen; and both had recognizable contacts with Lollardy. John Foxe praised Frith's learning, and recent scholarship has shown him to be the most competent theologian of the early Tudor Protestants.[49] It was while at Cambridge, and as a teacher in the Cardinal's College, Oxford, that Frith's mind moved to a distinctly evangelical position. This made it convenient for him to flee to Marburg, where he was in the company of François Lambert and other reforming scholars. Patrick Hamilton, whose noteworthy little book the *Loci* Frith translated, had been there before him but had already returned to Scotland and given his testimony in the flames. Frith returned to England, and in 1533 he, too, steadfastly died at the stake with a no less resolute disciple Andrew Hewet, a tailor's apprentice, tied to his back. Froude's view of the Reformation as "a revolt of the laity against the clergy" [50] seems subject to exceptions!

Such a statement is in fact grossly misleading. Nor can we be quite happy with Trevelyan's phrases about "Henry VIII's anti-clerical social revolution." This author recognizes that "a religious aspect" was embraced in the movement, but in accordance with what Henry approved. He finds, indeed, a "permanence" in the religious Reformation, but for him this has its "seed-time" in Edward's reign. Henry's anti-clerical drive had lacked a moral basis, but there now emerged a new expression of religion in which:

> The religious home was the Protestant ideal, with family prayer and private Bible reading in addition to the services and sacraments of the Church. These ideas and practices were by no means confined to the dissident Puritans. . . . The religion of the home and of the Bible

[49] Clebsch offers a valuable study of Frith's theology, *England's Earliest Protestants*, chaps. 7–8. R. E. Fulop's unpublished Edinburgh dissertation *John Frith and His Relation to the Origin of the Reformation in England* may also be read with profit. It is the most comprehensive and searching work on Frith. Clebsch dissents from Fulop only in minor factual details.

[50] James Anthony Froude, *Lectures on the Council of Trent* (London: Longmans, Green & Co., 1905), Lecture 1.

> became a social custom common to all English Protestants.

"The martyrs recorded in Foxe's book" provided the moral basis previously lacking, and "when Elizabeth came to the throne, the Bible and the Prayer Book formed the intellectual and spiritual foundation of a new social order."[51]

The social historian sees the Reformation as something else than "an act of state." The new social order itself rested on the Prayer Book and the Bible. Now of these two only the English Prayer Book is in the main a product of Edward's reign, and most of its content is of much earlier date. Actually the spread of the English Bible in a variety of translations during the 1520's and 1530's had made many Englishmen of all ranks Bible readers well before the end of Henry's reign. Bilney and the Cambridge gospellers were Bible men, reading it in Latin and preaching it in English. Tyndale's sense of a divine obligation to translate the Bible regardless of all obstacles must have come upon him not long after 1520, and by 1526 his New Testament was being industriously circulated despite all prohibitions in England and Scotland. He had to live abroad, where Henry's long arm reached him in 1536. But he had done his important work, and Coverdale's Bible had followed, while other versions were on their way. It is an interesting point that on Easter Eve, 1527, in the house of Thomas More though apparently not in his presence, Thomas Cromwell and Miles Coverdale had what the latter calls "a godly communication" about projected Bible translation work. Cromwell was then Wolsey's assistant, but in this he did not speak with his master's voice. A decade thereafter the acquaintance of Englishmen with the English Bible had gone a long way.

In 1537 we have tell-tale evidence of this in the speech of a Henrician bishop. Edward Fox of Hereford had in youth been at times in the White Horse company but had steered a politic course and flourished under Henry. He was sent by Henry to head a deputation to the Schmalkald League and had recently

[51] G. M. Trevelyan, *English Social History* (London: Longmans, Green & Co., 1946), pp. 127 f.

returned deeply impressed by Luther and Melanchthon, whose emissary in England at this time was Alexander Alesius. In Scotland Alesius had been appointed to confute Patrick Hamilton but had been overcome by Patrick's arguments and testimony in death. He had escaped to the Continent and become Melanchthon's friend. He had exchanged pamphlets with the celebrated Cochlaeus over the issue of vernacular Bibles. In England he had been in close relations with both Cranmer and Cromwell. Early in 1537 he was taken by Cromwell to a meeting of a commission of bishops on issues chiefly connected with the sacraments. On this the bishops were sharply divided. John Stokesley of London, who had much to do with the condemnation of Frith four years earlier, strongly defended the Seven Sacraments (the position of Henry himself, as is well known). On invitation of Cromwell, Alesius rose to discourse against this view and was charged with falsehood by Stokesley. Whereupon Edward Fox broke into the debate. Turning to the topic of the lay use of the Scriptures, he taunted the conservatives in these sentences:

> Think ye not we can by any sophistical subtleties steal out of the world again the light that every man doth see. Christ hath so lightened the world at this time that the light of the Gospel hath put to flight all misty darkness. . . . The lay people do now know the Holy Scriptures better than many of us. . . . Wherefore, make yourselves not to be mocked and laughed to scorn in the world, that ye bring them not . . . to think evermore hereafter that ye have neither one spark of learning or of godliness in you. . . . Truth is the daughter of time, and time is the mother of truth, and whatsoever is besieged of truth cannot long endure.[52]

[52] The incident, with Fox's speech, is reported by Alexander Alesius in his book *Of the Auctorite of the Word of God.* This treatise was written in Latin and translated into English by Edmond Allen from manuscript. The English version was apparently printed before the Latin original, which appeared in Strasbourg in 1542. See my article "Alexander Alesius, Scottish Lutheran, 1500–1565" in *Archiv für Reformationsgeschichte,* 55 (1964): 161–91, and for this passage, pp. 180 ff.

Alesius, who preserves this discourse, calls it "a short and pithy oration." We may make some discount for the exaggeration of a debater; but the fact that these words could be uttered in 1537 by a bishop of Hereford who knew his England well from court to countryside is significant evidence that at that date the Bible in English was leavening the religious attitudes of the people. Although we look in vain for this speech in books of source readings, we may take it as marking the point of no return for the "religious" Reformation, just ten years before King Henry's reign ended.

Another revealing passage is given by Strype, possibly from unpublished notes by Foxe that were available to him. It refers to the reception of the Great Bible placed in the churches in 1539. Strype says it was joyously welcomed not only by the learned "but generally all England over." All who could do so bought the book and either read it or heard it read. Some old folk learned to read in order to use it, and children flocked to public readings of the Scripture. Some evidence against Strype's "all England over" report has been presented.[53] There was some indifference and some violent resistance. But the process went on. The later restrictions placed by Henry on the circulation and reading of the Bible were not effective; and in Edward's reign new printings multiplied.

The progressive saturation of the English mind with the teachings of the Bible, even on the most conservative view of its extent, was a powerful factor in the English Reformation. Its effect was augmented by the circulation of theological writings and by some popular preaching, a feature that became highly important under Edward's government. I must excuse myself from describing the influence of Martin Bucer, Peter Martyr, John à Lasco, and other learned foreign Protestant teachers in England, and also avoid any attempt to estimate the effect there of the writing, in Latin and in translation, of foreign Reformers, among whom Luther, Bullinger, and

[53] John Strype, *Memorials of Thomas Cranmer, Archbishop of Canterbury* (Oxford: Clarendon Press, 1840), 1:91. Cf. H. Maynard Smith, *Henry VIII*, pp. 342 ff.

Calvin were largely represented. England was religiously more a part of Europe than is sometimes recognized by her historians. But whatever was effected by the flood of persuasive treatises from the Continent, in England it was Englishmen who shed their blood in the cause.

Why does the fact that England produced a large and representative company of resolute martyrs for evangelical religion, as well as a considerable number in devotion to the Papacy, receive so little attention from most of the historians? Nothing can better establish the religious reality of a movement than the test of martyrdom freely accepted. It was not "the tyrant's brandished steel, the lion's gory mane" that confronted them, but a more agonizing death. Men who fought in that battle were not charlatans or profiteers. In the light of their utterances before their judges, it is unrealistic to regard them as fanatical or psychopathic extremists. They could render a reason for the faith that was in them and were not the victims of delusion. Many of them were the authors of weighty and still readable treatises or of guide books to a life of piety; others were humble, but convinced, layfolk. There were relatively few recantations, probably far fewer proportionately than in the days of Decius and Diocletian; and the defectors had a way of returning to do battle courageously. Nowhere else in the sixteenth century persecutions were the victims more resolute and valiant. Their testimony alone should be sufficient to furnish a devastating comment on the secularistic generalizations often applied to the Reformation of England.

In the study of the Scottish Reformation there has been less obscuring of the religious initiative. From the youthful Lutheran proto-Reformer Patrick Hamilton, the smoke of whose burning (1528), as a worried opponent remarked, "infectit as many as it blew upon," the line runs through the century of leaders whose religious motivation can hardly be questioned. As for Hamilton, every self-regarding consideration would have kept him in ecclesiastical safety. This is also true of the devout scholar George Wishart and of the venerable priest Walter Milne. In the more dominant Reformers John Knox and Andrew Melville, a deep religious zeal continued to burn, though both of them at times took a vigorous part in matters political. James S. McEwen has discussed the "burning inward fervour" of Knox, making note of his allusions to his favorite passage of Scripture, the seventeenth chapter of John.[54] It has always been known, and recent studies have made it more apparent, that some of the opponents of the Scottish Reformation were also men of genuine religious motivation.[55] Even if they were not put to death for their beliefs, some of them chose exile rather than conformity with the Reformed Church and lived out their lives abroad. The rough struggle for the establishment of the Reformed Church was not without much proof of religious faith and commitment. The men who were greedy to possess Church property were secular-minded nobles faithful neither to the old establishment nor to the new. At the same time many of the nobility sincerely espoused the cause of the Reformers.

A little before the time of Patrick Hamilton's burning, through the cooperation of merchants and ship-masters, the first shipments of Tyndale's New Testament entered Scotland's North Sea ports and, despite the episcopal ban, were carted across the land. The teaching of Hamilton was a joyous message of the faith which not only justifies but "makes God and man friends." People responded to this doctrine as if they had been waiting for it. In W. Croft Dickinson's words, "A new belief in faith began to course through men's veins like new wine." [56] They read the Bible and took guidance from its very words. A gentleman David Stratoun, hearing his son the Laird of Lauriston read in the New Testament the words of Jesus, "He that denies me before men . . . ," broke forth in the prayer: "Let me never deny Thee for fear of death." Being called to account to Holyrood, he was sentenced with another to hanging and burning, despite the king's known wish to have him freed. In one act three friars, a canon regular, and two

[54] James S. McEwan, *The Faith of John Knox* (Richmond, Va.: John Knox Press, 1961), chap. 6.

[55] David McRoberts, ed., *Essays on the Scottish Reformation* (Glasgow: Burns, 1962).

[56] W. Croft Dickinson, ed., *John Knox's History of the Reformation in Scotland*, 2 vols. (Edinburgh: Nelson, 1949), 1:xxiv.

gentlemen suffered in the fire together.[57] The unnumbered adherents of the new teaching were of all social ranks. Some, like Sir James Scrymgeour of Dundee, were in a strong enough political position to disregard the bishops and lend aid to "New Testamenters" making their escape abroad.

Admittedly, there existed in Scotland a good deal of mere anti-clericalism that had little of positive religion in it. But there was also a ground swell of Protestant belief and piety that fed upon the Scriptures, and in this we should recognize the roots of the Scottish Reformation. Not many country villagers could read; but where they could, it is not absurd to imagine scenes like that of The Cotter's Saturday Night even before John Knox took leadership in the Kirk. In December, 1557, some of the Protestant nobility, along with commoners, in order to protect the now numerous new believers, banded together in a solemn covenant, pledging before the Majesty of God to maintain and defend, with their property and their very lives, the people of "Christ's Congregation" and those who ministered to them Christ's Holy Evangel and Sacraments.[58] In the strife that followed the nation was set free from foreign control and the way opened for the formation of the Reformed Church of Scotland.

Eight years later a score of Netherlands nobles formed at Brussels a somewhat similar covenant, which may be thought of as the beginning of the Netherlands rally against Spanish rule and of a contest that was to win freedom for the Northern Provinces.[59] The most obvious comment is that in these in-

[57] Knox recites these among other instances of firm witness to a newfound evangelical faith. *Ibid.*, 1:24–30.

[58] Knox's text of the "Common Band" or Covenant of 1557 is found in Dickinson, *Knox's History*, 1:136 f.

[59] Maurice G. Hansen, *The Reformed Church in the Netherlands* (New York: Reformed Church in America, 1884), p. 56, dates this meeting October 2, 1565, but this is evidently an error for November 2. See Geraert Brandt, *History of the Reformation in the Low Countries*, 4 vols. (London: T. Childe, 1720–23), 1:162. The names of Philip of Marnix, lord of Ste. Aldegonde, and of the eminent theologian Franciscus Junius (François du Jon), both of whom had studied in Geneva, are associated with this meeting. It was after a sermon by Junius that the decision was taken. In this critical hour in the Netherlands, when William of Orange was not yet giving vigorous leadership, "the Calvinists alone knew what

stances religion was not shaped by politics; rather, religion was reshaping the political world.

I have led you on flying visits to a number of the countries in which one must study the phenomena of the Reformation, and in each situation I have shown evidence for the priority and generating force of religion. The Reformation arose with men who were concerned to the depths of their being with their own spiritual problems, while sensitive to the religious needs of their fellows and primarily seeking for them religious objectives, amid which temporal concerns were incidental and minor. The movement was charged with power because it freshened and invigorated Christian belief. If it made demands upon conduct, these rested upon a basis that was solely religious.

We have had reason to lay some emphasis on the role of the Bible in the formation of Reformation piety. For the Reformers, not only was the authority of the Bible supreme, but a knowledge of its contents was for every Christian highly important. The common use of the Bible required that it be made available in languages understood by the lay people everywhere. In the sixteenth century we are never far from this issue. During the first few decades of the Reformation it held a prominent place in the controversial literature and could be no less divisive than the more strictly theological revisions. In this connection it is sometimes overlooked that the defenders of the old order, like their opponents, recognized the authority of Scripture. But it was, they said, to be interpreted to the lay people by the clergy and not put in their hands. Here the Reformers enjoyed the advantage of advocating what the people craved, and their success turned partly upon this advantage. It was already widely believed that most of the clergy were too unfamiliar with the Bible to be its interpreters. There was no convincing answer to the argument for the translated Bible short of a repudiation of the authority of the sacred book. But this was an unthinkable solution, even for the most ardent advocates of hierarchical ecclesiasticism.

they wanted." Cf. Pieter Geyl, *The Revolt in the Netherlands* (London: Williams & Norgate, 1932), p. 84.

In this situation we have, I think, one key to an understanding of the dazzlingly rapid spread of the movement in many lands.

What I have said above is far from a comprehensive treatment of the religious dynamic and motivation of the Reformation. I am anxious to affirm that the Reformation is not to be explained on any "Great man theory." In fact no Reformer, not even Luther, considered himself and his associates indispensable to it. There was something in it which the leaders themselves could not fathom, and which they could only refer to the purposes of God. The historical inquirer does not profess expertness in relating the Reformation narrative with the divine purpose. We have all been very eager to get at the background of the movement, but there are some lines of approach here that have been only touched upon by most of us. Some questions will lead us to the basic consideration to which I would now call attention. Why was it that just over three years after Luther's Ninety-Five Theses, Aleander, representing the pope in Germany, to his astonishment found nine out of ten Germans crying "Luther" and all ten demanding a Church council for reform? Why was it that before Calvin ever saw or thought of Geneva, under the ardent evangelical preaching of Farel, the Genevan citizens, meeting in the Cathedral, without any dissent formally voted that with God's help they would live according to the Holy Evangel? It will not do to explain this on the ground that the act was essentially a part of Geneva's spirited resistance to Savoy. The Savoyan bishop had already been expelled, and his clergy, whom Franz Wilhelm Kampschulte thought cowardly and unfit, quailed before Farel.[60] The resolution of the citizens was a religious decision. Why was it that in England during the late 1520's "great numbers of the working classes" became possessors of Tyndale's New Testament at a price equal to two weeks' pay?[61] Why, in short, was the Reformation eagerly welcomed by all sorts of people? It is possible that we have been a little misled through

[60] Franz Wilhelm Kampschulte, *Johann Calvin, seine Kirche und sein Staat in Genf* (Leipzig: Duncker & Humblot, 1869), 1:2, iv.

[61] G. G. Perry, *A History of the Church of England* (New York: Harper & Bros., 1879), pp. 38 ff.

our fascination with the genius of Luther and the brilliance of Calvin. Of Luther, Wilhelm Dilthey remarked, after well-expressed astonishment before his gigantic personality: "He was master of the people of his time because they believed that they recognized in him their own self raised to a higher power."[62] Joseph Lortz brings us nearer to the point in the words: "When Luther came, he appeared to thousands and to tens of thousands as the final redemption of the demands for reform which were long due and long generally recognized as justified."[63]

Another Roman Catholic historian Jean Delumeau put forth a book in 1965 that deserves wide reading, *Naissance et affirmation de la réforme*.[64] Delumeau begins his inquiry into the origins of the Reformation with some vivid evidence of the religious depression and insecurity that afflicted the late medieval man. He takes as typical of this the *Dies irae*, with its relentless portrayal of man's plight as helpless and alone before the divine Judge, and its final outcry for mercy.[65] If you have read the *Dies irae* with reference to its supposed thirteenth-century author Thomas of Celano, a kindly Franciscan, you may have missed some of its dismal accent as it was sung at funerals in later times. This masterpiece of medieval rhymed Latin verse is a prayer out of the depths of man's helplessness,

[62] Wilhelm Dilthey, "The Interpretation and Analysis of Man in the Sixteenth Century," translated from Dilthey's *Gesammelte Schriften* by Edna Spitz, in Spitz, *Reformation*, p. 11.

[63] Joseph Lortz, "Why Did the Reformation Happen?" in Spitz, *Reformation*, pp. 50 f.

[64] Jean Delumeau, *Naissance et affirmation de la réforme* (Paris: Presses Universitaires de France, 1965). We are here concerned especially with his chapter entitled "Le Reforme: Pourquoi?" pp. 47–76.

[65] Delumeau, *Naissance de la réforme*, pp. 55 ff. The text of the *Dies irae* is conveniently available in *The Oxford Book of Medieval Latin Verse* (Oxford: Clarendon Press, 1928), pp. 149 f. The various English renderings I have seen come short of being adequate translations. Delumeau regards the poem as a product of the late fourteenth century. What was perhaps an even more vivid experience of the fear of death and judgment was afforded by the seasonally enacted Dance of Death. The awesome figure of Death emerged from the charnel house bearing a scythe, followed by his train, and led a dance with many macabre features. John Lydgate's version of the French original play is in *The Dance of Death*, ed. Florence Warren (London: Oxford University Press, 1931).

a prayer of trembling hope, not of confident faith. Set it side by side with English Cynewulf's poem on the Last Judgment, written about A.D. 800, and you will, I think, be struck by a great difference in outlook. Cynewulf celebrates the heavenly joys in store for the faithful and is not horrified over the woes of the damned.[66] Delumeau takes the *Dies irae* as a literary expression, familiar to all, of the low religious mood and haunting doubt of the pre-Reformation era, when men had lost confidence in the prescriptions offered by their clerical guides. To this depression of soul there came no response from the clergy—no satisfying reassurance or comforting message—until Luther's proclamation of the doctrine of justification by faith. Delumeau points to the frequency and duration of interdicts affecting whole populations. When the sacraments were thus withheld as a penalty, man learned to do without them and ceased to prize them. The people were still attracted by the colorful processions of the clergy but did not feel the earlier reliance upon their functions. This does not, he insists, indicate lay indifference to Christianity. Ockham's teaching had encouraged the hope that laymen might obtain a larger place in Church matters, but this expectation had faded with the failure of the reforming councils. From the beginning of printing many people individually sought help from the Bible and other religious books. Editions of the Vulgate, some vernacular Bible texts, and many books of piety were already being printed in 1500. Here it may be noted that the Chronicle of Cologne under date of 1499 says optimistically: "The eternal God has out of his unfathomable wisdom brought into existence the laudable art, by which men now print books, and multiply them so greatly that every man may for himself read or hear read the way of salvation."[67] Delumeau states that at least seventy-five percent of all books published between 1495 and 1520 were on religious themes. We may be sure that the printers were responding to the religious cravings

[66] Cynewulf, *The Last Judgment*, in *An Anthology of Old English Poetry*, trans. Charles W. Kennedy (London: Oxford University Press, 1964), pp. 149–54.

[67] A. P. Usher, *A History of Mechanical Inventions*, rev. ed. (Cambridge: Harvard University Press, 1954), p. 242.

of the people. But while the demand for Bibles was in millions, the supply was in thousands only.[68] The Reformers, then, did not create the craving for the sacred Word. But they supplied vastly improved translations, utilizing the textual scholarship of Erasmus and others. The printers were their allies in producing these in quantity; and the problem of their circulation was met, often at great risk, by merchants and colporteurs.

The French scholar's approach helps me to press home the point that in the Reformation scene laicization is not to be equated with secularization. The Reformers achieved what they did because they understood and shared the impatient religious craving and felt need of the mass of lay people and of many in religious orders — the literate or illiterate folk who, in the chronicler's words, desired "to read or to hear read the way of salvation," and who sensed that the clue to this lay in the Scripture.

If a Church Father could discern in the pre-Christian culture a *praeparatio Evangelica*,[69] we can equally recognize a forecast of the Reformation in the unanswered yearning of many for assurance of salvation. The scandalous abuses in the Church were not their primary concern, though these added to their perplexity. They were outside the range of the materialistic trends of thought represented by the late Averroists; and Pietro Pomponazzi's disbelief in the soul's survival was not for them. No doubt those whom we often call "Pre-Reformers," such as Rudolph Agricola and Wessel Gansfort in the Netherlands, John Colet in England, and Jacques Lefèvre in France, within their limited range of influence had been helpful to the anxious seekers; and the Reformers had good reason to be grateful to all such forerunners. But with all these there was, as with Erasmus, an emphasis on scholarship that was foreign to the common man. Luther's emphasis was on religion and on

[68] Delumeau, *Naissance de la réforme*, pp. 67–70.

[69] Eusebius of Caesarea, in his labored work under the title Προπαρασκευὲ εὐαγγελική, was concerned to show that the Greeks borrowed their best thought from the Hebrews. If he is responsible for the phrase, Justin Martyr and Clement of Alexandria had, long before him, thought of Greek philosophy as, through its conception of the Logos, leading to Christ.

those aspects of religion over which multitudes were troubled. He and the other Reformers were, themselves, along with the common people, concerned about an endless future life to be lived in separate compartments of agony and bliss. Whatever twentieth-century sophistication may say of this, it represents a motivating belief among sixteenth-century men. On a higher level of thought their concern was to be accepted of God and to escape the hell which Calvin described as alienation from God. Martin Luther in his own anguish shared to the depths the haunting disquiet and distress of an uncounted number, and when for him the light of faith shone he was equipped as none before him to speak to the condition of distressed souls with a liberating voice.

9

Anabaptism and the Social Order

CORNELIUS J. DYCK

In describing the persecution of Christians under Nero following the great fire of Rome in July, A.D. 64, Tacitus reported that they were convinced "not so much of the crime of arson, as of hatred of the human race." [1] The Christians, of course, knew themselves to be completely misunderstood. They would likely have preferred the image created by the second century *Epistle to Diognetus*, that "what the soul is in the body Christians are in the world." [2] The attitude of sixteenth-century Anabaptism to society has usually been understood in much the same way as Tacitus reported, but they too would likely have preferred the Diognetian analogy as a part of their self-image.

Anabaptism has generally been characterized as antisocial or, at best, asocial. Three different methods of inquiry seem to have led to a consensus about this description. For many years historians have considered Anabaptism to be synonymous with Thomas Münzer and the Peasants' Revolt of 1525 and also with the Münster tragedy of 1534–35. This identified them as apostles of violence and social revolution. In working to correct this interpretation, more recent historiography has taken us to the other end of the continuum, where Anabaptism is described as a peaceful, withdrawn (*die Stillen im Lande*) movement, the adherents of which wanted only to be left alone. In either case, the social revolutionary and the quietist can be, and have both been, characterized as antisocial.

[1] J. Stevenson, *A New Eusebius* (New York: Macmillan Co., 1957), p. 2. Quoted from *Tacitus*, Annals, 15. 44. 6.

[2] *Ibid.*, p. 28. Quoted from *The Epistle to Diognetus* 6. 1.

From another perspective sociologists have arrived at the same conclusion through the use of the sect typology. At the heart of sectarianism, according to Ernst Troeltsch, lies the protest against secularization; the sect would rather perish than compromise with the world.[3] In general agreement with this view, H. Richard Niebuhr identified the Anabaptist-Mennonites as a type of Christ against culture social organization.[4] Social protest is seen as leading to theological dissent, which in turn leads to sectarian withdrawal from the world. Since churches and states together represent the institutionalization of violence and fraud, the true believer cannot identify himself with them. The sectarian text, from this perspective, has usually been 1 John 2:15, "Do not love the world or the things in the world." Niebuhr believed culture to be what the New Testament means by world.

The third approach, which might be called theological, also leads to the conclusion that Anabaptism was *sui generis* asocial, or even antisocial. According to this view Anabaptism "sought to replace the *Corpus Christianum* as a socio-political unity with a voluntary non-political reality called the *Corpus Christi.*"[5] Persecution was a sign that the two orders were mutually exclusive. Thus, in identifying themselves with this new radical obedience to Christ, the Anabaptists rejected all responsibility for the social and political affairs of their environment. Their citizenship was in heaven, and the new community of grace was a colony of heaven on earth. From this perspective the Hutterite movement is seen as the logical and most faithful interpretation of the Anabaptist vision. Withdrawal is seen neither as an historical accident nor as the result of severe persecution, but as the inevitable corollary of the ethic of absolute nonresistance. Coercion is necessary in sinful

[3] Ernst Troeltsch, *The Social Teaching of the Christian Churches* (New York: Macmillan Co., 1913), pp. 331 ff, 692 ff.

[4] H. Richard Niebuhr, *Christ and Culture* (New York: Harper & Bros., 1951), p. 56. The author seems to have the Amish in mind rather than the Mennonites.

[5] J. Lawrence Burkholder, "The Anabaptist Vision of Discipleship," in *The Recovery of the Anabaptist Vision*, ed. G. F. Hershberger (Scottdale, Pa.: Herald Press, 1957), p. 137.

society but outside of the perfection of Christ, so the withdrawn church becomes the new frame of reference for the life of the believer. Sometimes the believer must be hostile to the world because he sees it as a personification of the devil. Sometimes he is simply indifferent to it, but never is the world affirmed as *here*, as a part of the believer's real work; it is always *over there*, separate from the things that really count in life.

The evidence of these historical, sociological, and theological inquiries is corroborated by the simple fact that the persecuted Anabaptists did indeed withdraw from the world—whether for the sake of survival, or because of the inexorable determination of the sect cycle, or for theological reasons—after the initial thrust of the movement had spent itself, and the heirs of Anabaptism continued to remain aloof from society in succeeding generations and centuries. It is tempting, therefore, to accept this asocial or antisocial description as normative and authentic, and to explain deviations from it as regional or periodic variations of the central thesis. There is, however, a large and growing collection of Anabaptist source material which has not been adequately used. Furthermore, the ordering of this history under specific motifs has led to incongruities which obscure rather than clarify our understanding of the movement. How, for example, could Anabaptism be withdrawn and at the same time be a radical and effective missionary movement? how could it be antisocial and yet make a positive pioneer contribution to social theory and practice in the areas of religious liberty, voluntary church membership, and the separation of church and state as Ernest Payne, Harold S. Bender, Franklin H. Littell, Roland H. Bainton, and others have shown?

It is clear that church and world are major themes in Anabaptist thought. It is not the purpose of this essay to propose counter arguments to the above-mentioned studies in the hope of delineating the structures of an Anabaptist "social gospel," nor to read into their history equivalents of our modern notions of "involvement" or "holy worldliness." The intention of this study is simply to add, if possible, to our understanding of

Anabaptist thought about the social order by examining the nature of their church-world dualism and exploring the historical implications this had for them in relation to their sense of mission, their understanding of vocation, and the conduct of their economic life. It is possible to talk of an Anabaptist social consciousness even apart from church-state and nonresistant issues. We might, if we were bold, suggest the hypothesis that Anabaptism was, in fact, a vigorous, this-worldly movement which was successful initially precisely because it met people at the place and level of their real need. We might add that perhaps it was the only real social option people had in the sixteenth century, and against which the programs of the magisterial reformers were only variations on a medieval establishment theme. If on the other hand the Anabaptists died for a vision which was ultimately shown to be irrelevant to the individual and collective needs of people, we need to return to an earlier historiography which characterized the movement as misguided rather than pioneering and as tragic rather than glorious.

The Doctrine of the Two Worlds

A church-world dualism is basic to Anabaptist thought. While the early humanist-trained Swiss and South German Anabaptist leaders did not reject their Erasmian heritage, it was his *ad fontes* concern which led them to a depth encounter with the Scriptures. From this there arose among them a new understanding of the true, viz. biblical nature of the church of Christ which made a church-world polarity inevitable. This dualism was eschatological as well as ethical; in the believers' church the new aeon has come, calling forth a new ethic of personal and corporate discipleship. But in Michael Sattler (d. 1527), possibly also in Menno Simons (d. 1561) and others, one occasionally senses another kind of dualism reminiscent of a flesh-spirit ontological dualism. Where this emerged the emphasis on separation from the world seems to have become more radical, and the charismatic gifts are placed under congregational control. Sattler's *Schleitheim Confession* of 1527 is an inner-directed rather than outer-directed document.

Similarly, under the leadership of Menno Simons in the Netherlands, there was no room for the Hans Denck (d. 1527) or Hans Hut (d. 1527) kind of itinerant ministry, though this may in part have been the unique problem of second-generation Anabaptism.

The first protests of Conrad Grebel (d. 1526) and Felix Manz (d. 1527) in Zurich from 1523 to 1525 were directed against Zwingli's continuing identification of church and society despite his own deep Reformation insights into the nature of New Testament Christianity. They did not say that the state was bad nor did they identify society as demonic. They were engaged in a jurisdictional dispute on a matter of principle: the state had no right to interfere with, much less control, the life of the church. They had gradually come to see that a willingness to use political authority to initiate church reform meant, in fact, a subordination of the church to the state. This they rejected on Biblical and practical grounds. But they did not thereby reject the civil order. They were eager to do more for society than to pray for it, though they regularly did that too. The growing awareness that persecution would follow their separation from Zwinglianism, and their consequent delineation of suffering as a mark of the true church, indicate that they had no intention of finding a haven of refuge where they might live in peace. They were not forming a conventicle for the personal edification of a few but establishing in the midst of society a faithful community for all who would listen to and obey the witness of the Bible.

A similar pattern can be observed in South Germany. After his expulsion from Nuremberg on January 21, 1525, Hans Denck continued to teach and preach. In Strassburg he debated with Martin Bucer and Wolfgang Capito; from Switzerland Vadian wrote about Denck's work that "he could cite Scripture passages sharply and above understanding."[6] His writings reflect a man fully at home in the world of his day as well as in the world of the Bible and the *Theologia Deutsch.*

[6] Jan J. Kiwiet, "The Life of Hans Denck (Ca. 1500–1527)" *Mennonite Quarterly Review,* 31 (October, 1957): 242, quoted from Johannes Kessler, *Sabbata,* ed. Emil Egli and R. Schoch (St. Gallen, 1902).

In a different way the same was true of Hans Hut, where we again look in vain for signs of sectarian exclusivism and other-worldliness. His great missionary zeal was not spent in consolidating a few reliable congregations but in preaching to all who would hear. The great popular response to his apocalyptic message showed him to be speaking to the needs of the broad masses of society. The same might be said of Balthasar Hubmaier (d. 1528). He was, in fact, so relevant to society that he almost established an Anabaptist state church in Waldshut and again later in Nikolsburg.[7]

The congregations arising from the work of these men were heterogeneous, almost *ad hoc* in character, though complete and binding in their functioning. The dividing line between faith and unbelief was seen in obedience; those who walked in the obedience of faith were in the church of Christ, those who did not were in the world. The frame of reference for this ethic was the order of redemption rather than the order of creation, but they were not ascetics, as the Anabaptist modification of the Augustinian understanding of original sin also shows. They sat loosely to the social order in a kind of healthy indifference rather than rejecting it out of positive hostility. They had the kind of freedom which often characterizes a pioneering first generation. Their writings reflect a much more positive tone than, for example, the later more polemical writings of Menno Simons and others. They did, of course, reject the *corpus Christianum* as a valid structure for society. It was this, i.e. the refusal to baptize infants, which branded them as antisocial revolutionaries because it threatened to undercut the very structure of society.

A stronger dualism is evident in Sattler. In his letter to Bucer and Capito he proposes twenty theses to show that Christ and Belial, i.e. the world, have nothing in common. Among these Number 9 stated: "The believers have been chosen out of the world; therefore the world hates them." Number 10 said: "The devil is the prince of all the world; through him all the children

[7] John H. Yoder, "Balthasar Hubmaier and the Beginnings of Swiss Anabaptism," *Mennonite Quarterly Review*, 33 (January, 1959): 5–17.

of darkness reign." Theses 16 and 17 state that the believer is not a citizen of earth, but of heaven.[8] An equally pessimistic view of the world characterizes the *Schleitheim Confession*, of which he was undoubtedly the author. In it primary attention is given to shoring up the bulwarks of the congregation against encroaching evil from without *and* from within. The church has almost become a fortress to be defended. This is particularly evident in article four:

> We have been united concerning the separation that shall take place from the evil and the wickedness which the devil has planted in the world, simply in this: that we have no fellowship with them, and do not run with them in the multitude of their abominations. So it is; since all who have not entered into the obedience of faith and have not united themselves with God so that they will to do his will, are in great abomination before God, therefore nothing else can or really will grow or spring from them than abominable things. *Now there is nothing else in the world and all creation than good or evil, believing and unbelieving, darkness and light, the world and those who are come out of the world, God's temple and idols, Christ and Belial, and none will have part with the other.*[9]

It is possible that the pressure of persecution led to agreement on this article at Schleitheim as a logical response to suffering and a necessary defense against the persecuting world. By now the Anabaptists were obviously under no illusions about the reality of evil in the world; the binding and loosing community was needed precisely because of the temptations of the world, the flesh, and the devil. But there is more than development here, if indeed one can speak of development at all over this short, two-year period. Sattler seems to hold to a stronger, if not even a different, kind of dualism than

[8] Manfred Krebs and Hans Georg Rott, eds., *Quellen zur Geschichte der Taufer*, vol. 7: *Elsass, I Teil* (Gutersloh: Verlagshaus Gerd Mohn, 1959), pp. 68–69.

[9] John H. Yoder, ed., "The Brotherly Union of Schlaten-am-Randen (Schleitheim) 1527" (Unpublished manuscript, Elkhart, Indiana, 1966), pp. 14–15.

do Grebel, Manz, Denck, Hut, Marpeck, and others. To believe as Sattler did meant to be extremely pessimistic about society—to give up all hope even for improvement. It reflects a priestly rather than prophetic orientation. We know, of course, that the Anabaptists all had an eschatological rather than a programmatic or utopian vision for society, but the Sattler kind of ontological dualism provided an impetus for withdrawal in a way the work of the others did not. The *Schleitheim Confession* was widely circulated and played an important part in the life of the Anabaptists. The radical explicit and implicit separation from the world which its articles embody made it increasingly difficult to work redemptively in it. This dualism is, then, the basic category for understanding their withdrawal rather than nonresistance, as some have proposed. Also, if the suggested distinction between different kinds of dualism is tenable, we can correlate the extent of missionary and other involvement in society with the kind and degree of dualism which prevailed among them; the reasons for the rapid growth of sterile ethnicism among them must then be sought as much within the theological life of the Anabaptists as in the externals of persecution.

A Sense of Mission

At no point in their life and theology is the Anabaptist relation to society more apparent than in their sense of mission. A free and willing witness to the faith was inseparable from their understanding of the nature of the church; it was synonymous with discipleship as a vocation. It is apparent that the intensity of their missionary zeal was in large measure responsible for the persecution to which they were subjected.

Given the church-world dichotomy and eschatological sensitivity, it is not surprising to find real urgency in their witnessing. The new age will make all things new. Why concentrate on hopeless attempts to redeem the present order, they said, when the true church as a visible sign of the new order was already breaking in? This emphasis is most noticeable in Hut. In the spring of 1527 the Turk will come to the gates of

Vienna.[10] "The last and most dangerous time of this world has now come upon us." [11] The high and the mighty will be destroyed by the invaders under the hand of God. The faithful too must suffer to complete the passion of Christ, but eventually God's own shall rule the world.[12] The learned do not understand this, since it has pleased God to announce judgment through the preaching of those whom people call foolish *schwaermer*.[13] Therefore those who are called to proclaim must work while there is time, for difficult days will come and then the judgment.[14] Hut is not rejecting society; his eyes are focused on the coming glorious age which makes the present seem very unimportant. All structures will be changed in the day of judgment, and most people will be lost. Therefore as many as possible must hear the gospel before it is too late.

The centrality of the doctrine of the church in Anabaptism should not be allowed to obscure evidences of a strong personal concern for the lost—not an impersonal, theological concern but the compassion manifest in a one-to-one relationship. At his trial Manz said, "When some came to me weeping and asking for baptism I could not refuse them but did according to their desire." [15] From one of his journeys Jakob Hutter wrote about the chain reaction triggered by faithful witnessing. "One child of God wakes another and thus many are brought to God." [16] Hans Schmidt, who had been sent out by the Moravian brotherhood, wrote from his prison cell, "God has revealed His counsel to the Church. The primary

[10] Joseph Beck, *Die Geschichte-Bücher der Wiedertäufer: Fontes Rerum Austriacarum* (Vienna, 1883), 43:51.

[11] Lydia Müller, ed., *Glaubenszeugnisse Oberdeutscher Taufgesinnter* (Leipzig: M. Heinsius Nachfolger, 1938), p. 13.

[12] *Ibid.*, p. 22.

[13] *Ibid.*, p. 16.

[14] Paul Wappler, *Die Täuferbewegung in Thüringen von 1526–1584* (Jena: Verlag Gustav Fischer, 1913), pp. 240–43.

[15] Leonard von Muralt and Walter Schmid, eds., *Zurich*, vol. 1: *Quellen zur Geschichte der Täufer in der Schweiz* (Zurich: S. Hirzel, 1952), no. 42a.

[16] A. J. F. Ziegelschmid, "Unpublished Sixteenth Century Letters of the Hutterian Brethren," *Mennonite Quarterly Review*, 15 (April, 1941): 138.

and greatest task is to bring this counsel to the unknowing nations . . . to proclaim repentance to the sinner . . . so that at the last there may be no excuse."[17] Two excerpts from the writings of Menno Simons vividly summarize this concern for the lost:

> I have sometimes with Jeremiah resolved in my heart not to teach anymore in the name of the Lord because so many seek my life. Yet I could remain silent, for I am moved as was the prophet; my heart trembles within me and my joints quake when I consider that the whole world, lords, princes, learned and unlearned people . . . are so far from Christ Jesus and from eternal life.[18]
>
> Therefore we preach, as much as is possible, both by day and by night, in houses and in fields, in forests and wastes, hither and yon, at home or abroad, in prisons and in dungeons, in water and in fire, on the scaffold and on the wheel, before lords and princes, through mouth and pen, with possessions and blood, with life and death . . . for we feel his living fruit and moving power in our hearts. . . . We could wish that we might save all mankind from the jaws of hell, free them from the chains of their sins, and by the gracious help of God add them to Christ by the gospel of his peace.[19]

Most of the Anabaptists believed that most of the people in their day were eternally lost because of unbelief. It is likely that Menno Simons considered Anabaptism to be the only true church, but neither he nor any others insisted that membership in it was required for salvation. This position was considerably qualified, however, by their belief that anyone who had genuine faith in Christ would certainly seek believers' baptism as a seal of the covenant with God. Menno repeatedly stressed the importance of the new birth. "There is nothing

[17] Wilhelm Wiswedel, "Die alten Täufergemeinden und ihr missionarisches Wirken," Archiv für Reformationsgeschichte (Leipzig: Verlag Karl W. Hiersemann, 1943), 40:197.

[18] Menno Simons, *The Complete Writings of Menno Simons, ca.* 1496–1561, ed. John C. Wenger (Scottdale, Pa.: Herald Press, 1956), p. 298.

[19] *Ibid.*, p. 633.

under heaven that can or will endure before God but the new creature."[20] He believed too that all are lost who ". . . are not in the pure doctrine of Christ and in the Scriptural usage of his sacraments."[21]

The Anabaptist conviction that most people were lost was based primarily on the way people lived. "O Lord," Menno wrote, "I am not ashamed of my doctrine . . . before this rebellious world."[22] He frequently refers to "this poor, blind generation."[23] Leonhard Schiemer and Hans Schlaffer insisted that all nominal Christians are heathen; they have not placed their entire life under the Cross of Christ, they have not identified themselves with God's holy community, and, therefore, they proceed from the devil and antichrist. Even their prayers are blasphemy and a mockery of the divine.[24] True faith, they believed, could not help but produce disciplined Christian conduct. Sattler, for example, did not condemn the office of the magistrates but the incumbents themselves when he called them "Turks after the spirit."[25] Leonard Verduin has shown recently that moral earnestness in sixteenth-century Europe invariably made people suspect of being Anabaptists.[26] Marpeck was likely a little more tolerant than most of the others when he said that those who do not believe are lost but that God, not man, will judge unbelievers.[27] The frequently dis-

[20] *Ibid.*, p. 96.

[21] *Ibid.*, p. 158.

[22] *Ibid.*, p. 80.

[23] *Ibid.*, p. 91.

[24] Müller, *Glaubenszeugniss*, pp. 68–71. See also Robert Friedmann, "Leonard Schiemer and Hans Schlaffer: Two Tyrolean Anabaptist Martyr-Apostles of 1528," *Mennonite Quarterly Review*, 33 (January, 1959): 31–41.

[25] Müller, *Glaubenszeugnisse*, p. 39.

[26] Leonard Verduin, *The Reformers and Their Stepchildren* (Grand Rapids, Mich.: Wm. B. Eerdmans Publishing Co., 1964), pp. 95–131.

[27] Johann Loserth, ed., *Quellen und Forschungen zur Geschichte der oberdeutschen Taufgesinnten im 16. Yahrhundert* (Vienna: Verlagsbuchhandlung Carl Fromme, 1929), p. 170. "Wir haben niemant zu verdammen, wir bezeugen aber umb menschliches heyls willen die warheit gottes, wird yemant drunder troffen oder gericht, kunden wir nit für. Wir haben auch niemant selig zu sprechen . . . sonder bevelhem solche alle gott in sein gericht, der wirt die dausigen [ungläubigen] richten."

cussed Anabaptist emphasis on religious liberty must not be interpreted to mean tolerance in an Enlightenment sense; they were as convinced of the lostness of most others as the others were of the lostness of the Anabaptist. The difference was one of method of conversion-persuasion on the one hand, persecution and death on the other.

Coupled inseparably with the eschatological emphasis and the personal concern for the lost was another compelling motive for their sense of mission — the Great Commission of Jesus. They held to an epistemology of obedience, believing that understanding in spiritual affairs stood in direct correlation to obedience to the known will of God. This stress on obedience arose out of an unequivocal acceptance of the plain meaning of Scripture and a personal participation by faith in the life of Christ — Christ *in me* and *through me* as well as Christ *for me*. We notice an inner joy in Marpeck, for example, which compels him to say:

> Who can prevent the living stream of the heart from expressing itself through the mouth? Does not faith move? Does not the Holy Spirit compel? Does not love urge? Does not Christ command? Who then will prevent or forbid? Christians are all priests and therefore all proclaim the virtue of Christ (1 Peter 2), each one according to the measure of his faith. All this, by the grace of God and the witness of the Holy Spirit in our conscience before God and man, we must proclaim.[28]

Grebel was confident that he spoke "from" Christ with divine commissioning, stating *ideo ego te per Christum adiuro, no me contemnas ex Christo loquentem monentem.*[29] Blaurock asserted that since Christ had died for his sheep, he too would lay down his life and limb and soul for his sheep.[30] Perhaps

[28] *Ibid.*, p. 105.

[29] Grebel to Vadian, May 30, 1525, *Zurich*, no. 70.

[30] *Ibid.*, no. 123. In his further reference to the sheepfold passage recorded in John 10:1 he adds that all those not entering by the door, i.e., Christ, are thieves and robbers. As examples he cites Luther and Zwingli.

the most noteworthy, though somewhat later, example of missionary obedience is Leenaert Bouwens (d. 1582) of the Netherlands, who apparently baptized 10,251 persons, according to his own list of names.[31]

Many of the early accounts seem to witness more to perseverance under persecution than to intensive preaching because of the involvement of most of the baptized. The first mark of the priesthood of all believers was a willingness to witness. The rapid spread of the movement from 1525 to 1550 obviously depended on the faithfulness of more than a handful of leaders. There were first of all contacts with friends and relatives. There were also the daily contacts with others at the place of work, particularly for the wandering tradesmen. There were secret meetings in homes and listening to the defense of their own number before the courts. A tremendous missionary weapon also lay in the way the Anabaptists met torture and death as victors rather than victims. The gospel was carried into everyday life as a viable option for all to choose; the workshop became the cathedral and the village pump or a nearby stream the baptistry. Often women were as successful as men in winning converts.

The *Schleitheim Confession* remains an enigma in this picture unless it is seen, at least in part, as a product of the dualism referred to earlier. There is in it no trace of even implicit concern for the lost or for the world. It reflects the life of a congregation ready to settle down with a salaried pastor and other "unsectarian" accoutrements. Discipline is a primary emphasis and the concluding paragraph again urges the rule of the ban "that entry of false brothers and sisters among us might be prevented."[32] If the *Confession* was to serve as a unifying factor among the Anabaptists, one might expect it to have been concerned for their primary *raison d'être* rather than for establishment; if it was intended

[31] Karel Vos, *Menno Simons, 1469–1561* (Leiden: Drukkerij Brill, 1914), p. 130. Also S. Blapot Ten Cate, *Geschiedenis der Doopsgezinden* (Leeuwarden: W. Eeckhoff, 1842), 1:50 ff.

[32] Yoder, "Brotherly Union," p. 21.

to stress the uniqueness of Anabaptism over against other Reformation movements, an emphasis on mission might again have been anticipated. There is none.

An intriguing possibility exists, nevertheless, for insisting that Sattler had a sense of mission, perhaps even more than all the others. In his dualism the options regarding faith and unbelief were clearly delineated in black and white terms; to become an Anabaptist was actually a major decision, because people had to choose between the conventional and this new, radical form of Christian life. The *Confession* gives an impression of exclusiveness to the Swiss Anabaptists, but we might say that this was what was unique about their sense of mission—intense zeal coupled with an emphasis on a select fellowship of faith in the new society, the church. The seeming paradox of desiring to win converts on the one hand and a willingness to exclude them on the other may have been precisely what attracted people to them—a synthesis of zeal and love, of intense witness and rigorous demand. Theologically, this is an attractive option; historically, exclusiveness won out; Anabaptism lost contact with the world.

It is clear that the missionary response was for the Anabaptists the primary alternative to the methods of the magisterial reformers and that the believers' church was an attractive alternative to the *corpus Christianum*. Not coercion but persuasion, not primary emphasis on reforming society but on establishing a new society, not individualistic or sacramental salvation but personal experience and corporate faith were their alternatives. In opposing the Anabaptists the magisterial reformers rejected not only the Anabaptist vision for society but equally their method of achieving it. The Great Commission was intended only for the apostles and fulfilled by them, Schwenckfeld said with Luther. Marpeck replied that to neglect its command would inevitably lead to a deterioration of the inner life of faith, and he added, "The Church still stands on the first foundation and therefore in the power of the first commission. . . . No other power, or command, or commission is known to faithful Christians even today, nor will be known unto the end of the world."[33] This was, in a real sense, a program for society; not for the creaking social, political, and ecclesiastical machinery inherited from the Middle Ages, but for the people who were caught in it.[34]

Vocational and Economic Life

We have said in the preceding paragraphs that the Anabaptist layman was the primary carrier of the faith. This did not mean that the local emerging Anabaptist congregations did not take it upon themselves to send out certain members as their representatives in the world. The Hutterite communities frequently did this at the spring and fall communion services.[35] These persons were ordained and commissioned to go. From the perspective of the magisterial reformation, however, the Anabaptists were all laymen, since they had not been called by a legitimate church and since they could not pass the other apostolic test—they could not perform miracles.[36] From the perspective of the Anabaptists, however, they were all called to witness to what God had done for them in Christ. There is no discussion of a theology of the laity or of the priesthood of all believers in Anabaptist writings, because these terms assumed the old structure of church and society. In basically redefining the nature of the church, and therefore of society, the Anabaptists eliminated these old, corrective attempts, a fact which their opponents never understood. "Each one of you considers himself called to preach but you know that this is impossible, as Paul also states in 1 Corinthians 7:20. Most

[33] Loserth, *Quellen und Forschungen*, p. 105.

[34] For a discussion of Luther's understanding of the Great Commission, see Walter Holsten, "Reformation und Mission," *Archiv für Reformationsgeschichte* (Gütersloh: C. Bertelsmann, 1953), 44:1–32. Holsten asks us to judge modern missions in the light of the Reformers and not vice versa. He holds modern missions to be closely related to humanism and Catholicism, both of which were movements with which the Reformers had to break. Luther was more concerned to reform the church and thus also the mission program than he was to send out Protestant missionaries.

[35] Beck, *Geschichte-Bücher*, p. 39.

[36] Simons, *Complete Writings*, pp. 666–75.

of you are not called or sent by anyone, you are vagabonds [*Lant-loopers*]."[37]

Most Anabaptists continued in their vocational occupation after joining the movement, but it now became a choice opportunity to win others. Tradesmen talked with their fellow workers and invited them to the meeting in an Anabaptist home that night; servants shared their faith with curious employers. These natural contacts and conversations were often more significant than the sermon to which inquirers would be invited. The Christian calling became more important than the occupation, not *Beruf* but *Berufung*. The Anabaptists were indeed called to serve God in the world but not as transformationists seeking to sacralize the secular; God was, to be sure, also Lord of secular history, but the place where his sovereignty was seen and acknowledged was in the church. The true church of believers was seen as God's original and continuing will for all men, for society. It was in the church that Christ could manifest his glory and power rather than in the world. It was likely this emphasis which kept the English dissenters from joining the Dutch Mennonites in large numbers early in the seventeenth century; as new creatures, Christians were to remain in the world, they said, rather than withdraw into the spiritual safety of the church.[38] This reminder of the true nature of the church would not have been necessary in early Anabaptism.

Several studies have been made of the actual vocations represented among the Anabaptists.[39] These all reflect a wide

[37] Guy de Bres, *De Wortel, Den Oorspronck, Ende het Fundament der Wederdooperen, oft Herrlooperen van onsen tyde* (Amsterdam: Jan Eversz, Cloppenburgh, 1585), p. 43.

[38] Cornelius J. Dyck, "Hans de Ries: Theologian and Churchman: A Study in Second Generation Dutch Anabaptism" (Unpublished Ph.D. dissertation, Divinity School, University of Chicago, 1962), pp. 162–71. See also Irvin B. Horst, "Anabaptism and the Early English Reformation, 1534–1553" (Unpublished Th.D. dissertation, University of Amsterdam, 1960).

[39] Paul Peachey, *Die soziale Herkunft der Schweizer Taufer in der Reformationszeit* (Karlsruhe: Mennonitischer Geschichtsverein, 1954), pp. 22–72, 109–43; Peter James Klassen, *The Economics of Anabaptism, 1525–1560* (The Hague: Mouton & Co., 1964), pp. 83–97; W. L. C. Coenen, *Bijdrage tot de Kennis van de Maatschappelijk Verhoudingen*

spread of occupations and make impossible the belief that Anabaptism was a movement of the disinherited. A study of the Swiss Anabaptists during the years 1525–40, for example, showed the following categories among the 762 cases examined: 49 were classified as well educated, including one medical doctor, printers, teachers, 14 former priests, and 6 former monks; 9 were members of the nobility; 100 were city tradesmen and laborers; 75 were village tradesmen and laborers; the remaining 452 were farmers or peasants; the vocations of 77 could not be documented.[40]

Closely related to their vocational life was their understanding of economics. Most of their opponents felt extremely threatened by it and roundly charged them with being communists. Among these was Melanchthon, who identified their views erroneously as "Christen sind schuldig, ihre Güter in gemein zu geben, und sollen nicht Eigentum haben."[41] As a group, however, only the Hutterites practiced communalism; they did not differ from other Anabaptists in their understanding of the basic issues of Christian economic life, but carried their interpretation further than most Anabaptists felt Biblical warrant to go.

Anabaptist economics might be described as belonging more to the redemptive than to the natural order; only the obedient child of God could really understand that all the gifts of creation were given to men to use but not to own. The believer was to walk lightly in the world, not attaching himself to things which might divide his loyalty. The court records show that most Anabaptists tried on economic issues defended the right to private property, provided it was not used selfishly.[42] The attitude of believers to earthly possessions was for them a valid test of faith and one which could be easily identified. They did not consider themselves to have been deprived

van de Zestiende-Eeuwsche Doopers (Amsterdam: J. H. & C. van Heteren, 1920).

[40] Peachey, *Die soziale Herkunft*, pp. 109–43.

[41] Quoted in Wappler, *Die Tauferbewegung in Thuringen*, p. 152, from *Werke*, 1:312.

[42] See the evidence collected in Klassen, *Economics of Anabaptism*, pp. 28–49.

of their rights by fate and developed their theology to compensate for such loss;[43] they knew they had found the pearl of great price which put all other possessions into true perspective.

Putting possessions to right use meant first of all sharing them with all who were in need, inside and outside the fellowship of faith. Willingness to share was a sign of Godly love, without which there could be no true faith. Even as the believer prays "Our Father," so he recognizes that his possessions are not "mine" but "ours."[44] Instead of being forced to share their possessions in the manner of modern communism, they gave what they had voluntarily, gladly, before they were even asked. Possessions were no longer essential to their self-identity; their pilgrim consciousness had overcome covetousness. In 1526 Hubmaier said before the Zurich council:

> Concerning community of goods, I have always said that everyone should be concerned about the needs of others, so that the hungry might be fed, the thirsty given to drink, and the naked clothed. For we are not lords of our possessions, but stewards and distributors. There is certainly no one who says that another's goods may be seized and made common; rather, he would gladly give the coat in addition to the shirt.[45]

Georg Schnabel, a Hessian Anabaptist tried for heresy in 1538, wrote: "Economic practices in the congregation of believers are thus, that everyone who has food and clothing to spare shares it with his poor brother even as Paul writes about it in

[43] As suggested, for example, in H. Richard Niebuhr, *The Social Sources of Denominationalism* (New York: Meridian Books, 1957), pp. 34 ff.; also by Charles Y. Glock, "The Role of Deprivation in the Origin and Evolution of Religious Groups," in Robert Lee and Martin E. Marty, eds., *Religion and Social Conflict* (New York: Oxford University Press, 1964), pp. 24–36.

[44] Karl Schornbaum, ed., *Quellen zur Geschichte der Wiedertaufer, Bayern* (Leipzig, 1934), 1:49.

[45] Quoted in Klassen, *Economics of Anabaptism*, p. 32, from Joseph von Beck, *Die Geschichte-bücher der Wiedertauffer in Oesterreich-Ungarn* (Vienna: Carl Gerold's Sohn, 1883), p. 72.

Romans 15:26 and 27."[46] In the congregations of the "new pope," he adds, meaning Luther, it is worse than under the old pope. Members of the church not only do not help each other but become rich at each other's expense. Such practices, he concludes, are not even heard of among the heathen. A similar position is seen in the writings of Menno Simons:

> All those who are born of God . . . called into one body and love in Christ Jesus, are prepared by such love to serve their neighbors, not only with money and goods, but also after the example of their Lord and Head, Jesus Christ, in an evangelical manner, with life and blood. They show mercy and love, as much as they can. No one among them is allowed to beg. They take to heart the need of the saints. They entertain those in distress. They take the stranger into their houses. They comfort the afflicted; assist the needy; clothe the naked; feed the hungry; do not turn their face from the poor. . . .[47]

There are many records of the Anabaptists helping both friend and opponent in need, as for example, the help given to the Reformed refugees from Marian England at Wismar on December 21, 1553. On the other hand there are no records where they seek justice with the authorities through the prosecution of others. It is doubtful whether they could have achieved anything if they had tried, given the attitudes against them, but it is significant that they helped others without expecting or receiving help in return. The classic illustration might well be Dirk Willemsz, who escaped across the thin ice of a river but returned to pull out the guard who wanted to arrest him and had broken through the ice in his pursuit. He was burned in spite of his act of mercy, in 1569.[48]

Most of the Anabaptists believed that the taxpaying examples of Jesus required that they too pay all government

[46] Günther Franz, *Urkundliche Quellen zur Hessischen Reformationsgeschichte* (Marburg: N. G. Elwersche Verlagsbuchhandlung, 1951), 4:174.

[47] Simons, *Complete Writings*, p. 538.

[48] T. J. van Braght, *Martyrs Mirror* [1660] (Scottdale, Pa.: Mennonite Publishing House, 1950), pp. 741–42.

taxes except those used for the prosecution of war and those used only to enhance the pride and sinfulness of the ruler. When civil authority took it upon itself to raise "blood money" (*Henkergeld*) for war, believers should not pay, said Peter Riedemann, lest they become "partakers of other men's sins." [49] Christians are commanded to love their enemies. Some felt differently, however. A group of Anabaptists examined at Sorge in 1533 had no qualms about paying any kind of taxes, since God would clearly hold the government responsible, not the taxpayer.[50]

Obviously, these examples of Anabaptist vocational and economic life do not mean that the magisterial reformers did not believe in the priesthood of all believers or did not concern themselves with the needs of the poor. Luther too wanted all begging to be eliminated through the generosity of those who had abundance. There were, nevertheless, significant differences in both theory and practice between them and the Anabaptists on these issues which are not germain to this context. The discussion is intended to show only that, both in their vocational life as lay missioners and in their free sharing of material possessions, the Anabaptists were not antisocial but, on the contrary, showed a high degree of sensitivity to the spiritual and material needs of their fellow citizens in general as well as of their co-religionists in particular.

Summary

It has been suggested in the preceding that the basic theological factor shaping Anabaptist social consciousness was a church-world dualism which was found to be more pronounced in some than in others and which determined the degree of their withdrawal from the world as well as the rapidity of the transition from an aggressive protest movement to becoming the quiet of the land. Their understanding of the nature of the church as both eschatological and visible in time

[49] Quoted in Klassen, *Economics of Anabaptism*, p. 100, from Peter Riedemann, *Account of Our Religion*, trans. Kathleen Hasenberg (London: Hodder & Stoughton, and Plough Publishing House, 1950), p. 110.

[50] Klassen, *Economics of Anabaptism*, p. 103.

and space was likewise rooted in this church-world dualism, as was their ethic of discipleship and their insistence on the separation of church and state.

It is clear from this basic premise that we look in vain for signs of Calvinist transformationism among the Anabaptists; they were much closer to the pessimistic realism of Luther on society, but they did not think in his terms. There was no desire to adapt the personal ethic of discipleship to fit the requirements of a social ethic for the needs of all men in society; they had no intention of running society according to the Sermon on the Mount, as Luther charged.[51] They were content to witness and to serve in the world, but that was not the epitome of their interest. The church of true believers was for them the new social and cultural option as well as the only valid theological reality. This new society was the coming total society of the future – in God's own time; meanwhile they were willing to serve and witness in the old society, the world, as best they could.

We need to ask whether this new pattern of social organization was really antisocial or asocial, as has often been claimed, simply because the majority of the people did not follow this path to the new society? Is there not presented in it a full option, albeit radical, for society to consider? The Anabaptists knew from experience that they were and would remain a minority movement, but their theology of the remnant was not based on the a priori assumption that people would not respond to their witness anyway; they coveted their vision for everyone. Theirs was not a gnostic doctrine for the select few. In Anabaptism a bold new socio-religious model was presented to the world and tested in the fires of martyrdom. In a way, therefore, Anabaptism can be considered antisocial and socially irresponsible only if by social consciousness and responsibility we mean that for which the majority in fact opted historically. This raises the question of what criteria may be used to measure success. We know that Luther and Zwingli

[51] Clarence Bauman, "The Theology of 'The Two Kingdoms': A Comparison of Luther and the Anabaptists," *Mennonite Quarterly Review*, 38 (January, 1964): 41.

both had real doubts, at the end, whether they had actually achieved what they set out to do, whereas the Anabaptists were convinced that they had succeeded. Their only regret was that so few had caught the vision.

Aside from these normative considerations, however, the discussion of the Anabaptist sense of mission and also their ordering of vocational and economic life was introduced to show that there was a genuine social concern among them. Their missionary zeal was not motivated by a stiff and arid obedience to the divine command but characterized by a genuine love for people and a real desire to see them in the kingdom. Their sharing of material possessions with the needy was a logical corollary of this compassion, a footnote to authenticate their profession of faith and love. In a way Menno Simons epitomizes this new love for the world in the following words:

> While I served the world I received its reward; all men spoke well of me, even as the fathers did of the false prophets. But *now that I love the world with a godly love, and seek its welfare and happiness*, rebuke, admonish, and instruct it with Thy Word . . . it has become unto me a grievous cross, and the gall of bitterness.[52]

There were other signs of social consciousness among the Anabaptists which need further study. We know, for example, that Menno and others repeatedly called for the abolition of capital punishment; the issue is not really resolved by commenting that this seems rather natural for those who themselves faced execution. What, if any, was the influence of their emphasis on integrity by refusing to swear oaths of any kind? In which way did their frequently exceptional skills in specific trades and crafts influence social and economic life as seen, for example, in the experiences of the Hutterite communities in Moravia, as well as in the Lowlands, the Vistula Delta, and other places? The history of the Dutch Anabaptist-Mennonites provides an unusual opportunity for a study of their relationship to society; many of their church divisions arose over this

[52] Simons, *Complete Writings*, p. 80. (Italics mine.)

issue, yet many of the seventeenth-century Dutch national figures in painting, poetry, business, and philanthropy were Mennonites.[53] Also remaining for considerable further study is the actual Anabaptist contribution to modern social theory in their emphasis on freedom of religion, voluntary church membership, and the separation of church and state.

[53] Cornelius J. Dyck, ed., *A Legacy of Faith* (Newton, Kans.: Faith & Life Press, 1962), pp. 119–35. Also Hershberger, *Recovery of the Anabaptist Vision*, pp. 219–36.

10

The Reformation and the Rise of Modern Science

B. A. GERRISH

The first half of the sixteenth century witnessed two revolutionary movements in the intellectual history of the West. Twenty-six years after Luther's theses on indulgences had shaken the Western Church (1517), the strange theories of Nicholas Copernicus were published at Nuremberg (1543) and called in question the medieval picture of the cosmos. Of course, neither event was a revolution in itself. Copernicus was fully aware of his forerunners in the ancient world, and his heliocentric theory required the criticisms and observations of his successors before the scientific revolution was complete. Others, before Luther, had tried to reform the Roman Church; and it could be argued that, viewed in the context of European intellectual history as a whole, his religious "revolution" was not much more than a minor disturbance within medieval thought. Not until the Enlightenment were Christian ways of thinking about God and man radically transformed. Still, the Protestant Reformation and Copernican astronomy were, at the very least, parts of two incomplete revolutions, and their coincidence in time invites inquiry into the relations between them. The later development of Copernican astronomy and the wider question of Protestantism's place in the modern world may be left outside the limits of this enquiry.

The relations of religion and science in the Reformation Era were not confined to astronomical matters. Andreas Carlstadt, for example, had his doubts about medical science and suggested that the sick should turn to prayer, not to the physician.[1] Again, the man who discovered the pulmonary

[1] See the "table talk" reported in *D. Martin Luthers Werke kritische*

circulation of the blood, Michael Servetus, was burned in Protestant Geneva.[2] Of course, he was not condemned for his physiological opinions. But one may still wish to argue that Calvin's religious fanaticism delayed the physiological advances that might have resulted from the discoveries of Servetus.[3] Moreover, if there was nothing in the Christian revelation to contradict the pulmonary circulation of the blood, one of the charges brought against Servetus was that he had cast doubt on revealed geography: whereas the Old Testament called Palestine a land flowing with milk and honey, Servetus reproduced a statement of Ptolemy's, according to which Judaea was notoriously barren.[4] In his widely read work, *A History of the Warfare of Science with Theology in Christendom*,[5] Andrew Dickson White quite properly took

---

Gesamtausgabe (Weimar, 1883 ff.); *Tischreden*, vol. 1, no. 360. The *Weimarer Ausgabe* will be cited by the standard abbreviation "W.A." (with reference to volume, page, and line); the *Tischreden*, by "W.A.TR." (with volume and entry numbers).

[2] ". . . and after all Calvin did burn one of the few scientists of the age": Quirinus Breen, *John Calvin: A Study in French Humanism* (Grand Rapids, Mich.: Wm. B. Eerdmans Publishing Co., 1931), p. 155.

[3] So, at least, A. Wolf, *A History of Science, Technology and Philosophy in the 16th and 17th Centuries* (New York: Macmillan Co., 1935), p. 411. The English translation of Taton's history of science makes P. Delaunay say that "Calvin banished the physician Jerome Bolsec, with whose medical doctrines he disagreed": René Taton, ed., *The Beginnings of Modern Science, from 1450 to 1800: History of Science*, trans. A. J. Pomerans (New York: Basic Books, 1964), 2:170. This, however, is a mistranslation of the French original, which does not state that Calvin's disagreement was with Bolsec's medical doctrines: *La Science moderne de 1450 à 1800: Histoire générale des sciences* (Paris: Presses Universitaires de France, 1958), 2:178.

[4] See Roland H. Bainton, *Hunted Heretic: The Life and Death of Michael Servetus 1511–1553* (Boston: Beacon Press, 1953), pp. 118 ff. (on Servetus' discovery of the "circulation" of the blood), and pp. 94–95 and 184–85 (on the charge of impugning Biblical geography). As Bainton points out, nothing was said about Ptolemy in the actual sentence on Servetus (*ibid.*, p. 207).

[5] Originally published in 2 vols. (London: Macmillan & Co., 1896), White's fascinating study has recently been reissued as 2 vols. in one (London: Arco Publishers Ltd., 1955). He discusses Servetus' geographical heresy in 1:113. In the sixteenth century itself, "science" would have included the "humanities" (the *Geisteswissenschaften*). Indeed, Choisy suggests that science for the man of the sixteenth century meant above all the firsthand acquaintance with ancient literature; and scientific

note of such aspects of his subject. It is only for reasons of manageability that attention is focussed, in the present essay, on Luther and Calvin and their attitudes towards astronomy. Other reformers and other sciences could have been chosen.

Even when the theme "the Reformation and the rise of modern science" has been so circumscribed, opinions about it are sharply divided. On the one side, it has been argued that the Continental Reformation, in each of its two major branches, proved itself hospitable to the new science. Lutheran men of learning played a prominent role in the publication of Copernicus' theories, and the principles of Reformed (or Calvinistic) theology were supposedly an important incentive to scientific research. On the other side, it is alleged that Protestant biblicism greeted the new astronomy with enraged opposition, and that by their obscurantism Luther and Calvin delayed acceptance of the heliocentric hypothesis. The Reformers, it is said, repudiated Copernicanism by quoting Scripture and initiated a campaign of suppression which was as vehement, but not as effective, as the Roman Church's silencing of Galileo. Bias, perhaps, has played its part in the debate, and even among the defenders of Protestantism interest may sometimes be divided along confessional lines. Be that as it may, the question has to be faced whether, in actual fact, Luther and Calvin really were Biblical literalists in their attitudes towards natural science. The answer is that Luther in his so-called "doctrine of twofold truth" and Calvin in his "principle of accommodation" were operating with theories of theological language which made a conflict of Biblical and Copernican science unnecessary. The relation between Reformation and science thus appears to be many-sided, and it is still perhaps an open question.[6]

---

method was the direct appeal to the sources instead of citing "authorities." Eugène Choisy, *Calvin et la science*, Université de Genève, Recueil de la faculté de théologie protestante, no. 1 (Geneva, 1931), p. 10.

[6] As far as I can ascertain, there is no treatment in the literature which brings together all the various aspects of the theme as outlined above. Several of the problems are briefly discussed by John Dillenberger in his useful and discerning study, *Protestant Thought and Natural Science: A Historical Interpretation* (Garden City, N.Y.: Doubleday & Co., 1960). The subject was also sketched in two articles of mine, "Luther" and

I

Copernicus boldly dedicated his major treatise to Pope Paul III. But the dedicatory preface reveals the author's misgivings.[7] He is trying, in fact, to obtain the Pope's protection against the expected slanderers, hence the judicious flattery of his holiness as himself a learned mathematician. Diplomatically, Copernicus mentions the interest of Cardinal Nicholas Schönberg, of Capua, and Tiedeman Giese, bishop of Culm, together with "not a few other most eminent and learned men." Moreover, he represents his theory, not as an unprecedented novelty, but rather as a return to a neglected strand of antiquity, made necessary by difficulties in the accepted mathematics.[8] Copernicus anticipates that there will be those who oppose him on the basis of "some place of Scripture wickedly twisted to their purpose." But he hints, too, that his findings may be of practical utility to the Church, since efforts, under Leo X, to reform the ecclesiastical calendar had failed for lack of accurate astronomical data. Copernicus did not live to witness either the religious controversy over his work or its ecclesiastical utility. The first copies of his *De revolutionibus orbium coelestium* (1543) reached him on his deathbed.

Among the "eminent and learned men" who showed interest in Copernicus' researches were certain Lutherans, whom he wisely neglected to name in his dedicatory letter. Although the *De revolutionibus* was not published until 1543, the manuscript was apparently completed much earlier (possibly by

"Reformation," written in the spring of 1964 for *The Encyclopedia of Philosophy*, 8 vols., ed. Paul Edwards, which has been announced for publication in 1967 by The Macmillan Company.

[7] The author's preface to *De revolutionibus* is reproduced in Leopold Prowe, *Nicolaus Coppernicus*, 2 vols. (Berlin: Weidmannsche Buchhandlung, 1883–84), 2:3–8. Translations from the sources and literature are mine.

[8] The ancient authorities are Nicetas (whom Copernicus found mentioned in Cicero) and Philolaus, Heraclides and Ecphantus (all named by Plutarch). A reference to Aristarchus of Samos appears in Copernicus' manuscript, but was struck out before publication. Cf. Dorothy Stimson, *The Gradual Acceptance of the Copernican Theory of the Universe* (New York: Baker & Taylor Co., 1917), p. 27, n. 7.

1530), and the ideas it contained were not unknown in learned circles. A preliminary account had appeared in the *Commentariolus*, which Copernicus had written during the first decade of the century and distributed in manuscript among his friends.[9] In the spring of 1539, a young Wittenberg professor of mathematics Georg Joachim Rheticus was sufficiently intrigued by the rumors to pay a personal visit to Frauenburg in East Prussia (Ermland), where Copernicus was a prominent canon in the cathedral chapter. Rheticus became one of the keenest advocates of the new astronomy. The next year he published a preliminary report on Copernicus' findings,[10] and when he returned to Wittenberg (1541) he had been commissioned by Copernicus to publish the *De revolutionibus*. The suggestion that Rheticus found himself *persona non grata* at Wittenberg has not been demonstrated from the sources.[11] The

[9] Stimson says of the *Commentareolus*: "probably written soon after 1530." – *Acceptance of Copernican Theory*, p. 30. But Wilhelm Norlind dates the work "probably between 1504 and 1509": "Copernicus and Luther: A Critical Study," *Isis*, 44, pt. 3, no. 137 (September, 1953): 273. The *Commentareolus* is given by Prowe, *Nicolaus Coppernicus*, 2:184–202. In his *Three Copernican Treatises*, Records of Civilization, no. 30, ed. Austin P. Evans (New York: Columbia University Press, 1939), p. 7, Edward Rosen notes that the heliocentric system of the *Commentareolus* does not fully agree with the system taught in *De revolutionibus*.

[10] *De libris revolutionum Nicolai Copernici Narratio prima*. Rheticus' report, in the form of an extended letter (dated September 23, 1539) to John Schöner of Nuremberg, is reproduced in Prowe, *Nicolaus Coppernicus*, 2:293–377. The first volume of Prowe's monumental work is a biography of the astronomer (in two parts), and constitutes the leading authority for information concerning Copernicus' life and writings. The second volume is a collection of major documents. For Rheticus' journey to Frauenburg see 1, pt. 2:387–405; for the publication of the *De revolutionibus*, see 1, pt. 2:490–542.

[11] Rheticus' alleged troubles at the University of Wittenberg are suggested, e.g., by Stimson, *Acceptance of Copernican Theory*, p. 31, and Thomas S. Kuhn, *The Copernican Revolution: Planetary Astronomy in the Development of Western Thought* (Cambridge: Harvard University Press, 1957), p. 196. The salient facts, however, are these: (1) Rheticus resumed his professorship at Wittenberg after his return from Frauenburg and after publication of his *Narratio prima*. Almost immediately, he was made dean of the arts faculty. (2) To supervise the printing of *De revolutionibus* in Nuremberg, he was granted leave of absence, with

truth is that Copernicus' great work was published through the good will of the Lutherans, even—remarkably enough—the good will of those Lutherans who disapproved of Copernicus' thesis. Of course, Rheticus did not stand alone as the solitary Copernican among the associates of Luther. It was the Lutheran theologian Andreas Osiander who furnished *De revolutionibus* with an anonymous preface. One of Luther's closest friends and co-workers Casper Cruciger, professor of theology at Wittenberg, made no secret of his admiration for Copernicus. Erasmus Reinhold, a mathematician at the University, openly praised Copernicus and based a set of astronomical tables (the *Tabulae Prutenicae*) on his calculations.[12] The evidence, then, seems perfectly plain: Copernicus won some of his keenest advocates among the Lutherans; and those Lutherans who remained unconvinced at least tolerated their more adventurous colleagues, even encouraged them.

salary, from his duties at the University. For this privilege he had the approval both of the Lutheran Elector of Saxony and of Philip Melanchthon, who gave him letters of commendation to friends in Nuremberg. (3) Nothing sinister can be inferred from the fact that publication was undertaken in Nuremberg, since Rheticus had a shorter work of Copernicus published in Wittenberg itself by the printer of Luther's German Bible (Hans Lufft). (4) Though Rheticus eventually left Wittenberg, he did so in order to assume a post at the University of Leipzig, which had also become Lutheran. In addition to the literature already cited see: Werner Elert, *Morphologie des Luthertums*, vol. 1 (München: C. H. Beck'sche Verlagsbuchhandlung, 1931), pp. 396 ff.; Heinrich Bornkamm, "Kopernikus im Urteil der Reformatoren," *Archiv für Reformationsgeschichte*, 40, nos. 1–3 (1943): 171–83, esp. p. 181. Leopold Prowe promised a third volume in which he would furnish evidence that Rheticus and Reinhold were obliged, in the course of their teaching duties at Wittenberg, to abide by the Ptolemaic astronomy; further, that Rheticus moved from the University to escape the conflict between duty and conviction, and that Reinhold continued to edit work based on the older system so as not to deprive himself of a source of income (Prowe, *Nicholaus Coppernicus*, 1, pt. 2:280 n.; cf. 1, pt. 2:232 n. and 2:395 n.). Unfortunately, this third volume seems never to have been completed.

[12] For Cruciger and Reinhold see Elert, *Morphologie des Luthertums*, pp. 370 ff., and Bornkamm, "Kopernikus," pp. 180–81. Kuhn's suggestion that Reinhold kept silent about the validity of the system on which his tables were based (Kuhn, *Coperican Revolution*, p. 196) may strike the reader as decidedly odd.

Reformed scholars were not so intimately involved in the early dissemination of Copernicanism. It is possible that at Geneva, as in Wittenberg, champions of the old and the new astronomy taught side by side during the sixteenth century.[13] But with regard to Calvinism the somewhat different claim is made that Reformed theology was in some degree a nursing mother to scientific research. Attention has been drawn to evidence that Protestants in general have predominated over Roman Catholics among the leading scientists of modern Europe and that within Protestantism the Reformed Churches (at least until the nineteenth century) played the larger role in nurturing men of science.[14] In this connection, the case of Calvinist Holland is particularly interesting. The telescope and the microscope are both claimed as Dutch inventions; the Reformed Christians of the Lowlands expressed their gratitude to God for deliverance from Roman Catholic powers by founding the University of Leyden; and many Dutch Calvinists distinguished themselves by their passion for the natural sciences.[15] Even when allowances are made for patriotic and

[13] It has been suggested that Michel Varro, a pupil of Jean Tagaut at Geneva, anticipated the discoveries of Galileo, Kepler, and Newton. This seems to indicate at least a certain openness to astronomical novelties at Calvin's Academy. See Charles Borgeaud, *L'Académie de Calvin 1559–1798: Histoire de l'Université de Genève* (Geneva: Georg & Co., Libraires de l'Université, 1900), 1:67.

[14] See, for example, S. F. Mason, *Main Currents of Scientific Thought: A History of the Sciences*, The Life of Science Library, no. 32 (New York: Henry Schuman, 1953), chap. 16. Mason's authorities are Alphonse de Chandolle, *Histoire des sciences et des savants* (1873); and R. K. Merton, "Science and Technology in 17th Century England," *Osiris*, vol. 4 (1938). By studying the records of scientific societies Chandolle was able to argue that even in France a disproportionately high number of leading scientists were Huguenot by religious persuasion. The special role of the Calvinists is corroborated, so Mason argues, by the fact that in Lutheran Germany no scientist of the caliber of Johannes Kepler appeared again until the nineteenth century: Mason, *Scientific Thought*, p. 141.

[15] W. F. Dankbaar, "De verhouding van Calvinisme en wetenschap in de 16de eeuw, bepaaldelijk aan de Leidsche Universiteit," *Vox Theologica*, 15 (July, 1944): 121–28; Abraham Kuyper, *Calvinism* (Edinburgh: T. & T. Clark [1899]), pp. 143–88.

confessional loyalties, the evidence may seem sufficient to catch the historian's attention, though not every historian is likely to be impressed.[16]

Various attempts have been made to explain the evidence by analysis of the Calvinist mentality. In fact, there is a parallel here to the attempts of Max Weber and others to establish a correlation between the Calvinist "ethic" and the "spirit" of modern capitalism.[17] It is noteworthy that S. F. Mason's attempt to explain the historical correlation of Protestantism and science echoes, in part, Weber's explanation of the connection between Protestantism and capitalism. The followers of Calvin, according to Mason, "experienced an imperative need to know whether they were predestined." They obtained this assurance through the performance of good works, including scientific activity, which was valued as beneficial to mankind. Hence the Calvinistic-Puritan mentality was not merely congruous with scientific activity but provided it with "a positive impulse," since it was able to use science for the attainment of religious ends.[18]

Other features of the Calvinist tradition have been highlighted as possible incentives to scientific activity. Mason finds a further "congruence between the early Protestant ethos and the scientific attitude" in Protestantism's anti-authoritarian appeal to religious experience and individual interpretation of the Scriptures.[19] W. F. Dankbaar maintains that the most sig-

[16] "Voor de opkomst der wetenschap . . . heeft het Calvinisme geen specifieke beteekenis gehad. . . ." — J. Huizinga, as quoted by Dankbaar, "Calvinisme," pp. 121–22.

[17] An outline of Weber's thesis and the subsequent debate is offered in my essay, "Capitalism and the Decline of Religion," *McCormick Quarterly*, 18 (January 1965): 12–19. The titles of both this and the present essay are deliberately suggestive of R. H. Tawney's study, *Religion and the Rise of Capitalism* (New York: Harcourt, Brace & Co., 1926).

[18] See Mason, *Scientific Thought*, pp. 138–40. Mason himself does not allude to Weber's researches on the relation between Protestantism and capitalism.

[19] *Ibid.*, pp. 138–39. This, of course, is a point which Mason makes of Protestantism generally, not of Calvinism alone. Whether the original Protestantism of the sixteenth century was really so non-authoritarian and individualist is at least debatable.

nificant feature of Calvin's Academy at Geneva was the way in which the entire pursuit of science was subsumed under the religious duties of glorifying God and christianizing society. Similarly, Prince William the Silent desired that at the University of Leyden science, in the service of God and for His glory, should dedicate its powers to the good of both church and society, religion and freedom. The scientific enterprise was given a certain religious dignity through its inclusion under the rubric of glorifying God.[20] Others have sought the clue in the Calvinistic doctrine of common grace, according to which truth in every domain comes from God, so that the quest for truth is an act of piety which honors Him.[21] Finally, it is claimed that the doctrine of predestination, so boldly emphasized in the Reformed tradition, was "the strongest motive in those days for the cultivation of science." For God's decrees are the sure foundation of nature's laws, and scientific enquiry depends on confidence in the unity, stability, and order of nature.[22]

None of these attempts to explain the sympathy between Calvinism and the scientific temper amounts, I think, to a convincing demonstration, even if we grant the historical correlation which they seek to explain. Both the explanations and the correlation itself need further research. Mason's thesis

[20] Dankbaar, "Calvinisme," pp. 123, 125, 128.

[21] Choisy, *Calvin*, p. 12. The significance of *gratia universalis* for the relations of Calvinism and science is also noted by Dankbaar, "Calvinisme," pp. 126–27, and Kuyper, *Calvinism*, pp. 159 ff., though both put the accent elsewhere.

[22] Kuyper, *Calvinism*, pp. 146, 150–51. Mason attaches a somewhat similar significance to the doctrine of predestination, and he notes the agreement of Calvinist theology with natural science in their common rejection of the medieval celestial hierarchy of angelic beings (Mason, *Scientific Thought*, pp. 141–43). In a sense, the Reformed view of the relation between Creator and creature means a "disenchantment" of nature, as T. F. Torrance has argued, though without appealing to the doctrine of predestination: "The Influence of Reformed Theology on the Development of Scientific Method," in *Theology in Reconstruction* (London: S.C.M. Press, Ltd., 1965), pp. 62 ff. But it seems to me an oddity in Torrance's argument that he refers to Francis Bacon as evidence for Reformed theology.

concerning the Calvinistic use of science in the quest for assurance is not substantiated.[23] Dankbaar's argument, though more persuasive, is qualified by the admission that the University of Leyden was modeled on humanistic and medieval patterns, so that one cannot speak of a distinctively Calvinistic style of scientific activity.[24] Further, it may be asked, what makes even the "Calvinistic" concept of glorifying God anything more than a Christian commonplace, a vision shared by medieval educators as well? Nevertheless, the glory of God, common grace, and predestination—though none of them individually is without its counterparts in other Christian traditions—do seem to me, when taken together and given a special prominence, to be indicative of a distinctively Calvinistic view of the world and a corresponding Calvinistic "ethic." The vocation of the scientist receives a religious dignity,[25] and it may even be that the mechanics of providential working in Calvinist theology furnished a kind of midway point between the unpredictable angel- (and demon-) filled world of the middle ages and the deterministic order of seventeenth-century science. This much could be maintained without claiming that science everywhere had to cross over this particular bridge.

[23] Mason's quotation from the Puritan John Cotton (p. 141) hardly proves his main thesis. If anything, it would confirm Dankbaar's argument, since the reasons Cotton advances for interest in nature are (1) that the glory of God may be viewed in the created order and (2) that the understanding of nature (e.g., in medicine and economics) has utilitarian value for society.

[24] Dankbaar, "Calvinisme," p. 128.

[25] Cf. the remarks of Auguste Lecerf on science as a Christian calling: "De l'Impulsion donnée par le calvinisme a l'étude des sciences physiques et naturelles," *Bulletin de la société de l'histoire du protestantisme français*, 84 (April–June, 1935): 192–205, esp. 194–95. (The article appears, with the same pagination, also in *Études sur Calvin et le calvinisme* [Paris, 1935]). Lecerf rightly views Calvinism as more than a theological school: it became a *principe universal* (p. 193), a kind of *Weltanschauung*, and Lecerf himself was an exponent of a "Reformed philosophy." Cf. also William Young, *Toward a Reformed Philosophy* (Grand Rapids, Mich.: Piet Hein Publishers, 1952), which discusses the philosophy of the Dutch Calvinists, particularly Dooyeweerd. What Calvin himself might have made of these attempts at a "Calvinist philosophy" is another question.

II

If, then, some of Copernicus' key advocates were enlisted from Lutheran circles, and if there seems to have been a certain affinity between Calvinism and the scientific temper, why has it been repeatedly maintained that Protestantism arrested the advance of modern science? The answer is that a kind of sacred tradition has been faithfully transmitted in the literature, both English and foreign,[26] according to which the first generation of Reformers initiated a campaign to suppress the new astronomy. The origins and foundation of this tradition are seldom examined by those who pass it on. And it has to be conceded that some who write as the avowed champions of science have been strangely reluctant to transfer the scientific temper and method into the domain of history.

The five main features of the tradition can be readily enumerated, though they do not always appear together. First, Luther, Melanchthon, and Calvin rejected the heliocentric hypothesis.[27] Second, they refuted Copernicus by quoting Scripture.[28] The first and second points, as we shall see, are

[26] In what follows I have concentrated on the literature in English. A similar tradition in the German literature is traced by Elert, *Morphologie des Luthertums*, p. 367, n. 1., who mentions Franz Beckmann, Franz Hipler, Adolf Müller, J. H. von Mädler, R. Wolf, and L. Lohmeyer. He finds that even Prowe has not entirely escaped the influence of Beckmann and Hipler. Bornkamm, "Kopernicus," is mainly concerned with the more recent work of Ernst Zinner.

[27] See, e.g., A. Wolf, *History of Science*, p. 25, and the references cited in our following note (n. 28). In providing these references, I am only concerned to support the claim that a particular "tradition" has been disseminated in the literature – works ranging from rationalist propaganda to important monographs in the history of science. Frequently, allusions to the Reformers are only incidental. Of course, some historians of science display little or no interest in the relations of the Reformers and Copernicanism: cf., e.g., A. R. Hall, *The Scientific Revolution 1500–1800: The Formation of the Modern Scientific Attitude* (London: Longmans, Green & Co., 1954).

[28] John William Draper, *History of the Conflict between Religion and Science*, new ed. issued by the Secular Society, Ltd. (London: Pioneer Press, 1923 [first published in 1874]), pp. 214–15; White, *Warfare of Science with Theology*, 1:26, 97, 126–27; 2:176–77, 212–14; Bertrand Russell, *Religion and Science*, The Home University Library (London: Thornton Butterworth, Ltd., 1935), p. 23; Kuhn, *Copernican Revolu-*

two-thirds correct: Luther and Melanchthon did reject Copernicanism on Biblical grounds. But from this evidence it is assumed, third, that the Reformers were in principle opposed to scientific investigation[29] and, fourth, that they sought to suppress the Copernican viewpoint.[30] This, as far as I can judge, is an unwarranted inference from the first point and is already refuted by our previous discussion. Finally, it is suggested that, if Copernicanism nevertheless flourished in Protestant lands, this was only because the Protestants were less effective than the Roman curia in silencing scientific heretics.[31] This, too, is a suggestion which seems unnecessary in the light of our previous conclusions, since no campaign of repression was in fact undertaken during the Reformers' life-

---

tion, pp. 191 ff.; Stimson, *Acceptance of Copernican Theory*, pp. 39–41, 48, 99 ff.; A. C. Crombie, *Medieval and Early Modern Science*, vol. 2: *Science in the Latter Middle Ages and Early Modern Times, XII–XVII Centuries* (New York: Doubleday & Co., 1959), p. 168; Marie Boas, *The Scientific Renaissance 1450–1630*, vol. 2: *The Rise of Modern Science*, ed. A. Rupert Hall (New York: Harper & Bros., 1962), p. 126; Herbert Butterfield, *The Origins of Modern Science 1300–1800* (London: G. Bell & Sons, Ltd., 1958), pp. 55–56; Mason, *Scientific Thought*, p. 141. Mason shows how the Puritan John Wilkins evaded the clash of science and scripture (*ibid.*, pp. 147–48), but he does not seem to be aware that Wilkin's exegesis was anticipated by the Reformers themselves.

[29] See, e.g., White's remark that the Reformers "turned their faces away from scientific investigation" (White, *Warfare of Science with Theology*, 1:213–14). The drastic statement attributed to P. Delaunay in the English version of René Taton's history of science, that "Calvin denounced science as nothing but 'impudent curiosity and impertinence'" (Taton, *History of Science*, 2:170), turns out to be an over-enthusiastic translation of the original (see p. 178 of the French). Delaunay actually said that Calvin denounced the impudence and audacity of it (*sc.*, science) – a sufficiently prejudiced selection of evidence, which needed no further embellishment.

[30] According to Kuhn, "Protestant leaders like Luther, Calvin and Melanchthon led in citing Scripture against Copernicus and in urging the repression of Copernicans." The Protestants "provided the first effective institutionalized opposition." – Kuhn, *Copernican Revolution*, p. 196.

[31] *Ibid.*: the Protestants lacked the "police apparatus" available to Rome. Cf. White, *Warfare of Science with Theology*, 1:126; Russell, *Religion and Science*, pp. 42–43; Stimson, *Acceptance of Copernican Theory*, pp. 99, 104; William Cecil Dampier, *A Shorter History of Science* (Cambridge: At the University Press, 1944), p. 49. (Calvin was as bad as any Roman inquisitor, but he lacked comparable power.)

time.[32] It remains, then, to examine the actual sources in which Luther, Melanchthon, and (allegedly) Calvin expressed opposition to Copernicus on Biblical grounds.

By 1539, even before the publication of his major work, Copernicus had become a topic for conversation in Wittenberg. It was in the spring that Rheticus left for Frauenburg, to obtain firsthand information from Copernicus himself. The same year, on June 4, Copernicus and his theories came up for discussion in Luther's household, and the Reformer's admiring disciples jotted down notes on the master's astronomical opinions. Here is Lauterbach's version of the discussion:

> Mention was made of some new astrologer [*sic*], who would prove that the earth moves and not the heaven, sun, and moon, just as if someone moving in a vehicle or a ship were to think that he himself was at rest and that the earth and the trees were moving. But [Luther's response] this is the way it goes nowadays: anyone who wants to be clever, should not be satisfied with the opinions of others (*der soll ihme nichts lassen gefallen, was andere achten*). He has to produce something of his own, as this man does, who wants to turn the whole of astrology upside down. But even though astrology has been thrown into confusion, I, for my part, believe the sacred Scripture; for Joshua commanded the sun to stand still, not the earth.[33]

The parallel passage in Aurifaber's version of the *Table Talk* includes the remark greatly beloved and faithfully reproduced

[32] Since it is sometimes supposed that Johannes Kepler was persecuted by the Lutherans as was Galileo by Rome, it is worth noting that he was held unacceptable as a teacher in his native Württemberg, not because of his astronomical views, but because he doubted the ubiquity of Christ's body. See Elert, *Morphologie des Luthertums*, pp. 375 f., who also alludes to Kepler's efforts at reconciling his astronomy and his faith. Elert does not mention, however, that the thought of invoking the power of the authorities against the upstart astronomer at least occurred to Melanchthon. But the thought, expressed in a piece of private correspondence (October 16, 1541), was not implemented, as we have shown. See *Corpus Reformatorum* (henceforth abbreviated "C.R.") 4. 679.

[33] W.A.TR. 4, no. 4638.

in the secondary literature: "The fool wants to turn the whole art of astronomy upside down."[34] In general, Lauterbach is to be considered the more reliable reporter, so that there must be some doubt about the authenticity of the notorious "fool" clause.[35] Nevertheless, even without it the passage seems to be plainly anti-Copernican. To be sure, Wilhelm Norlind has read Lauterbach's version as complimentary to Copernicus. "Now it is very curious," he remarks, "that, according to Aurifaber, Luther may *first* seem to praise the man ('er muss ihm etwas Eigens machen') and *then* blames him as a 'Narr'!" Since the disparaging expression *der Narr* was not in the corresponding passage of "the more trustworthy Lauterbach," we are bound, so Norlind maintains, to "regard the 'famous' expression given by Aurifaber as an interpolation not consistent with the text."[36] It could be replied that Luther is not commending Copernicus for his inventiveness, but disparaging him for wanting to be thought clever. But in any case the main point is sufficiently clear: Luther thought he could refute Copernicus by quoting Scripture, though he did not therefore try to prevent the spread of Copernican astronomy.[37]

Melanchthon, too, like Luther, adduced Scriptural arguments against Copernicanism.[38] But Melanchthon was not simply a theologian. He was also a philosopher of the humanistic type, and he held astronomical opinions on non-theological grounds. For him, the study of nature rested upon the authority of the approved ancients — that is, Aristotle and Ptolemy. Hence the greater part of his case against Copernicus con-

[34] W.A.TR. 1, no. 855: "Der Narr will die ganze Kunst Astronomiae umkehren." It is this version which is quoted by White, Stimson, Kuhn, Russell, Crombie, and Boas.

[35] Lauterbach's version represents *die ursprüngliche Nachschrift;* Aurifabers, *eine spätere Bearbeitung*, though it was the edited version of Aurifaber that was first printed (in 1566). So Bornkamm, "Kopernicus," p. 173. Cf. also Elert, *Morphologie des Luthertums*, p. 372; John Dillenberger, *Protestant Thought*, pp. 37–38.

[36] Norlind, "Copernicus and Luther," pp. 275–76.

[37] Cf. Bornkamm, "Kopernikus," p. 173.

[38] See the *Initia doctrinae physicae* (1549): C.R. 13. 216. Cf. Elert, *Morphologie des Luthertums*, pp. 367 f.; Dillenberger, *Protestant Thought*, pp. 39–41.

sisted of arguments drawn from antiquity.[39] In other words, Melanchthon believed himself to be taking up the debate against a misguided effort to revive outmoded science. Nonetheless, he did not permit his disagreements to intrude upon his friendships nor even to detract from his respect for Copernicus.[40] So far was he from initiating a campaign of repression, that he somewhat mitigated his criticisms after 1549.[41] Still, it must be admitted that Melanchthon, like Luther, thought it legitimate to refute a scientific theory with scriptural arguments. Moreover, he repaired the fateful alliance of theology and Aristotelianism which Luther had shattered; and thereby he created for later Protestantism a problem which did not exist for Luther and Calvin.[42]

As notorious as the "fool" passage in Luther's *Table Talk* is the rhetorical question commonly attributed to Calvin: "Who will venture to place the authority of Copernicus above that of the Holy Spirit?" But although the question is faithfully transmitted in the English literature, the exact reference does

[39] C.R. 13. 217 ff. "Es sind die alten ptolemäischen Argumente, aber vor allem auch weithin dieselben Gründe, mit denen die alexandrinischen Jünger des Aristoteles den antiken vörganger des Kopernikus Aristarch von Samos widerlegt hatten." – Bornkamm, "Kopernikus," p. 179.

[40] Melanchthon's support of Rheticus has already been noted. It should be added that he was equally generous in his friendship for Reinhold. He commended the *Tabulae Prutenicae*, and he composed an address for Reinhold to read in honor of Caspar Cruciger. The address speaks of Copernicus with frank admiration. See Elert, *Morphologie des Luthertums*, pp. 370–73. Bornkamm notes other passages in which Melanchthon gave expression to his respect for Copernicus: Bornkamm, "Kopernikus," p. 180.

[41] *Ibid.*, in dependence upon Emil Wohlwill.

[42] I have discussed elsewhere Luther's relationship to Aristotle and to philosophy in general: *Grace and Reason: A Study in the Theology of Luther* (Oxford: Clarendon Press, 1962). Though Calvin may be said to have shared Luther's reservations about Aristotelian philosophy, it has often been pointed out that the Platonic tradition influenced him more positively: Roy W. Battenhouse, "The Doctrine of Man in Calvin and in Renaissance Platonism," *Journal of the History of Ideas*, 9 (October, 1948): 447–71; Joseph C. McLelland, "Calvin and Philosophy," *Canadian Journal of Theology*, 11 (January, 1965): 42–53; Albert-Marie Schmidt, "La Doctrine de la science et la théologie calviniste au XVIe siècle," *Foi et vie*, 36 (April, 1935): 270–85, esp. 279.

not accompany it, and it has so far proved impossible to locate it in any of Calvin's known writings. I have not come across it (or its equivalent) in the foreign literature,[43] and I suspect that its currency in English and American studies is the most striking proof of the influence of A. D. White. In White's own words:

> Calvin took the lead, in his *Commentary on Genesis*, by condemning all who asserted that the earth is not at the centre of the universe. He clinched the matter by the usual reference to the first verse of the ninety-third Psalm, and asked, "Who will venture to place the authority of Copernicus above that of the Holy Spirit?"[44]

Where, then, did White himself find Calvin's question, since it cannot be found either in the *Commentary on Genesis* or in the exposition of Psalm 93? In a splendid piece of detective work Edward Rosen has tracked the citation back to F. W. Farrar, who likewise offered only the "quotation," not the reference.[45] Rosen explains this omission by giving a rather mischievous turn to a eulogy of Farrar by his son, who wrote: "Quotation with him [F. W. Farrar] was entirely spontaneous, almost involuntary, because his marvellous memory was stored, nay saturated with passages." The famous Calvin quotation seems, in fact, to be a fiction due to Farrar's overconfidence in his marvellous memory. Rosen concludes: "What then, . . . was Calvin's attitude toward Copernicus? Never having heard of him, Calvin had no attitude toward Copernicus."[46] This, per-

[43] Lecerf apparently presumed that Calvin had no knowledge of Copernicus: Lecerf, "De l'Impulsion," pp. 193–94.

[44] White, *Warfare of Science with Theology*, 1:127. Ps. 93:1 reads (in the King James version): "The world also is stablished, that it cannot be moved." Calvin's alleged question is repeated by Stimson, *Acceptance of Copernican Theory*, p. 41, n. 1; Kuhn (with express acknowledgments to A. D. White), *Copernican Revolution*, p. 192; Russell, *Religion and Science*, p. 23 (also in his *History of Western Philosophy* [London: George Allen & Unwin Ltd., 1946], p. 550).

[45] Frederic William Farrar, *History of Interpretation* (London, 1886), p. xviii. See Edward Rosen, "Calvin's Attitude toward Copernicus," *Journal of the History of Ideas*, 21 (July–September, 1960): 431–41.

[46] Rosen, "Calvin's Attitude toward Copernicus," p. 441. John Dillenberger had already written of the alleged Calvin quotation, as given by

haps, says too much. It is hardly necessary to suppose that Calvin had never heard of Copernicus. What is plain, however, is that, if he knew of Copernicus, he felt no compelling need to quarrel with him. It cannot even be established that Calvin once mentioned Copernicus in all his voluminous writings.[47]

III

It remains true, however, that the Lutheran Reformers, at any rate, did oppose Copernicanism with arguments drawn from Scripture. A. D. White and others were perfectly right in seing here a phase in the warfare between science and theology, even though they constructed false inferences upon the evidence, some even magnifying rejection of the Copernican theory into an imaginary campaign of suppression. Luther and Melanchthon set the pattern for later Protestant biblicism, according to which the Sacred Scriptures furnish inerrant information on scientific matters. The basis was already laid, by the first generation of Lutheran Reformers, for what Draper called "the fatal maxim that the Bible contained the sum and substance of all knowledge useful or possible to man." [48] Luther

White: "I have been unable to find the passage in Calvin and doubt that it exists." – Dillenberger, *Protestant Thought*, p. 38, n. 33. The reference to Rosen's article by Boas, *Scientific Renaissance*, p. 357, n. 31, indicates that his conclusions will gradually be appropriated in the textbooks. That White's influence nonetheless persists is suggested by the fact that Boas still charges Calvin with Biblical literalism and refers to White for the usual Melanchthon quotation (p. 126).

[47] According to Quirinus Breen, Calvin's "only possible reference to Copernicus" occurs in his commentary on Ps. 46, "where he appears to criticise the new astronomy." – Breen, *John Calvin*, p. 155. At most, this could only be an oblique reference, and Copernicus is not mentioned by name.

[48] Draper, *Conflict between Religion and Science*, p. 215. Cf. White: "At the Reformation the vast authoriy of Luther was thrown in favor of the literal acceptance of Scripture as the main source of natural science." – White, *Warfare of Science with Theology*, 1:26. On occasion, White notes a more critical attitude to Scripture on Luther's part, whom he considers (despite everything!) to have been characterized by "strong good sense" (*ibid.*, 2:305). The remarks of White and Draper on the Reformation use of the Bible are so plainly out of date that one would ignore them, were they not so widely disseminated in nonspecialist literature. I have discussed Luther's and Calvin's use of Scrip-

and Melanchthon assumed that not only the meaning of the Gospel, but also the scientific picture of nature could be read off from the pages of Scripture, literally interpreted. This much is clear enough in the sources used by White. It must now be pointed out, however, that gross injustice is done to Luther by the extraordinary procedure of isolating a solitary passage from the *Table Talk* and assuming that his entire attitude towards the natural sciences—and indeed the Sacred Scripture—is adequately presented in this stray, offhanded remark.

According to White, the Reformers "turned their faces away from scientific investigation."[49] Even in the narrow sense of modern English usage, which virtually identifies "science" with natural science, this statement is incorrect. Luther had a lively interest in scientific progress and explicitly raised the question of the relationship between science and theology.

It is true that a superficial reading of Luther could uncover further apparent evidence of hostility towards science. Part of the difficulty is resolved when one recalls that the natural sciences in the sixteenth century were entangled in sorcery, alchemy, and astrology. Some of Luther's judgments can only be understood as an attempt to disentangle science from quackery. What looks at first like an obscurantist assault on "natural philosophy" may turn out to be a protest against unwarranted procedures in science. "Those who lie about far-distant lands, lie with all their might, there being none with experience to contradict them." But science is tied to experience. For Luther, the two sources of knowledge were experience (*erfarung*) and revelation.[50] They correspond to philoso-

ture in "Biblical Authority and the Continental Reformation," *Scottish Journal of Theology*, 10, no. 4 (1957): 337–60.

[49] White, *Warfare of Science with Theology*, p. 214.

[50] See Luther's postil on the Gospel for Epiphany (Matt. 2:1–12), W.A. 10$^{1, 1}$. 555–728, esp. pp. 565 ff. The quotation (a proverbial saying) appears at 566. 13. Of course, "experience" in Luther's parlance has other meanings in addition to sense-experience. Sometimes it refers to the inward appropriation of spiritual truth (e.g., W.A.TR. 1, no. 701; W.A.TR. 3, no. 3503). But in the postil for Epiphany he clearly has in mind an exercise of the intelligence which is tied to observation.

phy and theology respectively, or to reason and faith (the two modes of cognition).[51] And by "philosophy" Luther understood the sum total of the human "sciences." Hence he admired astronomy as an empirical science, but had no respect for astrology;[52] and he contrasted the astrologer's predictions with the physician's prognosis, which has "symptoms and experience" as its guide.[53]

Luther was not ignorant of the fact that he lived in an age of scientific progress. He greeted the new science with enthusiasm and liked to contrast himself in this respect with the Humanist Erasmus. In the advance of scientific knowledge he saw the gradual recovery of Adam's dominion over the world of nature.[54] Reason was understood by Luther as the divinely given organ by which man was to move out into the world and have mastery over it.[55] Hence he did not need to become defensive when science and Scripture ran into apparent conflict. He was willing, for example, to accept the astronomers' conclusion that the moon was the smallest and lowest of the "stars": perhaps the Scriptures, in calling the sun and the moon two great lights, were simply describing the moon as it looks to us.[56] Luther recognized that religious and scientific interest in nature are two different things. The light of the moon was for him, religiously, a token of divine care; but he acknowledged

[51] "Philosophia versatur circa cognoscobilia ratione humana. Theologia versatur circa credibilia, id est, quae fide apprehenduntur" (W.A. 39². 6. 26).

[52] W.A.TR. 2, no. 2413. That the actual terms "astronomy" and "astrology" are not always so sharply distinguished is clear in the passage already cited from W.A.TR. 1, no. 4638. In another passage from the *Table Talk* (W.A.TR. 1, no. 17) Luther suggested that the benefits Melanchthon derived from astrology he himself found in a strong draught of beer.

[53] W.A.TR. 4, no. 5113.

[54] W.A.TR. 1, no. 1160.

[55] See esp. the *Disputatio de homine* (1536): W.A. 39¹. 175–80. As the organ of man's dominion, reason is inventress and mistress of all the sciences (Theses 4–8). She remains queen of the earth even after the Fall (Thesis 9).

[56] "Quare credo Mosen locutum esse ad captum nostrum, quia nobis ita videatur." – W.A.TR. 5, no. 5259. This is the thought which Calvin developed in his theory of accommodation.

that the astronomer's concern was to show how the moon's light was in fact reflected from the sun.[57] In other words, even when theology and science are directed to a common object, as are the heavenly bodies, they talk about it in different, but not necessarily exclusive, ways. Faith penetrates beyond the visible object to the unseen God, whose gracious care the object attests.[58]

It is the attempt to distinguish the proper spheres of theological and philosophical language that lies behind Luther's interest in the so-called medieval "theory of double truth."[59] As usually formulated, the theory maintains that a proposition may be true in theology but false in philosophy, and vice versa. It seems to have been not so much a consciously formulated doctrine as an accusation leveled against theological opponents,[60] and it is commonly assumed that the accused were guilty of a dishonesty which tokened the bankruptcy of scholastic theology.[61] In his important *Disputation on the*

[57] W.A. 42. 31. 8 ff.

[58] Sometimes, according to Luther, the visible sign is in contradiction to the grace of God, whose "yes" is hidden in a "no." But this opens up the question of Luther's *theologia crucis*, which cannot be discussed here even though it is of some importance for his understanding of nature. See, for example, Walther von Loewenich, *Luthers Theologia crucis*, 4th ed. (Munich, 1954). For further discussion on Luther's picture of nature, see Heinrich Bornkamm, *Luther's World of Thought*, Eng. trans. (St. Louis, Mo.: Concordia Publishing House, 1958). Cf. Bornkamm's essay "Faith and Reason in the Thought of Erasmus and Luther," in *Religion and Culture: Essays in Honor of Paul Tillich*, ed. Walter Leibrecht (New York: Harper & Bros., 1959).

[59] See Karl Heim, "Zur Geschichte des Satzes von der doppelten Wahrheit," *Studien zur systematischen Theologie*, Theodor von Haering zum 70. Geburtstag von Fachgenossen dargebracht (Tübingen, 1918), pp. 1–16; Bengt Hägglund, *Theologie und Philosophie bei Luther und in der occamistischen Tradition: Luthers Stellung zur Theorie von der doppelten Wahrheit* (Lund: C. W. K. Gleerup, 1955), pp. 87–102; Gerrish, *Grace and Reason*, pp. 49 ff.

[60] Cf. Étienne Gilson, *Reason and Revelation in the Middle Ages* (New York: Charles Scribner's Sons, 1954), p. 58.

[61] Cf. Clement C. J. Webb on the Renaissance philosopher Pietro Pomponazzi (1464–1525): *Studies in the History of Natural Theology* (Oxford: Clarendon Press, 1915), pp. 319 ff. Apart from Pomponazzi, the theologian Robert Holcot (d. 1349) is most often singled out as an adherent of the double-truth theory.

Proposition, "The Word was made flesh" (1539),[62] Luther states explicitly, though without using the expression "double truth," that the same thing is not true in different disciplines. And yet his intention is not to allow, but to exclude, the possibility of contradiction between two disciplines. It remains axiomatic that one truth agrees with another.[63] Luther begins by affirming that the proposition "The Word was made flesh" is true in theology, but simply impossible and absurd in philosophy (Thesis 2). In the course of the disputation the objection is made that if the same thing is true in theology and false in philosophy, then philosophy and theology contradict each other. Luther's reply, in effect, is that there can only be contradiction *within* a particular language system, not *between* one system and another.[64] "God is man" and "God is not man" would only be contradictory if both were asserted in the same discipline.[65] The fact is that the words "God is man" do not *mean* for the theologian what they mean for the philosopher. The philosophical sense of the word "man" is "self-subsistent person," but when the theologian speaks of the Incarnation he has in mind "a divine person bearing humanity." [66] Similarly, in

[62] W.A. 39². 3–5 (the forty-two theses); 6–30 (three different transcripts of the disputation); 30–33 (notes prepared against the theses by an unknown hand). In my discussion I have not discriminated among the three transcripts.

[63] "Etsi tenendum est, quod dicitur: omne verum vero consonat, tamen idem non est verum in diversis professionibus." – Thesis 1: W.A. 39². 3. 1. "Sapientia non pugnat sibi ipsi, hoc nos quoque dicimus." – *Ibid.*, 13. 5.

[64] "Contrarietas debet fieri et esse in eodem genere et in eadem propositione. Deus est homo. In philosophia est falsa, quod sit Deus et homo." – *Ibid.*, 16. 11.

[65] "Deus homo et Deus non homo sunt contraria non in eodem ordine." *Ibid.*, 16. 23. "Deus et homo sunt 2 propositiones, in theologia verum. Si essent ambae in theologia, tum consisteret argumentum." – (16. 33). The second of the two quotations is not entirely clear, but the general drift of the argument is plain enough.

[66] "Hic enim fit novum vocabulum significans personam divinam sustentantem nostram humanam, ut albus significat hominem sustentantem albidinem." – W.A. 39². 10. 30. The illustration seems to require the insertion after *humanam*, not of *personam*, but of some such word as *naturam*. One of the parallel transcripts has the phrase *Deum sustentantem humanam creaturam* (10. 10). Luther goes on to say that God is man

the syllogism "Every man is a creature, Christ is a man, therefore Christ is a creature" there are really four terms, not the required three, since "man" has a different sense in the major and the minor premises.[67]

In his distinction between the two uses of the word "man" Luther was borrowing from the schoolmen. But he turns a scholastic distinction against the Paris schoolmen themselves and argues that if they find it necessary to invoke the notion of equivocalness, then they ought really to agree with him. That is, they should not attempt a reconciliation of theology and philosophy, but should concede his point, that the same thing is not true in both theology and philosophy. A proposition could only be said to be true in both contexts if the terms of the proposition were used with the same significance.[68] In answer to a further objection, Luther insists that the propositions "God is man" and "Every man is a creature" are both "simple." He means, I take it, that they are unambiguous within *either* context, theology *or* philosophy.[69] But if you compare their meaning across disciplines, so as to say, they are not strictly the same propositions, because (as Luther has already shown) the terms are differently used. We cannot admit ambiguity into our syllogisms *within* any discourse: we have to keep them unambiguous by distinguishing the disciplines.[70] When we observe the necessary distinction, then the fact that one discipline seems to affirm what another denies proves not to be a genuine contradiction.[71] The need to maintain the distinction of the disciplines is what Luther intends

by *communicatio idiomatum* (11. 25, 12. 4). Later, he adds: "Ego capio hominem dupliciter, uno modo pro substantia corporali per se subsistente, alio modo pro persona divina *sustentante humanitatem*." — 17. 4 (italics mine).

[67] *Ibid.*, 10. 3, 11. 8.

[68] ". . . sic ipsi Parisienses distinguunt, et tamen dicunt, idem esse verum in philosophia et theologia. Cur ergo distinguunt? Si esset idem, deberet etiam esse univocatio, idem verbum, eadem significatio. Nescientes ergo, quid dicant, tamen distinguunt a philosophia theologiam." — *Ibid.*, 11. 30.

[69] *Ibid.*, 17. 28.

[70] *Ibid.*, 17. 32; cf. 11. 15.

[71] "Sunt diversa, non contraria." — *Ibid.*, 26. 31.

by Thesis 14: Lady Reason must do as the Apostle says, and keep quiet in Church.[72]

What Luther suggests, then, against the Sorbonne—that "mother of errors"—might properly be called a "theory of multiple discourse" rather than a "theory of double truth." Neither "double" nor "truth" expresses his position accurately. He is concerned with various disciplines, not just two (since "philosophy," in his parlance, is the sum of the departmental sciences); and with truth only indirectly, as a consequence of his theory of meaning. His thesis is that each of the various disciplines (*professiones*) operates with its own special discourse. Words and propositions do not have a fixed meaning in a universal language. Their meaning is relative to a particular discourse. A word transferred from one discourse to another may have a different meaning in its new context or even no meaning at all. Hence it is a mistake to ask how many lines there are in a pound or how many feet there are in a pint; and in geometry you do not reckon up pounds and ounces.[73] If this principle holds true within philosophy—that is, among the various sciences (*artes*)—it is all the more true when we com-

[72] "Sed ubiubi impingit vel forma syllogistica vel ratio philosophica, dicendum est ei illud Pauli: Mulier in Ecclesia taceat . . ."—*Ibid.*, 4. 19. In the course of the disputation Luther asserts and illustrates the point that the procedural rules of philosophy do not apply in theology. But his interest, I think, is really in what we should call "informal," rather than "formal," logic. He does not deny that dialectic is needed as the handmaid of theology (*ibid.*, 24. 24). And yet syllogisms which would be valid in philosophy break down in theology because *proprietas verborum* is relative to a particular discourse. See *ibid.*, 19. 7 (on *proprietas*); 19. 24 (not everything that follows in philosophy follows also in theology); and the various particular arguments on pp. 20 ff. Even the threeness of Father, Son, and Spirit is not a simple arithmetical three: "Longe alia trinitas est in theologia, quam in mathematica accipitur."—22. 23. Hence: "Mathematica est inimicissima omnino theologiae . . ."—22. 1. And the disputation comes back, in the end, to the starting point: ". . . hominem, carnem etc. fieri nova vocabula, quando referuntur ad Christum."—30. 18.

[73] See Theses 30–32 (*ibid.*, 5. 15–20). Luther uses these examples to illustrate the principle that the same thing is not *true* in all the sciences (Theses 29, 36, 38). But it is clear that the principle is really a matter of *meaning*.

pare philosophy with theology, which works from a wholly different kind of data.[74]

The conclusion is, then, that much more can be said about Luther and science than is contained in the notorious fool-passage. Not only did Luther take a lively interest in scientific progress, he also reflected about the relation of science and theology; that is, about the place of theology among the various university disciplines. And his overriding intent is plain: to give each discipline autonomy in its own "sphere." Admittedly, his reflections in the *Disputation* are not fully developed. But they are not out of harmony with his general theological position, in which theology and philosophy are related to the doctrine of the two realms. The thesis that the same word or proposition changes its meaning (and therefore its truth-value) if transferred from one realm to the other is fundamental to Luther's discussion on justification and ethics.[75] Words are like coins, which are acceptable currency only in the area where they are minted;[76] and the various disciplines are like the distinct spheres which God has placed in the heavens.[77] Clearly it was Luther's intention to allow the various disciplines full autonomy within their own limits. But

[74] "Quanto minus potest idem esse verum in theologia et philosophia, quarum distinctio in infinitum maior est, quam artium et operum." — Thesis 39. Cf. also Theses 40–41.

[75] For further discussion see my *Grace and Reason*, p. 21 (on the proposition "Fallen man can do no good"); pp. 72 ff. (on the scholastic formula *facere quod in se est*); p. 96 (on the term *habitus*); and p. 112 (on *iustitia*). Heiko Oberman, in a valuable article on Robert Holcot (*Harvard Theological Review*, 55, no. 4 [October, 1962]: pp. 317–42), has discussed Luther's rejection of the Nominalist doctrine *facere quod in se est*. Strictly speaking, however, Luther never abandoned the formula itself, but transferred it to the *regnum mundi*.

[76] W.A. 39.^{1}. 232. 13 (the *Promotion-Disputation of Palladius and Tilemann*, 1537). This Disputation is concerned, in part, with the same problem of "double truth."

[77] "Fides non est regulis seu verbis philophiae adstricta aut subiecta, sed est inde libera. Et sicut Deus multas sphaeras in coelo creabit, ita etiam in his facultatibus distinctae sunt." — W.A. 39^{2}. 7. 36. "Nam ut Deus condidit sphaeras distinctas in coelo, sic et in terra regna, ut unaquaeque res et ars suum locum et speciem retineat necque versetur extra suum centrum, in quo positum est." — *Ibid.*, 8. 5. Elsewhere Luther makes it a general "principle" that the sciences are both inde-

apparently he forgot at the dinner table on June 4 what he had argued in a public disputation on January 11. Or, at least, he failed to draw the consequences. Even so, an obvious injustice is done to him if his dinner conversation is treated as the better source for his opinions on theology and science.

IV

The features of Calvinistic theology which may be viewed as inducements to a scientific interest in nature have already been noted. It hardly needs to be demonstrated that they have their source in Calvin's own thinking, even though later Calvinists may have developed the master's thoughts beyond the limits he himself imposed.[78] Calvin was intensely interested in the world of nature, on which he saw the manifest traces of God's handiwork. The world is a "mirror," in which God may be viewed.[79] It is the "theater" of God's glory, and men are placed in it as spectators.[80] True, since Adam's fall most people walk like blind men in this divine theater. But the Word of God is given to restore our eyesight—to furnish us, as Calvin puts it, with spectacles.[81] And although the evidences are open even to the unlearned, men of science are privileged to penetrate more deeply into the secrets of divine wisdom.[82] We should be guilty of base ingratitude if we failed to acknowledge the bountiful hand of God both in the works of nature[83] and in the human intelligence which comprehends

pendent in their terminologies and yet interdependent in their utility: W.A. 42. 36. 11.

[78] I do not see, for instance, in what sense Calvin could have valued philosophy as the "natural foundation of supernatural knowledge": Dankbaar, "Calvinisme," p. 127.

[79] *Corpus Reformatorum, Calvini Opera* (henceforth "C.O."), 6, 15–16 (Geneva Catechism). Cf. *Christianae religionis institutio*; ed. of 1559 (henceforth "*Inst.*"), 1. 5. 1. For the *Institutio* I use the Latin text in the *Opera Selecta*, vols. 3–5, ed. Peter Barth and Wilhelm Niesel, 2d ed. (Munich, 1958–62).

[80] *Inst.* 1. 6. 2; 14. 20.

[81] *Inst.* 1. 5. 8; 2. 6. 1; 1. 6. 1.

[82] *Ibid.*, 1. 5. 2. Presumably the scientist needs the light of the Word to make him aware of what he is doing.

[83] *Ibid.*, 1. 14. 21.

them.[84] Of course, Calvin was not himself a "scientist" in our sense; that was not his special calling.[85] And only a faithful admirer could describe him as a *savant*, of prodigious erudition, who knew just about all there was to be known in his day.[86] It is hardly true, however, that Calvin "appears to have had no taste for the sciences."[87] On the contrary, he writes almost enviously of the astronomer, to whom the intricate workings of Providence were more openly displayed than to other men.[88] And, like Luther, he felt a corresponding disdain for the astrologers, who abused the study of the heavens.[89]

It still has to be asked, however, whether Calvin left the scientists free from theological interference. Did he recognize the *autonomy* of science as well as its religious *utility*? It seems that, unlike the Lutheran Reformers, he did not oppose the new astronomy on Biblical grounds. But this is not necessarily to his credit and may indicate only that he was less well informed than they. The real question is whether or not he believed that there are theological criteria for statements about the natural order. He ought, in principle, to have been freed from the practice of using Scripture as a source of scientific information, since he could present the Christological content of the Bible as, so to say, an intellectual limit. That is, he affirmed that the function of the Bible was to furnish knowledge of Jesus Christ, so that our minds, as we read the Scripture, should come to a halt when this goal is attained.[90] From

[84] *Ibid.*, 2. 2. 14–16, where all the arts and sciences are traced to what later Calvinism called *gratia universalis*. Cf. *ibid.*, 1. 5. 5.

[85] Cf. Lecerf, "De l'Impulsion," pp. 194–95.

[86] Choisy, *Calvin*, p. 18.

[87] Breen, *John Calvin*, p. 155.

[88] As Kuyper, *Calvinism*, p. 158, says, "Thus vanished every dread possibility, that he who occupied himself with nature, were wasting his capacities in pursuit of vain and idle things."

[89] Cf. his *Avertissement contre l'astrologie qu'on appelle judiciaire*, 1549 (C.O. 7. 509–42).

[90] The most remarkable affirmation of this principle appears in Calvin's preface to Olivétan's New Testament: "Voila ce qu'il nous fault en somme cercher en toute l'Escriture. C'est de bien congnoistre Iesus Christ. . . . Mais fault que nostre entendement soit du tout arresté à ce poinct, d'apprendre en l' Escriture à congnoistre Iesus Christ tant seulement. . . ." – C.O. 9. 815.

which one might fairly infer that the Bible does not furnish, in addition, revealed information about astronomy. But in actual fact Calvin was no more consistent than Luther in maintaining a "Christocentric" view of the Bible.[91]

It has been suggested by Albert-Marie Schmidt that Calvin bequeathed to his disciples as a criterion of scientific truth, not the letter of Holy Scripture, but "the test of God's glory as Scripture reveals it generally."[92] To which it must be replied that such a criterion would end the autonomy of science just as effectively as the Biblical literalism of Luther's notorious *Table Talk*. But not one shred of evidence is advanced to demonstrate that this was in fact Calvin's approach to questions of secular learning. It is one thing to believe that the pursuit of science will give access to the glory of God, quite another to use God's glory as a test for scientific truth. Further, although Schmidt treats the opinions of Lambert Daneau (Danaeus) under the rubric *rédaction de la doctrine*, he is obliged to begin by drawing attention to the differences between the author and the redactor. Calvin considered as true all the scientific information contained in the Bible, but he set no limits on the scientific activity of the human spirit by which the information was to be elucidated. Daneau, on the other hand, spoke as though there were no need to look beyond the letter of Scripture, and he expressly opposed "those who deny that a knowledge of physics can truly and properly be learned from sacred scripture."[93] If, then, Calvin's disciple performed the useful service of gathering what Calvin himself had sown throughout his various writings, it remains true, as Schmidt concedes, that he ruined the crop (*il dénature la récolte*). More important is the fact, not mentioned by Schmidt, that Daneau explicitly rejected, or at least qualified, the hermeneutic principle by which Calvin was able to maintain simultaneously the truth of *Biblical* science and the autonomy of *natural* science. True, Daneau admitted that there were some par-

[91] I have argued the point elsewhere. See n. 48 above.

[92] Schmidt, "Doctrine de la science," p. 271.

[93] *Ibid.*, p. 276. Daneau's major work, *Physica christiana*, was published at Geneva in 1576.

ticulars concerning nature on which it is necessary to consult physicians and natural historians, "since that *Salomons* Bookes whiche were written copiously of the Nature of all thynges, are, through the negligence of men, perished." Cosmological questions, however, are not of this kind, but are chiefly to be settled by appeal to Scripture, inasmuch as the Author of Nature is best qualified to discourse about it. The contrary view, Daneau points out, rests on two arguments: that natural philosophy and divinity are two distinct disciplines and that, because Mosaic science is "fitted to our capacitie," an exact knowledge of nature is "other whence to bee drawne." In rejecting these contrary arguments, Daneau claims that Moses wrote "barely [i.e., in a plain style], but rightly." Calvin, on the other hand, went further, as did Luther, and made the language of Mosaic astronomy relative to the viewpoint of an untutored observer.[94]

According to Calvin, the forms of revelation are adapted in various ways to the nature of man as the recipient. His general term for the several types of adaptation is "accommodation."[95] It is axiomatic for Calvin that God cannot be comprehended by the human mind. What is known of God is known by revelation; and God reveals himself, not as he is in himself, but in forms adapted to man's capacity.[96] Hence in preaching he communicates himself through a man speaking to men,[97] and in the sacraments he adds a mode of communication adapted to man's physical nature.[98] Now, in speaking of the Bible,

[94] My quotations are from the sixteenth-century translation of Daneau's *Physica christiana*, since I do not have access to the original: Lambertus Danaeus, *The Wonderful Workmanship of the World: wherein is conteined an excellent discourse of Christian naturall philosophie . . . especially gathered out of the fountaines of Holy Scripture*, trans. T[homas] T[wyne] (London, 1578), pp. 2, 6, 8 f.

[95] I do not know of any comprehensive treatment of "accommodation" in Calvin's theology. For a general discussion of his views on revelation see Ronald S. Wallace, *Calvin's Doctrine of the Word and Sacrament* (Edinburgh: Oliver & Boyd, 1953).

[96] C.O. 31. 741 (on Ps. 78:60). Revelation is therefore indirect: C.O. 25. 111 (on Ex. 33:21).

[97] C.O. 51. 565 (on Eph. 4:11–14). Cf. *Inst.* 4. 1. 5.

[98] *Inst.* 4. 1. 1, cf. 14. 3; C.O. 29. 168 (On Deut. 33:18–19), 48. 153 (on Acts 7:40).

Calvin extends the idea of accommodation beyond the mode to the actual content of revelation and argues that the very diction of Biblical language is often adapted to the finitude of man's mind. God does not merely condescend to human frailty by revealing himself in the prophetic and apostolic word and by causing the Word to be written down in sacred books: he also makes his witnesses employ accommodated expressions. For example, God is represented anthropomorphically as raising his hand, changing his mind, deliberating, being angry, and so on.[99] Calvin admits that accommodated language has a certain impropriety about it.[100] It bears the same relation to divine truth as does the baby talk of a nurse or a mother to the world of adult realities.[101]

Now, Calvin allows for yet another form of accommodation, which is a concession not to the finitude or sensuousness of human nature as such, but rather to the special limitations of the people to whom the scriptural revelation was originally given. For example, under the old dispensation spiritual benefits were depicted as earthly goods, and this is no longer necessary since the manifestation of the Gospel in Jesus Christ.[102] Again, because of the uncultured state of the ancient Israelites, not only language about God and salvation, but also language about the created order had to be "accommodated." Just as anthropomorphisms represent God, not as he is in himself, but

[99] C.O. 29. 70 (on Deut. 32:40); 29. 356 (on 1 Sam. 2:27–30); 36. 134 (on Isa. 6:8) *attemperat* is used rather than *accommodat; Inst.* 1. 17. 13; 2. 16. 2. Cf. also C.O. 43. 161 (on Amos 9:4), where it is said that Scripture speaks *humano more* of God as seeing or not seeing.

[100] C.O. 55. 11–12 (on Heb. 1:3). Cf. Calvin's view of the *communicatio idiomatum* as a figure of speech which uses language improperly, but not without reason: *Inst.* 2. 14. 2.

[101] Calvin frequently speaks of Scripture as (so to say) God's "prattle." ". . . Dieu s'est fait quasi semblable à une nourrice, qui ne parlera point à un petit enfant selon qu'elle feroît à un homme . . . nostre Seigneur s'est ainsi familierement accommodé à nous." – C.O. 26. 387–88. See also C.O. 29. 356 (on 1 Sam. 2:27–30) and *Inst.* 1. 13. 1, where the Latin word used by Calvin for God's accommodated speech is *balbutire.*

[102] C.O. 43. 161, 172 (on Amos 9:13–15). Cf. 38. 660 (on Jer. 31:12), where the same notion is expressed without use of the term "accommodation."

as he seems to us,[103] so Biblical statements about nature may represent the heavenly bodies as they appear to a simple-minded observer, not as the astronomer would describe them scientifically.[104]

The principle of accommodation in this sense—that is, in the sense of condescension to the unlearned—underlies Calvin's entire exposition of the "History of Creation." He expressly points to a number of statements in Genesis, chapters 1–3, as accommodated to the mentality or the received opinions of a simple folk.[105] And he repeatedly affirms that throughout the entire narrative Moses spoke in a popular, not a scientific, manner.[106] The story has, in fact, a strictly religious purpose: to make the believer aware by *revelation* of what he would see, were it not for the dulness of his vision, simply by *observation*; namely, that he is placed in the world as a spectator of God's glory.[107] Biblical affirmations about the heavens and the planets are not scientific statements, but inducements to thankfulness, and they are therefore expressed in a homely style which even the simplest believer can understand. They are made from the standpoint of an unlettered man, who is simply using his eyes. For instance, the expression "great lights" in Gen. 1:16 does not refer to the actual size of the sun and the moon but to the amount of light that an ordinary person observes coming from them. The expressions are rela-

[103] *Inst.* 1. 17. 13: "Haec est porro submittendi [ad captum nostrum] ratio, ut se talem nobis figuret, non qualis in se est, sed qualis a nobis sentitur."

[104] Rosen, "Calvin's Attitude Toward Copernicus," p. 441, notes Calvin's view that the Biblical writers sometimes adopted a popular style, but does not relate this to the principle of accommodation. Dillenberger, *Protestant Thought*, p. 32, makes much the same point and does mention the relevance of accommodation (*ibid.*, p. 38).

[105] *Commentarius in Genesin*, C.O. 23. 17 (on Gen. 1:5); 36 (on 2:8); and 40 (on 2:10, where Moses' topography is said to be accommodated). Not merely the language of the narrative, but even God's decision to create over a period of six days is traced to his consideration for man's limited comprehension: *ibid.*, col. 18 (on Gen. 1:5).

[106] *Ibid.*, cols. 20–23 (on Gen. 1:14–16), *passim*; cf. cols. 40 (on Gen. 2:10); and 53 (on 3:1).

[107] *Ibid.*, cols. 9–10 (on the "argument" of Genesis). Note that this religious purpose requires us to regard the heavenly bodies as "signs," but not in the astrological sense: *ibid.*, col. 21 (on Gen. 1:14).

tive to the observer. The moon simply *looks* bigger than the other planets, though in fact Saturn *is* bigger. Nor was it relevant to Moses' purpose to mention that the moon borrows light from the sun.[108] If any are disdainful of this Biblical simplicity, they will "condemn the entire economy of God in ruling the Church."[109] On the other hand, it would also be wrong to oppose the science of astronomy just because its conclusions are contrary to popular opinion. Astronomy is both enjoyable and useful, since it unfolds the marvellous wisdom of God. The astronomer is worthy of our praise, and those who have the leisure and the ability should not neglect "this sort of exercise."[110] The Bible, however, is the "book of the unlearned." Anyone who wants to learn about astronomy must therefore look elsewhere.[111]

Calvin's cosmology was, of course, geocentric. But it was geocentric because he accepted the established astronomical views of his day.[112] Had he been confronted—as nobody in fact was during Calvin's lifetime—with convincing evidence for the heliocentric hypothesis, there is no reason to assume that he would have found the evidence embarrassing. He considered it an act of accommodation when the Psalmist spoke of the sun as passing from one end of the sky to the other. The Psalmist's aim was to evoke thankfulness by pointing to what the eye sees. Had he been talking among philosophers, he might have mentioned that the sun completes its revolution around the other hemisphere.[113] Would it have been so difficult for Calvin to assimilate the new ideas and admit that the

[108] *Ibid.*, cols. 21–23 (on Gen. 1:15–16). Note especially "Nos enim potius respexit [Moses] quam sidera, ut theologum decebat."—col. 22. Cf. col. 40 (on Gen. 2:10). Luther, too, recognized that Biblical language about the natural order may be *secundum visionem oculorum* (W.A. 31[1]. 370. 15, on Ps. 24:2).

[109] C.O. 23. 53 (on Gen. 3:1).

[110] *Ibid.*, col. 22 (on Gen. 1:16).

[111] *Ibid.*, col. 18 (on Gen. 1:6).

[112] See, e.g., *ibid.*, cols. 9–10: "Nos certe non ignoramus finitum esse caeli circuitum, et terram instar globuli in medio locatam esse" (on the "argument"). He was non-Copernican because he was well informed! Occasionally, he qualifies the accepted views for non-Biblical reasons; see *ibid.*, col. 22 (on Gen. 1:15).

[113] C.O. 31. 198 (on Ps. 19:4–6).

Psalmist's language was rather *differently* accommodating than he had imagined? As Calvin remarks on another Psalm, it was not the Holy Spirit's intention to teach astronomy: he preferred to use "baby talk" (*balbutire*) rather than close the door of learning against the uneducated.[114]

V

The relations between natural science and the Protestant Reformation prove to be much more complex and fascinating than the standard quotations (and pseudo quotation) have allowed. A complete discussion would need to take account of the contrast between Reformation and later Protestant attitudes towards science.[115] Worthy of attention, too, are the opinions of other Reformers—of Andreas Osiander, for example, whose anonymous preface to the *De revolutionibus* presented the heliocentric theory as a method of calculation, not as a claim to objective truth. Osiander's account of an astronomical "hypothesis" was not just a piece of shrewd diplomacy, but deserves to be taken seriously as an interpretation of scientific language different from Copernicus' own.[116] Further, the cosmologies of Luther and Calvin themselves are not fully considered until their use of such theological terms as "heaven" and "hell" has been examined. They recognized that the theological and the cosmological use of the terms are not to be confused. Hence Luther refused to think of Christ's Ascension as comparable to climbing up a ladder.[117] And Calvin could only understand the Descent into Hell as Christ's experiencing in his soul the torments of a man forsaken by

[114] C.O. 32. 364–65 (on Ps. 136:7).

[115] Dillenberger's study, already mentioned, is particularly valuable for this aspect of the problem (see esp. chap. 2).

[116] On Osiander's understanding of a scientific hypothesis see especially Prowe, *Nicolaus Copernicus*, 1, pt. 2:519–39; Rosen, *Three Copernican Treatises*, pp. 22–23. The text will be found in Prowe's second volume, pp. 13–14. Osiander is also discussed by Bornkamm, *Luther's World of Thought*, pp. 174–78; Dillenberger, *Protestant Thought*, pp. 41–47; and Elert, *Morphologie des Luthertums*, pp. 369 f.

[117] W.A. 19. 491. 7, 26. Cf. the *Consensus Tigurinus*, art. 25: C.O. 7. 743.

God.[118] The theology of the Reformers was less closely tied to a particular cosmology than might be expected: "demythologization" has already set in. The doctrine of twofold truth (to retain the usual designation) and the principle of accommodation by no means exhaust their reflections on the nature of religious language. It is true that neither of them had a comprehensive theory of religious language: Calvin's principle of accommodation, for instance, was used chiefly as a problem-solving device, to be rolled out only when needed. But it is also true that the problems of theological discourse had occurred to them, precisely in the context of scientific questions. Their tentative moves towards a solution are not without historical interest, whether or not they make a permanent contribution to the debate between religion and science.

But what impact, if any, did their theological ideas make upon the actual development of science? Our conclusions have been partly negative: Luther and Calvin did nothing to *hinder* scientific progress. And there was no theological reason why they should. The Reformers were not literalists in the sense that they took all Biblical statements about nature as literal reports of the plain truth. They were literalists in the sense that they insisted on taking the Scriptures in the meaning intended by their authors (or author). A. D. White himself gives a good example of the kind of non-literal exegesis which the Reformers deplored. He tells us that a Dominican preacher countered the researches of Galileo and his disciples with a sermon on Acts 1:11: "Why do you Galileans stand gazing up into heaven?" A "wretched pun," as White justly remarks.[119] The "literalism" of Luther and Calvin was designed to rule out allegories and other forms of fancy exegesis, but it still left room for maintaining the autonomy of natural science. Where the reigning astronomical opinions seemed to conflict with Scripture, they knew how to make the necessary adjustments.

[118] *Inst.* 2. 16. 10. Cf. also Luther's remarks on the "Christus Victor" theme: W.A. 37. 63. 23.

[119] White, *Warfare of Science with Theology*, 1:133. For the Reformer's literal – or, more correctly, "historical" – exegesis, I may refer again to the article mentioned above (in n. 48).

But this meant that they had to make the adjustments to Ptolemaic, not Copernican, science, precisely because the scientific revolution remained incomplete during their lifetime.[120] Moreover, if Calvin himself did not apply the principle of accommodation to the problem posed by the new science, no others than Kepler and Galileo did so apply it[121]—which raises intriguing historical questions about the origins and dissemination of the principle. Not only did scientific interest in nature find a congenial ally in Calvinistic theology, but the principle by which leaders of the new science sought to avert a conflict between science and religion was a key notion in Calvin's theology. The currency of this principle in some circles—in Puritan England, for example—may have owed something to John Calvin.[122] In any case, the principle of accommodation, whatever the means of its transmission, assumes an historical importance not shared by Luther's reflections on double truth. But, of course, by the time the scientific revolution was complete—let us say by the time Newton's *Principia* was published (1687)—the problem of religion and science had moved to a deeper level. It was no longer a question of reconciling Scripture with the heliocentric hypothesis but of finding a place for God in the cosmos. The Newtonian world was causally self-contained, needing God only to set the mechanism in motion and to solve (at least temporarily) one or two problems that continued to resist

[120] Dorothy Stimson, *Acceptance of Copernican Theory*, p. 41 notes this fact, but does not do justice to its importance. Lecerf, "De l'Impulsion," p. 198, on the other hand, rightly insists that primitive Calvinism was geocentric for the same reason that modern Calvinism has been Newtonian or Einsteinian: because Reformed theologians have accepted current astronomical doctrines. Cf. also Dillenberger, *Protestant Thought*, p. 29; Edwin Arthur Burtt, *The Metaphysical Foundations of Modern Science*, rev. ed. (Garden City, N.Y.: Doubleday & Co., 1955), pp. 36 ff.

[121] Dillenberger, *Protestant Thought*, pp. 84, 88–89. For others who used the same solution to the conflict of Bible and science, see the same work, pp. 72, 101, 107 f., 129.

[122] Paul H. Kocher, however, in his study *Science and Religion in Elizabethan England* (San Marino, Calif.: Huntington Library, 1953), has noted that the principle had patristic antecedents and was common among Renaissance interpreters (pp. 38–39).

scientific explanation. Was it, then, enough to concede the methodological autonomy of science?[123] Or does the scientist also demand an actual autonomy of the physical universe?[124]

[123] Cf. Jaroslav Pelikan's expression "technical autonomy" in his study *The Christian Intellectual*, Religious Perspectives, vol. 14, ed. Ruth Nanda Anshen (New York: Harper & Row, 1965), p. 58.

[124] Cf. Bertrand Russell, *The Impact of Science on Society* (London: George Allen and Unwin Ltd., 1952), pp. 18 ff.

11

Oliver Cromwell and the Quest for Religious Toleration

GEORGE A. DRAKE

Early in 1652 a committee of the Rump was appointed to discuss John Owen's scheme for a new ecclesiastical establishment in England. In the course of the committee's debates, Oliver Cromwell burst out against the narrow-mindedness of his colleagues: "I had rather that Mahometanism were permitted amongst us than that one of God's children should be persecuted."[1] Cromwell was one of the most tolerant men of his age; a fact which assumes greater interest when it is recalled that he was also the most powerful man in England from 1644 until his death in 1658 – actually ruling during the last four and one-half years of that period.

One can produce few figures in European history who better exemplify "The Impact of Christianity on Its Culture." Oliver Cromwell's puritanism was unquestionably the dominant force in his life. Through the application of puritan principles of discipline he was to rise from his amateur beginnings to become the outstanding soldier of the English Civil Wars.[2] Even the briefest glance at his collected letters and speeches[3] overwhelms one with the intensity of Cromwell's religious

[1] Samuel Rawson Gardiner, *History of the Commonwealth and Protectorate 1649–1660*, 3 vols. (London: Longmans, Green & Co., 1897), 2:30.

[2] George Drake, "The Ideology of Oliver Cromwell," *Church History*, 35 (1966): 263–65.

[3] W. C. Abbott, *The Writings and Speeches of Oliver Cromwell*, 4 vols. (Cambridge: Harvard University Press, 1937); or: Thomas Carlyle, *The Letters and Speeches of Oliver Cromwell*, ed. S. C. Lomas, 3 vols., 3d ed. (London: Metheun & Co., 1904).

preoccupation; and on occasions primarily devoted to secular concerns, such as the Putney Debates in 1647, he appears almost to be out of step because of his obsession with religious side issues.[4]

The salient features of Cromwell's puritanism were: his belief in the autonomy of local congregations gathered together under a covenant and loosely associated in an established national church; the belief that dissent from this establishment should be tolerated and that neither church nor state ought in any way to abridge freedom of conscience; and, finally, his doctrine of providence. With that doctrine, Cromwell assumed that the realms of Grace and Nature are closely related, so that God governs the course of human events. The implications of this doctrine were that if one were reasonably sure that he was following the dictates of God, he could test this assumption by its results. Success meant approbation, and failure, disapproval. Cromwell used this test throughout his public life, becoming convinced by the success of the Parliamentary revolution and his personal role in it that it was indeed the work of God and he God's special instrument.[5] Oliver Cromwell's doctrine of providence sharply focused the unbreakable connection between religious belief and public act which marked his rule in England. In fact, Cromwell's life was a study in the impact of Christianity on its environment; for he was the leading Puritan in what Samuel Rawson Gardiner has called with some justification, "The Puritan Revolution."

Oliver Cromwell, though usually recognized as one of the titanic figures in western history, has not been regarded widely with affection. Preoccupation with the will of God, often justifying his own policy, exposed him to the charge of hypocrisy. His arbitrary military rule in England was a bitter reward to the promise of parliamentary revolution. The cruelty and injustice of Cromwell's suppression and settlement of Ireland left a legacy of hatred for the English and their govern-

[4] A. S. P. Woodhouse, *Puritanism and Liberty* (London: J. M. Dent & Sons, 1938), pp. 1–124.

[5] Drake, *Ideology of Oliver Cromwell*, pp. 266–69.

ment which did not abate until the twentieth century. In fact, there is but one prominent aspect of Oliver Cromwell's rule with which the modern mind can form an immediate and unreserved attachment: his religious tolerance.

The first half of the seventeenth century was not notable for its display of religious toleration. The Continent produced the Thirty Years War out of festering hatred between Protestants and Roman Catholics. In England, the Elizabethan definition of the Anglican Church was widely accepted as normative. As a result, many Puritans had given up hope of being comprehended or even tolerated by the establishment. The seventeenth century, particularly after the elevation of William Laud to the primacy in 1633, saw the first great wave of Protestant emigration since Mary's reign. Oliver Cromwell himself had seriously contemplated emigrating to New England.[6] At the outbreak of the Civil Wars in 1642 few people, particularly those with political or religious power, even entertained the idea of tolerating a variety of religious opinion and practice in England. Uniformity in religion was normally regarded as a prerequisite to political unity. Moreover, it was asked, how can there be more than one set of religious truths?

Neither Oliver Cromwell nor his fellow Independents reflected the usual contemporary attitude of intolerance. Most contemporary observers agree that the common denominator among all Independents was their desire for toleration. In this, as in so many things, Cromwell was the premier Independent. On several occasions he spoke of tolerance as the primary cause for which he had fought in the Civil Wars. He said it at Putney in 1647,[7] and he reiterated it to his second Protectorate parliament in a speech delivered on January 20, 1658. He told them that "a freedom to worship God according to their consciences . . . [is the] thing [that] hath been the state and sum of our Quarrel, and of those Ten Years Wars wherein we have been exercised."[8] Earlier he had told his first Protectorate

[6] Charles Firth, *Oliver Cromwell and the Rule of the Puritans in England*, 4th ed. (London: Oxford University Press, 1958), p. 61.

[7] Woodhouse, *Puritanism and Liberty*, p. 76.

[8] Carlyle, *Letters and Speeches*, 3:152.

Parliament that religion had become the issue which was "most dear to us" in the Civil Wars. And, he continued:

> Wherein consisted this more than in obtaining that liberty from the tyranny of the Bishops to all species of Protestants to worship God according to their own light and consciences, for want of which many of our brethren forsook their native countries to seek their bread from strangers, and to live in howling wildernesses; and for which also many that remained here were imprisoned and otherwise abused, and made the scorn of the nation.[9]

More impressive even than Cromwell's own statement about the importance of religious toleration is the galaxy of testimony by contemporaries. Men as widely divergent as the Earl of Clarendon, Robert Bailie,[10] Richard Baxter,[11] Henry Marten, and Thomas Edwards[12] agreed that toleration had, in Clarendon's words, "become the great charter; and men who were inspired, preached and prayed when and where they would. Cromwell himself was the greatest preacher."[13] The Republican Henry Marten regarded toleration as the glue which bound Cromwell and the Independents. "He (Cromwell) got a crew about him of blades that would follow him through any fire to avoid the fire of persequition."[14]

There is abundant evidence of Oliver Cromwell's activities in favor of toleration. During the Civil Wars he was a leading advocate of religious toleration in the House of Commons. He took the lead in September, 1644, to defend the Dissenting

[9] *Ibid.*, 2:417. This is a part of a speech delivered on January 22, 1655.

[10] William A. Shaw, *A History of the English Church During the Civil Wars and Under the Commonwealth 1640–1660*, 2 vols. (London: Longmans, Green & Co., 1900), 2:37.

[11] Woodhouse, *Puritanism and Liberty*, pp. 388–89.

[12] Robert Barclay, *The Inner Life of the Religious Societies of the Commonwealth* (London: Hodder & Stoughton, 1876), p. 142.

[13] Edward, Earl of Clarendon, *The History of the Rebellion and Civil Wars in England*, ed. W. Dunn Macray, 6 vols. (Oxford: Clarendon Press, 1888), 4:312.

[14] Great Britain, *Historical Manuscripts Commission: Thirteenth Report*, Appendix, pt. 4 (London: Her Majesty's Stationery Office, 1892), p. 400.

Brethren against the majority opinion of the Westminster Assembly that non-conformity should not be tolerated by the projected Presbyterian establishment. He moved that the opinion of the Dissenting Brethren be recognized and considered and that some means be discovered to protect "tender consciences" which cannot submit in all things to the "common rule."[15] This was but one amidst a raft of pleas with which Oliver Cromwell besieged the Long Parliament and its successors. To the Barebones Parliament, in a speech delivered on July 4, 1653, he said that the judgment of truth should teach them to be "as just towards the unbeliever as towards the believer," adding, "and it's our duty to do so."[16] Later in the same speech he informed this Parliament, so eager to establish a rigorous rule of the "Saints," that, "if the poorest Christian, the most mistaken Christian, shall desire to live peaceably and quietly under you,—I say, if any shall desire but to lead a life in godliness and honesty, let him be protected."[17] The following year Cromwell exclaimed, "When shall we have men of a universal spirit? Everyone desires to have liberty, but none will give it."[18] This outburst was directed at the first Protectorate Parliament, which had attempted to reduce Cromwell's power to grant religious toleration. It is illuminating to discover that he was consistently more tolerant than were his Parliaments, though they contained a preponderance of Independents.

The opening shot in this particular struggle over religious toleration was fired by Parliament on December 15, 1654, when it voted that the consent of the Protector need not be requisite for bills restraining "atheism, blasphemy, and damnable heresies."[19] This was a frontal assault on the Protector's power to protect religious offenders. The dispute centered around clauses thirty-six and thirty-seven of the Instrument of Government. This, the constitution of the Protectorate,

[15] Samuel Rawson Gardiner, *History of the Great Civil War*, 4 vols. (London: Longmans, Green & Co., 1893), 2:30.

[16] Carlyle, *Letters and Speeches*, 2:292.

[17] *Ibid.*, p. 294.

[18] Gardiner, *Commonwealth and Protectorate*, 3:63.

[19] *Ibid.*, p. 64.

drawn up in early 1653 by the council of army officers, which included Cromwell, officially established a broad policy of religious toleration. Clause thirty-six insured that no one would be compelled to adhere to the "public profession," but that sound doctrine and good example should be used to persuade the recalcitrants.[20] Clause thirty-seven further insured that all who professed Jesus Christ, even though they differed from the doctrine, worship, or discipline of the establishment, would not be restrained from professing their religion. To the contrary, they would be *protected* so long as "they abuse not this liberty to the civil injury of others and to the actual disturbance of the public peace . . . provided this liberty be not extended to Popery or Prelacy, nor to such as, under the profession of Christ, hold forth and practice licentiousness."[21] The principle here established was one of almost complete freedom of religious belief, placing restrictions, however, upon religious practice—particularly if it caused a breach of the peace. As we shall see, the Protector agreed with these principles of toleration, but his practice often was even more liberal than his profession. This was resented by his Parliaments, beginning with the first, which took the steps already described to limit his freedom of action.

The Instrument of Government was ambiguous about the administration of its toleration clauses. Was the Protector to have an entirely free hand, or was he to be limited by his parliaments when they were in session? Cromwell believed that his magisterial powers encompassed the administration of toleration and he acted on this belief throughout his rule. On January 22, 1655, in a speech dissolving the first Protectorate Parliament, he chided them for having wasted time disputing his powers over toleration. After assuring them that he would not tolerate civil disturbance or licentiousness in the name of religion, he once more strongly defended liberty of conscience, attacking the members of Parliament for their

[20] Samuel Rawson Gardiner, *The Constitutional Documents of the Puritan Revolution 1625–1660*, 3d ed. (Oxford: Clarendon Press, 1906), p. 416.

[21] *Ibid.*

unwillingness to grant others that for which they themselves had fought and suffered.

> It is ingenuous to ask liberty, and not to give it? What greater hypocrisy than for those who were oppressed by the Bishops to become the greatest oppressors themselves, so soon as their yoke was removed? I could wish that they who call for liberty now also had not too much of that spirit, if the power were in their hands! [22]

The Protector closed this episode by issuing, on February 15, 1655, a "Proclamation on Religious Liberty." [23] After rehearsing the blessings of religious toleration, which were almost uniquely the possession of England under the Protectorate, Cromwell promised that he would "take all possible care" to continue this freedom to all persons who feared God, even though they be of differing judgments. However, he added, he would not protect those who abused this liberty by exceeding the "bounds which the royal law of love and Christian moderation have set us in our walking one towards another." The Proclamation ended by naming the Quakers and Ranters in particular as men whose conduct overstepped the "bounds," requiring that henceforth they cease their "irregular and disorderly practices."

That Cromwell singled out the Quakers for a special warning in his Proclamation is scarcely surprising. They were a thorn deeply imbedded in the side of the Protectorate. There probably was no religious group in England which posed a more agonizing problem for Oliver Cromwell. He was profoundly sympathetic with the "inwardness" and spirituality of their religion. Furthermore, he respected their courage. Yet, they persistently transgressed the recognized bounds of order and decency. It incensed the Puritans to see their ministers reviled by Quakers who would rise in the midst of divine service, hat on head, to denounce them as "priests." This was a common occurrence, since a Quaker would remove his hat for no man (only Divinity merited that honor), and worship

[22] Carlyle, *Letters and Speeches*, 2:417.
[23] Gardiner, *Commonwealth and Protectorate*, 3:107–9.

was in their eyes an opportunity to gather to discuss and dispute the revelations of conscience, or, in their terms, "the inner light." On at least one occasion Cromwell gave vent to his disgust, ordering the arrest of several Quakers who had disrupted a religious service he had attended at Whitehall in April, 1656. He charged them with breach of his Proclamation on Religious Liberty.[24] There can be no question that legal grounds existed for the persecution of Quakers under the Instrument of Government. They did disrupt public order. Yet, the Protector rather consistently either refused to initiate proceedings against them or shielded them from the machinery of justice. On at least two occasions[25] he released the leader of the Quakers, George Fox, from imprisonment, granting him a pardon for his offences. Fox's *Journal* records several interviews with Cromwell revealing the Protector as a man seeking accommodation rather than confrontation with the Quaker leader.[26]

The dispute between the Protector and his first Parliament which has been sketched was primarily inspired by Cromwell's alleged softness toward the Quakers. A similar confrontation took place during the second Protectorate Parliament in late 1656 and early 1657, and once again a Quaker was the cause.[27] This was the famous case of James Naylor, who, in the fall of 1656, made a triumphal entry into Bristol with women strewing branches in his path and crying "hosanna." Naylor's behavior was too eccentric even for Fox, who disavowed any connection with him. Condemned from all sides, Naylor was arrested by the Bristol magistrates and sent to London for trial, where the matter was brought before Parliament on October 31, 1656. Naylor's plea was offensive in the extreme, as he argued that what he had done had been at the express command of God. Without a division, Parliament voted that

[24] *Ibid.*, p. 215.

[25] February, 1655, and August, 1656.

[26] George Fox, *An Autobiography*, ed. Rufus M. Jones, 2 vols. (Philadelphia: Ferris & Leach, 1906), 1:212, 215, 267, 275–76.

[27] See the account in Charles Hardin Firth, *The Last Years of the Protectorate 1656–1658*, 2 vols., reprint ed. (New York: Russell & Russell Inc., 1964), 1:85–106.

Naylor was guilty of "horrid blasphemy" and that he was "a grand impostor and a great seducer of the people." The members, fearing that Cromwell might intervene, proceeded hastily to sentence and punish Naylor. They feared that the Protector would veto a bill sentencing Naylor, so they tried him on the basis of their alleged judicial powers drawn from pre-civil war precedents. By a vote of 96–82 the death penalty was rejected, so that Parliament proceeded on a more "merciful" course of condemning Naylor to be pilloried and whipped and to have his tongue bored through with a hot iron and his head branded with the letter *B* for Bristol. He was then to be sent to Bristol for display and further whipping. Finally, he would be returned to London for imprisonment under conditions of hard labor at the pleasure of Parliament. On December 18 the first part of Naylor's sentence was executed. He was whipped so severely that a few extra days were granted for his recovery before boring his tongue with a hot iron.[28]

At this juncture Cromwell intervened in response to a petition in favor of Naylor which had been presented to him on December 23. On the twenty-sixth he sent a letter to Parliament asking them by what authority they had proceeded against Naylor. Once again the dispute over jurisdiction on matters of toleration had been raised. Parliament responded to the Protector's letter by executing the second part of Naylor's punishment. On the twenty-seventh his forehead was branded and his tongue bored. The House never did answer the Protector's query. Cromwell, choosing not to press the issue into an open constitutional quarrel, decided rather to work behind the scenes to lighten Naylor's imprisonment. He saw to it that the strictures against visiting Naylor were not enforced and appointed a special attendant to aid Naylor in his confinement. A month before his own death in 1658, he ordered a doctor to attend Naylor, who was ill.

Obviously, Cromwell was more tolerant than his Parliaments. He was willing to avoid the constitutional issue be-

[28] The hangman counted 310 stripes.

cause he held the ultimate weapon—the right to dismiss his Parliaments after they had sat a minimum of five months. Though he regarded Naylor as being guilty of blasphemy, he was unwilling to see a man of sincere religious conviction cruelly persecuted. This incident reveals above all else that Oliver Cromwell was compassionate, particularly toward religious enthusiasts.

According to the Instrument of Government, toleration was not to be extended to either "Popery" or "Prelacy." Legally, then, Roman Catholics and Anglicans were denied toleration. It would be a dramatic illustration of Cromwell's tolerance could it be established that he deliberately refrained from persecuting either group. The evidence is not conclusive, but what we have indicates that the Protector under ordinary circumstances turned a blind eye toward clandestine Roman Catholic and Anglican worship. In 1655 the Venetian ambassador, Sagredo, reported that the policy of the government was "to deprive the Catholics of their possessions, but to let them hear as many masses as they would."[29] The French ambassador Bordeaux wrote to his government in September, 1656, that though the laws against Catholics had been modified, the number of priests at large and the traffic in the chapels of foreign embassies demonstrated that Roman Catholics had fared better under Cromwell's government than under any former government whether Royalist of Parliamentarian.[30] Previously he had written that, though it was impossible for him openly to do so, the Protector nevertheless tried to be as tolerant as possible to Roman Catholics.[31]

However, Cromwell's toleration of Roman Catholics should not be divorced from his foreign policy. From March, 1654, until the autumn of 1655, he negotiated with two Catholic powers France and Spain, with an alliance to the highest bidder in mind.[32] During that time it patently was good policy

[29] Gardiner, *Commonwealth and Protectorate*, 3:225.

[30] *Ibid.*, p. 226.

[31] Firth, *Oliver Cromwell*, 1:77.

[32] We have an abstract of two meetings of the Protector's Council which shows that a balance sheet of the advantages and disadvantages

to create good will by ignoring the restrictions on Roman Catholic worship. When Cromwell did opt for war—with Spain—he rallied support by launching a vicious attack against Spain's "popishness" in his opening speech to the second Protectorate Parliament, on September 17, 1656.[33]

The war stirred up an already virulent anti-Catholic sentiment in England. Cromwell reaped the harvest of his inflammatory opening speech when Parliament brought forth a new recusancy bill in November. According to this bill the justices of the peace and justices of assize were to demand that all Roman Catholics abjure their faith. The penalty for refusal was confiscation of two-thirds of one's estate. Furthermore, any English subject caught attending mass at a foreign embassy was to be fined one hundred pounds.[34] In June, 1657, the Protector gave his assent to the bill, but there is little evidence that either this act or the old recusancy laws were seriously enforced during the Protectorate.[35] Even so, a new stringency toward Catholics prevailed. Bordeaux's letters reflect this change beginning in December, 1656.[36]

There can be little doubt that Cromwell was not as tolerant of Roman Catholics as he was of other religious groups. There is every reason to suppose, however, that he should have been absolutely intolerant of Catholicism. It was officially proscribed by the Instrument of Government. Its relations with English governments had been undermined since the days of Elizabeth and the Bull of Pius V. From that time Catholicism could be—and was—defined as treason, particularly by the Puritans. Since the 1580's the Counter Reformation under the aegis of the Hapsburgs had become the national enemy.

of each alliance was drawn up. Sir William Clark, *The Clark Paper*, 4 vols. (London: Printed for the Camden Society, 1891–1901), 3:307–9.

[33] Carlyle, *Letters and Speeches*, 2:510–15.

[34] Firth, *Oliver Cromwell*, 1:74.

[35] For example, in December, 1656, eight priests were arrested in Covent Garden, but none was indicted or punished. *Ibid.*, p. 71. Between 1641 and 1646 twenty-one Catholic Priests were hanged; but between 1649 and 1660 only two were hanged; and Cromwell would have spared one. Geoffrey F. Nuttall, *The Holy Spirit in Puritan Faith and Experience* (Oxford: Blackwells, 1946), p. 131.

[36] Firth, *Oliver Cromwell*, 1:77–78.

Finally, there was one particular group of Catholics whom Cromwell despised: the Irish: His cruelty in 1649 was untempered by the glimmers of compassion which we have detected in his dealings with most opponents. He regarded the Irish as a subhuman species; as "barbarous and bloodthirsty wretches" who in no way merited the consideration which Cromwell ordinarily extended to all men as "children of God."

With the important exception of the Irish, Oliver Cromwell's policy toward Roman Catholics was remarkably tolerant[37] – particularly since the Puritans were constitutionally anti-Catholic.[38] Only when his foreign policy dictated it did his government persecute Catholics, and then, half-heartedly.

The evidence about Episcopalian worship is less conclusive than that for Roman Catholicism. Anglicans such as Archbishop James Ussher, Thomas Fuller, George Hall, and Jeremy Taylor continued to preach during the Protectorate;[39] and John Evelyn recorded that he was not obliged to receive the sacrament in conventicle until August, 1656.[40] We know also that the Oxford conventicle across from Merton College was not interrupted during the Protectorate.[41] On the other hand, soldiers stopped an Anglican service on Christmas day, 1657, because it broke the ordinance against celebrating Christmas.[42] The weight of this evidence makes it seem likely, however, that Anglicans were permitted freedom of worship in most places and at most times during the Protectorate.

Finally, of course, as evidence of Cromwell's tolerance, one can point to the well-known return of the Jews to England in early 1656. Manasseh Ben Israel, a Dutch Jew, had taken the initiative to persuade the Protectorate to allow the Jews once again to take up residence in England – one of the few European countries still denied to them. Cromwell's Council of

[37] Cromwell's tolerance was extended to Roman Catholics as individuals, not to their church, which he consistently opposed.

[38] Perhaps the most consistent principle binding all the Puritan groups was "anti-popery."

[39] Nuttall, *Puritan Faith*, p. 129.

[40] Gardiner, *Commonwealth and Protectorate*, 3:227.

[41] *Ibid.*

[42] *Ibid.*

State refused the request, but the Protector gave Ben Israel a private assurance that the Jews would be admitted and that the recusancy laws would not be enforced against them.[43] Once again, Cromwell had proven to be more tolerant than his fellow Independents.

This catalog of Oliver Cromwell's policies should be sufficient to prove that he was indeed far more tolerant than were most seventeenth-century Englishmen; not excepting his fellow Independents. The leading authorities on Cromwell—S. R. Gardiner, C. H. Firth, and W. C. Abbott—all posit that Cromwell's practical tolerance exceeded his theoretical tolerance. Cromwell certainly was not a theorist to anything like the degree of, for instance, John Milton. He was forced constantly throughout the Civil Wars and Interregnum to *act*—often without adequate time for consideration. It is painfully clear that events continually outraced Cromwell as they did most of his contemporaries. Cromwell was the first to admit that often he was overwhelmed. He remarked to Sir Philip Warwick and Sir Thomas Chichely early in the Civil Wars, "I can tell you, Sirs, what I would not have; tho' I cannot what I would."[44] This attitude also was to characterize his quest for political and religious settlement during the Interregnum. Clearly the most valid test of Cromwell's principles is to be found in their application; so that, if indeed Cromwell's practical tolerance outran his theory, he may well have been far more tolerant than even he supposed.

Oliver Cromwell said enough about toleration in his letters, speeches, and official pronouncements to give us a clear idea of his views on the subject. The capstone was his belief in the authority of the individual Christian conscience. For most Independents, and no less for Oliver Cromwell, the Christian conscience was the ultimate judge of God's revelation; that revelation being contained almost exclusively in the Scriptures. Often Cromwell alluded to the Christian conscience as

[43] *Ibid.*, pp. 216–22.

[44] Robert S. Paul, ed., *An Apologetical Narration*, facsimile ed. (Philadelphia: United Church Press, 1963), p. 60.

the mediator of revelation.[45] At Putney, for example, he said: "No man receives anything in the name of the Lord further than [to] the light of his conscience appears."[46] Having substituted the conscience for an external authority such as the Church, Cromwell followed the logic of his position, insisting that there is absolutely no external authority which can override the individual Christian conscience as it interprets Scripture. This was a radical belief, and many Puritans, the Presbyterians for example, were not willing so to free the conscience from external restraints. Cromwell was well aware of his differences with the Presbyterians on this point. For example, in 1650, he chided the Scottish General Assembly, saying that "in matters of conscience . . . every soul is to answer for itself to God."[47] The idea that conscience is the authority in matters of Christian belief is what led Cromwell and the Independents to their insistence on religious toleration. If indeed "every soul is to answer for itself to God," then, as Cromwell further explained in his letter to the General Assembly, the soul does not answer to man. Though it certainly is not free from God's judgment, the conscience must be free from human restraints. Cromwell went even further, saying that "liberty of conscience is a natural right."[48]

Oliver Cromwell's belief in the authority and consequent freedom of the Christian conscience was formed before the Civil Wars, for it underlay his utterances on religion throughout that period. Furthermore, it may have been the cause of his Independency, as this concept was the tenet which most sharply separated the Independents from the Puritans to their right. Having fought along with the Independents to establish the rights of the Christian conscience, Cromwell lost all patience with them when, during the Protectorate, they tried to

[45] For example, in his speech of January 27, 1655, closing the first Protectorate Parliament. Carlyle, *Letters and Speeches*, 2:427. Or, during the Putney Debates. Woodhouse, *Puritanism and Liberty*, pp. 17–104.

[46] Woodhouse, *Puritanism and Liberty*, p. 101.

[47] Abbott, *Writings and Speeches*, 2:302. The letter was dated August 3, 1650.

[48] Carlyle, *Letters and Speeches*, 2:382. From the speech of September 12, 1654 to his first Protectorate Parliament.

deny this freedom to others. Once in power, as was so often the case, desire for uniformity and order erased the memories of years of persecution. Not so, Cromwell. As he told his first Protectorate Parliament:

> Is not liberty of conscience in religion a fundamental? So long as there is liberty of conscience for the Supreme Magistrate to exercise his conscience in erecting that form of church-government he is satisfied he should set up, — why should he not give it, "the like liberty," to others? Liberty of conscience is a natural right; and he that would have it, ought to give it. . . . Indeed that hath been one of the vanities of our contests. Every sect saith: "Oh, give me liberty!" But give him it, and to his power he will not yield it to anybody else. Where is our ingenuousness? "Liberty of conscience" — truly that's a thing ought to be very reciprocal! The magistrate hath his supremacy, and he may settle Religion, "that is, church-government," according to his conscience. And "as for the People" — I may say it to you, I can say it: All the money of this nation would not have tempted men to fight upon such an account as they have "here been" engaged in, if they had not had hopes of liberty "of conscience" better than they had from Episcopacy, or than would have been afforded them from a Scottish Presbytery, — or an English either.[49]

One discovers in this passage that Cromwell's belief in liberty of conscience had not nullified his assumption that there should be an established church. In his opinion, establishment and toleration were not mutually contradictory. Hence, the Protectorate's loosely established state church with a liberal allowance for dissent was in keeping with Cromwell's own ideas.

Willingness to tolerate dissenting opinions did not mean that Oliver Cromwell conceived that there is more than one set of Christian truths. He consistently maintained that there is but one truth of God. However, our *knowledge* of it is fallible and often contradictory. As he said at Putney, "certainly God

[49] *Ibid.*, pp. 382–83.

is not the author of contradictions. The contradictions are not so much in the end as the way."[50] Ultimately, to be sure, God will unite all Christians in the truth, but in the interim men shall have to wait upon him.[51] Thus, no man or group of men can be sufficiently certain of God's truth to warrant their persecution of others for doctrinal error. In fact, an open mind should be the characteristic attitude of the true Christian in order that he be receptive to the truths of God.[52] Too often these truths cannot penetrate the filters of prejudice and error with which men guard their consciences.

Though liberty of conscience was the crux of Cromwell's tolerance, it turns out that he placed some limitations upon it. He defined these limits when he told the Socinian John Riddle in September, 1655, "that the liberty of conscience provided for in those articles[53] should never, while he hath any interest in the Government, be stretched so far as to countenance them who deny the divinity of our Saviour, or to bolster up any blasphemous opinions contrary to the fundamental verities of religion."[54] The Protector was well aware of the dangers inherent in liberty of conscience, occasionally admitting that this freedom had been abused.[55] Nevertheless, he was prepared to run the risk of having this principle perverted. He was pragmatic enough to realize that the existence of a median necessarily entails latitude for the extremes. In other words, if one is utterly devoted to the implementation of a principle,[56] he discovers that he must allow the existence of aberrations in order to preserve enough ground for his own principle.

Though Oliver Cromwell's doctrine of the authority and hence, integrity, of the individual Christian conscience was the sheet anchor of his insistence on toleration, there were other important causes. Most Independents, including Crom-

[50] Woodhouse, *Puritanism and Liberty*, p. 104.
[51] *Ibid.*, p. 107.
[52] *Ibid.*, p. 17.
[53] Clauses thirty-six and thirty-seven of the Instrument of Government.
[54] Gardiner, *Commonwealth and Protectorate*, 3:210.
[55] Carlyle, *Letters and Speeches*, 2:345.
[56] See above, pages 269f., where Cromwell declared that freedom of conscience was the primary cause for his participation in the Civil Wars.

well, argued that Christ was the model for the exercise of religious authority; and his was a spiritual, not a physical authority.[57] The Protector himself said that the spirit of Christ means affection for all men.[58] In particular, he went on, it means that unless I can love the Presbyterians as well as the Independents, I am not a faithful Christian.[59] On another occasion he said: "Here is a great deal of 'truth' among professors, but very little 'mercy.' They are ready to cut the throats of one another. But when we are brought into the right way, we shall be *merciful* as well as orthodox."[60] Apparently one of the wellsprings of Oliver Cromwell's tolerance was simply the basic Christian injunctions to charity, love, and mercy.

There were some quite practical and, I suspect, personal reasons for Cromwell's attitudes on toleration. Not the least of these were his vivid memories of the consequences of persecution. As we have seen,[61] he remembered the religious exiles who were driven to a "howling wilderness" to seek freedom of conscience. He himself nearly emigrated to New England. We should not overlook the impact of seeing neighbors and friends leaving settled and comfortable lives for an unknown and almost certainly arduous existence in a wilderness across three thousand miles of ocean. Cromwell's references to these scenes leave little doubt that they made a permanent and profound impression on him. He was determined to create an England from which no Christian would be forced to flee to secure freedom of conscience.

Much of Puritanism can be understood quite simply as anti-Catholicism. The movement originated in the reign of Elizabeth from fears that too much "popery" had remained in the Anglican church. The Puritans wanted a complete "re-formation" of the English church, leaving not a trace of "popery." John Milton, for instance, argued that because Catholics persecute, persecution is *ipso-facto* a bad thing and ought not

[57] Milton's was the classic argument. See below, pages 286ff.

[58] Carlyle, *Letters and Speeches*, 2:292.

[59] *Ibid.*, p. 294.

[60] *Ibid.*, p. 552. From a speech delivered on September 17, 1656 to the second Protectorate Parliament.

[61] See above, page 270.

to be found among truly reformed Christians.[62] Oliver Cromwell nowhere that I have found fashions the same argument. Yet, I suspect that he harbored a sentiment similar to Milton's: persecution in the name of The Truth is a "popish" practice; therefore, a true Christian ought to avoid persecution as he would avoid all "popish" practices.

Another belief which helped to account for Cromwell's tolerance was his assumption that Christian unity is possible in the absence of uniformity. Uniformity, he said, is outward and physical, while unity is inward and spiritual.[63] Therefore, uniformity of profession and practice, which was so important to many Christians, was of little or no importance to Oliver Cromwell. Consistent with his belief in the inner nature of true religion, he was content to wait upon the Holy Spirit to overcome the visible malice of the world, bringing all Christians together into an invisible spiritual unity.[64]

The pre-eminence of Cromwell's desire for liberty of conscience did not go unchallenged within the hierarchy of his own religious values. Along with toleration, he had a deep desire for the reformation of morals. Like John Calvin, he argued that the glory of God demands holiness of life in those who worship him.[65] Furthermore, he regarded purity as essential to human dignity. Otherwise, "I would very fain see what difference there is betwixt him and a beast."[66] That Cromwell did more than talk about reformation of morals is well known. It was reported that he fined, placed in stocks, or even cashiered his soldiers for swearing and drunkenness,[67] with the result that he was very proud of the decorum of his troop-

[62] See below, page 288.

[63] Carlyle, *Letters and Speeches*, 1:218. From a letter to William Lenthall, written on September 4, 1645, after the successful storming of Bristol.

[64] Abbott, *Writings and Speeches*, 2:283.

[65] Carlyle, *Letters and Speeches*, 3:115. From the speech of April 21, 1657, to the second Protectorate Parliament. See also, Abbott, *Writings and Speeches*, 2:171. A letter to William Lenthall dated November 25, 1649.

[66] Carlyle, *Letters and Speeches*, 2:541. From the speech of September 17, 1656, delivered to the second Protectorate Parliament.

[67] Abbott, *Writings and Speeches*, 1:321.

ers.[68] One of his first acts upon landing in Ireland in 1649 was to issue a proclamation against swearing and drunkenness.[69] Finally — and this by no means exhausts the list of his reforming activities — he was a staunch supporter of the commissions of Triers and Ejectors set up in 1654 to reform the manners and morals of the clergy.[70]

The Protector's desire for reformation meant that he supported the clauses in the Instrument of Government which called for the suppression of those who were blasphemous or disturbed the peace in the name of religion; and Cromwell had held this belief long before it was constitutionally enshrined.[71] There is, in fact, every reason to suppose from Cromwell's utterances that he would have been a hammer of groups such as the Quakers whose "manners" were outrageous. Yet, we already have seen that he was more lenient toward them than were most who shared the responsibilities of government. Why did Cromwell's actions belie his attitudes? One can only conclude that his care for tender consciences was nearly always an overriding concern. He recognized that it was extremely difficult to separate questions of belief from those of practice. Under no circumstances would he persecute anyone simply for his beliefs, though he was, in theory, willing to proceed against erroneous practice. Where malpractice was clear-cut — swearing or drunkenness for example — his response was immediate and unambiguous. When, on the other hand, it was difficult to divorce practice from belief — as, for example, was the case with the Quakers, who were driven to disrupt religious services by what they interpreted to be the dictates of conscience — Cromwell was genuinely confounded. He could see that the Quakers acted in good conscience and he sympathized with them. In fact, he often was willing to overlook their breach of the Instrument of Government. Actually, the Protector's inconsistency in his dealings with the Quakers

[68] *Ibid.*, pp. 256–58.

[69] *Ibid.*, 2:110. The Proclamation was issued at Dublin Castle on August 23, 1649.

[70] Carlyle, *Letters and Speeches*, 2:539.

[71] In 1650, for example. Abbott, *Writings and Speeches*, 2:335.

was more apparent than real; for Oliver Cromwell was thoroughly consistent in his efforts to preserve liberty of conscience. Where the case was ambiguous, with conscience and practice hopelessly intertwined, he consistently opted for toleration. If err he must when confronted with religious fanaticism, it would be on the side of too much, rather than too little, liberty. This made him nearly unique among rulers in the first half of the seventeenth century.

Finally, since Oliver Cromwell was much more the practical than the theoretical man, it is not surprising that his tolerant practices outstripped his theories. The practice of toleration is the avoidance of persecution. Thus the Protector's practical tolerance was the aggregate of those cases in which he refused to persecute. Faced with concrete situations and confronted by living men of profound religious convictions, abstract principles usually gave way to his feeling of identification with those who would defy all worldly authority to pursue the dictates of conscience.[72]

Though Oliver Cromwell's name frequently emerges when one thinks of toleration in seventeenth-century England, there are two major figures who come to mind even more readily: John Milton and Roger Williams. A brief comparison with the most famous contemporary theories of toleration should further refine our understanding of Cromwell's position.

There was a fairly close identity of interests between Milton and Cromwell. Both were Independents, and Milton was a civil servant of the Commonwealth, acting as Latin Secretary to the Council of State until his blindness incapacitated him in 1652. In May of that year, Milton addressed his famous sonnet to Cromwell, enjoining him to:

> Help us to save free conscience from the paw
> Of hireling wolves, whose Gospel is their maw.[73]

John Milton's ideas about toleration were most clearly expressed in *Areopogitica* (1644), *A Treatise of Civil Power in*

[72] It will be recalled that Cromwell believed the individual Christian conscience to be the locus of religious authority.

[73] Gardiner, *Commonwealth and Protectorate*, 2:33.

Ecclesiastical Causes (1659), and *Of True Religion, Heresy, Schism, and Toleration* (1673). His position was remarkably consistent in these works, written respectively amidst the turmoil of the Civil War, at the close of the Interregnum, and after more than a decade of restored Stuart monarchy.

The similarities between Milton's and Cromwell's ideas easily outweighed the differences, though Milton, to be sure, was the more systematic advocate of toleration. Both men regarded freedom of conscience as the essential reason for religious toleration. They agreed right to the very roots of this idea, since Milton also argued that the locus of religious authority is the light of Scripture as revealed to the individual conscience. In *A Treatise of Civil Power in Ecclesiastical Causes,* he wrote: "What can there else be named of more authority than the church but the consciences, than which God only is greater?" [74] He continued:

> But if any man shall pretend that the scripture judges to his conscience for other men, he makes himself greater not only than the church, but also than the scripture, than the consciences of other men; a presumption too high for any mortal, since every true Christian, able to give a reason of his faith, hath the word of God before him, the promise of the Holy Spirit, the mind of Christ within him, . . . a much better and safer guide of conscience, which as far as concerns himself he may far more certainly know, than any outward rule imposed upon him by others, whom he inwardly neither knows nor can know . . . for belief or practice in religion according to this conscientious persuasion, no man ought to be punished or molested by any outward force on earth whatsoever.[75]

Cromwell would have agreed with Milton's entire argument.[76]

Another important idea on which Milton and Cromwell

[74] Frank Allen Patterson, ed., *The Student's Milton* (New York: Appleton-Century-Crofts, 1957), p. 865.

[75] *Ibid.*

[76] See above, pages 268–74, for my discussion of Cromwell's tolerance of religious practices based on conscientious persuasion.

agreed was the belief that Truth is absolute, but that man's knowledge of it is distorted and incomplete. Milton stated that Truth had come into the world once in the form of Jesus Christ, but that when he departed deception again reigned supreme.[77] Nevertheless, through free debate, men, however falteringly, once more may draw near to the Truth:

> Where there is much desire to learn, there of necessity will be much arguing, much writing, many opinions; for opinion in good men is but knowledge in the making. . . . There must be many schisms and many dissections made in the quarry and in the timber, ere the house of God can be built.[78]

Truth, then, as men know it, is always a process, a quest; it is, in Milton's metaphor, as water which while dammed is stagnate, but when released to flow freely is fresh and pure.[79] "A man," he said, "may be a heretic in the truth." That is, if he believes a thing only because he is told by some authority to believe it, then, "the very truth he holds becomes his heresy."[80] John Milton could not have underlined more dramatically the dynamic quality of Truth as the Independents — Cromwell included — understood it.

Because their truths were implicit and not dynamic, the Roman Catholics were condemned to wallow in error. In fact Milton regarded them as the only bonafide heretics in Christendom. "Heresy, therefore, is a religion taken up and believed from the traditions of men, and additions to the word of God. Whence also it follows clearly, that of all known sects, or pretended religions, at this day in Christendom, popery is the only or the greatest heresy."[81]

With all this Oliver Cromwell would have agreed. There were, however, lines of divergence between Milton and the

[77] John Milton, *Areopagitica*, ed. George H. Sabine (New York: Appleton-Century-Crofts, 1951), p. 41.

[78] *Ibid.*, pp. 45–46.

[79] *Ibid.*, p. 37.

[80] *Ibid.*

[81] John Milton, *Of True Religion, Heresy, Schism, Toleration*, ed. Frank Allen Patterson, *The Student's Milton*, p. 915.

Protector. For example, Cromwell would not have supported Milton's proposition that evil must be tolerated in order, by contrast, to know the good.[82] However much he might have sympathized with the idea that the Christian who knows evil and yet refrains from it is the best Christian, Oliver Cromwell could not bring himself voluntarily to permit the existence of evil. In this he was an orthodox Calvinist, holding the honor of God above the maturation of man.

The major disagreement between the poet and the Protector was over the relationship of church and state. Oliver Cromwell believed in an established church which permitted wide latitude for dissent. John Milton, on the other hand, argued that since Christ's rule is entirely spiritual it is not in any way to be upheld by the external forces of the world.[83] Hence, the magistrate may protect the church, but he may not establish it. His jurisdiction ceases with his protective function.[84]

There is a curious reversal of roles in another area of disagreement between Cromwell and Milton. From what has been written so far, it appears that Milton's theory of toleration was if anything broader than Cromwell's. However, when it came to the subject of Roman Catholicism, Milton was adamant. *No* exercise of Catholicism was to be tolerated under any circumstances, because, as we have seen, Catholicism was the only authentic Christian heresy. There can be little doubt that John Milton, had he the authority of the Protector, would not have averted his attention from the discreet exercise of Roman Catholicism as Cromwell seems to have done. Cromwell may well have agreed with Milton's theories, but he would not practice them.

Despite important areas of disagreement, Cromwell's and Milton's attitudes toward toleration were remarkably similar. There possibly was no other articulate Independent of the time with whom Cromwell was more compatible on this issue.

With the other famous contemporary treatise on toleration, Roger Williams' *The Bloody Tenet of Persecution* (1644),

[82] John Milton, *Areopagitica*, p. 18.

[83] John Milton, *Civil Power*, ed. F. A. Patterson, *The Student's Milton*, p. 870.

[84] *Ibid.*, p. 877.

Oliver Cromwell had a fundamental disagreement. "Fundamental" is the accurate word, for Williams and Cromwell held radically different presuppositions. A. S. P. Woodhouse, in his brilliant introductory essay to his collected documents on *Puritanism and Liberty*, has defined these presuppositions as either the acceptance or rejection of the "principle of segregation." The radical, separating Independents, of which Williams was one, assumed that the realms of Grace and Nature are sharply separated or "segregated." The main body of Independents to which Cromwell belonged assumed that Grace and Nature are closely related, even to the extent of Grace intermixing with Nature. Thus, for Cromwell, what happens in this world is important because God moves in human affairs. On the other hand, Williams, at bottom, did not take the events of this life seriously because they have little if any connection with God or salvation.

Because it was grounded on these contradictory presuppositions, the tolerance of these men, though professed with equal passion, was quite dissimilar. For Roger Williams religion was utterly a spiritual phenomenon. Christ said, "My kingdom is not of this world," so, argued Williams, the civil power has absolutely no authority over religion.[85] Furthermore, Christians need not worry about anti-Christian behavior; God is not dishonored by it because His Kingdom is in no way "of this world."[86] This means that the Christian need not be concerned even about those most in error, the Roman Catholics, for God will deal with them at the last judgment when the reign of Grace shall begin.[87] Intolerance, Williams argued, is the result of confusion. Men have mistakenly assumed that God's dominion is of this world. Hence, they worry about the regenerate being contaminated by the unregenerate. Cease worrying, he counseled; the saints are of God and cannot be contaminated by anything of this world.[88]

Roger Williams' plea for tolerance arose from his percep-

[85] Woodhouse, *Puritanism and Liberty*, p. 282.
[86] *Ibid.*, pp. 270, 277.
[87] *Ibid.*, p. 280.
[88] *Ibid.*, p. 288.

tion of the *futility* of persecution. Persecution is futile because it stems from an attempt on the part of Nature to regulate Grace. This attempt is doomed to failure because the two realms are sharply "segregated." Oliver Cromwell did not regard persecution as futile—he thought of it as *error.* It is error because it inhibits Christians in their *temporal* quest to find the truths of God by the light of their consciences.

Cromwell, as a man of tolerance, was not unique. There were many Independents, Separatists, Anabaptists,[89] Levellers, and others who argued for liberty of conscience during the English Civil Wars and the Interregnum. Yet, his contribution to the history of toleration was an important one—more important perhaps than those of more articulate men like Milton. Indeed, his was, and still is, a rare example: the example of a man of passionate religious belief and of dictatorial power who tolerated a wide range of disagreement with his perception of religious truth even though he possessed the power to proscribe and perhaps to suppress that disagreement. Furthermore, the groups other than the Independents which asked for religious toleration represented the extreme left wing of Protestantism. Cromwell and the Independents were only slightly left of center, so they gave religious toleration a new degree of "respectability." Of course, modern history has witnessed the triumph of religious toleration; but in large part it has been the result of indifference rather than principle. In Oliver Cromwell we have a man who was tolerant from principle—never from indifference.

[89] The idea of toleration had traditionally been the preserve of the radical wing of the Protestant Reformation. In the mid-seventeenth century it was still thought to be a radical doctrine; so that opponents of Cromwell and the Independents often tarred them with the brush of radicalism because of their preoccupation with tolerance. Clement Walker, for example, called Cromwell a "new John of Leyden" and accused the Independents of trying to set up a "new Munster" in England. Cf. Clement Walker, *The History of Independency* (London, 1649), 2:154. Cromwell, of course, was not an Anabaptist, nor was he even a bonafide religious radical. Walker's was typical of the common belief that religious toleration implied radicalism. Oliver Cromwell and the Independents were among the first to demonstrate that this was not necessarily a correct assumption.

12

Piety and Invention: A Study of the Dynamic Roots to Intellectual Creativity in Schleiermacher

JAMES D. NELSON

One could hardly devise a more difficult realm in which to make judgments of psychological or historical causation than that under consideration in this study. To the difficulty, not to say impossibility, of making such judgments at all must here be added the confusion that has risen between the realm of thought and that of piety as a direct result of millennia of human experience during which a simple identification was assumed between religion and all culture. To this basic confusion one must add the powerful counterconfusions created in the course of recent centuries, the birth pangs of a new secular culture. From these ambiguous relationships we find emerging a plethora of counterinfluences and borrowings which make the task of the observer anything but simple, and that of the theorist nigh to impossible.

The intellectual context in which we must understand Friedrich Daniel Ernst Schleiermacher (1768–1834) poses a particularly difficult problem, since in Germany the identification between theology and the general intellectual culture was extremely close and long-lived. This gave to the Enlightenment in Germany a unique character, and one may rightly say that until the middle of the nineteenth century there was no major thinker in Germany that was not "some kind" of theologian. To this must be added the fact that, through the transformation of the Lutheran concept of faith into intellectual assent to right doctrine, the realm of theology and that of religion had become almost hopelessly tangled. That a distinction was in due course drawn, and religion was ultimately recognized as something other than a theological exercise, is in no small degree an outgrowth of Schleiermacher's own efforts—all of which brings us to a working definition of the terms involved in our discussion.

Piety is here defined as the human enterprise of fostering and giving expression to a relationship with a higher being by means of cultic action and communal life. Intellectual creativity here means the ability to formulate and express mental concepts of reality as experienced and reflected upon, which both remain faithful to human experience and recommend themselves to human understanding. The presence of echoes of an earlier religious domination of culture which extend into our time, coupled with a natural inclination of historians to seek formal rather than dynamic influence, has tended to divert the attention of the historian of thought from the question of a biographical continuity underlying the question of influence between these two far from simple realms of human experience and activity. The dual implications of the German term and concept of spirit or *Geist* suggest such a dynamic continuity between the two within the human spirit itself. Modern adherents of religion have been tempted to take a rather perverse pleasure in the discomfort of their secular cohorts in attempting to separate these implications from one another in translation and interpretation. The fact is, however, that if this concept, bridging as it does the spiritual and the intellectual categories in English terminology, is based upon a historical misapprehension rather than upon a psychological reality, we may be certain that the discomfort of the secularist will soon enough be resolved. Thus, if there is indeed any reflection of reality in the dual significance of this concept, it should be sought out and brought to light, and if there is not, it had best be dropped. This enigma of *Geist* may be seen as the general problem area of this essay.

Thus we come to the putting of the question out of which this study takes its genesis. How may one account for the coincidence of conversion and intellectual creativity in a number of major theological figures?[1] The basis for this question is the observation that Schleiermacher, like a number of other persons outstanding for their theological creativity—e.g., Paul, Augustine, Luther—had experienced a profound change of religious condition and situation prior to the onset of his period of intense and creative intellectual activity. For the sake of our discussion here the traditional term "conversion" will be used for this change, while according it a much broader definition than it has generally enjoyed.

In immediate response to this question, which seems to recognize the possibility of such a conversion as a positive factor relating to intellectual creativity and productivity, it is necessary to point out that in several rather notorious cases conversion played precisely the opposite role, e.g., Tolstoi and Newman. Which leads to the recognition of the two-directional character of religious conversion, i.e., that one may at least in regard to a piety scale be either converted "in" or "out." It seems quite clear that in certain cases the convert moves from a highly complex cultic and communal religious structure to a less complex and engrossing one, while in others quite the opposite takes place. The general thesis that arises from this question and the distinctions that have been made is that when the movement in conversion is from a more to a less highly developed structure of piety, intellectual creativity tends to appear, but when the opposite direction is followed, such creativity tends to end. It must be immediately admitted that this thesis is a shot in the dark (and what historical thesis is not?), but in the case of Schleiermacher himself it is possible to muster evidence both from his writings and his career which makes the thesis—if not inevitable—at least credible.

Before examining the rise of this proposed thesis in the life and writings of Schleiermacher, however, let us set forth at least two conclusions that could rightfully be drawn from it. First, we must recognize that this interpretation of the relationship between piety and intellectual creativity lends itself

[1] This question was first raised for me in a tutorial session with Professor Pelikan in 1961.

all too readily to the Marxist understanding of religion. It might with justice be concluded that one could more simply state that "piety is the opiate of the intellect," that religion puts the mind to sleep, that the internal tumult and tensions which give rise to works of intellectual or artistic genius are put to rest in the structure of cultus and community, that the Gordian knot is loosed and the great sleep ensues, or, on the other hand, that an ingenious mind is awakened from its pious slumber and, responding at last to the real world, the creative tension is awakened that lies at the heart of intellectual expression. This is indeed an interesting and reasonable conclusion from the problem as it has been described and the solution as it has been formulated, but at the same time, when taken by itself it assumes too static and mechanical a view of human creativity; it views the prerequisites for intellectual creativity as a quantity given which either wakes or sleeps. It must certainly be recognized that overt works of genius do not rise from repose, but as a matter of fact, neither does what I would present as a much more profound and many-sided fruit of the human spirit—piety. I would rather propose that we deal here, not with intellectual wakefulness and pious slumber, but with two modes by means of which wakefulness and intense activity of the human spirit are expressed and stimulated. This interpretation of the basic thesis affords a character of vitality to the principle of human creativity and expression, recognizing it as a continuity in a state of perpetual activity and growth rather than as a static given. By this means we are able to understand the passage from one mode of spiritual expression and activity to the other, bearing all the sensitivities and capacities from one to the other.

To this I would add a general observation that again rises from the career of our central figure. For some reason, possibly owing to the longer history of that mode of spiritual activity, it would seem that in the time of Schleiermacher, or at least in his spiritual career, piety was a more adequate and satisfactory mode of expression for the spiritual forces available to, and at work in, man. Insofar as this may be judged to be true, the intellectual history of man may be seen as a grand process of demythologization, and insofar as it may still be judged possible to give vent to spiritual aspirations and instincts which are not fully expressible in intellectual categories, that process is not yet complete. The question remains whether it ever will be. So much for the definitions of terms and characterizations of a general cultural framework in which the central thesis of a positive relationship between piety and intellectual creativity may be interpreted and expanded. We must now turn to the life in which it found its origin and in which its credibility is to be defended.

Although the blood of an eighteenth-century *Schwärmer* flowed in his veins, the gift of his paternal grandfather,[2] the young Schleiermacher was, until the middle of his tenth year, the product and resident of a home dominated by Enlightenment influences. Raised in the confines of an extreme left-wing pietist community, his father had nevertheless reached a high degree of skepticism about the Christian religion in its orthodox form. While remaining a Reformed army chaplain and accommodating himself to the beliefs of the masses, he yet found his real religious satisfaction in an extremely active career as a Freemason.[3] The mother, upon whom fell the major part of bringing up young Fritz and his siblings, stemmed from the Stubenrauchs, a family whose name stands with the Sacks and the Spaldings as an inner circle of clergy, churchmen, and theologians in the King's church—the Reformed Church of Brandenberg-Prussia. Though her family descended from deeply religious Saltzberger stock, Schleiermacher's mother and the ecclesiastical set in which she had her place were in the avant-garde of the Enlightenment in Germany. The thoroughness of this orientation is to be ob-

[2] Daniel Schleiermacher.

[3] Father to Schleiermacher, Schweidnitz, May 7, 1790; Georg Reimer, Ludwig Jonas, and Wilhelm Dilthey, eds., *Aus Schleiermacher's Leben in Briefen*, 4 vols. (Berlin: Georg Reimer, 1858–63), 1:89. All citations of vol. 1 are from the first edition; English translations of quotations from vols. 1 and 2 are revised from Friedrica Rowan, trans., *The Life of Schleiermacher* (London: Smith, Elder & Co., 1860). This work will be cited hereafter only as *Briefe*. See also E. R. Meyer, *Schleiermachers und C. G. Brinkmanns Gang durch die Brudergemeine* (Leipzig: Friedrich Jansa, 1905), pp. 2–4.

served in the identification which she made between human virtue and immortality, both to be realized through moral living and the education of her beloved children.[4] This gentle lady to whom Schleiermacher's early education almost exclusively fell harbored pedagogical views far advanced of practices in her own time. Against the authoritarian atmosphere and rote memorization of data which dominated the German academic world, Frau Schleiermacher favored the new "philanthropic" views then being advanced by Basedow in Germany, with emphasis laid upon the development of the sensitivities and interests with which it was assumed the child himself was endowed. It was out of this Enlightenment emphasis upon the development of the natural attributes of the student that Schleiermacher's mother first developed her anxiety concerning the education of her son and the harm that was being done to his "heart" by the exclusive emphasis upon mental gymnastics in the German school system, an anxiety which grew as the religious climate in their home changed, until it led to an overt attempt to thwart that precocious intellectual advancement and finally to his placement with the Herrnhuters.[5]

The intellectual brilliance of Schleiermacher as a child was a major burden of the letters writen by his mother to her brother Theodore Stubenrauch, who was personally to play an important role in the later life of the boy.[6] It is probably better here to allow Frau Schleiermacher to speak for herself, after noting that the context in which these statements stand reflects upon her part a remarkable objectivity and honesty in her analysis and evaluation of her children. She worked very hard at understanding them, and her letters reflect her remarkable success. The outbreak of the War of the Bavarian Succession in 1778 had begun an epoch in the life of Schleiermacher and his family. First of all, it caused the removal of

[4] Mother to Stubenrauch, Breslau, n.d., *Briefe*, 1:18.

[5] This concern constitutes a major theme in her letters and came to dominate her activity in the education of her children. See *ibid.*, 1:17–27.

[6] "ein väterlicher Freund"; see "Selbstbiographie," *ibid.*, 1:12–16. Hereafter cited as *SB*.

the entire family from his native city of Breslau, with its superior schools, to Silesia (first to Pless, then in the following year to Anhalt), with marked effect on Friedrich's life and education. Second, the mobilization of the Silesian regiment to which his father was attached and its quartering in a settlement of the Moravian Brethren led finally to the conversion of the entire family, all this during Schleiermacher's tenth year. Most revealing among a number of letters which Frau Schleiermacher wrote on the intellectual state of her son is one addressed to her brother from Anhalt in 1780, in which she reports:

> Fritz busies himself with French and Latin translations and teaches arithmetic and writing to Carl. In that time which remains we allow the boys a good deal of freedom that they may strengthen their bodies with exercise and fresh air. The two boys are quite opposite natures. Fritz is all spirit (*Geist*), and Carl all body; therefore we still keep the former at home, for he has knowledge enough for his age, and we only wish that his heart (*Herz*) was as good as his understanding (*Verstand*); but his heart has been corrupted by the constant praise bestowed on his intellect at Breslau, and he has become vain and conceited. Had we left him in Breslau, he would probably have been quite ready for the University in his fourteenth year so quickly does he progress in everything. Mr. Sch., the headmaster in Pless, has as a result of his industry become quite fond of him and marvels that although he had not yet studied mathematics in Breslau still he has grasped the subject so quickly. I have much confidence in Mr. Sch. and hope that we can board Fritz with him. He loves the boy and the lad loves him very much and one can accomplish a great deal through love with Fritz.[7]

We have been involved thus far in seeing the sensitivity of the future theologian's mental endowment and the power of his intellect with regard to the contemporary norms. Beside

[7] *Ibid.*, 1:21; also pp. 4, 17, 19; "Schleiermacher's Curriculum," in Meyer, *Schleiermachers*, pp. 147–48.

this we must now place a remarkable capacity for inner spiritual-intellectual criticism which, with his vigor in this area, was later to constitute a determinative factor in his inner development both in piety and in intellectual achievement. The ability to seriously reflect upon his own inner state, to be aware of what was going on inside himself, seems to have been a part of Schleiermacher's natural, or at least early, endowment dating from the period before piety as such came to be a determinative force in his spiritual existence. It was also, in my opinion, the object of intense cultivation and massive development in the particular cultic and communal pattern into which he moved at about this time. Early in his academic career, begun at the tender age of five years,[8] this capacity of self-examination expressed itself in a deep anxiety at his inability to comprehend the Latin authors to whom he had been introduced.

> Here I saw nothing but darkness; for although I learnt to translate the words mechanically into my mother tongue, I could not penetrate into the sense, and my mother, who directed my German readings with much judgment, had taught me not to read without understanding. When I endeavoured to collect into a whole the detached pieces, which I had read at school, my deficiency in the necessary preliminary knowledge frequently rendered me incapable of forming a vivid conception of the subject, a fact which made me very uneasy; and as I perceived none of this uneasiness in my comrades, I began seriously to doubt the much-lauded greatness of my natural faculties, and was in a state of constant fear lest others also should make this unexpected discovery.[9]

Thus it was already with a definite capacity for self-examination and analysis on the part of this young lad that he along with his entire family came into contact with a religious movement that had brought the exercise, development, and exami-

[8] At the Friedrichs Schule in Breslau, *SB*, p. 4.
[9] *SB*, pp. 4–5.

nation of the inner state in the self and in others to an extremely high state of perfection. This brings us to the other environmental revolution of Schleiermacher's tenth year.

This change was precipitated by the circumstance of his father being quartered in the midst of a community which consciously sought to respond to the particular intellectual-religious problem with which he had been struggling since youth. Gottlieb Schleiermacher had become morally and intellectually disillusioned with an earlier, extreme Pietism in which a substantial sectarian certainty had been his birthright. The irrelevance of the original wave of Pietism in the present development of European culture had joined itself to moral disillusionment with the leader of the sect to which he had been attached,[10] causing his rejection of Pietism and the basic orthodoxy it had retained.

Classical Pietism had attempted to supplant the intellectual concept of religion fostered by the political-ecclesiastical structure of post-Westphalia Germany with what it thought of as true "heart religion," for validation of which it went back to Luther and the New Testament. The times, however, had changed, and, partly as a result of the success of classical Pietism's onslaughts upon the old theological-ecclesiastical structure, a new "head religion" had come into the picture, and by the middle of the eighteenth century the one-note knell of classical Pietism was no longer a relevant option. Count Zinzendorf had anticipated this shift from the "old belief" to the "new unbelief" and had become the founder of a new movement (or reshaper of an old one) which may properly be denominated "Neo-Pietism." Therein we find a heavy emphasis upon the cultic and communal experience of salvation, and continuance and development of that experience in a monastic type of social and religious structure. Against the rational doubts of modern man is affirmed the empirical fact of its internal and external life, both individual and corporate. Against the intellectual fragmentation of man in the development of the new science is proposed the union

[10] Reference here is to his experience with Elias Eller and the so-called Ronsdorfer Sect.

of humanity in the incarnation of the Saviour and its continuation in the Church (particularly, but not exclusively, in their congregations). This was the work of a unique religious genius, Count Nicholaus Ludwig von Zinzendorf (1700–1760). And it was into the lap of such a community and under the influence of just this teaching that Gottlieb Schleiermacher fell at a time when he was fully ripe to hear the solution that it proposed. The immediate result of this constellation of chance and destiny in the life of the Schleiermacher family is reported by the elder sister Charlotte several years later.

> From my father, who during the war stopped for some time in the neighborhood of Gnadenfrei and had experienced through the addresses of the late Brother Heinrich von Bruiningk[11] a powerful seizure, we received comforting letters in which he exhorted our good mother and us children to trust in the Saviour, very often deplored the lost time in Breslau, and urgently bade our mother to yield herself to the Saviour.[12]

The degree to which Friedrich Schleiermacher became involved with the Brethren has been variously understood by interpreters of his development, some seeing it only as a matter of having been sent to a boarding school—an educational expedient—others looking upon it as a total family commitment. The latter is generally shared by those who have troubled to familiarize themselves with the sources in any thoroughness. The former position, conceiving a relatively superficial relationship, apparently stems from the fact that it is directly, and I believe intentionally, fostered in the two major original documents interpreting this move which are readily available in English.[13] In view of the available sources

[11] Heinrich von Bruiningk (1738–85), a protege of Zinzendorf's, the outstanding preacher of the movement during this period; see *Nachrichten aus der Brüder-Gemeine: 1845* (Gnadau, 1845), pp. 502–30.

[12] "Lebenslauf der ledigen Schwester Friedrike Charlotte Schleyermacher" (hereafter cited as "Charlotte's Lebenslauf"), in *Nachrichten aus der Brüder-Gemeine: 1834* (Gnadau, 1834), p. 505.

[13] Reference here is to the Rowan translation of *SB* and to the letter,

as a whole, set into the context of the Brethren movement at the time, there can remain no serious doubt that, from Schleiermacher's tenth year until his nineteenth, his family and he were committed to that new-Pietist group and its approach to life. The simple fact is that Schleiermacher was becoming, and indeed did become, a Herrnhuter during those very years in which the sensitivities and faculties of his spirit were making their most rapid growth and reaching their extensive maturity.

That Schleiermacher underwent a struggle with regard to religion during the years of his association with the Brethren is obvious from the most incidental view of the sources, but its extent, character, and significance pose an extremely complicated hermeneutical problem. The fact is that the sources do not agree. We can, I believe, refer to at least three interpretations which emerge from his own letters and papers, insofar as they have come to print.[14] It shall be our purpose here to reconstruct the growth and maturity of that association, setting it in the contemporary context of the movement itself and understanding the divergence of interpretation as it relates to Schleiermacher's changing awareness of his own development. A careful examination of the sources suggests that this religious struggle, like the doubts and difficulties which occasioned it, was by no means so continuous as Schleiermacher indicates in the autobiographical sketch of 1794, and his period of relatively undisturbed involvement in the religious life of that remarkable brotherhood is a far more predominant condition than is suggested by that document. That the initial struggle, which indeed extended over several years, and the final tumult, which marked the end of his direct involvement with the movement and extended even well beyond that point, should have given color to the entire relationship and cast doubt upon the validity of the era of relative

Father to Stubenrauch, Anhalt, n.d., in *Briefe*, 1:21–23. Both reflect a conscious effort to minimize commitment to the Brethren.

[14] (1) The letters written to, by, and about him during the years 1779–87; (2) the *SB* of 1794; and (3) his writings from 1802 to the end of his life.

peace separating them is only natural. At the same time, the account which he gives us in that extremely valuable document portrays those periods of struggle with such pungency that it must remain an important key in our understanding of the ultimate significance of this period of his life.

The religious influence of the Brethren spreads itself over the face of Protestant Europe by means of a kind of work called the Diaspora. This arm of the Brethren program was made up of individuals, families, and voluntary ecclesiastical fellowships in sympathy with the Herrnhuters. They were nurtured by their literature and were visited by itinerant workers, and in turn they visited the settlement congregations from time to time, especially at the Christian festivals. One of the major bulwarks of this Diaspora work was the establishment of the so-called *Haus-Kirchlein* as the basic cell of devotion and discipline.[15] It was felt that such cells could constitute the nucleus from which religious revival could affect the ecclesiastical establishment.

An examination of the moves which Gottlieb Schleiermacher made following his return from the Bavarian War indicates that he set out to establish in his household just such a "little house-church." It was within the context of this home, which had formerly been definitely oriented toward Enlightenment values and ideals, that the ten-year-old Schleiermacher was, during the next five years, subjected to a steady, saturation diet of Brethren piety. We find Pastor Schleiermacher, in the parochial duties which he at this time took up at Anhalt, utilizing typical neo-pietist themes in his preaching[16] and introducing the standard Brethren catechism in the parish religious instructions at which at least his two

[15] "Verlass der vier Synoden der evangelischen Brüder-Unität, von den Jahren 1764, 1769, 1775, and 1782," a manuscript in four volumes, hereafter cited as "Verlass," found in the Moravian Archives in Bethlehem, Pa.; par. 784,18. See also general treatment in John R. Weinlick, *The Moravian Diaspora* (Nazareth, Pa.: Moravian Historical Society, 1959).

[16] Meyer, *Schleiermachers*, pp. 271–73, surveys the sermons which remain among the papers of the son.

elder children were in attendance.[17] But these stand only as relatively external factors. The Brethren did not leave a stone unturned in the organization of such a household for instruction and development of the young. In a contemporary manual for guidance of parents in this movement we may find a regimen outlined which took advantage of forces from every dimension of human experience for the rearing of the young.[18] In this regimen an important role is to be played by a program of daily private instruction periods carried out in connection with the regular family devotions, or with meals. Schleiermacher's elder sister recalls for us her own experience with this mode of instruction by her father.

> In this time he dedicated each morning at breakfast one hour to special conversation with me, chiefly in order to impart gospel exhortation to my heart. He often read also addresses from the Brethren, especially from Count Zinzendorf, and then explained that which I had not properly understood. In this I became powerfully permeated by the truth that an intimate acquaintance of the soul with its Saviour must take place in order that one might finally be able to taste the blessedness which is prepared for us.[19]

A letter from the mother to Fritz during his stay at boarding school in Pless indicates that he, too, participated in such instruction, the center of which was to be a concern with "the meritorious life, and suffering of our Lord and Saviour,"[20] and the object of which was to be that touchstone of Herrnhut piety, "an intimate relationship with the Saviour" (*Umgang mit dem Heiland*).

The sister, in reflecting upon this transition in her family

[17] "Charlotte's Lebenslauf," p. 505; reference is there to Samuel Lieberkühn, *Die Lehre Jesu Christi und seiner Apostel zum Unterricht der Jugend in den Evangelischen Brüdergemeine* (Barby, 1774).

[18] Paul E. Layritz, *Betrachtungen über eine verständige und christliche Erziehung der Kinder* (Barby, 1776); often bound with the Lieberkühn catechism.

[19] "Charlotte's Lebenslauf," p. 505.

[20] Layritz, *Betrachtungen*, p. 140.

and the struggle which accompanied it, reports the despair of her mother, for which an inherent combination of sensitivity and criticism set the stage.[21] We have already pointed to this very combination in her clever and impressionable son Friedrich. It was to the conflict of these two faculties that we may best point as source for his inner struggle during these crucial years, and later. From the first year of his life as member in a household committed to the way of the Brethren we find Schleiermacher later recalling in his autobiography: "In my eleventh year I spent several sleepless nights in consequence of not being able to come to a satisfactory conclusion concerning the mutual relation between the sufferings of Christ and the punishment for which these sufferings were to substitute."[22] Nor were his critical intellectual misgivings during these years limited merely to matters of Brethren doctrine in the narrower sense, but ranged to the broadest contexts of human historical knowledge. In reference to this period, apparently while a resident in the school at Pless, Schleiermacher recalls:

> . . . I had a peculiar thorn in the flesh. It consisted in a strange skepticism, the origin of which I can no longer recollect. I conceived the idea that all the ancient authors, and with them the whole of ancient history, were suppositions. The only reason, indeed, that I had for this belief, was that I was not acquainted with any proofs of their genuineness, and that all that I knew about them seemed to me disjointed and unreal.[23]

That the promising schoolboy again kept these views a secret from his fellows and his teachers in order to protect his reputation for brilliance is not so striking as is the fact that such radical and extensive doubts should present themselves at precisely the time when the "verities" of Brethren orthodoxy were being pressed on him in his home life. The emergence of this general skepticism was no mere coincidence, but

[21] "Charlotte's Lebenslauf," p. 506.
[22] *SB*, p. 7.
[23] *Ibid.*, p. 6.

may be seen as an intellectual rebellion against the closed system of truth conformed to orthodox formulations which dominated Herrnhut during its second generation.[24] Here, already at the threshold of his involvement with the Brethren, we find planted the seeds which in due time were to result in his expulsion from that fellowship. The fact that he was troubled from first to last by what he came later to name the "exoteric" side of the Herrnhuters – their commitment to traditional theological statements[25] – is probably illustrated best by the difficulty he had with this very matter at the time when he was prepared to sacrifice even his dreams of a scholarly career if only he might become a brother. In the midst of a "love at first sight" engagement with the cultus and communal structure of this movement, at Gnadenfrei at Easter of 1783 we find the expectant young *Schwärmer* reflecting a deep inner conflict concerning the doctrines of human corruption and the supernatural means of grace which eventuated for him, as for his mother, in "that state of torture, with producing which our reformers have so frequently been taunted,"[26] namely "*Anfechtung.*" The consistent problem of the young Schleiermacher with this doctrinal emphasis and the role it played in his eventual "conversion" from the Brethren naturally raised the question what might have been if his relationship with that movement had been in its first, rather than in its second, generation. Though no answer is possible for such a question, it does point to the fact that this troubling emphasis was neither the historical nor logical genius, the mystique or "esoteric" of the movement, as Schleiermacher himself was later to judge. But we have as yet presented only one side of the conflict within the future theologian. Judging by what has thus far been disclosed, the ultimate outcome of this initial struggle is incomprehensible.

The fact is that, despite certain surface appearances, the

[24] In this the Moravians anticipated the alliance between Pietism and orthodoxy against "modern unbelief," which characterized popular Protestantism in Europe during the following century.

[25] Schleiermacher to Brinkman, Stolpe, December 14, 1803, *Briefe*, 4:87.

[26] *SB*, pp. 7–8.

final commitment of Schleiermacher, not just as a sympathizer of the Brethren but as a full-fledged member dedicated to a career in the ministry thereof, was no mere response to parental pressures maintained over several years. Although such indoctrination and pressures did, to be sure, have a part in the eventual outcome, Friedrich Schleiermacher's becoming a Herrnhuter was no simple submission of the will. It was no passive compromise for the sake of domestic peace, even as on the parents' part it was no mere boarding out of the children to a "safe" academic refuge. If Schleiermacher subjected his intellectual genius to an inferior level of intellectual crystallization, it was not in trade for the sake of rest but rather for the acquisition of what appeared for him to be the greater value to be gained through immersion in the cultic and communal life of the Herrnhuters. The truth of this position is perhaps best illustrated by the fact that, although he assiduously attempted to "sell himself" on the Brethren religion that his father imported into their home, it was for the son, as for the mother, not until he had seen its operation in a settlement community that he could accept it wholeheartedly.[27] It was really on the basis of the superiority of their academic institutions that Friedrich was convinced by his father to apply to the *Paedagogium* for admission.[28] But once a participant in the most richly wrought segment of Herrnhut cultic life – the Passion Week in a settlement congregation – it was from engrossment in the advantages of such piety that he became determined to remain even if the school were closed to him. The change in attitude, the first "conversion" of Schleiermacher, is associated with his first profound religious experience, which occurred in that place and at that time as a result of his decision not merely to reject the dangers of the world but to choose the Brethren as he had at last come to see them.[29] With regard to this event we may understand Schleiermacher's ultimate identification of Gnadenfrei as the birthplace and home of his inner life. And it was definitely with

[27] "Charlotte's Lebenslauf," pp. 507–10.

[28] Father to Stubenrauch, Anhalt [1782], *Briefe* 1. 21–23.

[29] *SB*, pp. 6, 8.

conscious regard to this initial contact with the Herrnhuters in their "natural habitat" and to the experience which it brought forth that the mature Schleiermacher came to an understanding in this very place of his religious-intellectual Odessy.

It was thus in the spring of 1783 that all three of the Schleiermacher children were brought into the inner circle of this extremely active religious movement, and, although we have no information concerning the attitude of young Carl, the elder brother and sister looked upon their ultimate acceptance as permanent residents of one of these settlements as the most desirable thing in all creation.[30] That they received their wish when at last the Lot was resorted to is a matter of historical record,[31] and in June the two boys removed to Niesky, where they took up residence in the central schools of the Brethren. The sister remained at Gnadenfrei, where she was received into the residence of the single sisters, the so-called choir house. To simply say that Schleiermacher thus "joined" this church, or sect, or monastic order, or whatever you wish to call it, is to say nothing of any significance. To fill such a hollow statement we must attempt to gain some clear impression of the kind of movement it was and what it implied to be caught up in the machinations of its common life and cultus during this period.

A settlement congregation of the Brethren in the eighteenth century bore in its outward appearance a distinctive stamp.[32]

[30] "Charlotte's Lebenslauf," p. 508; *SB*, p. 8; and *Briefe*, 2:22–23.

[31] "Charlotte's Lebenslauf," p. 512; *SB*, p. 7. The use of the "Lot" as a divine oracle during this period for the decision of such matters is an extremely interesting religious phenomenon.

[32] The reconstruction here given of religious life among the Brethren is based chiefly upon [Heinrich Lynar], *Nachricht von dem Ursprung und Fortgange, und hauptsächlich von dem gegenwärtigen Verfassung der Brüder-Unität* (Halle: Johann Jacob Curt, 1781); *Reise durch Kursachsen in die Oberlausitz nach den Evangelischen Brüdergemeinorten, Barby, Gnadau, Herrnhut, Niesky und Kleinwelke* (Leipzig, 1805); and A. G. Spangenberg, *Kurzgefasste historische Nachricht von der gegenwärtigen Verfassung der evangelischen Brüderunität augspurgischer Confession* (Frankfort, 1774). See also James David Nelson, "Herrnhut: Friedrich Schleiermacher's Spiritual Homeland" (Unpub-

In a central square stood the Prayer Hall or church surrounded by four or five large buildings, each generally with its own courtyard, and these in turn were surrounded at the outward edges by several dozen private dwellings and structures to house small industry. The almost invariable rule was that such a settlement would be a social, economic, and political unit set off from all habitation, as a village, or perhaps more like a monastery surrounded by dwellings for retainers. Within the borders of these settlements existed as thorough and as well-thought-out and instituted a structure for the promotion and execution of religious piety as is likely in any age to be found anywhere. During the period under discussion the time of adventurous religious experimentation by Count Zinzendorf, based upon a very broad knowledge of other such experiments, was over.[33] The results of this experimental time had been consolidated, and a half century of usage had tended to smooth out the rough places and fill the loopholes. Although the movement was just at this time theologically losing its nerve,[34] its cultic and communal life continued on with most of its primitive vigor, if not its innovation, until about the end of the first decade of the next century.

For devotional and disciplinary purposes, and no real distinction was made between the two here, the entire community was divided up in several different ways. First of all, it was seen as a unity, and for some of the most important cultic acts its members were viewed in this generally corporate fashion. The most stable divisions in such a congregation were constituted by the so-called "choirs," the primary unit in

lished Ph.D. dissertation, Divinity School, University of Chicago, 1963), pp. 17–422.

[33] Although Zinzendorf's contacts with earlier monastic and liturgical experiments have never been fully investigated, even a casual observation of his experiments reveals that they must have been extensive. See *Kurze zuverlassige Nachricht von der . . . Kirche Unitas Fratrum, etc.* (1757).

[34] Symbolic of the theological retrenchment of the period are the "Fundamentalist" position taken by the Synod of 1775, "Verlass," par. 9; and the decision to remove the Seminary from Barby to Niesky to place it farther from Halle; "Gemein Nachrichten" (1788), I. Theil, 20. Woche, 1 (MS periodical available at Moravain Archives in Bethlehem, Pa.).

which the religious life was nurtured.[35] There were generally nine such units—the little boys, the little girls, the big boys, the big girls, the single brothers, the single sisters, the married, the widowers, and the widows. The buildings surrounding the square on which the church stood were, besides the inn and manor house, the residence and industrial complex of the single brothers and the single sisters, who were the bulwark of the settlement, and those also of the widows and widowers. If there were an educational institution of the Brethren in the settlement, it would be housed in a similar building to be added to this number. The married choir members lived in their private residences along with their minor children, and any children who could not be kept by their parents generally resided in the single choir house of their respective sex and were the wards of their choir. It is revealing to note that in this society infants were presented for baptism, not by their parents, but by the choir "helper" or spiritual leader in the single choir of which they would eventually become members.

Inside each choir house were to be found a refectory, dormitory halls, industrial shops, and a prayer chapel generally equipped with a small organ. In the Prayer Hall at the middle of the square one found arrangements for seating the men on the left and the women on the right side of the hall, each with a separate entrance and all facing a raised platform which extended along one wall and on which was to be found a table at which the speaker or liturgical leader sat. The spiritual leaders of the congregation and of the choirs also found their places on this platform. The choirs sat as bodies in this hall, the youngest at front. At some distance from this building, usually separated from it by an avenue of trees, stood the cemetery or *Gottesacker*, which was laid out in exact imitation of the distribution of the congregation in the Prayer Hall. It was looked upon literally as "God's field" which was planted in anticipation of the harvest at the general resurrection. This spot was the cultic center, not for veneration of the past, but

[35] These monastic units should not be confounded with a *chorus musicus*.

for celebration and contemplation of the church triumphant. This communal and corporate emphasis runs through the entire Brethren conception of religion.

Yet another way in which a congregation was divided was within the choirs themselves, where one found circles established, composed of from six to ten persons. The circles met for mutual confession, prayer, and admonition almost daily during the winter months, when the evenings were long and agriculture was at a standstill, but not so regularly as the days became longer. The personnel of these groups generally changed each quarter. Beside these divisions involving the entire congregation, there were others for devotional and administrative purposes. Among these we find the society which carried on perpetual prayer and intercessions, the council of the spiritual leaders or helpers, and the council of the administrators. These latter two bodies decided on all administrative and disciplinary matters and reached far into the private lives of each one of the residents and members of such a settlement congregation. All these "disciplines" of place and structure are important, but much more central in understanding what it meant *to be* what Schleiermacher *was* during this time is the functioning of all these provisions as a cultic organism.

Basic to any understanding of Moravian liturgical life is a comprehension of the role which music in general, and hymnody in particular, play in it. Arising in the German national culture in an age when it was unique for its production of ecclesiastical music, this movement under the leadership of Zinzendorf made an effort to appropriate to its cultic usage both the great Protestant storehouse of hymnic tradition utilizing the chorale, which was the musical idiom thereof, and the potentialities of the new classical forms and instrumentation. The rise of the Herrnhuters and especially the career of Zinzendorf marked a renaissance in German hymnody,[36] and it was this which may best be seen as an index of the spiritual quality of the movement, rather than any doctrinal formula-

[36] See Joseph Müller, "Moravian Hymnody," and "N. L. Zinzendorf," *A Dictionary of Hymnody*, ed. John Julian (New York: Charles Scribner's Sons, 1892), pp. 765–69, 1301–5.

tions which emerged. The role which the singing of chorales played in the cultic life of the Brethren must be literally observed to be credible. In each of the several thousand religious services held in a settlement congregation during a year, one discovers the presence of several well-chosen hymn verses, each usually set to a different chorale tune. These were in no case, even when the service featured a sermon or spiritual address, simply incidental or tacked on, but rather they set the tone of the meeting. In services of a more narrowly liturgical character, of which there would be several hundred during the year, only two were dominated by the spoken word – the usual Sunday morning usage of their Church Litany and the Eastern Morning Litany – and even these were richly endowed with sections which were sung. The remainder of the cultic gatherings – Lovefeasts, Holy Communion, Singing Hours, Evening Liturgies, Choir Liturgies, Cup of Covenant – some of which occurred each day, some once a week, some each month, and others yearly – could be carried out with the utterance of no more than a dozen spoken words, and many of them were composed entirely of hymns and anthems.

From a musical point of view, the manner in which these services were executed became legendary throughout the Protestant world.[37] The softness and full, harmonious execution of congregational singing among the Moravians is, even to this day, a pleasant surprise. The mention of anthems brings us round to a consideration of the function of more specialized musical groups, of which there were usually several. One generally found a trombone choir which served both for the announcement of such communal events as birth, death, and hours of worship and as executor of the prelude and introit for festal services in the Prayer Hall. For services within the Prayer Hall it was not unusual also to have a string ensemble. There might be several musical choirs in a congre-

[37] Johann Friedrich Reichardt (1752–1814), a noted contemporary musician, expressed his impression of this feature in Brethren piety. Christian G. Frohberger, *Briefe über Herrnhut und die evangelische Brüdergemeine* (Budissen: Georg Gotthold Monse, 1795), p. 348.

gation, and, in fact, a number of the liturgical settings that come down to us from this period call for the functioning of two within a single service. Most important among these musical organizations, however, were the organist and his instrument. Even under frontier conditions in America the Herrnhuters brought with them the art of building and using excellent pipe organs, and the organist's role was conceived by those who knew it best to be parallel, not inferior to, that of the chief pastor of such a congregation. The presence and exercise of all this musical art as the chief motif of Brethren worship contributed a spiritual quality to their devotion which stirred human feeling and action and, finally, thinking to a remarkable degree. The music of the Moravians and the extremely imaginative poetry which they set to it may be executed softly and harmoniously, but it does not have a somnic effect on the human spirit—quite the opposite is the case!

The truly monastic character of Brethren piety may best be seen in their application of religious "disciplines" to time. Time became here a carefully and richly woven cultic tapestry. Each day had its official "hours" dedicated to the acts of thanksgiving and edification. Beginning and ending in the choir prayer hall with services of benediction, the industrial activities of the day were interlaced with at least three additional public acts of worship: a morning children's service; and in the evening, two services—the first featuring a spiritual address, the second entirely composed of music. Each day of the week had its own specific pattern, with two morning services added on Sunday along with specialized services for the various choirs in the afternoon. During one year in such a congregation, one hundred and twenty-three special days of a weekly, monthly, or yearly character came to interrupt the simple weekday schedule of liturgical activity.[38] At such times we find alterations very like those seen for Sundays. During each four-week period there occurred at least a children's prayer day, a congregational prayer day, and a celebration of Lovefeast and Holy Communion. Each year we find regular

[38] The year was 1783 at the settlement in Bethlehem, Pa. See Nelson, "Herrnhut," pp. 330–33 for a table of these observances.

celebrations of feasts little observed in Protestant circles, such as Michaelmas and Candlemas, as well as, of course, the great feasts of the Christian year. To this were added a wide variety of special days for the individual choirs and for special groups, but the capstone of the yearly cycle was the celebration of Passion Week and Eastertide. Using a scriptural reconstruction in the form of a harmony of the four Gospel accounts of the events of Christ's life during the week of his passion,[39] by means of services of reading interspersed in the usual fashion with music, footwashing ceremonies in the choirs, Holy Communion, Lovefeasts, and festive benedictions and liturgies, reaching a dual climax at three o'clock on Friday afternoon and at sunrise on Sunday in the *Gottesacker*, the Herrnhuters liturgically relived that crucial period in their understanding of Jesus and his career. It should be recalled that it was during this celebration that the young and receptive Schleiermacher had his first immediate contact with the Brethren, and this served as the context of his first "religious" experience. Thus it seems wise here to speak of the view of religious experience in this movement.

For Moravian piety the experience of God par excellence was feeling (*Gefühl*), not of "utter dependence" or of the "World Spirit,"[40] but of being with Jesus of Nazareth who is also "very God" as he walked on this earth. One was to be transported into an association with the earthly-heavenly Saviour, which was the key to a continuing relationship then carried into modern life. This Zinzendorfian "*Umgang mit dem Heiland*"[41] still dominated Brethren religion during this time, and as we see their cultic celebrations, particularly of the Holy Week, the corporate implications of this ideal become

[39] Samuel Lieberkühn, *Die Geschichte der Tage des Menschen-Sohne von der Marter-Woche an bis zu Seiner Himmelfahrt* (Barby, 1765); for present day practice see *The Passion Week Manual* (Bethlehem, Pa.: The Moravian Book Shop, 1933).

[40] This is not to suggest that there is no genetic connection between the concept in Zinzendorf and that in Schleiermacher.

[41] The best summary of Zinzendorf's theology is still that in Albrecht Ritschl, *Geschichte des Pietismus*, 3 vols. (Bonn: Adolph Marcus, 1880–86), 3:404–38.

clear. It was, after all, not to be cultivated in solitude, but in this place, among these people, arranged in terms of these structures, and living this life of common song and prayer. Here a way of life developed which, through its concentration on the inner state, stimulated a remarkable degree of sensitivity to one's own thoughts and feelings as well as to those of others. In, with, and under the more formal devotional and communal operations of the congregation developed a vast complex of extremely intimate human relationships which gave and preserved the life of the whole. Here the divination of the inner state of human beings as a dimension of friendship aiming at a mutual religious end became a highly sophisticated art. Thus a great amount of energy was given to the development of the religious individual, but always within the communal context. Against the richness of this cultic and communal structure we must now examine the experience of Schleiermacher and its significance for his career of intellectual creativity.

The line of interpretation of his experience with the Brethren which is incorporated in the 1794 autobiography casts serious doubt whether Schleiermacher ever actually became a Herrnhuter. To be sure, there is no question even there that he had tried to be one, but in that document he denies the objective validity of any and all religious experience which he enjoyed there. We find him reporting from his early days there that

> in vain I aspired after those supernatural experiences, of the necessity of which every glance at myself with reference to the doctrine of future retribution convinced me—of the reality of which, *external to myself*, every address and every hymn, yes, every glance at the Brethren so attractive while under their influence, persuaded me. Yet me they seemed ever to flee, though at times I thought that I had seized a shadow of them at least; for I soon perceived that it was no more than the work of my own mind, the result of the fruitless straining of my imagination.[42]

[42] *SB*, p. 8.

And of his last efforts in this direction he reports later in that same document:

> We (Schleiermacher and his "other self") were still striving in vain for supernatural experiences, and for that which in the phraseology of the Brethren was termed intercourse with Jesus (*Umgang mit Jesu*); the most violent tension of our imagination remained fruitless, and the voluntary aids which it lent were always discovered to be deceptive.[43]

That this is not at all the picture one gets through examination of documents from Schleiermacher's own hand dating from the period of his residence at the *Paedagogium* at Niesky and subsequently at the Seminary at Barby is not convincing evidence of the inaccuracy of this interpretation. The interpretation in the "autobiography" is plainly an effort to deal fairly and objectively with that very critical problem. The fact is that Schleiermacher's father had apparently made a specific accusation of falsehood in the earlier reports from his son's hand when the eventual "apostasy" from the "true faith" took place.[44] Thus we find Schleiermacher, seven years after his overt break with the Brethren, advancing this theory that he had honestly deceived himself. In this we should more or less have to take his word if he had not later, on further reflection, maturity, and renewed contact with the movement in question, changed his interpretation from the judgment that he had deceived himself concerning the genuineness of his experience to a sustained view that he and the movement itself had merely misunderstood the true nature of the Brethren religion and its place in his life and the life of the entire culture. Although this final judgment would lead him to conclude that he could not live among the Herrnhuters, as he apparently so much wished that he could, without either deceiving them or offending them, it did not suggest that what he saw as their "esoteric" genius, which he identified with the "Sav-

[43] *Ibid.*, p. 10.

[44] Father to Schleiermacher, Anhalt, February 8, 1787, *Briefe*, 1:49.

iour" and the "Church," was in any way invalid.[45] In view of this final position, which made it possible to become "once again a Herrnhuter," we are required to look at his experience as "then a Herrnhuter" in a more confident manner.

A very few soundings will be adequate to project the degree to which Schleiermacher participated in the life of the Brethren as it has been sketched briefly above. After a phenomenally short time — only one year — Schleiermacher was admitted to full communicant relationship in the congregation at Niesky.[46] This final step of admission to Holy Communion was traditionally a high point in the life of a Herrnhuter. In Schleiermacher's case we have a relatively clear picture of his condition at this crucial time. He was, as he recalls thirteen years later, "all aflame with imagination."[47] Less than a week before his confirmation, which apparently took place on Palm Sunday, the fifteen-year-old wrote the following letter to his sister:

> Dearly beloved Sister!
>
> The congregation here has celebrated the office (Eucharist) a week later than in Gnadenfrei and other congregations; consequently yesterday I was for the second time, by the grace of the Saviour, permitted to be a looker on. In the afternoon, before the Lovefeast, I received your letter. I am assured that you will rejoice with me — that with me you will thank our good and merciful Saviour, and also pray to him to bestow upon me his grace, more especially during the fortnight between this and Maundy Thursday, when I am to partake of his flesh and blood in the Holy Communion, so that it may day by day show forth more gloriously in me. "I will draw all men unto myself," John 12:32b, was the text yesterday; and as

[45] Schleiermacher to Brinkman, Stolpe, December 14, 1803, *ibid.*, 4:87–88.

[46] Meyer, *Schleiermachers*, pp. 137–42. There were three distinct steps involved, each accompanied by the most careful examination and the drawing of the "Lot": (1) Residence, (2) Membership, and (3) Communion.

[47] "lauter glühende Phantasie," Schleiermacher to sister Charlotte, Berlin, August 18, 1797, *Briefe*, 1:151.

regards me also he will graciously fulfill this promise. He has risen from the dead to help all miserable sinners on earth, and therefore I also have a part in him; he alone is my stay, the God who died for me upon the cross.

On the occasion of your approaching birthday, the first that you will celebrate in the congregation, I wish you the special peace of the Saviour, and many blessings; I will think of you on that day. Ah! did but the love of Christ fill our hearts day and night! Were we but always pleasant in his sight, were we but in constant, uninterrupted communion with him, did we but cling to him so that not even for one moment could we be drawn away from him! With these wishes for us both I conclude. Remember me, and love your brother, who loves you in Jesus.

[Fritz] [48]

In reflection upon the events which he was then anticipating, we find Friedrich a little over three weeks later writing:

> I quite agree with what you say about the recent beautiful festivals, and to me also they brought a blessing. It is true that all days that God gives, ought, in the community, to be days sacred to the memory of his martyrdom; but on occasion of such holidays and memorial festivals we feel nevertheless a greater and more lasting blessing.[49]

A letter several months later may be seen as perhaps the classical expression of Schleiermacher's attachment to this movement. "When I find," says he,

> that I do not love the Saviour enough, that I do not sufficiently honour him; when the daily intercourse with him does not go on uninterrupted, then I am disturbed. But as often as we draw near to him feeling ourselves sinners, who can only be saved by his mercy — as often as we pray to him for a look of grace, we never go away from him

[48] [Niesky, March 28, 1784], *ibid.*, 1:34 (John 12.32b, the daily text for March 27, 1784, dates this letter).

[49] Niesky [Late April, 1784], *ibid.*, 1:35.

> empty. He never abandons us, however much we may deserve it; yet the more undisturbed our minds the better, the more consistent, the more tranquil, the nearer to heaven—happiest for us would it be, were we there altogether. But his will be done; it is the best.[50]

It may without fear be stated that in this outpouring the changes are rung in some way on every important theme of theology, practice, and terminology characteristic of the Brethren during this period. One is tempted here to develop the exact bearing of this document on that movement as a valid representation, but our point is rather to gain a glimpse at the completeness of Schleiermacher's commitment to this religiously saturated system of life.

It should at the same time be supposed that during the period from his fifteenth to his nineteenth year Schleiermacher's intellectual capacity was in a state of suspended animation. The level of his performance at Niesky was almost unique, being paralleled in his time only by him to whom we have already referred as his "other self"[51]—Johann Baptist Albertini (1769–1831). These two brilliant young men formed a friendship which became famous in that narrow world of the Brethren, where such close personal attachments and relationships were a well cultivated art. Known within the Brotherhood as "Orestes and Pylades,"[52] Albertini and Schleiermacher privately shared the reading and study of the Greek poets and the Hebrew Old Testament as well as their spiritual struggles and endeavors of a more specifically religious character. They were Herrnhuters together and they developed together their theological and vocational problems and doubts which were to hurl them headlong into collision with the then more and more rigid theological discipline of this movement.

[50] Niesky [September, 1784], *ibid.*, 1:30. Dated correctly by Meyer, *Schleiermachers*, p. 140.

[51] This English designation was applied to Albertini in a German context by a former teacher at Niesky; Horn to Schleiermacher, Gnadenfeld, April 4, 1784, *Briefe*, 3:4.

[52] *SB*, p. 9. Schleiermacher to sister Charlotte, Berlin, August 2, 1798, *Briefe*, 1:191.

Most interesting for us in this relationship of Schleiermacher and his "other self" is that, with the stimulation of Neological doubts and of the then birthing German classical literature, and the collision which the development of heterodox "philosophical" views brought with the ecclesiastical authorities, one of these "selves" departed from the Brethren, the other did not. Schleiermacher was deprived of the cultus and the community in which his spiritual life had during those crucial years been fostered and expressed, and returned to a world which had become strange and fearful to him.[53]

The theological doubts which Friedrich poured out to his father in January of 1787 at the insistence of his superiors at the Seminary at Barby had apparently emerged in the much freer atmosphere of that school during the second semester at that place. The actual expression came in the midst of his third and final semester there, a time which their discovery by the authorities of the school was to make a veritable hell for Schleiermacher and his friends, particularly his closest friend Albertini. "I cannot believe," confessed the eighteen-year-old Friedrich,

> that he, who called himself the Son of Man, was the true, eternal God; I cannot believe that his death was a vicarious atonement, because he never expressly said so himself; and I cannot believe it to have been necessary, because God, who evidently did not create men for perfection, but the pursuit of it, cannot possibly intend to punish them eternally, because they have not attained it.[54]

These doubts had developed in the bosom of the friendship of these two youths, now joined in their endeavours by several other lads forming a "philosophy club."[55] It will readily be noted that these specific doubts struck at the very roots of Brethren theology. It is not to be anticipated that a religious

[53] *SB*, p. 12.

[54] Schleiermacher to his father, Barby, January 21, 1787, *ibid.*, 1:45.

[55] Albertini and Schleiermacher had been joined at Barby by Samuel Okely, Johann Jacob Beyer, and Emanuel Zäslein. See Meyer, *Schleiermachers*, pp. 204–5. In *Briefe*, 3:9–25, we find letters from these young men to each other.

order just then responding in a rigid fashion to a massive challenge from outside in these very concerns should deal gently or patiently with such a challenge from within. Schleiermacher's father makes reference to the isolation of the "mangy sheep" so as to avoid infection of the whole flock,[56] and this is just was happened.

This is not to suggest that no effort was made to rescue Schleiermacher from his own folly. During the winter semester 1786–87 no expedient was neglected by the authorities at Barby in an effort to "save" this misguided brother from the poison of his own doubts. The disciplinary structure of the Brethren was an extremely versatile and many-sided affair, and those who exercised it were virtuosos in the analysis and manipulation of the emotional state of their charges. That no possible pressure was spared, from the most subtle appeal to the boy's inner consciousness to the almost overt threat that if he failed to turn from "destruction" he would be expelled from the community and abandoned by his family, is obvious from the agonizing testimony of his letters from this time. That he was vulnerable to such pressures is also obvious from such almost symbolic submissions as his voluntary excommunication and finally his voluntary withdrawal from the community so as to avoid burning the bridges by which he actively hoped to return once he had conquered his doubts.[57] Seven years later he reflects on those days and what they cost him. "In vain," says he,

> was every means of conversion employed. I could no longer be drawn out of the path I had entered; but long after, I still felt the exhaustion consequent upon the immense exertions I was obliged to make to conquer the numerous obstacles and impediments that were placed in my way as soon as it was discovered that I had entered this path.[58]

[56] "dass nicht ein räudiges Schaf die ganze Heerde anstecke"; Father to Schleiermacher, Anhalt, March 19, 1787, *ibid.*, 1:62–63.

[57] Schleiermacher to his father, Barby, January 21, 1787, *ibid.*, 1:47–48. This intention also reflected Albertini's concern in: Schleiermacher to his father, Barby, June 29, 1788, *ibid.*, 3:21.

[58] *SB*, pp. 11–12.

This shipwreck to which his career as a Herrnhuter had brought him is the basis for the negative judgments he makes of his entire experience, as reflected in his autobiography, and his continuing ambivalence, exemplified in a comparison of the *Reden* with the *Monologen*,[59] in regard to this episode in his life. Another immediate contact with the movement was required in order to stimulate his reevaluation thereof. This came in the spring of 1802 at Gnadenfrei. From this point we can date his deeper appreciation of the contribution that this movement had made to his spiritual formation and development.

There are, in fact, a number of formal elements in Schleiermacher's later theological formulations which may be traced directly or indirectly to his experience among the Herrnhuters. Not the least of these is the whole central methodological bulwark of "*Frömmigkeit*" or Piety itself, but this is not our interest here. We are primarily interested in an examination of the role which his experience of religious piety contributed to the formation of his spirit and, in particular, with regard to its creativity. How did it equip and stimulate him in his subsequent career?

The statement of yet another ex-Herrnhuter who went on to scholarly fame, the philosopher Jacob Friedrich Fries, made thirty-one years after his separation from the Brethren, expresses with remarkable fidelity Schleiermacher's condition in this regard. "For a runaway child of Herrnhut," confesses Fries, "the shoe never ceases to pinch."[60] The Herrnhuters were for Schleiermacher a perpetual source of religious frustration; he simply could neither do with them nor without them. Although this dilemma did not come to overt expression in his extant correspondence until a relatively late date, its presence is easily discernible through his life after separation from the community. He keeps harking back to it, and at some level of his being he never completely gave up a hope that

[59] In his *Reden über Religion* (1799) we find strong and pervasive sympathy reflected for the Brethren, while the *Monologen* (1800) is at points critical of the lack of freedom in that movement.

[60] Meyer, *Schleiermachers*, p. 280.

some day he could return to that place.[61] Why should this be so when he had manifestly been treated so badly? Let us first listen to what he himself says about it, then attempt to place it into the context of his career of remarkable intellectual creativity and influence.

On seven occasions that we know of Schleiermacher visited a settlement of the Brethren subsequent to his withdrawal from Barby.[62] Of most of them we know very little, but on one occasion he stated the significance of these pilgrimages to him. "My state of mind while amid a congregation of the Brethren Unity," he states in 1817,

> is always very peculiar. The greater part of my youth and the decisive moment in regard to the entire development of my life, are forcibly recalled to my mind. This point of transition, however casual it may appear on the one hand, seems to me on the other to have been so strictly necessary, that I cannot at all conceive of myself without it.[63]

The truth of these words spoken during a stay in Ebersdorf is best demonstrated by the effects of a crucial stay at Gnadenfrei just after Easter in 1802. It was of this place that he had indicated that

> here were laid the germs of an imaginativeness in matters of religion which, had I been of a more ardent temperament, would probably have made me a visionary (*Schwärmer*), but to which I am nevertheless indebted for many a precious experience, and which is the cause, that while in most people the disposition of the mind is formed unconsciously by theory and observation, in my case it bears

[61] Schleiermacher to Grunow, Gnadenfrei, May 3, 1802, in Wilhelm Dilthey, *Leben Schleiermachers*, 2d ed. (Berlin: Vereinigung wissenschaftlicher Verleger, 1922), pp. 580–82; Schleiermacher to Brinkmann, Stolpe, December 14, 1803, *Briefe*, 4:88; and Schleiermacher to his wife, Ebersdorf, August 30, 1817, *ibid.*, 2:331. For an excellent collation of references and visits of Schleiermacher to the Brethren after 1787 see Meyer, *Schleiermachers*, pp. 257–68.

[62] In 1787, 1795, 1802, 1805, 1809, 1817, and 1821.

[63] *Briefe*, 2:331.

> the impress, and is the conscious product, of my own mental history.[64]

A few short months before this visit he had referred to Gnadenfrei as the one locality in his native Silesia where "I feel really attached though I spent no more than a few months there; but these were very remarkable months; during that period occurred the first movements in my inner life."[65] Schleiermacher returned here at the close of the period of his most active intellectual stimulation – the period of his immediate contact with the Romantic circle at Berlin. On the last day of April, 1802, Schleiermacher poured out his feelings about this "homecoming" to his friend and publisher Georg Reimer, in the famous "Herrnhuter of a Higher Order" letter. "I feel myself very happy here," confesses the young Romantic,

> in the society of a beloved sister, in a beautiful country, and amid the wonderful impressions of an earlier period of my life. There is no other place which could call forth such lively reminiscences of the entire onward movement of my mind, from its first awakening to a higher life, up to the point which I have at present attained. Here it was that for the first time I awoke to the conscious relations of man to a higher world – in a diminutive form, it is true, just as it is said that spirits sometimes appear in the form of children and dwarfs; but they are nevertheless spirits, and as regards essentials thereof, it comes to the same thing. Here it was that that mystic tendency developed itself, which has been of so much importance to me, and has supported and carried me through all the storms of skepticism. Then it was only germinating, now it has attained its full development and I may say, that after all I have passed through, I have become a Herrnhuter again, only of a higher order.[66]

[64] *SB*, p. 7.
[65] Schleiermacher to Von Willich, June, 1801, *Briefe*, 1:294.
[66] Schleiermacher to Reimer, Gnadenfrei, April 30, 1802, *ibid.*, 1:308–9.

In a letter written a year and a half later to another ex-Herrnhuter Schleiermacher gives an account of his effort to communicate his feelings, while visiting at Gnadenfrei, to the widow of a former teacher, and he thus makes confession of his spiritual debt to the Brethren.[67] Although his efforts were frustrated by the stubbornness of the lady in question, this letter directs our attention to at least two important contents of what had been described earlier as a "mystical tendency." He here states: "I could not even get so far with her that I could make her realize how much it would be worth that one should early learn to view the world from a single idea,"[68] a capacity certainly not unrelated to Dilthey's recognition of Schleiermacher as the German Plato.[69] In this same letter we find Schleiermacher speaking of yet another spiritual capacity for which he thanks the Brethren. He here observes:

> There are many men who as a matter of fact have no mean capacity but yet are not in a position to discover the truly inner in another man. This is the reason why we are often not so well understood by people who are of some worth to us as we wish, and why *our* talent of understanding must appear to us as somewhat distinctive if we would be honest. Insofar as one can attribute something inner to outward circumstances I believe that we can always in this matter attribute something to the reckoning of the congregation. The early practice of looking into oneself (*in sich selbst schauen*) and in such detail as it is almost nowhere else possible, certainly forms the most mature observer of man.[70]

Thus in this single effusion of reflective gratitude we find Schleiermacher tracing the two mental capacities which may

[67] Reference is to a conversation with Frau Tschiersky; see Schleiermacher to Brinkmann, Stolpe, December 14, 1803, *ibid.*, 4:87.

[68] *Ibid.*

[69] Reference here is not to the Schleiermacher translation of Plato's *Dialogues* but rather to the position which Dilthey ascribes to Schleiermacher in the development of German philosophy. See Dilthey, *Leben*, pp. 191–217, 588–604.

[70] *Briefe*, 4:87.

be judged most pivotal for his intellectual approach—the faculty to develop a coherent *Weltanschauung* and the faculty to observe the workings and contents of the human spirit in the self and others—to his spiritual experience as a youth with the Herrnhuters. But I would still wish to press even beyond these faculties, crucial as they are, to a yet more dynamic factor in his intellectual creativity.

Time after time Schleiermacher resorts to statements which reflect a longing to return to the Brethren, or rather to a more timely version thereof, and pours out his admiration for the cultic and communal provisions of their congregations.[71] To be sure, this extremely active and much troubled thinker, churchman, and academician had cause enough to desire solitude, but this alone does not account for his rather pungently expressed longing. In view of the biographical context in which these longings are expressed it seems quite clear that after his separation from the Brethren Schleiermacher suffered from a varying degree of religious frustration. The massive stimulation of the Moravian cultic and communal life had developed a natural spiritual capacity, which was indeed great, to a keen and intense vitality. Even the brief glimpse of the religious life in such a settlement which has been granted to us here must reveal what a magnificent and versatile tool it was for the stimulation and expression of an already sensitive mind and heart. The satisfaction which Schleiermacher enjoyed here is reflected by the statements he made at the time, but still more later, as he looked back. The woodenness of his existence in the years that followed, I submit, was not merely a result of exhaustion, but even more a result of his passage from the lurid three-dimensional world of the Herrnhuters back to the drab, black and white, two-dimensional spiritual world of university life in late eighteenth-century Germany.

[71] Schleiermacher to Charlotte von Kathen, Halle, May 5, 1805, *ibid.*, 2:21–24; and *Zwei unvorgreifliche Gutachten in sachen des Protestantischen Kirchenwesens zünachst in Beziehung auf dan prussischen Staat* (1804), in *Friedrich Schleiermacher's sämmtliche Werke*, erste Abtheilung, *Zur Theologie* (Berlin: G. Reimer, 1846), 5:41–156; are the best reflections of his views on Moravian cultus in his mature years.

I further submit that beside the basic capacities of sight to which the Brethren had contributed so greatly we must place a spirit stretched to such a degree, and spoiled to such a degree, by the stimulative and expressive possibilities of Brethren piety that he literally could not abide within the intellectual modes that traditional theology afforded him. He had feelings to feel and thoughts to express for which the usual intellectual forms had no adequate capacity. Saddled with a spiritual development and no means to express it except the tools of intellect, Schleiermacher burst the "old wineskins" and fashioned new ones. Romanticism came to his assistance, as he to its, and the same might be said for ideological nationalism, but in the end he still longed back to the expressive tools of his youth. On the way, however, he created a new epoch in the intellectual *lingua franca* of contemporary Germany—he became the "Father of Modern Theology."

While Pylades wrestled with the frustration of a half-tied spiritual tongue and created a new age for the now sorely troubled queen of the sciences, Orestes, his spiritual twin, was left behind, either too cowardly or too courageous to pursue his doubts out into the world. The historical accident which has preserved for us in the case of Schleiermacher a "control" as touches this matter of piety and creativity has presented us with an almost unique possibility. Not only were Albertini and Schleiermacher involved in an almost completely parallel career, even down to sharing the same involvement with the new thought and classical literature and the same new doubts which they produced, but they were immediately and profoundly involved with each other's spiritual character and development to such a degree that, despite the failure of direct communication between them, Schleiermacher could speak years later as if he knew exactly what Albertini was thinking and feeling at any given moment or situation.[72] The two youths, only three months apart in age, had gone the whole

[72] Schleiermacher to sister Charlotte, Berlin, August 2, 1798, *Briefe*, 1:190–91; see also Okely to Schleiermacher, Northampton, March 23, 1787, *ibid.*, 3:13.

way together in both piety and in intellectual pursuits—they had arrived at the same crisis together—but while Schleiermacher passed over into the world of understanding and thought, Albertini turned back to the world of cultus and community. As he was later to confess, the vision of Christ at Gethsemane—the symbol par excellence of Brethren piety—overwhelmed his doubt.[73] And although he was never to speak of the "philosopher" within him that he had put to death at that moment of decision, it is quite clear from what he did with his life that he consciously chose to abandon the world into which he had begun to enter for the world to whose edge he had moved dangerously close.[74] The fact that he wished his spiritual biography to be read in his poetry rather than in any discursive account stands as a profound symbol of the parting of the ways for him.[75]

If the lad with the grotesque nose who so dearly loved the diminutive Schleiermacher had quietly crept back to the "womb" and fallen into a devout and exhausted spiritual sleep, the story would be over. But this is not at all the case. Albertini went on to become the spiritually perceptive leader of his movement during a crucial period of its development—a bishop and an administrator of his order.[76] He also was to be the great interpreter of Brethren principles, as the master of spiritual address and preaching during his lifetime, an exercise in which the influence of his encounter with the Kantian approach as a fellow "club" member with Schleiermacher is easy

[73] "Albertini's Lebenslauf," in *Nachricht aus der Brüder-Gemeine: 1832* (Gnadau, 1832), p. 161.

[74] Albertini's motives in turning his back on "philosophy" and remaining with the Brethren are extremely difficult to sort out. We have reasons to believe that at first he remained because of his fears of a rift with his father (*Briefe*, 3:22), and that only after his father's death did he discover that he was remaining for religious reasons (*ibid.*, 3:23–26). In retrospect on Albertini's whole career, Schleiermacher concluded: "In spite of all the skeptical tendencies that had been developed in us, he had, even at the time of our separations, firmly determined to remain in the congregation."—Schleiermacher to Reichel, Berlin, April 31, 1832, *ibid.*, 2:457.

[75] "Albertini's Lebenslauf," p. 157.

[76] *Ibid.*, pp. 160–71.

enough to trace.[77] But most significant for us here is his greatest claim to fame inside and outside the congregations. Albertini, Schleiermacher's "other self," found the fullness of his spiritual expression in becoming "the holy Bard"[78] — the sweet singer of the Brethren. The influence of his romance with classical German literature, rather than causing Albertini to seek expression in thoughts and principles, merged itself with the cultic language of the Herrnhuters — the spiritual song — and in him brought that mother tongue to a newly elevated status and capacity for the stimulation and expression of future Schleiermachers.

Friedrich Schleiermacher is here the example, and Albertini the foil against which we see him. Yet there are others in this same time who could well deserve our attention. The rebellion of the Romantics against the cerebral mechanism and moralism of the Enlightenment may not, I believe, be separated from that similar rebellion by Neo-Pietism. In this movement our principal does not stand alone. One may point to that darling of the German Romantics, Novalis, also a former Herrnhuter, and even to the impact of this movement upon Goethe himself. One might also look at Kant and his background in the more classical Pietism of his youth. Still closer to our own time we may observe the strange vitality in nonreligious realms of the pious and their children. It is with the greatest seriousness to be hoped that our age will not allow an adolescent resentment of the ways of our fathers to cut off this dimension from objective examination. If we indeed live in a day of a secular culture come of age, we cannot satisfy

[77] The emphasis upon moral fidelity and the importance of experience for knowledge which are reflected in Albertini's preaching and spiritual addresses can only be understood in this context. See [Albertini], *Dreissig Predigten für Mitglieder u. Freunde der Brüdergemeine* (Gnadau, 1829); *Sechs u. dreissig Reden an die Gemeine in Herrnhut in den Jahren von 1818 bis 1824* (Gnadau, 1832); and *Sechs u. dreissig Reden . . . von 1825 bis 1831* (Gnadau, 1833).

[78] This term was applied to Albertini by Schleiermacher's wife; *Briefe*, 2:403. For Schleiermacher's own extremely high estimate of Albertini's *Geistliche Lieder für Mitglieder u. Freunde der Brüdergemeine*, 2d ed. (Bunzlau, 1827), see *Briefe*, 4:290.

ourselves with a defensive rejection of our spiritual forebearers; we must examine carefully the strange springs of human creativity lest we, in a misguided rage, stop forever that which drives us onward in our search for the good, the beautiful, the TRUE!

13

Jozef Miloslav Hurban: A Study in Historicism

JAROSLAV PELIKAN

In a little-known essay on "Herder and the Enlightenment Philosophy of History," Arthur Lovejoy has pointed out two normative principles implied in the view of history set forth by Johann Gottfried Herder:

> (a) Towards all the elements of all cultures other than one's own—whether of some earlier period in history or of another race or region—one should cultivate a catholicity of appreciation and understanding, based upon . . . historical necessitarianism and historical optimism. . . . But (b) [this also implied] . . . a kind of particularism. Nature, having through the supposedly necessary and benign process of historical development, placed you in a particular situation, that situation is the best for you.[1]

The incompatibility of these two principles, Lovejoy maintains, becomes evident in Herder's interpretation of the relation between continuity and change in the historical process. It is evident also in the historicism of Herder's disciples, not only in Germany but in the other parts of Europe where there was a response to his philosophy of history.[2]

Nowhere was the response to Herder more enthusiastic or far-reaching than in the Slavic lands. For in the sixteenth book of his *Ideen zur Philosophie der Geschichte der Menschheit* Herder had interpreted the place of the Slavs in the history

[1] Arthur O. Lovejoy, *Essays in the History of Ideas* (Baltimore: Johns Hopkins Press, 1948), pp. 172, 181.

[2] See the discerning comments of Robert T. Clark, Jr., *Herder: His Life and Thought* (Berkeley and Los Angeles: University of California Press, 1955), pp. 336–38.

of humanity in such a way as to show that their hour was now about to strike. Now that legislation and politics were replacing warfare as the means of settling disputes, the peaceful virtues of the Slavs would come into their own:

> Thus you [Slavic] peoples, once so industrious and happy but now so deeply depressed, will finally be roused from your long and deep slumber and set free from the fetters of your slavery. [You will be restored to] your beautiful lands from the Adriatic Sea to the Carpathian Mountains, and there you will be able to celebrate your ancient festivals of peaceful labor and commerce.[3]

As recent studies have shown, this theory of history was directly responsible for the rise of a romanticist historicism in several of the Slavic peoples, notably among the Czechs and Slovaks.[4] *Slávy dcera,* the great epic of the Slovak poet, Ján Kollár (1793–1852), which was originally published in 1824 and was then expanded in 1832, was the poetic statement of this historicism.[5] In Kollár's poem, as a recent history of Slovak literature has pointed out,

> the parallel between the past of the Slavs and the present of his own nation was able to call forth a mighty poetic image, in which the poet also made room for his faith in the future, which proceeded from his philosophical conception of the development of humanity, as he had formulated it on the basis of the ideas of J. G. Herder.[6]

[3] Johann Gottfried Herder, *Ideen zur Philosophie der Geschichte der Menschheit* (Riga and Leipzig: Johann Friedrich Hartknoch, 1792), 4:42. This and all subsequent translations are my own.

[4] Konrad Bittner, *Herders Geschichtsphilosophie und die Slaven* (Reichenberg: Gebrüder Stiepel, 1929); *idem,* "Herder und die Tschechen," *Geist der Zeit,* 17 (1939): 227–38, 426–31.

[5] Cf. Karol Rosenbaum, "Ideový charakter Kollárových rozpráv o slovanskej vzájomnosti," introduction to Ján Kollár, *O literárnej vzájomnosti,* new ed. (Bratislava: Slovenská akadémia vied, 1954), pp. 57 ff., for a recent Marxist interpretation of Kollár's dependence upon Herder; for a bibliography of the extensive literature on *Slávy dcera,* cf. Ján V. Ormis, *Bibliografia Jána Kollára* (Bratislava: Slovenská akadémia vied, 1954), pp. 38–50, nos. 129–233.

[6] Milan Pišút, Karol Rosenbaum, and Viktor Kochol, *Dejiny sloven-*

But that same volume points out also that the most effective exploitation of that parallel between past and present was in the work of Jozef Miloslav Hurban (1817–88), especially when, after being "exclusively preoccupied with the past, he breaks with historicism and pays attention only to the Slovak present."[7] And it was Hurban who, in 1852, published Herder's chapter on the Slavs in a Slovak translation as part of his campaign to provide the ideological foundation for the Slovak revolution and the struggle of Slovak nationalism against the Magyars.[8] During most of the half century from 1840 to 1890, when that struggle dominated the culture, literature, and religion of the Slovaks, Hurban was their leading intellectual figure. The development of his thought and action is therefore an index to the situation of the minorities in the Austro-Hungarian empire, and, if one can make sense of the twists and turns in his development, one is on the way toward understanding the ideology that inspired the distinctive forms of nationalism among these minorities. But these twists and turns in Hurban's development are hard to understand, harder still to harmonize with one another on the basis of the simple assumptions about nationalism, historicism, and romanticism which have come to enjoy almost canonical status among intellectual historians.

The first book Hurban published was written in 1839 and appeared in 1841: *Cesta Slowáka ku bratrum Slowanským na Morawě a v Čechách.*[9] As the title suggests, the book was a travelogue, describing Hurban's journey to Moravia and Bohemia. The title also indicates that a major theme of the book is the fraternal relation between the Slovaks and the Czechs. A symbol of the relation was the language in which the book was written. For Hurban, though a Slovak, used a

skej literatúry, vol. 2: *Literatúra národného obrodenia* (Bratislava: Slovenská akadémia vied, 1960), p. 184.

[7] *Ibid.*, p. 463.

[8] *Slovenské Pohladi*, 3 (1852): 173–75.

[9] The book is now available in a new edition in Slovak translation: Jozef Miloslav Hurban, *Cesta Slováka k slovanským bratom na Morave a v Čechách*, tr. Jozef Ambrus (Bratislava: Slovenské vydavateľstvo krásnej literatúry, 1960).

form of Czech, the literary language usually called *bibličtina.*[10] It was the language of the Bible of Kralice of 1579–93, a translation which Hurban, many years later, was to call "a model of the perfection and purity of Slavic style."[11] The six-volume Bible of Kralice was the literary masterpiece of the Unity of Bohemian Brethren.[12] To the Protestant minority among the Slovaks, it represented a bond with the Czechs and a symbol of the bond between Luther and Hus. On the other hand, the hegemony of its language in the literature of the Slovaks represented, to the Roman Catholic majority in Slovakia, an intolerable subservience to the Reformation, which had managed to conquer the literature, even if it could not permanently reform the churches, of Slovakia.

Hurban's *Cesta* both employed and vindicated the Czecho-Slovak language of the Bible of Kralice, by means of which he had made his way through the cities and towns of Bohemia and Moravia as one who belonged, not as a stranger.[13] Although his comments on Czech and Moravian monasteries and churches in the *Cesta* are quite charitable,[14] it is evident that he found it congenial to identify himself with *bibličtina* against its Slovak Roman Catholic detractors. This defense of *bibličtina* came just at the time when leading Slovak intellectuals and literati were agitating for the establishment of a distinct literary Slovak. In 1787 Anton Bernolák, a Roman Catholic priest, had published a *Dissertatio philologicocritica de literis Slavorum,* to which was appended a *Linguae Slavonicae per regnum Hungariae usitatae compendiosa simul, et facilis Orthographia.*[15] Taking as the literary basis for his

[10] Milan Hodža, *Československý rozkol: Príspevky k dejinám slovenčiny* (Turčiansky Sv. Martin: Milan Hodža, 1920), pp. 39–63.

[11] Hurban, "Slavische Bibelübersetzungen," *Real-Encyklopädie für protestantische Theologie und Kirche,* 2d ed. (Leipzig: J. C. Hinrichs'sche Buchhandlung, 1877–88), 14:363–64.

[12] Jan Jakubec, *Dějiny literatury české,* 2 vols. (Prague: Jan Laichter, 1929–34), 1:687–90.

[13] *Cesta,* pp. 21, 26, 29.

[14] *Ibid.,* pp. 30, 37.

[15] This has recently appeared in a new edition, together with a Slovak translation and an introduction: *Gramatické dielo Antona Bernoláka,* ed. Juraj Pavelek (Bratislava: Slovenská akadémia vied, 1964).

proposal the extensive Slovak literature that had been produced by the Counter-Reformation, largely at Trnava, Bernolák had argued for the distinctiveness of Slovak as a language and therefore for the desirability of codifying its orthography and grammar.

In opposition to the theories of Bernolák about Slovak, Hurban defended *bibličtina*. Yet within a few years *bibličtina* gave way to literary Slovak, and one of the principal architects of the new style was—Jozef Miloslav Hurban! As editor of the literary periodical *Nitra*, he stated the principles which had prompted him and his associates, after publishing the first volume of the journal in *bibličtina*, to switch to Slovak in the second volume. In an essay dated April, 1844, he explained that the manuscript for the second volume of *Nitra* had originally been written in *bibličtina*, but that after further reflection he had, "with the help of several excellent younger authors," put in into Slovak. "I know beforehand," Hurban wrote, "that when Slovaks write Slovak, this will not please the Czechs. . . . But a literary bond [between Czechs and Slovaks] is not itself the authentic bond; only the spirit creates the substance of an authentic bond."[16] He was especially critical of those Slovaks who disdained the forms and accents of the Slovak language as fit only for peasants and common laborers, but not for intellectuals. In conclusion he promised that there would soon appear a full-length defense of the adoption of literary Slovak and a proper grammar of Slovak.

The two promised books appeared in 1846. They were written by Hurban's associate and former teacher Ľudovít Štúr (1815–56). Like Hurban himself, Štúr had been inspired by Hegelian historicism as well as by Herder. As Hurban said of Štúr, "if Štúr was already a Slav under the guidance of his previous historical studies, he really became one after he had digested in his spirit Hegel's views of history."[17] These views enabled both Štúr and Hurban to transcend the superficial rationalism of their youth and to learn to look at the issues of

[16] *Nitra*, 2 (1844): 310–12.

[17] Hurban, *Ľudovít Štúr* and *Rozpomienky*, ed. Jozef Štolc (Bratislava: Slovenské vydavateľstvo krásnej literatúry, 1959), p. 169.

philosophy and theology historically. On this basis they also developed their sense of the destiny of the Slavic peoples. In his description and defense of Štúr's Hegelianism, Hurban went back to Hegel's great-grandfather, who, because of his Protestant allegiance, had emigrated to Württemberg from his native Carinthia. Thus Hegel, the philosopher of Prussian absolutism, was actually of Slavic descent, and, by a turn of history which only a philosopher of history such as Hegel could appreciate, he eventually came to Berlin, to a land which had originally been Slavic.[18] Therefore it was not an alien philosophy which Štúr and Hurban were bringing into the intellectual life of Slovakia, but one that had its roots in Slavic history. The glorification of that history was a central motif in Štúr's justification for the new literary Slovak. Kollár—together with present-day students of Slavic linguistics—believed that the Slavs were divided into four branches: Russian, Polish, Czecho-Slovak, and Serbo-Croatian.[19] Štúr, on the other hand, found eleven branches, one of them the Slovaks as distinct from the Czechs; and, Hegelian that he was, he saw in language the embodiment of the genius of a people.[20] As we have seen, Hurban professed at this point to see a unity of spirit between Czechs and Slovaks in one people, a unity which could not be jeopardized by any divergence of literary usage.

It was, however, the problem of another kind of unity that was now to demand Hurban's attention. The lay superintendent or "general inspector" of the evangelical church, Count Karl Zay, proposed in 1840 that the Reformed and Lutheran churches in the Magyar lands be united, and in 1842 there began to appear a journal, in Hungarian, devoted to the cause of this union.[21] The cause grew rapidly, so that, as Hurban himself admitted many years later, "by 1845 . . . all the presbyteries and districts had expressed themselves in support

[18] *Ibid.*, pp. 173–74.

[19] Kollár, *O literárnej vzájomnosti*, pp. 114–15; he uses the term "Illyric" for "Serbo-Croatian."

[20] Hodža, *Československý rozkol*, pp. 169–72.

[21] The title of the journal was *Protestáns Egyházi és Iskolai lap.*

of Zay's plan of union."[22] The convention of the district to which Hurban's parish belonged decided on August 14, 1844, to abolish the requirement of subscription to the Lutheran confessions and thus to prepare the way for the unification of the two Protestant groups.[23] Following some of the patterns set by the Prussian Union of 1817,[24] the union of Reformed and Lutheran in Hungary aimed to create a catechism, a hymnal, and an agenda which would transcend the old differences between the confessions. The trouble was that one of the differences between the confessions was national: Reformed usually meant Magyar and Lutheran ordinarily meant Slovak. The plan of union contemplated the abolition of service books and sermons in *bibličtina* and their gradual replacement by Magyar.

Although other leaders of Slovak Lutheranism also spoke out against the plan of union, it was Hurban who became the leader of the opposition. In 1845 he published a book entitled *Unia,* attacking Zay's plan of union.[25] The book is basically a historical essay on the Reformation which seeks to interpret the meaning of the sixteenth-century Reformation in the light of the events that preceded and followed it. A large section is devoted to the development of the dogmatic differences between Reformed and Lutheran theology during the sixteenth century and to the history of various plans of union from the sixteenth to the nineteenth century. These dogmatic and confessional objections to the proposed union are interwoven with nationalistic objections. Hurban speaks as an orthodox Lutheran and as a patriotic Slovak, and the boundaries be-

[22] Hurban, "O poměrech evanjelicko-slovenského kněžstva ku vnitřní Missii," *Církevní Listy,* 4, no. 30 (January 28, 1868): 233–34.

[23] Cf. Samuel Štefan Osuský, *Filozofia Štúrovcov,* vol. 2: *Hurbanova Filozofia* (Myjava: Daniel Pažický, 1928), pp. 19–29, quoted from the minutes of local and district conventions.

[24] See Hurban's comments on the Prussian Union, *Církev Evanjelicko-Lutheránská v její vnitřních živlech a bojích na světě se zláštním ohledem na národ slovenský v této církvi spasení své hledající* (Skalica: U Františka Škarnycla Synu, 1861), pp. 290–91, note.

[25] Cf. Johannes Borbis, *Die evangelisch-lutherische Kirche Ungarns in ihrer geschichtlichen Entwicklung* (Nördlingen: C. H. Beck'sche Buchhandlung, 1861), pp. 208–15, for a summary in German.

tween these two concerns are drawn with no more precision than are the boundaries between Magyar and Reformed on the other side of the question. The Slovak Lutheran clergy, emboldened by Hurban's stand, began to express their opposition to the union; and at a convention of the presbytery of Nitra on July 28, 1847, several of them came to his support.[26] Suddenly, the entire campaign in support of the plan of union and against Hurban was interrupted by the violent events of 1848, when the accumulated resentments against the Hungarians erupted in the Slovak national revolution.

The leader of the Slovak national revolution of 1848 was Jozef Miloslav Hurban. On May 5 he journeyed to Liptovský Svätý Mikuláš for an assembly of Slovak patriots. There, as he wrote to his wife, he demonstrated that he was "the first of the Slovaks to know how to make use of freedom."[27] Now events moved rapidly. Instead of returning home, Hurban went to the congress of Slavs convoked at Prague by František Palacký (1798–1876), at which, on June 7, he represented the cause of Slovak nationalism. From Prague he went to Vienna to plead that cause, and thence to Zagreb, where on August 6 he addressed the Croatian diet and received its support. Upon his return to Vienna he became convinced that negotiation with the Hungarians was useless. From the autumn of 1848 to the autumn of 1849 he pressed his campaign on two fronts, the military and the political. He himself battled on the barricades on September 17, 1848, and his fiery oratory continued to stir the patriotism of his Slovak followers throughout most of 1849.[28] But when the military phase of the September revolution had come to its tragic end, Hurban concluded that the hope of the Slovak cause lay with the emperor in Vienna, who was also being threatened by the Hungarians. And so, as Daniel Rapant has summarized Hurban's appeal of November, 1848, "at stake in the battle are the freedom and the

[26] Osuský, *Hurbanova Filozofia*, pp. 28–29.

[27] Hurban to his wife, May 10, 1848, printed in *Slovenské Pohľady* (1906), p. 4.

[28] Daniel Rapant, *Slovenské povstanie roku 1848–49: Dejiny a dokumenty*, vol. 3, pt. 1: *Zimná výprava* (Bratislava: Slovenská akadémia vied, 1956), p. 240.

nationhood of the Slovaks, the unity of the Austrian monarchy, the emperor and the ruling house, public order and peace."[29] Eventually, of course, this hope was disappointed, and on November 21, 1849, the Slovak national revolution was over. Hurban was not able to return to his home and parish until the following May. The years of his part in the revolution are probably the most exciting chapter of his life, as is evident from his memoirs, written in 1886 and 1887, when he was almost seventy years old.[30]

Hurban's memoirs also give evidence of a deep and intransigent conservatism, both political and theological. As Andrej Mráz has put it, "after the revolution, with all its disappointments and bitterness, he saw the guarantee for the attainment of Slovak rights in Vienna, and more and more there appear in his political and cultural thought the beginnings of a reactionary position, based on Hurban's deepening ecclesiastical dogmatism."[31] His reactionary and moralistic condemnation, in 1871, of the new Slovak poets, specifically of Koloman Bansell (1850–87),[32] alienated him from many of the leaders of the rising generation, including the most eminent figure in the history of Slovak literature, Pavel Orsagh-Hviezdoslav (1849–1921)[33] and, to some extent, even Hurban's own son Svetozár Hurban Vajanský (1847–1916).[34] In 1861 Jozef Miloslav Hurban expanded some of the material that had originally appeared in *Unia* into a full-length defense of Lutheran confessionalism, entitled *Církev Evanjelicko-Lutheránská*;[35] and in 1863 he began the publication of a journal for theology and the church, called *Církevní Listy*, which continued to appear, partly in Slovak and mostly in

[29] *Ibid.*, p. 50.

[30] *Rozpomienky*, pp. 645–780.

[31] Andrej Mráz, "Hurbanov životopis Ľudovíta Štúra," *ibid.*, p. 9.

[32] "Literatúra," *Církevní Listy*, 9, no. 20 (October 30, 1873): 315–16.

[33] Andrej Mráz, "Živy básnik," *Hviezdoslav v kritike a spomienkách: Sborník* (Bratislava: Slovenské vydavateľstvo krásnej literatúry, 1954), pp. 152–53.

[34] Cf. the manuscript letters of Jozef Miloslav Hurban to Svetozár Hurban Vajanský, quoted in Osuský, *Hurbanova Filozofia*, pp. 352–54.

[35] Cf. note 24 above.

bibličtina, for just over ten years, until it was suppressed by the authorities.[36]

These two publications summarized his orthodox theology, polemicizing against all the trends which Hurban regarded as dangerous. The clergyman who had manned the barricades in 1848 now attacked political preachers for mixing into civil affairs and asserted that "Christianity has never been the servant of any political partisanship, but has always been the improver of human conditions under any secular government whatsoever."[37] The translator of Herder and disciple of Hegel now attacked the very idea of an autonomous philosophy and declared that "the Christian Church helps philosophy to attain its sublime goal. . . . [Theology] is the subject, the norm, and the boundary of true philosophy."[38] And the defender of the rights of the Slovak minority against the Magyars now indulged in violently anti-Semitic tirades, almost always referring to a Jew with the offensive term *Žiďák*[39] and ascribing all manner of anti-Christian movements, including Socialism, to a Jewish conspiracy.[40] It is not surprising therefore, that in the judgment of a modern historian "orthodox conservatism completely prevailed against his earlier democratic thought."[41]

This development of Hurban's attitudes is not easy to explain on any grounds. When Milan Hodža suggests that

[36] Since the original issues appeared in a small number of copies, some of which were confiscated, the complete set of *Církevní Listy* handed on to me by my family is probably one of relatively few and is perhaps the only one in the United States.

[37] *Církev Evanjelicko-Lutheránská*, p. ix. Cf. Hurban, "Církev evanjelicko-křestanská A. V. uvažená ze stanoviště jejího dogmatického i právního pojmu," *Církevní Listy*, 7, no. 29 (August 30, 1871): 247.

[38] "Poznamenanie Redakcie," *Církevní Listy*, 5, nos. 30–32 (November 10, 1869): 306; cf. "Úmysly a rady novoroční," *ibid.*, 9, no. 1 (January 20, 1873): 4–7.

[39] Cf. Štefan Peciar, ed., *Slovník slovenského jazyka* (Bratislava: Slovenská akadémia vied, 1965), 5:804, *s. v.*

[40] "The greatest supporters of the nonconfessional schools are the Jews, for it would be impossible to think of any better means than such schools for the eradication of Christianity, and the Jews are undoubtedly the most implacable foes of the name of Christ." — Hurban, "Protikřesťanské živly v křesťanstvě moderním," *Církevní Listy*, 5, no. 10 (June 9, 1869): 131.

[41] Pišút *et al*, *Literatúra národného obrodenia*, p. 468.

"Hurban's introduction of Slovak does not seem to breathe so much the spirit of a great decision arrived at after troublesome battles of spirit and intellectual struggles as rather the pressure of improvisation,"[42] this would seem to apply to his entire career. The Slovak historians of the late nineteenth and early twentieth century, inspired by Western democratic idealism, had great difficulty interpreting this career.[43] It is no simpler for the Slovak Marxist historians of the past two decades.[44] Any one stage of Hurban's development may perhaps be explicable either on the grounds of his ideology (so the earlier historians) or on the grounds of his real, though limited, awareness of the class struggle against feudalism (so contemporary historians). But how is one to account for all the stages of that development in a manner that will indeed recognize the shifts in Hurban's position as the exigencies of the situation changed, but will at the same time discover that continuity of outlook and belief which enables one to see the man within and behind the changes and chances of this present life? None of the explanations set forth in the current literature would seem to provide an answer to that question of continuity.

The obvious explanation of Hurban's most dramatic exploits is, of course, to relate him to the development of nationalism in the nineteenth century.[45] The first half of that century saw the explosion of nationalistic aspirations in many nations where these had been slumbering for centuries. Especially was this true of the *mélange* of nations in the Austro-Hungarian Empire, in which the three major ethnic stocks—the Germanic, the Magyar, and the Slavic—as well as their various subdivisions, were competing for recognition and for the achievement of national identity. A large part of Hurban's defense of Slovak identity against the Magyars may be read as

[42] *Československý rozkol*, p. 167.

[43] Cf. Osuský, *Hurbanova Filozofia*, pp. 276–364.

[44] Cf. Pišút *et al*, *Literatúra národného obrodenia*, pp. 467–69.

[45] The materials have been assembled in František Bokes, ed., *Dokumenty k slovenskému národnému hnutiu v rokoch 1848–1914*, vol. 1: *1848–1867* (Bratislava: Slovenská akadémia vied, 1962), containing many documents by and about Hurban

a declaration of independence, in the spirit of the nationalistic awakening. Nor was he the only leader of the new nationalism who had theological training. Much of the movement in Slovakia was inspired and led by clergymen, especially by Lutheran pastors but also to some extent by Roman Catholic priests.[46] After all, Hurban's most distinguished predecessor in the codification and defense of literary Slovak against *bibličtina* had been Anton Bernolák, a priest. Even in the conservatism of his later years Hurban remained a fervent Slovak nationalist. Plausible though this explanation may seem, it does finally seem to be too obvious an answer. It may account for Hurban the patriotic hero on the barricades, but it does not do justice to Hurban the theological scholar at the desk. Most of the work he did at that desk, as a historian and theologian, simply cannot be reduced to a function of his nationalistic fervor. Although his incredible literary output includes a large amount of Slavic nationalism or even chauvinism, most of the eleven volumes of *Církevní Listy*, for example, would defy classification under that rubric. Nationalism might explain the young Hurban, but it would not account for the whole Hurban.

Related to this explanation is the suggestion that Hurban is the Slovak version of the revolutionary movement of 1848—whether that movement is seen as the expression of a bourgeois resistance to feudalism or as an unsophisticated anticipation of the proletarian revolution. This suggestion would link Hurban with his Hungarian contemporary and *quondam* ally, Lajos Kossuth (1802–94).[47] Like Hurban among the Slovaks, Kossuth led the uprising of the Magyars against the Hapsburgs in 1848. The Magyar revolution was ultimately more successful than the Magyar revolutionary: Hungary achieved recognition in the *Ausgleich* of 1867 as a full-fledged partner

[46] Cf. Ľudovít Bakoš, "Ľudovít Štúr ako vychovávateľ" in the centennial symposium, *Ľudovít Štúr: Život a dielo 1815–1856* (Bratislava: Slovenská akadémia vied, 1956), pp. 255–81, esp. pp. 261 ff.

[47] For a Marxist view of Kossuth in relation to the development of Slovak nationalism, cf. Jozef Butvin, *Slovenské národnozjednocovacie hnutie (1780–1848)* (Bratislava: Slovenská akadémia vied, 1965), pp. 242 ff.

in the Dual Monarchy, but Kossuth himself spent the second half of his life in the bitterness and irrelevance of political exile. There are notable similarities between Kossuth and Hurban, not the least of which is the rhetorical magic described by their contemporaries.[48] Hurban's bitter comments on Kossuth suggest the hazards of too facile a parallel,[49] but those hazards are accentuated by Hurban's stand in his later years, when he sustained himself, not by the memory of the revolution, nor yet by the repudiation of that memory, but by his religious commitment. "Without Jesus," he wrote, "nationalism and patriotism are simply the tyranny of some over others." [50] If there had to be the difficult choice between the mother tongue and the faith, Hurban would, albeit painfully, opt for the faith; Hurban was sure that Kossuth would have opted for the mother tongue. Attractive though the parallels might seem, Hurban cannot be seen as the Slovak equivalent of Kossuth.

For Kossuth himself and for his Magyar colleagues, Hurban was to be explained in other terms, as "the fanatic among the pan-Slavs." [51] As has been suggested, pan-Slavism owed much of its inspiration to the historicism of Herder, who had proposed that the *kairos* of the Slavic peoples had come. Not only Kollár's *Slávy dcera*, but a large body of literature, both the purely poetic and the frankly political, owed its inspiration to this pan-Slavic idealism. It is obvious, moreover, that both Hurban himself and his mentor Ľudovít Štúr were brought to life by the vision of Slavic destiny. Like their Slavophil contemporaries in Russia, Hurban and especially Štúr sought an alternative that transcended the usual Western antitheses, and they found it in Slavic, specifically in Russian, culture. This explanation of Hurban's development has the advantage

[48] See the description in Rapant, *Zimná výprava*, pp. 240–41.

[49] Cf., for example, *Rozpomienky*, pp. 656–58.

[50] Hurban, "Ve jmeno Ježíše," *Církevní Listy*, 2, no. 2 (1865): 49.

[51] Lajos Steier, *Beniczky Lajos* (Budapest, 1924), p. 391, quoted in Werner Elert, *Morphologie des Luthertums*, vol. 2: *Soziallehren und Sozialwirkungen* (Munich: C. H. Beck'sche Verlagsbuchhandlung, 1932), p. 196.

over some of the others that there remain expressions of this pan-Slavism even in his later "reactionary" period. For example, in 1872, under the title "Pan-Slavism in the Development of the Church," he wrote an article defending the Orthodox churches of Bulgaria and of Russia against the dominance of the church of Greece; he concluded the article with the observation: "Whoever wants to dominate the Slavs in any respect, cries out against them: 'Aha, this is pan-Slavism!' "[52]

But as this polemical exchange suggests, the slogan of "pan-Slavism" was probably more important to Hurban's opponents than it was to him. And perhaps the most telling refutation of this slogan as an explanation of his stance is a comparison of the relatively cool things he says about Russian Orthodoxy with the endorsement he felt able to supply for German, and even Magyar, Lutheranism. The German adoption of the term "Evangelical-Lutheran" commended itself to him in place of the usual term "Evangelical" for "Protestant" in Czech and Slovak usage.[53] A believing Magyar, on the other hand, was as good a Lutheran as a believing Slovak.[54] He counseled the Slovak Lutherans to strengthen their confessional stand with the help of German theology. Hurban himself was acknowledged by that theology when, on May 10, 1860, he received the honorary degree of Doctor of Theology from the University of Leipzig.[55] Such an acknowledgment would seem difficult to square with a simple explanation of his development as "pan-Slavism."

The various explanations of Hurban's development all seem to have most difficulty accounting for the later, "reactionary" stages of that development, except perhaps by means of some psychological explanation, which provides something of an answer but only by begging the question. Thus the aforemen-

[52] Hurban, "Panslavizmus v rozvoji cirkevnom," *Církevní Listy*, 8, no. 21 (November 10, 1872): 330.

[53] Hurban, "Conferencia evanjelicko-luteránska," *Církevní Listy*, 6, no. 35 (August 31, 1870): 273.

[54] Hurban, "Předmluva," *Církevní Listy*, 1 (1864): 200–201.

[55] Cf. Osuský, *Hurbanova Filozofia*, p. 307.

tioned history of Slovak literature suggests as an explanation of the historicism in Hurban's novel *Gottšalk*, published in 1861:

> Hurban, obviously disillusioned by the present, takes his refuge in the distant past, the time of the Christianization of the Polabian Slavs in the eleventh century. . . . But the nationalistic motifs . . . are overshadowed by the religious motifs — further evidence of Hurban's growing theologism.[56]

Similarly, the principal monograph on Hurban's thought suggests that the events of the 1850's, after the revolution, brought Hurban to believe that the chief task now was to conserve in both the Church and the nation and that the death of Ľudovít Štúr on January 12, 1856, contributed to this conservatism.[57] It goes so far as to say that "on the basis of Hurban's philosophical development it is necessary to conclude that in his world view the young Hurban, before 1855, is not the same as the old Hurban, after 1855."[58] Yet the problem of continuity and consistency obliges one to look for some theme that will unify the disparate stages and elements of Hurban's thought.

As has already been suggested, there is much reason to see such a theme in Hurban's historicism, which caused him, in the words of Lovejoy already quoted, to "cultivate a catholicity of appreciation and understanding" toward other cultures and ideologies for a while but finally to affirm "a kind of particularism." Both the catholicity and the particularism, while deeply nationalistic in their expression, are ultimately theological in their lineage. What Hurban learned from Herder and from Hegel he put into the service of his specifically theological loyalties. And for the support of these he looked, among his contemporaries, to Leipzig and to its dominant theologian, Christoph Ernst Luthardt (1823–1902).[59] Of Luthardt's *Apologetische Vorträge* Hurban wrote:

[56] Pišút *et al*, *Literatúra národného obrodenia*, p. 468.
[57] Osuský, *Hurbanova Filozofia*, pp. 277–78.
[58] *Ibid.*, p. 66.
[59] Cf. Luthardt's preface to Borbis, *Kirche Ungarns*, pp. vii–xii.

> This is a thorough defense of the Bible and of our Christianity against rationalists, deists, pantheists, materialists, and other errorists of our time. Deep learning, combined with faith in the Lord Jesus Christ, presents to us very beautiful pictures of the development of the present-day world of learning.[60]

Shortly after receiving his honorary degree from Leipzig, Hurban wrote a German article on the state of the church in Slovakia, which appeared in the *Zeitschrift für die gesammte lutherische Theologie und Kirche* in Leipzig in 1861.[61] This article, too, shows Hurban's deep affinities, despite the national and nationalistic differences, with the Leipzig theologians and with their understanding of history.

A fundamental element both in their understanding of history and in his was the interpretation of Luther. To be sure, Hurban in his more conservative middle years looked for support to Luther in his conservative middle years, declaring that "we take our stand only on the later, mature, and more developed Luther."[62] But Luther was his mentor and model throughout his career. It does not seem to require an act of unrestrained fancy to note the parallel between Luther and Hurban, made explicit, for example, in Hurban's summary of Luther's historic achievement:

> Luther restored the pure Word of God to us. Luther restored to the nations their mother tongue. Luther powerfully united the school with the church, and the church with the nation. Let us hold to Luther in theology, in the church, in our administration, and in our life.[63]

That summary would not be an inaccurate statement of Hurban's own historic achievement, as he himself understood it

[60] Hurban, "Čo budeme čitať?," *Církevní Listy*, 2 (1865): 40.

[61] Hurban, "Die Kirchenparteien und die Kirche," *Zeitschrift für die gesammte lutherische Theologie und Kirche*, 1 (1861): 59–108.

[62] Hurban, "Ještě některé poznámky Redakcie," *Církevní Listy*, 7, no. 16 (April 22, 1871): 125.

[63] Hurban, "Na Neděli VII. po Sv. Trojici," *Církevní Listy*, 10, no. 14 (July 17, 1874): 202.

and as it has been interpreted by later historians. Hurban himself maintained, for example, that the acceptance of Luther's Reformation in Slovakia—more rapid than in any other land—was due to Luther's espousal of the rights of the vernacular in the church, which was, Hurban argued, "a new teaching in the Western world, [but] nothing else than the renewal of the form of Christianity originally brought to Slovakia by Cyril and Methodius." [64] Uniting his commitment to the principles of the Reformation with his romantic historicism about Cyril and Methodius, Hurban founded *Církevní Listy* as a journal of Reformation orthodoxy on the anniversary of the millennium of the Christianization of the Slavs by Cyril and Methodius. Here he saw the continuity of Slovak Christian culture, and here we may see the continuity of his own thought and teaching.

Historicism is an integral part of Hurban's philosophy of language, which was, as we have seen, a more persistent issue in his thought than any other. As a student under Štúr in Bratislava, he had been imbued with his teacher's passion for the history of the mother tongue, as Štúr, led by his Hegelianism, declaimed its poetic treasures to his students. Already on his youthful trip to Bohemia, Hurban had been captivated by the Augustinian friar František Matouš Klácel (1808–82),[65] a poet and a Hegelian, whose philosophical speculations about the genius of Czech manifest their presence in the language-mysticism of both Štúr and Hurban.[66] Yet it would be an oversimplification to explain Hurban's theory of language solely on this basis. He defended Slovak against the Magyars; he defended *bibličtina* against the Slovaks; he defended Slovak against the champions of *bibličtina*; he reverted to *bibličtina* in later years. The element that is common to all these mutually contradictory positions is his historicism about the Reformation. When he defended Slovak, it was because the Reformation had restored the vernacular; when he

[64] Hurban, *Církev Evanjelicko-Lutheránská*, p. 327.

[65] Hurban, *Cesta*, pp. 35–36 and *passim*.

[66] On Klácel, cf. Jakubec, *Dějiny literatury české*, 2:610–19, with a detailed bibliography.

defended *bibličtina*, it was on the grounds that it represented a bond with the Hussite Reformation. As he stated in the manifesto with which he introduced the first issue of his *Církevní Listy*, "the evangelical church will endure only as long as it has the pure preaching of the Word of God, the pure administration of the sacraments, worship in the mother tongue, and instruction in school in accordance with evangelical doctrine."[67] Restoration of pure preaching and restoration of the vernacular were not two separate items in the program of the Reformation for Hurban; they were completely interdependent.

Just how interdependent they were for him became clear during the battle over the proposed union between the churches of the Helvetic and those of the Augsburg Confession. In the manifesto just quoted, "Calvinization" and "Magyarization" are seen as two aspects of one program.[68] No one can read the polemical literature evoked by the controversy without sensing that for Hurban, also, resistance to "Calvinization" and resistance to "Magyarization" were two aspects of one program. But it is essential to a proper understanding of his thought to point out that these two aspects are not identical or interchangeable. For in the last analysis he was not defending the Augsburg Confession in the name of the Slovak language, but he *was* defending the Slovak language in the name of the Augsburg Confession and of Luther's Reformation. The two issues could become one issue only because the dignity of the vernacular was a basic tenet of the Reformation as Hurban's historicism interpreted it. Conversely, despite his violent polemics against Calvinism, he did not believe that the proponents of the union were defending the Magyar language in the name of the Helvetic Confession, but he accused them of using the Helvetic Confession and the union as instruments in the policy of the Magyarization of Slovak Lutheranism. Thus he explicitly identified his stand with that of Luther against Zwingli, maintaining, as had Luther, that "there is a

[67] Hurban, "Naměření a řád církevních Listu," *Církevní Listy*, 1 (1863): 14; in the original these words are in italics.

[68] *Ibid.*, p. 28.

greater and more fundamental difference between us [Lutherans] and the Calvinists than there is between us and the Roman Catholics or the Orthodox on the doctrines of the Word of God, the person of Christ, the sacraments in general and especially baptism and the Lord's Supper, and predestination."[69] Hurban's stand against the union in the early 1840's, the time of his so-called political liberalism, is an expression of his lifelong theological commitment to Luther and his Reformation—a commitment that survival Hurban's transition from political liberalism to political conservatism.

Indeed, that very transition, in both its constructive and its destructive aspects, also displays marked affinities with Luther's evolution. Hurban, the national hero who in his youth had embodied the political aspiration of his people, was disillusioned with the revolution he had helped to spark and with politics in general. During the Reformation the political leaders of Slovakia had "confessed their allegiance to Lutheranism in order not to have to believe; but when Luther insisted on the faith of the primitive church, they rebelled against him."[70] And the proof of this was a letter written by Luther to Count Francis Revaj of Turčianská on August 4, 1539.[71] Luther discovered in his later years, according to Hurban, that he had been exploited for political advantage; he turned to views of the political order that can only be regarded as reactionary. Hurban's development followed the same pattern and consciously took Luther as its model. Even the anti-Semitic tirades could have been written by either man! The revolution of 1848, he insisted in his memories, had not been inspired by the liberal *Zeitgeist*.[72] A recent investigation, written from a Marxist viewpoint by Andrej Mráz, confirms the method at work not only in those memoirs, but throughout Hurban's thought: "In general, Hurban's theological culture led him to express opinions in an exaggerated way also about non-religious questions

[69] Hurban, *Církev Evanjelicko-Lutheránská*, pp. 98–99.

[70] Hurban, "Naměření," *Církevní Listy*, 1 (1863): 26.

[71] *Luthers Werke* (Weimar: Böhlau, 1883 ff.), *Briefwechsel*, 8:258–61, where, for reasons cited in the introduction, the letter is dated 1538 rather than 1539.

[72] *Rozpomienky*, p. 662.

on the basis of parallels in the history of religion and of ecclesiastical ideology. In this respect, too, we regard Hurban's book on Ludovít Štúr as reactionary."[73] But the "progressive" as well as the "reactionary" features of Hurban's intellectual development are rooted in his theological culture and in his attitude toward church history. Important though all these other factors were, Hurban's historicism makes sense only when it is interpreted in the light of his theology.

[73] Mráz, "Hurbanov životopis Ludovíta Štúra," pp. 15–16.

14

"Ich bin kein Reformator," aber . . .

G. WAYNE GLICK

Since great men are not to be accounted for solely by times, and history is not made solely by great men, it is salutary to examine a great man's *influence* as a partial palliative to the dominant environmentalism which still pervades historiography today. Adolf von Harnack is a splendid example, for of no theologian is it probably more true that the borrowing sons ignored the contribution of the father.

Such an examination must take account of the process by which he arrived at an independent position, for it was this process which created the setting for his influence; and it must characterize his "achieved position," since in it, and primarily through it, he exerted this massive influence on his myriad followers.

Whatever the personal struggles which preceded the public establishment of his role as "representative man" of theological liberalism, that role was laid out for Harnack by the time he moved to the center of imperial Germany's cultural life. The personal travail had been present, of course, almost from the beginning of his student days at Leipzig. It had been intensified by his acceptance, at least in the main, of Ritschl's thought, laid onto a rich and generally conservative orthodox theological training. The bell had not cracked when he arrived at Leipzig in 1873; but by 1885, when the first volume of the *Dogmengeschichte* was completed, there was no longer any doubt that Dorpat had been overcome, so far as a viable personal basis of theological vocation was concerned. The poignant correspondence with his father proves that beyond a shadow of doubt.

The personal liberation preceded the public identification, but for so gifted and prolific a scholar as Harnack, the latter could not but come. From the chrysalis of conservative theology, a liberal had emerged, still somewhat naive with respect to the possibility of rapprochement between the "camps," and so writing to his mentor at Bonn of his hope for a new mediating theology.[1] Ritschl knew better, and as the decade of the eighties wore on, the lesson should have been borne in on Harnack as journal after journal and consistory after consistory cited him as a dangerous influence. Yet there is compelling evidence that he learned this lesson slowly, since, disclaiming the role of reformer, he lived through the furor caused by his *Dogmengeschichte*, the controversy over his choice (vetoed by the consistory) to a chair at Leipzig, the conflict over his call to Berlin, requiring an eventual imperial decision, and the Apostles' Creed controversy without conceding his optimism. Aber . . .

And in that disjunctive one finds as near a key as the historian is ever likely to find to the external reason for the impact of Adolf von Harnack on the culture of his time, and of subsequent time. That is to say, Harnack abjured the role of reformer within the church, choosing instead to be a mediator; *but* the response he met within the church forced him into a role of mediator toward the culture, and thereby he became a reformer, *cum sensu prorsus alieno*, within the church. For whatever disclaimers he may have entered, subduing these with an apt "*labora et noli contristari,*"[2] his role was fixed by the late eighties, he was categorized, and his fundamental referent was thereby set for him. In effect, he was forced into the role of prophet to the culture; and one could argue that thereby the consistorial functionaries who had initially opposed him guaranteed, lacking the prescience to identify his genius, the effect which they had thought to curb.

The emancipating instrument for Harnack, if one searches for concrete literary evidence, would be the *Theologische*

[1] Agnes von Zahn-Harnack, *Adolf von Harnack* (Berlin: Hans Bott, 1936), pp. 127–29. Hereafter this reference is designated AZH.

[2] *Ibid.*, p. 146.

Literaturzeitung. Conceived in 1873 by Harnack, Kaftan, and Baudissin, the journal was "to bear the firmly fixed stamp of Lutheran theology."[3] Such an identification of purpose (apparently suggested in the first instance by Luthardt) makes clear the continuing Dorpat influence. For though Engelhardt did *not* approve of a part of the stated purpose of the journal, and warned against it,[4] the fact that Schürer was excluded from the initial planning for the journal because of his less than complete commitment to the Lutheran theology indicates the vitality of these ties. By the time the journal actually began to appear, however, in 1876, Schürer was its manager and Ritschl, not Luthardt, or Engelhardt, was its mentor. In fact, so disparate had the position of the young Leipzigers become from that of Luthardt that he founded a counter journal, the *Theologische Literaturblatt,* four years after the *Theologische Literaturzeitung* began to appear.

Taking over the editorship of the journal in 1881 (and continuing it, with Schürer, for twenty-nine years), Harnack encountered a growing opposition as he began to take positions in his articles and reviews. The intriguing fact is that he *apparently* failed to recognize that this opposition was deep-seated and intransigent. As the criticisms began to flow in, in response to the position he set forth, Harnack established a massive correspondence with the theological leaders of the eighties, trying to hold together what the various proponents insisted could not be held together. To Ritschl he remarked of Luthardt that "you can accept him as an opponent who might *bona fide* come to an understanding," and advised Ritschl how this miracle might be brought about: "Take up the matter with a kind of restraint . . . let him pose questions *ad absurdum* . . . bring him to make concessions."[5] To Luthardt, he admits theological differences, but appeals to a deeper bond: "Both sides would recognize God only in Christ . . . and be-

[3] *Ibid.,* p. 84.

[4] *Ibid.,* p. 85. Specifically, Engelhardt believed the young men were overreaching in trying to offer the theological world such a comprehensive view as they projected.

[5] *Ibid.,* p. 127.

lieve what sacred history attests of him . . ."[6] To Engelhardt, he defends Ritschl; to a suspicious Ritschl, he lauds Engelhardt. And always, poignant and troubling, so long as he was alive, the words of the father were with him, advising against any rapprochement with Ritschl, or any attempt at mediation: "He will not get by with it . . . the fate of all so-called middle parties has been that they . . . were in time crushed . . . because I value your work highly, I do not want this judgment to fall on it."[7]

With the publication of the first volume of the *Dogmengeschichte* in 1885, Harnack's personal liberation was achieved, and the public identification of his position was inevitable. Foregoing all tendencies to read back to this period the later reputation of the man, it is yet clear that any work which brought forth reviews from so eminent a company as Loofs, Holtzmann, Lasson, Sabatier, and Rade, to name only a few,[8] must have had enormous influence. The fruits of this influence, not all sweet by any means, were not long delayed. There were first the reviews, from all points of the theological compass, the judgments of Harnack's professional peers. Second, the achievement of this first volume, added to an already estimable reputation derived from his earlier work, initiated calls from a number of universities. And finally, the wider German and international cultural community became aware of the name "Harnack" as representing—so it was believed—a significant option for those who no longer found the orthodoxy of the time satisfying.

Of the first influence, no more need be said. Regarding the university calls, it is noteworthy that Harvard University was sufficiently impressed to offer the thirty-four-year-old scholar a professorship. But it was with respect to another university, Leipzig, that the "first fruit of my Dogmengeschichte," as Harnack described it to Ritschl,[9] was revealed. The theological faculty at Leipzig voted in the winter semester of 1885–86

[6] *Ibid.*, p. 128.
[7] *Ibid.*, p. 130.
[8] *Ibid.*, p. 142.
[9] *Ibid.*, p. 146.

to recommend Harnack for appointment. The consistory opposed the nomination so strenuously, however, that the Ministry rejected the nomination, and Brieger was called. The incident in itself demonstrates that already there was advocacy "for and against" whenever Harnack was mentioned. But it is also noteworthy that his name was sufficiently known at this time that two of the giants, Nietzsche and Overbeck, took note of the action in their correspondence.[10] Yet, in the midst of the debate and the controversy, Harnack could declare "it is for me no disappointment. . . . I would be a knave if I allowed myself to be embittered."[11] And in his attendance at various pastoral conferences in Hesse, on which occasions he took a most active part in the discussions, he made it clear that he, at least, had not separated himself from the ecclesiastical affairs of the day.

The years at Marburg (1886–88) were characteristically filled with writing and lecturing, but they were hardly years of peace. Elsewhere I have expressed the judgment,[12] that the decade and a half between the publication of the first volume of the *Dogmengeschichte* and the delivering of the famous *Das Wesen des Christentums* lectures were "Harnack's *Sturm und Drang* period so far as the church is concerned"; and the last nine months of his stay at Marburg were filled with one of the bitterest fights in this emerging denouement. Again, it is important that one try to extrude the later Harnack from the present controversy; for at this time, he was still clearly of the opinion that "*labora et noli contristari*" would solve all difficulties. Not yet had he given up the hope of mediation.

As briefly as it can be told, the controversy over Harnack's appointment to the faculty at the University of Berlin developed as follows:[13] The Berlin faculty, on December 10, 1887, unanimously proposed Harnack for the chair in church his-

[10] *Ibid.*

[11] *Ibid.*

[12] In a monograph, *The Reality of Christianity*, published by Harper & Row in 1967.

[13] *Ibid.* The following summary is reprinted here with the permission of Harper & Row, to whom I express my gratitude.

tory vacated by Semisch.[14] In the old Prussian provinces, the Evangelical *Oberkirchenrat* had the right to express itself regarding the doctrinal and confessional position of anyone called to a university chair. The council was split, but one of those who took a neutral position, Brückner, wrote to Harnack, asking for a statement of his views on the Resurrection and on baptism as a sacrament. Harnack answered, referring him to his published writings. The ecclesiastical press of Prussia entered the fray against him, with Stöcker's *Deutsche Evangelische Kirchenzeitung* leading the pack. When the judgment of the council went to the Ministry, Harnack was voted against on three counts: that he had shattered the New Testament canon, that he left open the question of miracle, and that he denied that the Trinitarian formula for baptism had been instituted by Jesus. The Ministry of Worship now had a chance to reply, and Harnack's defenders were Althoff and Weiss. At this crucial juncture, Wilhelm I died and the young emperor inherited the problem. Through the active support of Bismarck in the Ministry of State, Wilhelm II, previously under Stöcker's influence, made a favorable decision, with a characteristic flourish: "Ich will keine Mucker!"[15] The decision came on September 17, 1888, over nine months after the recommendation of the faculty.

Harnack's expressed hope that he would be allowed to go about his work unimpeded proved again to be illusory. In 1892 the most bitter of all the controversies surrounding him, the *Apostolikumsstreit*, broke out. Though the problem was older than this, dating from the eighties, and included, as was customary, political factors, Harnack's involvement was precipitated when he was specifically asked for his judgment on the "Schrempf case." Schrempf, a young ecclesiastic, had performed a baptism without using the Apostles' Creed. Harnack answered the request with nine points, which he published in *Christliche Welt*. Among them, he held that the Church should prepare a shorter confession which would be grounded in the

[14] AZH, p. 156.
[15] *Ibid.*, p. 171.

Reformation position and also take account of later understandings of the Gospel. This confession should be required of everyone. Further, either the Apostles' Creed should be removed from liturgical worship, or its use should be left to the discretion of congregations. On specifics, he declared that certain elements of the Creed cannot be interpreted in their original sense, but must be seen in the light of evangelical belief, e.g. "the communion of saints"; and that the phrase of the Creed "conceived by the Holy Ghost, born of the Virgin Mary" cannot any longer be received by many believing Christians as fact. His generalization was that there should now be required of all future ecclesiastics the study of the history of dogma and of symbolics.[16] Harnack appended a statement in which he specified what he regarded as the essentials of any evangelical creed:

> The essential contents of the Apostles' Creed consists of the confession that in the Christian religion the goods "holy Church," "forgiveness of sins," and "eternal life" are given, that the possession of these goods is promised to those believing in God, the Almighty Creator, in his Son Jesus Christ, and in the Holy Spirit, and that these are won through Jesus Christ our Lord. This content is evangelical.[17]

With this statement the controversy flared into violence. Cremer of Greifswald, an opponent whom Harnack honored, argued, in *Christliche Welt*, against his position; but Stöcker requisitioned the columns of *Deutsche Evangelische Kirchenzeitung* to pour out his journalistic vitriol, accusing Harnack and his ilk of "no respect for history, no honor for the confessions, no regard for the Church and community. Hypotheses, quite often giddy hypotheses . . ., are given greater reality than the foundation beliefs of the Church."[18] Stöcker concluded with the declaration that "confession, biblical authority, and finally the historicity and the personality of Christ

[16] *Ibid.*, pp. 196–201.
[17] *Ibid.*, p. 201.
[18] *Ibid.*, p. 202.

himself are thrown into the witches' kettle of frothy criticism."[19] At Kassel a consistorial paper printed a sonnet ending with the lines:

> If Harnack is for you the light of the world,
> Then he must also now your Savior be.[20]

The Catholic press also joined the controversy, and an unbelievable number of letters appeared in the papers, most of them opposing Harnack's position. There were supporters, however: Rade through his influential *Christliche Welt*, and the *Akademie der Wissenschaften*. And Harvard University took occasion to offer Harnack, for the second time, a full professorship.[21]

Harnack was supported by the Ministry, and was not reproved.[22] It is significant that in spite of the many requests that poured in, including one from his brother Otto, asking Harnack to make explicit what he would put in the place of the Apostles' Creed, he refused. On the one hand, he confessed a great fear of agitators, for he held that in any agitation the truth suffers; on the other hand, he affirmed that he was not willing to destroy the faith that meant so much to so many people. Thus, though he was accused of a failure to follow through on his position, he took as his motto "Ich bin kein Reformator," and refused to say anything further.[23]

The *Apostolikumsstreit* can stand as a paradigm for Harnack's relation to the ecclesiastical authorities of his day, but there were many subsequent occasions when he came into conflict with them. After the publication of *Das Wesen des Christentums*, he was challenged from many sides for his statement that "the Father alone, and not the Son, belongs in the Gospel as Jesus preached it."[24] Two years previous to this

[19] *Ibid.*

[20] *Ibid.*, p. 203.

[21] *Ibid.*, p. 210.

[22] However, as a concession to orthodoxy, Adolf Schlatter, a conservative, was appointed to the Berlin faculty. *Ibid.*, pp. 208–9.

[23] *Ibid.*, p. 212.

[24] Harnack, *Das Wesen des Christentums* (Leipzig: Hinrichs, 1900). Translated by Thomas Bailey Saunders as *What is Christianity?* 4th ed.

he had declared to Rade his intention to continue in his vocation of serving the Church and serving science at the same time; [25] this in spite of the fact that the Church woud not even let Harnack act as examiner for his own students. A year after the publication of *Das Wesen des Christentums,* Harnack had desired to be appointed as the faculty representative to the meeting of the Brandenburg Synod, but when he contacted his friends to inquire whether this would be possible, they retorted that it would be an affront to the Synod if Harnack were appointed.[26] Even the liberal party among the churchmen did not find Harnack acceptable, for Harnack held that the Church was too much dominated by the ecclesiastics, and in his appeal for more lay participation he found few clerical supporters.

The sole place where his interest in action could be exercised was in extra-Church movements and organizations, and this doubtless accounts, in considerable measure, for his acceptance of the directorship of the Royal Library. When the call to this position came, in 1905, he wrote about it to Rade and, in the course of one of his letters, made a significant statement with respect to his relation to the Church:

> You learn to know the world only insofar as you influence it. My new position will not make me so much a "librarian" as an organizer. I hope that my friends will find that theology does not thereby lose anything, but that science, and theology also, will win. I have *done* so little in my life, and I would like to supplement my lectures and writings in a modest way by an *action* from which the entire community profits. The church has not offered me

rev. (New York: G. P. Putnam's Sons, 1923). The notation suggesting "revision" is misleading and amounts only to such trivialities as italicizing. In the German edition ("zum 45. bis. 50. tausend," issued in 1903), Harnack remarked that he deliberately left the text unchanged because he wanted it to remain as it had been delivered and transcribed (see p. iv). The Saunders translation is a good one, and I have used it. Hereafter the work is designated *WC.*

[25] AZH, pp. 295 f.

[26] *Ibid.*, p. 300.

> an opportunity in this regard, and such work would now come too late for me.[27]

This is certainly a classical understatement. Though Harnack had, in his writings, declared his concern to be the defense of Protestantism — to be sure, as understood under its Ritschlian form — though he had been actively interested since his Leipzig years in the "social question" in the Church; though he had supported foreign missions in numerous writings; though he had been president of the *Evangelisch-Soziale Kongress* for three years at the time of the writing of this letter and was to continue for five more; though he was active in the Inner Mission; though he was co-founder and president of the Evangelical Union; he remained *persona non grata* to the institutional church and its leaders.

It is clear that so far as Harnack's early conception of his vocation — the avoidance of "camps" and a mediating ministry to the church — was concerned, the door was closed for him as of the turn of the century. But this slamming of the door and his increasing involvement in the cultural life of Germany does not, however, in itself account for the role he was to play in the last twenty years of his career at Berlin. That explanation can be subsumed under the intention he had stated to Rade, "to serve science." And thereby one is involved in the consideration of a rich and variegated theory and practice of historiography.

Harnack insisted that what he meant by "Wissenschaft" was a dominant concern of his life, but he would permit no precise limitation to the scope of science. *Geisteswissenschaft* had as its object "life, the life of humanity, insofar as it is distinguished from and elevated above the stage of nature. This life can be grasped only through a study that includes not only the past but also the present."[28] If the historian lacks breadth and depth in his own life, he will lack responsible

[27] *Ibid.*, p. 325.

[28] Adolf Harnack, "Gedanken über Wissenschaft und Leben," *Reden*

conviction; and lacking this conviction, the historian "always lies, no matter what he says."[29]

Harnack dealt with "scientific knowledge" in a 1913 lecture, in which he defined "science" as "the knowledge of the Real turned to purposive behavior,"[30] and set forth its four "stages":

> (1) The first and most basic stage consists in *identification, analysis*, and *organization*. All knowledge begins with these operations.[31]
> (2) The second stage is to be designated as the *knowledge of the causal relations between things*. . . . In a word, it concerns itself with the knowledge of the powers of the world, insofar as they can be represented quantitatively and mechanically.[32]
> (3) To investigate life is the third stage of knowledge. A structure, analysis, and order is necessary here, as in the first stage, but in a higher estimate, and new questions are thereby raised, questions concerning the fleeting and the fit, the idea and the direction and the purpose. Here we have to deal with the living world *in its concrete reality*.[33]
> (4) The fourth stake of knowledge is closely related to this third stage, and one might be disposed to connect them, for epistemologically it at first uses the same means and methods as the third stage, and its object in any case is included in the concept of "life." But the knowledge of men . . . is lifted above the knowledge of "life" because we encounter something at this point which other living things do not manifest: conscious spirit.[34]

und Aufsätze, vol. 1; NF: *Aus Wissenschaft und Leben* (Giessen: Töpelmann, 1911), p. 4. Hereafter reference in this series are designated *RA*, with the appropriate volume number, NF in the case of the new series, and the title of the volume.

[29] Harnack, "Über Wissenschaft und Religion . . .," *RA*, 2:379.

[30] Harnack, Über Wissenschaftliche Erkenntnis," *RA*, vol. 3; NF: *Aus der Friedens- und Kriegsarbeit*, p. 178.

[31] *Ibid.*, p. 179.

[32] *Ibid.*, pp. 179–80.

[33] *Ibid.*, pp. 187–88.

[34] *Ibid.*, p. 191.

Specifically, what is encountered when we study men are the categories of "norms" and "worth." It is only in this fourth stage that we really can speak of history; for history is involved only when the spirit of an event is grasped. The creative leader among historians is the one who sets forth such "norms," which means to exercise the law of the spirit which gives freedom. "Through this law he creates above and in this life a second life, above and in nature another nature, a second world above nature — the human. It must express itself first in ideas, which appear to be as abstract as the ideology of mechanistic power-systems."[35] But as these ideas are grasped, they bring about a conquest of nature and thereby prove themselves to be of worth in the creation of "supermen" — for all those who live in this law of spiritual freedom are supermen. Does this provide a final measure of worth? There is only one answer, and it is absolutely crucial: "The measure and the directive for all higher life-motivation of man is the conviction that we are not mere fragments of nature, but also bear within ourselves an eternal life as the citizens and creators of a spiritual kingdom."[36] This is the measure, the standard of worth, the norm to which all activity is held accountable. Everything which contributed to the emergence of this new, "*überempirisch*" man, this true humanity, is worthful; everything that hinders it is evil. "And all history in its essence is nothing else than the leading forth of humanity from the gloomy depths of nature to the pinnacle of this knowledge."[37] Thus spoke Harnack in 1913; "da brach der Weltkrieg aus."[38]

In considering the elements of Harnack's historiographical theory, it is impossible to overemphasize his insistence upon source-work as the basis for any sound historical work. From beginning to end, critical, grammatical, philological competence is held to be a *sine qua non* for the historian. The evidence of his practicing this conviction is multiform; one can refer simply to the critical edition of early church documents

[35] *Ibid.*, p. 194.
[36] *Ibid.*
[37] *Ibid.*, p. 195.
[38] *Ibid.*, p. 174.

to which he contributed and which he edited in cooperation with a large company of scholars.[39] In his *Luke the Physician* he inveighs against those who attempt short cuts:

> The method which I have followed in this book is little in accord with the impressionism which is the style in biblical criticism today. . . . The problem before us . . . can be really mastered by a method which comprises close and detailed examination and discussion of vocabulary and style.[40]

Possessing full control of the sources, the historian must assess and distinguish the various factors that enter into and shape historical events. Harnack believed that there were three kinds of factors which must be assessed if the historian is to provide the necessary order to the fabric of his history. In the first place, there are "elementary" factors: the setting, the climate, the natural conditions, and those physical and mental givens which cannot be escaped. These constitute an important element in history, but to center on these alone, as do the materialistic historians, is indefensible. In the second place, there are "cultural" factors. These are the institutions which carry and preserve what we call tradition, ethico-religious strength, customs, art, and science. But there is a third, and crucial, factor if one is to fulfill the highest calling as a historian: the "individual" factor. "Individuality, personality, talent, and above all, genius, the *great men*, are here to be represented."[41] Indeed, "the great ideas and institutions . . . are, as a rule, the lengthened shadows of great men, and our spiritual, mental, and technical possessions are the capital which they have won, and which represents their continuing life."[42] It is not enough to say that "times produce men": "In history the rule obtains that a development is really *fulfilled*

[39] We refer here to the *Texte und Untersuchungen zur Geschichte der altchristlichen Literatur* series (Leipzig: Hinrichs, 1883 ff.).

[40] Harnack, *Luke, the Physician*, trans. J. R. Wilkinson (New York: G. P. Putnam's Sons, 1907), pp. vii–viii.

[41] Harnack, "Über die Sicherheit . . .," *RA*, vol. 4; NF: *Erforschtes und Erlebtes*, p. 10.

[42] *Ibid.*, p. 11.

and a *new situation created* only through great personalities, who do not come when they *must* come — ach! how often are they obliged to come! — but they come when they come!"[43]

It is in connection with this third factor that Harnack raises another important concern, one which might be denominated "the problem of continuity." The problem may be stated in this way: what assurance does the historian have that he can "get at" the life of the past and understand it? The answer lies in the fact that the key to the past is the institutions — here seen in the broadest sense — which have been bequeathed to us. But *all institutions stem from ideas.* There is no such thing as a cultural institution which did not have an idea behind it.

> To be sure, all history is institution-history; but behind these rest the idea and idea-history. Therefore: just as it is certain that what is mere ideology and has not been embodied in institutions can never be called history, it is equally certain that institution-history without the driving force of ideas would never penetrate; but the ideas are *mind.*[44]

It is because institutions are produced by ideas, and "all history is the history of the mind,"[45] that one can claim a continuity with the life of the past and can understand it. "How much or how little we may possess from it, it is always one and the same mind which works in all the products of history *and in us.* . . . A deep unity is discovered between all events and the essence of our own highest life."[46] There follows a sentence which may very well be the most revealing of Harnack's position with regard to the understanding of history: "*Homo sum, nil historicum a me alienum puto.*"[47] Or perhaps even stronger, "You yourself are all that has preceded and precedes you in

[43] *Ibid.*

[44] Harnack, "Was hat die Historie . . .," *RA*, vol. 4; NF: *Erforschtes und Erlebtes*, pp. 186–87.

[45] *Ibid.*, p. 187.

[46] *Ibid.*

[47] *Ibid.*

history, and it only depends upon your grasping it with your consciousness."[48]

Only when these three factors are considered with respect to the material is a true picture possible; and even so, to regard this as totally discharging the historian's responsibility is inaccurate. Epictetus had long ago said that it was not the facts, but the representation of the facts, that aroused men. Here all sorts of difficulties arise. Goethe had criticized history as resting on tradition, and all tradition, so he said, is falsified, or partisan, written out of blind hate or blinder love; and furthermore, the historian is always too late; the returns are already in! Harnack regards the situation as not so hopeless; though it is true that "*quo accuratius, eo falsius,*" if one goes on to ask the threefold question, "What *powers* were effective in a given epoch, in what *direction* did they proceed, and what was the *production* of the epoch,"[49] the decisive question of history can be raised, and the Goethean criticism met. What are the sources which provide the material for answering this question? *"The epoch-making events, the understanding of memorials, and the investigation of institutions constitute the backbone of history."*[50]

It is necessary to stress one further point as determinative of competent historiography. In order to pursue the factual investigation and to represent the facts properly, a historian must possess the practical wisdom which can grasp the inner relationships between facts, and a "rich, deep, and many-sided wisdom and experience of his own which he brings to the interpretation of the material."[51] A reflexive relationship is here involved: the wisdom and experience of the historian clarifies and arranges the historical material, and, in turn, the material strengthens his wisdom. He then can determine that which may still be useful from the past, declare what is to be done in the present, and how one may prepare responsibly

[48] *Ibid.*

[49] Harnack, "Über die Sicherheit . . .," *RA*, vol. 4; NF, p. 14.

[50] *Ibid.*, p. 15.

[51] *Ibid.*, p. 19.

for the future. These are the minimal conditions for gaining certainty in history.

The complexity of Harnack's conception and method is apparent. An attempt at summary would issue in something like the following:

Historical knowledge is knowledge of the material and spiritual structure of past life, to be seen as the progressive concretion of the spirit and its mastery of material circumstances. Such progression is undoubtedly present, but it is not inevitable. The historian should proceed to his task with a frank admission of the limits of historical knowledge and should seek, insofar as possible, to root out all preconceptions and prejudices; he would further be well-advised to seek the truth in the "mean" rather than the extreme. History is to be studied in order to intervene in the course of history and prepare for the future in a responsible way. Before one can engage in that responsible action which is the purpose of historical study, certain requirements must be fulfilled. These are: (1) the requirement that the historian possess a "practical wisdom" which can grasp the inner relationships between facts, and a "rich, deep, and many-sided wisdom of life" which contributes to, and is continually strengthened by, historical investigation; (2) source-work; (3) the analysis of the elementary, cultural, and individual factors as embodied in the memorials, events, and institutions which constitute the backbone of history; (4) the identification of the *Geist* of an epoch, made possible by the fact that "the same mind is at work in history and in us"; and (5) the representation of the facts, which is dependent upon all of the preceding steps and also requires an analysis of the power, the direction, and the result characteristic of a given epoch. This analysis in turn is based upon the source-study and centers upon the institutions produced by the ideas of the great men of an epoch. It is eminently clear that the method is highly contextual, the total framework being well-nigh presupposed in each part.

When one turns from Harnack's theory to his practice, it is *Christianity* understood historically which provides the subject-matter. When he was seventeen years old, Harnack had declared in a letter to a friend that one of the fundamental concerns that dominated his thought was "to understand Christianity historically and set it in living relation to all historical event." [52] Certainly that concern never left him. In an 1895 lecture, he begins with a question: "When all history seems to be a ceaseless process of growth and decay, is it possible to pick out a single phenomenon and saddle it with the whole weight of eternity, especially when it is a phenomenon on the past?" [53] Harnack began his answer with a quick glance at the process by which history had come to its present status. The eighteenth century had belittled history, exalted Nature and Reason, and subscribed with an antihistorical passion to Lessing's principle that "*historical truth, which is accidental in its character, can never become the proof of the truths of Reason, which are necessary.*" [54] From this principle it was deduced that all historical religions are in reality only the one, true, natural religion in disguise, whose content is Reason. This view was overcome, thanks to Herder, the romantic movement, Hegel and Ranke, and to a powerful reaction within Christian faith. "In the place of shallow talk about divine nature and profane history, about the 'eternal truths of reason' and casual records, we have arrived at the knowledge of *history*; of the history from which we have received what we possess, and to which we owe what we are." [55] Development and personality have been the two conceptions, apparently opposed, but actually determinative of the work of the historian, which are contained in the meaning of "history." When this came to be understood, religion was rightly seen as a growth that falls within the history of humanity.

In 1904, Harnack further developed this theme.[56] Pointing

[52] AZH, p. 40.

[53] Adolf Harnack, *Christianity and History*, trans. Thomas Bailey Saunders (London: A. & C. Black, 1896), p. 18.

[54] *Ibid.*, pp. 19–20.

[55] *Ibid.*, p. 24.

[56] Harnack, "Über die Verhältnis . . .," *RA*, vol. 2; NF: *Aus Wissenschaft und Leben*, pp. 41–62. Translated by Thomas Bailey Saunders as "The Relation between Ecclesiastical and General History," *Contemporary Review*, 86 (December, 1904): 846–59.

out the fact that the ancient and medieval Christian writers regarded the Church's history as different from the history of the world, and the fact that this view was continued to the present among the orthodox church historians, Harnack demurs: "The fact that there is absolutely no criterion by which we can distinguish two kinds of history is enough to destroy it." [57] It was not until this view was given up that any possibility of really understanding the *one* true history of the Church was effected. This view was challenged in the seventeenth century; further weakened in the eighteenth, and finally overcome in the nineteenth. Now we can say with assurance, "*The history of the Church is part and parcel of universal history, and can be understood only in connection with it.*" [58]

However, Harnack warns against the danger of *underestimating* the "*special character* which attaches to the history of the Church." [59] One question must remain central for the church historian: What is the Christian religion? If this is kept central, other matters may be investigated as contributory; but if church history loses this central concern, it will lose the right to be a special subject of study within the science of history. Only if one gives himself completely to this question will the secrets (*Geheimnisse*) become known, and, at the same time, the mysteries (*Heimlichkeiten*) will be seen to remain inviolate. Here Harnack affirms a variant of his "kernel-husk" theme, and of his principle that, though Christianity must be studied on the basis of the historical facts, it remains in essence an inner experience which cannot be finally represented in any historical form. Secrets we may know, mysteries, never. Should the latter then be avoided? Certainly not:

> In the history of the Church . . . these *Heimlichkeiten* go very deep and are very precious. We have seen that there is no such thing as a double history, and that everything that happens enters into the one stream of events. But there is a single inner experience which everyone can

[57] *Ibid.*, p. 847.
[58] *Ibid.*
[59] *Ibid.*, p. 859.

> possess; which to everyone who possesses it is like a miracle; and which cannot be simply explained as the product of something else. It is what the Christian religion described as the *New Birth*—that inner, moral, new creation which transmutes all values, and of the slaves of compulsion makes the children of freedom. Not even in the history of the Church can one get a direct vision of this inner evolution accomplished in the individual, nor by any external facts whatever can anyone be convinced of its possibility and reality. But the light which shines from it throws its rays on what happens on the stage, and lets the spectator feel in his heart that the forces of history are not exhausted in the natural forces of the world, or in the powers of head and hand. This is the *Heimlichkeit* of the history of the Church because it is the *Heimlichkeit* of religion.[60]

The *Ding an sich* we cannot know, but the power, the direction, and the purpose of a given epoch can be identified and described in their historical manifestation. This is a history which recognizes itself to be distinct from Nature, and therefore it must be investigated on the basis of a theory of historical causation, as opposed to simple natural causation. It cannot thereby pierce the veil which encompasses Reality, but, remembering its relativity, it can point to the historical effects which emerge from the *Heimlichkeit* of the New Birth.

Harnack's main point with respect to the relation of church history to general history is clear and needs no further emphasis: there is *one* history, of which church history is a part. What do need to be emphasized here are the identification of the Christian religion which Harnack makes, the specification of the controlling question, and the relation which he designates as prevailing between history and religion.

Religion is "a definite state of feeling and will, basing itself on inner experience and historical facts." Here, as in Harnack's claim of a "special character" for church history, a fundamental fissiparity is strikingly revealed. On the one hand, there

[60] *Ibid.*

is the involved theory of historical knowledge, demanding a scientific procedure; but on the other hand there is the appeal to an inner experience "which cannot be simply explained as the product of something else." This experience is identified as "that inner, moral, new creation which transmutes all values" but in itself remains an inviolate mystery. On the one hand, "everything that happens enters into one stream of events"; but on the other, there is the claim of a "special character" to church history, which, when identified, involves Harnack immediately in axiological prepossessions.

Second, the controlling question for the church historian, "What is the Christian religion?" innocent though it may appear, is charged with significance. For here (1) a nisus to essence procedure is implied in the way the question is stated, and (2) the answer to the question is stated solely in terms of a moral essence. Christianity, as concerned with "the inmost core" of the *Ego*—the transempirical *Ego*—in the "world of Freedom and the Good," speaks of a *New Birth* which is an inner experience, a mystery unreachable by historical study. "Everyone can possess" this, "it is like a miracle": yet it is inexplicable in terms of anything else. This is Harnack's Holy of Holies; when *Religionsgeschichte* attempted to make this also one relativity beside others, Harnack demurred: Jesus was *the* Master because he evoked the transmuting experience, and that's an end of it. This is the place where his lauded *Einheit* and *Sicherheit* finds itself. But what does this imply with respect to Harnack's stated purpose? "To understand Christianity historically and set it in living relation to all historical event" means to identify the essence of Christianity; but when this is done, the historically multiform phenomenon which is church history is judged by *a* particular moral norm! Harnack is correct, *cum sensu prorsus alieno*: "A single phenomenon [is saddled] with the whole weight of eternity";[61] but, fatefully, this phenomenon was *not* derived from Harnack's magnificent historical investigation. In the final analysis, it is Harnack's "inner experience," that which constituted his axiological a priori, which judged history.

[61] This quote is a paraphrase. Cf. above, note 29.

For, third, the relation between history and this *noli me tangere* is such that history can only lead one to the outer court, probing the *Geheimnisse*. The essence lies deeper, as an inviolate *Heimlichkeit*. Christianity, as concerned with the transempirical *Ego* and the world of Freedom and the Good, transcends scientific historical processes of understanding. One can, of course, see the effects of the Christian mysteries, and historical procedure can certify these effects. It cannot, however, point in a simple way to the source of these effects. History can destroy too-sure interpretations; it can say "not here" and "not there"; but history cannot explain the New Birth, nor describe the process leading to it, nor convince anyone of its possibility and reality. The *most* that history can do is to point to the effects and say, "There is something"; it is religion alone, religion as "a state of feeling and will," *not* first or primarily an intellectual process, which makes it possible for one to "feel in his heart" the morally transforming experience.

Yet even here, we note, the limits within which man lives his life remain firm. Harnack will not say "*Er gibt*" certainty of faith. He will say "*Es gibt*" a certainty of faith. This position has been described, not unfairly, as a "watered down version of justification by faith."[62] The quintessential New Birth is not, finally, given; everyone can possess it as an achievement. The Kantian limit of knowledge holds, and something closely resembling "the moral law within" prevails. Is this, then, "Christianity understood historically and set in living relation to all historical event"? No. It is Christianity understood morally, in terms of a particular axiological essence. Harnack's history can reduce; it is not, *pace* Harnack, history that overcomes. This honor is reserved for inner moral experience.

Harnack had been refused his desired role of mediator within the church; he had been forced, as it were, to a broader mediation. The talents required for this mediation, as we have

[62] This characterization comes from James Hastings Nichols, personal conversation.

seen, he possessed in profligate measure. And the motive was certainly there. For Harnack held as a cardinal tenet that *action* constituted the final responsibility of the historian. We are not in the world simply to contemplate it, but we are in it to prepare for the future in a responsible way.

Positively, this is the motivation. Were there negative reasons? If it is true, as we have declared, that at the time of *Das Wesen* a watershed had been reached, and from this point on, as it were, Harnack moved on a vast plateau that touched all facets of Wilhelmian and Weimar Germanic culture, was this not because the newer directions of theological science had turned to "system-building" and away from Harnack's "scavenger-labor" of historical investigation? And also because those who continued in his ways were simply mopping up? And still further, because the established church, governed as always by ecclesiastical politicians, went on its way as if there had never been a Baur, a Ritschl, or a Harnack? It is vastly instructive, in order to understand which of these reasons really controlled, if not all, to examine Harnack's own assessment of his "inner change" at the beginning of the twentieth century.

This change is described in a series of letters to Martin Rade, written in a two months' period in late 1899. On the direction of theological scholarship, he writes:

> They want today to get at things which in my opinion should remain a secret to general discussion as well as to science; for they are the secret of personality and its inner life. Whoever refuses to participate in this immodest and indelicate exposure is counted a pallid scholastic who has no feeling for "life." On the other hand, that work which makes real the ordering, the development, and the understanding of what is knowable, is little prized, as is the cultivation of the common resources of knowledge.
>
> Further, I cannot share in the whim of ignoring all that we have learned from history about religion and Christianity (although it may be that I myself, in my own personal development, have very imperfectly appropriated it), in order to introduce some sort of elementary,

> antediluvian frame of mind, as though we were as Titans. If anyone feels that way—and I do not doubt that some who represent Neo-Rousseauism do thus honestly feel—then I have neither the vocation nor the capacity to influence him. Perhaps history is preparing something actually new in and through these spirits. I am willing to believe it and, therefore I will not malign them. But personally I cannot go along with them.
>
> Finally, as to the structure which I have learned from Paul, Luther, and Ritschl—and I think they learned it from someone greater—faith in Christ, trust in God, peace in God, humility, patience and industry in one's calling and status, I pledge myself with all the strength which God has given me, and dare not let it be plucked to pieces, or regarded as belonging to a religion of secondary rank. In contrast to this, all high revelations, spirits and ecstasies are to me as nothing; they are merely individual protuberances.[63]

Against all attempts to interpret Christianity psychologically, or mystically, to interpret it according to its variations rather than its central principles, Harnack entered the strongest objection. *He never altered his position,* whether the opponent was the eschatological school, the *Religionsgeschichtliche* school (with whom he felt some affinity), the dialectical theology, the newer forms of mysticism, "neo-Buddhism,"[64] or the reviving pietistic influence within the church.[65]

Indeed, so committed was Harnack to his particular way of "understanding Christianity historically," that he courted the disfavor of his liberal colleagues in his rectoral address at the University of Berlin. The address bore the title "The Problem of the Theological Faculties and the General History of Re-

[63] *Ibid.*, pp. 285–96.

[64] See H. Weinel, "Religious Life and Thought in Germany Today," *Hibbert Journal*, vol. 7 (July, 1909), esp. pp. 732–37, for a fascinating analysis of the role of Schopenhauer, Wagner, and von Hartmann in this "movement."

[65] AZH, p. 297.

ligion," and in the address Harnack opposed that movement which "drew upon the popular traditions of the non-Christian religions for the interpretation of Christianity, . . . hoping to find in the mythology of the heathen religions a primitive religious property, from which Christianity would be seen as one derivative alongside other." Harnack's position was stated sharply: "Christianity is not *one* but *the* religion."[66]

Yet Harnack could not, on principle, oppose "new" directions:

> It is out of my line to be *laudator temporis acti*, and I believe I have a feeling for the progressive and the productive; but I look very cautiously into the future. I do not want nor do I have the ability to drive violently into it. Therefore I will remain absorbed in my work, and leave to the broader stream the course of its own development. . . . Perhaps something of importance may yet come out of the venture. Sometimes it all seems inhuman.[67]

He repeats to Rade—no, he protests—that his desire is to *serve* the church:

> I will at no point quench the spirit, nor will I let scholarship be cheapened; I want to serve the church, our much afflicted Reformation church. I want to do it because I feel the obligation to do so, and I cannot renounce that obligation so long as I stand in a semi-ecclesiastical position; further, I recognize no incompatibility between the two tasks. It would be much easier for me to let the church go its way, and who could blame me for doing it? The churches would rejoice; for they have never had anything for which to thank me. But my historical conscience and consideration for my students, which have been laid on my soul, forbid me to do that.[68]

[66] Harnack, "Die Aufgabe der theologischen Fakultäten und die allgemeine Religionsgeschichte," *RA*, 2:172.

[67] In a letter to Rade, AZH, p. 298.

[68] *Ibid.*, p. 299. As Harnack said of Luther, it could be said of him, "Never did he think to fight against the Church, but always *for the*

Yet this is the question: How can he most effectively serve the church? Harnack is very certain that the church as he meets it in his own *Sitz im Leben*, even among the liberals, is not a viable place for him to work. It "is completely encumbered with the mortgage of townhall free thought. Individually some of the men are excellent; as a group they are under the influence of the Communists. Perhaps I should make the attempt to change all this, but I have no inclination and no time for it." [69]

And so, his daughter records,

> He felt himself called to the task of administration; the heritage from his grandfather Ewers, reorganizer of the University of Dorpat and of the spiritual life of Livonia, was in his blood, and it drove him in this direction. He would not be untrue to himself, and he would not withdraw from the path marked out for him; rather, he followed the same law by which he had always walked when, at the height of his manhood, he undertook new tasks often far removed from theological science.[70]

One might choose from a number of minor or major alternatives as illustrative of Harnack's *practical* attempt to mediate between the church and the culture. But just because it represents most dramatically the divergence from theological historical work, we will use Harnack's work with the Kaiser Wilhelm Foundation as example.

As early as 1898 Harnack had presented a suggestion to the Ministry of Public Worship and Education regarding the naming of associates and assistants in the Royal Academy, the purpose being to support fundamental research that could not be carried out by those with professorial duties. A year

---

Church against a false and soul-dangerous practice; never did he dream that the Gospel had been really lost – no, but it was to be freed from a captivity into which . . . the theologians had led it." Quoted from Lyman Abbott *et al.*, *The Prophets of the Christian Faith* (New York: Macmillan Co., 1896), p. 115. Harnack's essay in this volume is entitled "Martin Luther, the Prophet of the Reformation."

[69] AZH, pp. 300–301.

[70] *Ibid.*, p. 302.

later he had expanded this suggestion to include the natural sciences. In the succeeding decade, many conversations with Althoff and succeeding ministers confirmed the judgment that the state should sponsor such fundamental research. Therefore, when the Kaiser, in 1909, sent to the ministerial director Schmidt-Ott a query "as to what could be done by him in the interest of science on the occasion of the jubilee of the University," Schmidt-Ott asked Harnack to prepare a memorandum "regarding the founding of institutes of research." [71] The memorandum was prepared, containing a strong rationale for the founding of such institutes, but also setting forth what was to become the organizational structure of the Kaiser-Wilhelm Foundation. Harnack had the help of a number of scholars, of course; but Schmidt-Ott later affirmed that "it bore the stamp of Harnack's genius" [72] in its structure.

In 1911, the Kaiser announced, at a convocation of world leaders in education, the founding of the Kaiser-Wilhelm Gesellschaft zur Förderung der Wissenschaften. Deissmann, who was present on that occasion, remarked that "the Kaiser spoke, but another had thought out and shaped the work." [73]

Harnack served as the first president of the Foundation and presided, for the succeeding years, over the establishment of a whole series of institutes. (In the first year alone, institutes of Chemistry, Coal Research [Krupp von Bohlen was vice-president!!!], Experimental Therapy, and Industrial Psychology were opened, and, in addition, support was extended in the areas of biological research, air traffic, and Islamic archaeology). Well might Harnack's friends ask, as they did ask, what justification there could be for one whose vocation was theology that he take on this "third" call. And that is, of course, the crucial question.

Harnack was not unaware of the question, and his answer to it is instructive. In 1929, at the dedication of the Harnack-Haus of the Foundation, he interpreted his eighteen-year presidency in this way:

[71] *Ibid.*, p. 425.
[72] *Ibid.*
[73] *Ibid.*, p. 427.

> It has been a deep concern of mine that wherever I see clefts, I should encourage the romance that will bring about a marriage. I have certainly made this my life's task. But I am not merely concerned that things should be joined together. They do not join themselves if men do not act, and I have had the splendid experience of seeing, in many areas, that not only industry but the industrialists, not only agriculture but the agriculturists, not only banks but the bankers, not only mining companies but the workers, not only cities but the burgomasters, have come into a hearty and occasionally inner relationship. . . . I have never observed such a mutuality developing where I have not also gained something for the life of the soul.[74]

That he sought to relate this work to his fundamental vocation is attested further in a letter to Rade written in 1929:

> The Kaiser-Wilhelm Foundation has laid on me great sacrifices, and does still. Yet I have not made a capricious choice, but have taken on me a destiny, and have then acted according to the principle: "Exactly or not at all." It has not been entirely without fruit for the evangelical church and Christianity, even if my professional colleagues do not discover it. For myself, I am still theologian as before, and my spare hours belong as from youth to our theological science.[75]

"I have not made a capricious choice, but have taken on me a destiny"—is this indeed the case? The writer of those lines was seventy-eight years old. The destiny had been "taken on" at least a quarter of a century earlier. Why?

"The culture," so he believed, demanded it. New and unforseen powers had brought their armies to the field, and these must be met—yes, even by a Christian theologian. Above all, these powers were represented in the variant forms of materialism which had grown apace in the last years of the

[74] *Ibid.*, p. 431.
[75] *Ibid.*, p. 432, n. 2.

nineteenth century. "Materialism": that representation of human life which rests on non-theistic assumptions. This view had been espoused in varying ways by Feuerbach, Schopenhauer, Vogt, Moleschott, Darwin (and his German interpreter Haeckel), Marx and his interpreters, and a veritable host of lesser personages. From the beginning of Harnack's scholarly activity he had been aware of their influence in the cultural background and of their challenge to any "religious" interpretation of human existence; thus they must be answered from the Christian point of view. Harnack explicitly admitted, in his essay on "The Double Gospel in the New Testament."[76] that the formulation of the position he there set forth had been determined by the contemporary situation: materialism had denied any validity to Christianity.

Two points need to be noted here. First, Harnack claims that this denial rests on a *false* historical view with respect to what Christianity *really* is.[77] He then proceeds to specify what it *really* is — in overtly Kantian terms. Second, this is, for better or worse, a utilitarian argument. Christianity *must* be defended against materialism; to do this, one must demonstrate on a scientific historical basis, against these thinkers (but also *for* these thinkers?), what the Gospel really is. Harnack claims to do this on the basis of historical truth. But what he is actually using as the basis of his argument is the contemporary *value* of the Gospel. The "second" Gospel cannot suffice to meet the contemporary challenge; the "first" Gospel, interpreted in terms of Kantian ethics, can. Therefore, the Gospel must be interpreted under this latter form.

It is to be noted further that the mode of development of his argument buttresses this conclusion. Scientific investigation is implicitly lauded as the only way to truth in the affirmation that any statement that does not begin, proceed, and end with his (Jesus') historical existence must be abjured.[78] Revelation

[76] Harnack, "Das doppelte Evangelium im Neuen Testament," *RA*, vol. 2; NF: *Aus Wissenschaft und Leben* (Giessen: Topelmann, 1911), pp. 211–24.

[77] *Ibid.*, pp. 223–24.

[78] *Ibid.*, p. 223.

is here cut to the necessary measure; it "can only take place in the uniqueness of personal life, and only the result that issues in history can tell us whether God has so acted through individuals."[79] These are "results" that can be studied "scientifically." Finally, then, even in his valiant and necessary attempt to save the uniqueness of Jesus, the apologetic situation with respect to the culture is apparent, perhaps to the detriment of the question of truth: Jesus is unique because history has found in him a way to a "personal higher life" which "overcomes the world."

We believe it is clear that Harnack is trying to "confess and defend" Christianity, but that he is caught in the necessities of a situation which subordinated even his fundamental question of truth to the question of contemporary efficacy and value in such a way that a certain content must be given in the answer.

It is obvious in this connection that what Harnack cannot say argues as decisively as that which he says. For though he had declared in numerous writings that there are two fundamental foci which are the objects of man's concern, "God and the soul,"[80] in actual practice these are not the true foci. Rather than God, the *world* is the "given" that confronts the liberal, and the relation of the soul to this world becomes his overarching problem. For of these two things one can speak, in an age when autonomous reason reigns, with some assurance that one will be heard. To speak of God is immediately to insert the concept of mystery into religion, at least from Harnack's point of view. The only option then is to speak of revelation in such a way that it can be drawn within the orbit of man's experience and therefore can be known by him. It is Jesus, in the full range of his humanity, as one who provides the power to overcome the world, to whom Harnack looks for the answer. And if the Church should agree, but claim that there is a mystery in the relation of Jesus as Christ and God as Father, Harnack could only say, with Ritschl, "Where I find

[79] *Ibid.*
[80] AZH, p. 516.

mystery, I say nothing about it."[81] Harnack then proceeds to examine Jesus' teaching in the light of the necessities of the situation, and what stands forth as the "first Gospel" is Kantian ethics with a nimbus.

Harnack's situation, then, with respect to the contemporary cultural challenge, was essentially ambivalent. He had to speak to culture, but he had to defend Christianity. The solution of this problem has been perennially vexing to Christian thinkers, and Harnack was no exception. But the fact that it was *this* problem that motivated much of his work is what we wish to emphasize here. He did not solve the problem, if indeed it is capable of "a" solution. But to understand him, one must be aware of the threat which he felt from the materialistic interpretation of life. This much is certain: Harnack did not evade, and he did not escape, involvement in the intellectual warfare that raged during his lifetime. Nowhere is this fidelity to "becoming involved" more patent than in his challenging of the materialistic interpretations of human existence which have dominated intellectual circles since 1850. But it may be argued that his own solution to the problem of Christianity and culture has proved to be as questionably valid as those against which he contended.[82]

[81] Quoted in H. R. Mackintosh, *Types of Modern Theology* (London: Nisbet & Co., 1937), p. 160.

[82] Cf. the critique of liberalism by H. Richard Niebuhr, *Christ and Culture* (New York: Harper & Bros., 1951) pp. 15–19.

Biographical Notes

JERALD C. BRAUER was born in Wisconsin in 1921, graduated from Carthage College and Northwestern Lutheran Theological Seminary, and received his Ph.D. from the University of Chicago in 1948. He taught at Union Theological Seminary, 1948–50. He is professor of the History of Christianity and dean of the University of Chicago's Divinity School. His publications are in the area of English Puritanism, Reformation, and religion in America.

QUIRINUS BREEN was born in Iowa in 1896. He did his undergraduate work at Calvin College and Seminary. In 1931 he received his Ph.D. in church history from the University of Chicago. Since 1964 he has been professor emeritus in history at the University of Oregon. At present he is teaching at the Grand Valley State College in Michigan. His publications pertain largely to Renaissance Humanism and the Reformation.

GEORGE A. DRAKE is assistant professor of history at Colorado College. Born in 1934, he graduated from Grinnell College in 1956. He received the B.A. in modern history from Oxford University where he was a Rhodes Scholar, 1957–59. He holds the B.D., M.A., and Ph.D. (1965) from the University of Chicago.

CORNELIUS J. DYCK was born in 1921 and is a native of Canada. He holds a M.A. in history from the University of Wichita and in 1962 was awarded the Ph.D. degree in church history by the University of Chicago. At present he is professor of historical theology at Mennonite Biblical Seminary, Elkhart, Indiana, and director of the Institute of Mennonite Studies.

B. A. GERRISH was born in England in 1931 and holds degrees from Cambridge, Union Theological Seminary, and Columbia University (Ph.D. 1958). He has been tutor in philosophy of religion at Union and taught church history at McCormick Theological Seminary 1958–65. Since 1965 he has been associate professor of historical theology at the University of Chicago Divinity School.

G. WAYNE GLICK was born in Virginia in 1921. He attended Bridgewater College and Bethany Theological Seminary. In 1957 he was awarded the Ph.D. in church history by the University of Chicago. He has taught at Juniata College, Franklin and Marshall College, and the Lancaster Theological Seminary. After serving as dean of the College at Franklin and Marshall for five years, he became President of Keuka College, Keuka Park, New York, in 1966.

ROBERT M. GRANT was born in 1917 and holds a Th.D. degree from Harvard University. For the past fourteen years he has been professor of New Testament and early church history at the University of Chicago Divinity School.

RICHARD LUMAN was born in Iowa in 1930. He holds the B.A. (1952), M.A. (1956), and the Ph.D. (1965) from the State University of Iowa. He has served as instructor in history, 1958–61, at the State University of South Dakota. In 1961 he came to the University of Chicago Divinity School and at present serves as assistant professor of church history specializing in medieval studies.

JOHN THOMAS MCNEILL was born in Elmsdale, Prince Edward Island, Canada, in 1885. He received his B.A. (1909) and M.A. (1910) from McGill University and studied theology in Vancouver and Edinburgh. In 1920 he received his Ph.D. in church history from the University of Chicago. From 1922 to 1927 he was professor of church history at Knox College in Toronto. He held a similar position at the University of Chicago Divinity School, 1927–44, and at Union Theological Seminary, 1944–53.

JAMES D. NELSON is assistant professor of theology at the United Theological Seminary in Dayton, Ohio. Born in 1930, he graduated from Westmar College, Iowa, in 1952 and received his B.D. in 1959 from the United Theological Seminary. He holds a M.A. (1961) and a Ph.D. (1963) in church history from the University of Chicago. He is an ordained clergyman (1959) of the Evangelical United Brethren Church.

JAROSLAV PELIKAN is Titus Street Professor of Ecclesiastical History at Yale University. Born in 1923, he received his Ph.D. in church history from the University of Chicago in 1946. He has taught at Valparaiso University, 1946–49; Concordia Seminary, 1949–53; University of Chicago, 1953–62; Yale University since 1962. He is the author of several books, editor, and a contributor to symposia and journals.

RAY C. PETRY was born in 1903 and received his Ph.D. in church history from the University of Chicago in 1932. At Duke University since 1937, he is currently James B. Duke Professor of Church History. He is a past president of the American Society of Church History and has published six volumes of medieval studies.

MASSEY H. SHEPHERD, JR. is Hodges Professor of Liturgics at the Church Divinity School of the Pacific in Berkeley, California. He was born in 1913 in Wilmington, North Carolina, and holds a B.A. (1932) and M.A. (1933) from the University of South Carolina. In 1937 he was awarded the Ph.D. in church history by the University of Chicago and served as instructor at the Divinity School, 1937–40. From 1940 to 1954 he was professor of church history at the Episcopal Theological School in Cambridge, Massachusetts.

MATTHEW SPINKA was born in 1890 in Stitary, Bohemia. He received his Ph.D. in church history (*magna cum laude*) in 1923 from the University of Chicago. From 1928 to 1938 he was assistant professor of church history at the Chicago Theological Seminary and the University of Chicago Divinity School. During the years 1938–43 he was associate professor in church history at the latter institution. Since 1958 he has been professor emeritus at the Hartford Seminary Foundation, Hartford, Conn.

Robert L. Wilken is one of the first Protestants to serve on a Roman Catholic theological faculty, having recently been appointed assistant professor of patristics at Fordham University. Born in 1936, he received his B.D. from Concordia Seminary (St. Louis) in 1960 and his Ph.D. in church history from the University of Chicago in 1963. Until 1967 he was assistant professor of the history of early Christianity at the Lutheran Theological Seminary, Gettysburg, Pennsylvania.

Acknowledgments

Most of the articles included in the present volume were presented at the Alumni Conference of the Field of History of Christianity, October 6–8, 1966, celebrating the seventy-fifth anniversary of the University of Chicago as well as the one hundredth anniversary of the Divinity School of the University of Chicago. The papers by Professors McNeill and Mead were given as public lectures. The following alumni served as discussants for the papers presented by their fellow alumni: Richard Baepler, Valparaiso University (for Massey H. Shepherd, Jr.); Allen Cabaniss, University of Mississippi (for Ray C. Petry); Albert L. Jamison, Syracuse University (for Winthrop Hudson); and Matthew Spinka, Southern California School of Theology (for Jaroslav Pelikan). Unfortunately limitations of space in this volume have made it impossible to include a summary of discussions by the participants. The papers have been revised, however, in light of the helpful comments made by the discussants and other participants.

We are very grateful to Mr. Trygve Skarsten, assistant professor of religion at Sweet Briar College, who not only assisted Miss Kathryn West in the planning of the Conference but also served as editorial assistant and helped prepare the manuscript for publication. Thanks are also due to the staff of the University of Chicago Press for their careful and thoughtful assistance and to Miss Kathryn West and Miss Nina Tweed whose meticulous typing made the editorial task a pleasant one.

Passages from the following book are quoted by permission of the publisher: G. Wayne Glick, *The Reality of Christianity* (New York: Harper & Row, Publishers, 1967).

Index